The Long Road

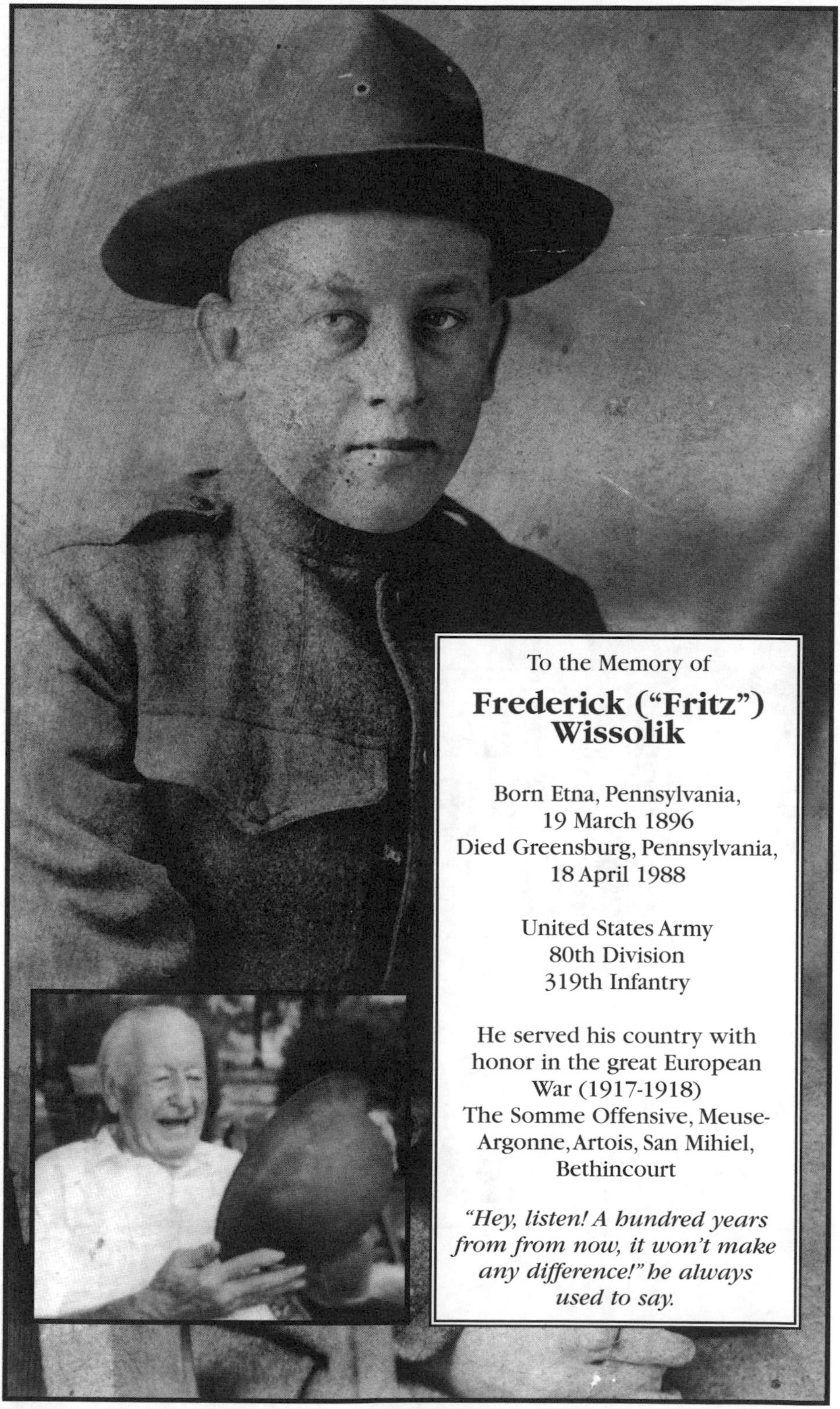

To the Memory of

Frederick ("Fritz") Wissolik

Born Etna, Pennsylvania,
19 March 1896
Died Greensburg, Pennsylvania,
18 April 1988

United States Army
80th Division
319th Infantry

He served his country with
honor in the great European
War (1917-1918)
The Somme Offensive, Meuse-
Argonne, Artois, San Mihiel,
Bethincourt

*"Hey, listen! A hundred years
from from now, it won't make
any difference!" he always
used to say.*

Le général Eisenhower s'adresse
aux peuples des Pays Occupés

LES ARMEES
ALLIEES
DEBARQUENT

11,000 PLANES BACK UP
4000 SHIPS IN BIGGEST
DRIVE IN ALL HISTORY

The Cincinnati Post

U. S. WEATHER FORECAST; Partly cloudy, cool tonight. Highest today about 77, low tonight about 55. Wednesday fair.

VOL. 127. NO. 135.   CINCINNATI, TUESDAY, JUNE 6, 1944.

LIBERATION
Late News
Home Edition
PRICE FOUR CENTS

ALLIES SMASH INLAND
FROM INVASION POINTS

*Photos: Courtesy of
Richard R. Buchanan*

To Mario DiPaul

Mario DiPaul's story appears later in this book. When he died in December 1998, the Saint Vincent Community lost a good friend. He came to the College often to work with SCORE, or in the monastery gift shop, or to help students with the school newspaper, or to talk with a class or two. We will miss him. *Ave atque vale*!

His army buddies called Mario "Tiny" because of his large stature. The nickname applied only to his size and not his courage, for according to Mario: "My buddies didn't know that I was really a coward inside!" My first impression of Mario was of a Santa Claus in the off-season! But after speaking with him for an hour during our first interview, I came to the conclusion that the nickname "Tiny" certainly did not equate with his courage or strength of character.

Mario was born in Greensburg, Pennsylvania in 1926. He was just a youngster of fourteen when Pearl Harbor was attacked. He watched with admiration and a little envy as all the "old guys" of eighteen and nineteen marched up to the court house in long lines to enlist. Mario's turn would come soon enough. In March of 1944 it did. After learning he had been selected to make his acting debut in the senior class play starring the cutest girl in the school, this shy and nervous young man decided he had to get out of making a fool out of himself at all costs. So he hurried down to the Greensburg Armory and asked to be taken early in the draft. Mario was soon cursing his decision as he crawled under barbed wire and live machine-gun fire in basic training. As he struggled through the mud of long field marches and bitterly cursed at the tough bayonet training, he thought to himself, "Why the Hell didn't I stay in that damn play!?"

However, he put all regrets aside when he learned his outfit, the 63rd Infantry Division would be shipping out soon. He knew he had a job to do; he didn't like the idea of it, but he went all the same. Mario was one of those rare individuals in a United States Infantry Division. He was a rifleman. Rare in that only about 3000 out of a 16,000 man division were riflemen, and rare also in that he lived long enough to tell about it. He was part of the exclusive group of men who had to go up into the front lines and do the fighting. These were the riflemen, and from June to December of 1944 they had suffered over 300 percent casualties in the American army. "I did a lot of praying," said Mario to me adamantly during one of our sessions, and as his story unfolded I could see why, because Mario became one of the countless decimal points in that percentage. He was wounded in the back and the stomach by shrapnel from a German artillery shell. His recovery was slow and painful, but the strength of this man never fell, though it occasionally wavered and he despaired. But hearing the voices of his parents again over the phone, granted to him a feeling of security, relief and renewed strength to see the crisis through. After long stays in numerous hospitals, continuous bouts with illness and not-so-difficult-measures he had to take in order to make himself "Tiny" again, that is, eating anything he wanted, he got back into shape and arrived home to the thankful embrace of his parents and brothers.

But the war was never truly over for Mario. He saw the worst of war and it stuck with him. Whether it's the nightmares he would often have in the years after the war or in his failed attempt to return to the place where he was wounded, he could never fully put to rest the ghosts of the battlefield. "It's just a deep, dark part of my past that I'd like to keep buried forever," he said to me in one of our last interviews. Despite his statement, I believe that by his willingness to impart to me his past, Mario somehow came to terms with those dark years and left behind the misery and pain of combat, the long fearful hours in a frozen foxhole and the endless days in the hospital. I saw that on his red, smiling face and heard it in his laughter as he traded good-natured cracks with his wife. Life was good for Mario, and he enjoyed it.

—David J. Wilmes

Brotherly Love

A younger brother's love and reverence for his older siblings is based on relationships formed at a very early age, usually exemplified in the caring little things that older brothers do for the youngest. And so it was in our family.

To me, Mario was not only an older brother; he was my childhood protector, guidance counselor, generous provider and friend. Those who knew Mario well will understand how my feelings toward him have lasted since we were children, for he continued throughout his life to help those in need.

I remember well that cold, February evening in 1945 when the telegram arrived from the War Department. As a young boy of twelve, I had hurried home after the Stations of the Cross ahead of my parents. A Western Union messenger arrived at the house at the same time I did and he handed me the dreaded news that Mario had been wounded in action. It was a scene that had been played out many times before in our community.

What I have read in this book about Mario's military experience is all new information to me. He simply never talked about it. Without this book, I would never have known the extent of his pain and anguish during that terrible time. Elsewhere in these pages we are privileged to read about the exploits of other young Americans from Southwestern Pennsylvania who found themselves in harm's way, in places far from home and hearth. They were all part of the heroic World War II generation. God bless them all.

—John DePaul

©PUBLICATIONS OF THE SAINT VINCENT COLLEGE
CENTER FOR NORTHERN APPALACHIAN STUDIES

With Financial Assistance from the Commonwealth of Pennsylvania, Department of Community and Economic Development and the Pennsylvania Historical and Museum Commission

Saint Vincent College
300 Fraser Purchase Road
Latrobe, PA 15650

The Long Road
From Oran To Pilsen
Oral Histories of World War II,
European Theater of Operations

General Editors:

David Wilmes, Fellow of the Center
Richard David Wissolik, Ph.D., Fellow of the Center
John Hill, Fellow of the Center
Gary E.J. Smith, Fellow of the Center

Editors:

G. Foster Provost, Ph.D., Fellow of the Center
Erica Wissolik, Fellow of the Center
Barbara Wissolik, Fellow of the Center
Ronald E. Tranquilla, Ph.D., Fellow of the Center
Mario Di Paul
Julie R. Platt
J.S. Downs and Associates

Introductory essays: G. Foster Provost, Ph.D.; Mark Gruber, O.S.B., Ph.D.; David J. Wilmes;
Charles J. McGeever, Ph.D.

Illustrations and Cover Design: J. Scott Downs; Jason Murch; Michael Cerce
Original photographs by the Interviewees

Printed in the United States of America by Braun and Brumfield, Inc.
Ann Arbor, Michigan

ISBN: 1-885851-13-8

Library of Congress Cataloging-in-Publication Data
The Long Road: From Oran to Pilsen: Oral Histories of World War II, European Theater of Operations / General Editors, David Wilmes [et. al.] / Editors, G. Foster Provost, [et. al.] / Joe and Henny Heisel Series 7 / Includes bibliographical references and index. 1. World War, 1939-1945--Campaigns--Western Front. 2. World War, 1939-1945--Personal narratives, American. 3. World War, 1939-1945--Veterans--United States---Interviews. 4. Veterans--United States--Interviews. 5. Oral history. I. Wilmes, David. II. Series. D756.L65 1999   940.54'1273--dc21   99-10637 CIP

The Long Road

From Oran to Pilsen.
Oral Histories of World War II,
European Theater of Operations.

General Editors:

David Wilmes, Fellow of the Center
Richard David Wissolik, Ph.D., Fellow of the Center
John Hill, Fellow of the Center
Gary E.J. Smith, Fellow of the Center

Editors:

G. Foster Provost, Ph.D., Fellow of the Center
Erica Wissolik, Fellow of the Center
Barbara Wissolik, Fellow of the Center
Mario Di Paul
Ronald E. Tranquilla, Ph.D., Fellow of the Center
Julie R. Platt
Downs and Associates

Publications of the Saint Vincent College Center for Northern Appalachian Studies with Financial Assistance from the Commonwealth of Pennsylvania Department of Community and Economic Development and the Pennsylvania Historical and Museum Commission

Joe and Henny Heisel Series VII

Latrobe, Pennsylvania
1999

Table of Contents

Front Cover Photographs

William King's squad at rest during a motor march. Soldier with glasses is William Meachan of Fort Worth, Texas.

V-Mail letter from John DiBattista to his parents.

The medical detachment of the 704th Tank Destroyer Battalion leaving Munich, Germany, on the Autobahn, heading for Marseilles, France, and home.

Editors' Note and Acknowledgments

The stories in this volume were prepared from the recorded interviews of the participants, their diaries, letters, and other appropriate material in their possession. Most of the photographs were taken by the interviewees themselves or their comrades, using their own cameras or cameras "liberated" from their adversaries. Some of the photographs were found among German prisoners of war or among Germans killed in combat.

The interviewees shared many common experiences concerning such areas as basic training, overseas journeys, weaponry, return trips to the United States, and others. These were edited in order to avoid redundancy. Only unique details were preserved.

The narratives which follow are not merely stories of combat. The interviewees were questioned about their families, their childhood, their work and educational experiences, as well as their military and post-military experiences. Their stories, though edited and arranged into narrative form, remain unadorned, and they are presented without editorial interpretation. Specific comments on the socio-historical circumstances the veterans witnessed may be found in the introductory materials. The Center has made every attempt to help the reader come to know the *person* as well as what the person did.

Each interviewee completed a general set of questions prepared by the Military History Institute at Carlisle, Pennsylvania. The Institute's aims and questions reflected and supported those of the Center.

Center staff conducted several interviews with each interviewee over a the period 1994-1999. Each assisted in the review and editing of transcripts. Each instance of an interviewee's written contributions (unit histories, diaries, articles from unit newsletters) is cited in footnotes. The wives and families of interviewees who died during the interviewing/editing process were of great assistance in providing photographs and other materials. They also assisted in editing final transcripts.

Audio tapes, completed questionnaires, and other materials appropriate to the interviews are archived at the Military History Institute, Carlisle Barracks, Carlisle, Pennsylvania.

The Saint Vincent College Center for Northern Appalachian Studies wishes to thank the following: Saint Vincent College, The Pennsylvania Historical and Museum Commission, The Pennsylvania Department of Community and Economic Development, and Dr. Richard R. Buchanan, for financial assistance in continuing the work of the Center.

Norman Hipps, O.S.B. (Provost, Saint Vincent College), Ms. Rita Catalano (Director of Research and Program Planning), Ms. Amy Stevenson-Mayfield (Grants Associate), and Ms. Marsha Jasper, Research and Planning secretary, for their invaluable assistance and advice in the development of grants for the Center.

Mrs. Patricia Dellinger, Mrs. Gina Nalevanko, Mr. John Kachmar, Reginald Bender (O.S.B.), Ms. Michele Pennesi, Ms. Julie D'Anna Parsons, Mrs. Carol McDowell, Ms Barbara Pushic, Mrs. Connie Philips, and Mrs. Evelyn Santone of the Saint Vincent College Business Office for their efficiency and patience in handling the accounts of the Center.

Mr. Don Orlando and Ms. Theresa Schwab of the Saint Vincent College Public Relations Office for arranging timely publicity for the Center's projects.

Chrysostom Schlimm (O.S.B.), Dr. Jack Macey, Mr. John Benyo, Mrs. Margaret Friloux, Ms. Denise Hegemann, Mrs. Pamela Reed; Mrs. Clydene Duran, and Mrs. Dolores Ghiardi, of the Saint Vincent College Library for their assistance to the Center during the process of research.

Ms. Shirley Skander, Faculty Secretary, and Ms. Lee Ann Deniker, Mailing and Duplicating for their prompt and uncomplaining assistance during the preparation of the manuscript.

Mr. Paul Steinhaus, Ms. Jenn Catullo, Ms. Kathy Curran, Mr. Joseph Ditch, Mr. Dennis Himic, Mrs. Nancy Ramaley, Mr. Randy Rhodes, Mr. John Sutton, Ms. Mary Williams, and Ms. Lori Sullivan, all from Information Services, for their prompt attention in keeping the Center's electronic equipment updated and running.

Colonel William Vossler (Ret.), Lieutenant Colonel Edwin M. Perry, and Ms. Angela Lehr, of the United States Army Military History Institute, Carlisle Barracks, for their continuing assistance in the development of the Center's veterans' projects, especially in the development of questionnaires and for archiving material gathered by the Center.

The Honorable Joseph Petrarca and the Honorable Allen G. Kukovich of the Pennsylvania legislature for advice and assistance in preparing grant requests for submission to the Commonwealth.

Finally, the Center is most grateful to the veterans for their willingness to tell their stories, not only for this volume, but to continue to do so for Saint Vincent College students in class visits, a generosity that enriches the educational milieu of the campus.

Preface

—*Foster Provost, Professor Emeritus*
Duquesne University

Although I served in the U.S. Navy from April 1944 to June 1946 and spent the final months of World War II as an aircraft radio and radar technician, by the luck of the draw I never went to sea while in the Navy and never approached a situation of combat in any other way. In reading the interviews which follow in this book, I have responded with a deep humility to these accounts of combat. The force of the accounts resides in the bald frankness with which the veterans acknowledge what they might have been inclined to conceal: their fear of battle and their lack of any desire to be heroes. Here the reader will find a sobering, yet frequently humourous, picture of the American Everyman at war, warts and buck teeth not airbrushed out.

These men were afraid of battle, but they were good soldiers. For weeks and months they exposed themselves daily to the prospect of death, even though in an exceptional situation they might decline to obey foolish commands from green officers who themselves did not understand the situation they were facing. The veterans speaking in these interviews convey perfectly the spirit of the citizens of the USA in the years 1941–1945, a spirit born on Pearl Harbor Sunday afternoon, December 7, 1941.

On that afternoon the entire country cast off the long hopelessness of the Depression and put hand and heart to the task of destroying the powers who had dared to commit such atrocities. The index of this country-wide spirit, born on that afternoon, appears not only in the prodigies of heroism achieved by a few conspicuous combatants, but also in the steady resolution of service personnel at every level who accepted the discomfort, and occasionally the outrage, or obedience to their military superiors day after day. They accepted their orders in training camps. And by and large they accepted their orders when sent into battle in conditions that invited some frightened neophytes to wound themselves just e-nough to be sent to a hospital and escape enemy fire. A very few American soldiers in this 1944–45 invasion of Europe did indeed shoot themselves in the leg or foot on purpose, but the typical GI accepted the fear and danger until he was wounded or killed by enemy action or until, like most of these interviewees, he was removed from the danger by the German surrender in May of 1945 and the collapse of Japan three months later.

It speaks well for the candor of these veterans that they openly acknowledge the attacking or victorious soldier's tendency to pay himself for the dangers he has weathered by helping himself to food, drink, and souvenirs in the cities and towns that the Army overruns. Had they denied or simply concealed this universal result of war, they would have compromised the frankness which makes this book a masterpiece.

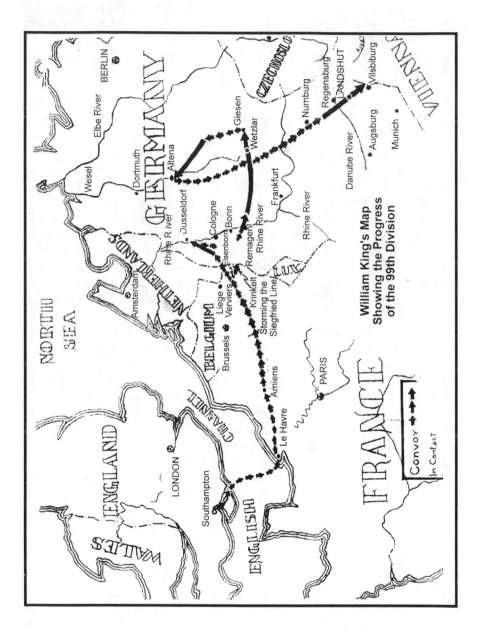

William King's Map
Showing the Progress
of the 99th Division

Convoy
In Contact

The Least We Can Do

—*Gary E. J. Smith*
Latrobe, Pennsylvania
January 1999

We, as a nation, owe much more than we can ever repay to the generation of Americans who, in combat or on the home front, won the Second World War. The generation of destiny, who survived the Great Depression, defeated fascism on two fronts, then forged a new and better nation for their children, is without peer in the annals of American history. We cannot easily measure the contributions they made to the continuance of the freedoms we often take for granted.

As a child, I would sit on our front porch on many a warm summer evening listening to uncles, grandfathers, neighbors and friends spin tales of their experiences during the War. These stories, told through the twin prisms of time and distance, were long on heroism and short on horror. Horror, after all, was what war really came to mean to each soldier, sailor, aviator, worker, and mother. Fresh-faced boys, who had never spent a day away from home, found themselves tasked with killing an enemy toward whom they harbored no personal enmity; mothers acquiesced as the government asked them for their sons, many thousands of whom never came home; young women cheerfully donned welding masks and took up riveting guns in dark and dangerous factories. The horror of war touched each participant differently, and it irrevocably changed each. It would be decades before I would come fully to grasp the fact that war was not tall tales, boisterous camaraderie, and glorious, bloodless victory.

Those summer stories fueled my passion for adventure and propelled me into my own enlistment in the service of my country. Both parents, both grandfathers (one in the Navy and one in the coal mines), and countless uncles and cousins had served. I could do no less. I looked upon national service as a familial obligation, much as the Depression-era generation saw the defeat of Germany and Japan as their national duty. After my service, I went to college seeking a degree in history. It was at Saint Vincent College that I was introduced to another form of "national service"—recording and publishing the spoken histories of the men and women who served the United States in World War II. Ironically, it was through the college's English department that I had the opportunity to do so. My first assignment was to prepare a history of Major Thomas J. Evans, a decorated hero who served with the 704th Tank Destroyer Battalion in the 4th Armored Division of Patton's Third Army. The Saint Vincent College Center for Northern Appalachian Studies ultimately published Major Evans' history under the title *Reluctant Valor*. Major Evans died in 1998.

Fifty-odd years after the surrender of the Axis powers, taps are being sounded over the graves of an ever-increasing number of World War II veterans. There were some fourteen million uniformed veterans of the war in 1945. In addition, there were countless civilians who participated in the war effort. Out of this vast, untapped natural resource, very few individual histories were recorded. Of course, there have been many books written concerning Patton, Bradley, Eisenhower, and Chennault, to name a few of the recognizable names. Most of the significant generals and world leaders from the era published their memoirs. But, sadly, the stories of men like the Catalfamos, the DiBattistas, the Gattos, the DiPauls, and the Bees, have been all too infrequently told. War is much different to the officer in the staff tent than it is to the soldier in the foxhole. The latter, more often than not, tells a truer story.

Very few of the veterans I have interviewed speak of glory, heroism and patriotism, because for them the heat of battle held none of those things. What battle meant to the dogface was his buddy in the next hole, the mail from home not yet read, the amassing of enough points to qualify for rotation home, or, barring that, the "million-dollar wound." To a man, none of the veterans admitted to acting heroically. Yet, that is what each of them did. That quiet, unassuming, everyday heroism is precisely why we must preserve their stories.

The Center's continuing oral history program and process is an arduous, yet rewarding, one. Typically, each veteran is pre-screened to determine what general experiences he had before, during, and after the war. This is done so that the interviewer can conduct in-depth research into the campaigns, theaters of operation, weapons, tactics and units of each oral-history candidate. The research enables the interviewer to prepare the right questions and to anticipate some of the experiences of each veteran. Experience has shown that when the interviewer can demonstrate a working knowledge of the material in question, the veteran tends to "open up," and provide more expansive answers to inquiries.

Interview sessions might last as long as two hours, and there may be up to six or more sessions per veteran. The tapes and transcriptions become a primary source for future researchers, as they contain not only names, dates and places, but, what is more important, the audible emotions of the interviewees. Beyond this, all of the transcriptions are edited into narrative form and published by the Center, together with whatever ancillary materials—diaries, photos, letters, reports—have been provided by the interviewees. Often the most difficult part of the interview process is seeing the pain in the veterans' eyes and hearing the anguish in their voices as they relive some terrible event, perhaps for the first time in fifty years.

Back Roads and Dark Detours

—Mark Gruber, O.S.B., Ph.D.
Saint Vincent College: Anthropology

Collective physical conflict has been a constituitive part of human social behavior since our kind emerged from the predatorial and territorial background of animal nature. For untold millennia the craft of fighting was largely improvisational. Pre-existing lines of social segments anticipated fissures within and between groups. Fissures opened up into a realm of behaviors utterly different from the kind which marked ordinary community cooperation. The momentum of violence, usually suppressed by customs and conventions of every kind, was occasionally exacerbated by special norms of behavior which suddenly asserted themselves when blood was let, women were molested, land use was usurped, or prestige was contested. Men found themselves not only in the altered affective state of sustained terror and rage, no doubt a matter of some blood chemistry, but also in the state of possessing a surprising clarity and understanding of the radically different rules in which they played. A spirit of the battle descended upon its participants.

As states evolved, the emergence of standing armies and total wars turned the spirit of battle into the gods of war. In war, men have always felt in-gathered into an angry or hungry, possessive cosmic force which exercised them to its own larger ends. Paradoxically, the more strongly the modern ethos is to repudiate this force and refuse its impulse, the more savagely it asserts itself. The wars of this past century are simply the most devouring, even while much of the rhetoric about war is the most critical ever voiced. Perhaps as the illusion of war's Divine nature is progressively dismissed, its residual ghosts must assert themselves with ever fiercer displays. How discouraging the reversals which deter moral progress!

When men are not actually fighting in wars, they are frequently satisfied to endlessly recount its drama. Years after the last battles have ceased, its combatants are still rehearsing their intricacies. The spirit of battle is generous with the enthusiasms it generates. Under the weight of poorly-told war stories, a genre of its own, families groan and friends flee. But a well-crafted story has the power to hold in its sway even the most pacifistic listener. One cannot deny the seductive powers of the old gods. Yet one more movie grips the nation about World War II; yet one more book is a best seller. Till now the veterans of war hold pride of place in politics, and the merchants of war hold highest court in commerce. In war, we are a people who "rally to presidents" and "support our troops" first, and then reflect upon the moral content of that behavior only a little and always late. We tell our stories and sing our patriotic marshal hymns with an intensity of affect which submerges all critical thought.

When I undertook the project of reading the vignettes and reflections on the Second World War by the veterans of the Northern Appalachian Region, I was expecting descriptions to fit well within the genre of the war stories heard long ago. I did not begrudge the survivors of battle their prerogative to formalize their accounts at last in prose. They are old now, and the blood which was once poured out in battle now quickens in the brain of recollection on far-away places and long-ago times. Memory has a passion all its own for them and if certain details are glossed over by time, other moments are raised into sharper and more poignant relief. The following accounts are rich in the wealth of compounded tellings and refined elaborations. But I found more than this in them.

Wars happen most intensely to young men whose senses are sharpest and whose sensibilities are still vulnerable. War stories told by old men are based upon such experiences and are fleshed out by the accumulation of the insight and wisdom gained through suffering. Youth is given to every unconscious excess of generosity and selfishness, affection and exploitation, violence and tenderness. War intensifies the opportunities for every excess in youth, and most practitioners of war will never participate in life so intensely thereafter. The sacrifices of friendship; the radiance of heroism; the abandonments to revelry; the exaltation of honor are the stuff of war stories to balance the horrors of the aftermath of battles; the guilt and anguish of surviving the fallen; the erosion of moral boundaries; the dehumanizing of the enemy-other; the rage at being manipulated; the terror of anticipations; and the loneliness for one's people at home: the stories recorded here are filled with this kind of description, but the observant reader should notice something even more.

Perhaps the interviewers of the Northern Appalachian Center asked the right kind of questions; perhaps the editors gleaned the right grain of phrases, but the men who tell their stories are talking with another spirit from what I have heard from veterans hitherto. Many voices are heard nowadays, to be sure, which disparage the modality of war as a means of global politic. Anti-war songs and protests were the winds which once blew across the face of a whole generation. But the protest of those who know war, the reasoned and seasoned voice of detachment which rises up from a sovereign soul who knows intimately the matter of which he speaks has a much truer ring than the voice of one who has simply refused war on principled ideas when he was drafted.

Over and over again, the following stories roam the back roads and dark detours of war and continue to arrive at questions of ultimate value. While their stories are filled with the details of an army's ordinary operations and soldiers' ordinary preoccupations, the men who remember them are also capable of transcending the limited horizons of their individual experiences and questioning the larger moral dimensions of war.

The conduct of whole armies and individual soldiers is subjected to repeated analyses as the men scrutinize events of cruelty to civilians and enemy soldiers which still trouble them five decades later. Trafficking in human misery, reveling while humans suffer near at hand; harvesting souvenirs from the dead; witnessing the atrocities of one's own army and wrestling with the responsibility thereof;

exploiting military status for sexual favors; disloyalties to friends; facing the spectacle of the aftermath of battles and the face of genocide; and all the ethical dilemmas which derive from exercising the highest degree of life-and-death sovereignty over others, while cut off from all familial, cultural and spiritual contexts: these are the complex issues which surface on every page of this work. Each soldier struggles while asking, "Am I the same person in this moment of battle, on this weekend pass, or beholding these unimaginable events as I was when I was formed in my home? Am I even recognizable to what I was then? And if I am not, what forms me now, and what will I be if I return to my homeland?"

In more recent military expeditions, the contemporary soldier is often detached from the moral gravity of what proceeds from the pushing of a button and the deployment of a machine. He may take the euphemisms of "collateral damage" and "personnel neutralization" too lightly and fail to grapple with the consequence of his military role. The veterans of World War II speaking here are our best moral compasses about where war takes us and from where war comes. They were still in the edge of war's movement and worked under the weight of its momentum.

To help us see beyond the thicket of details, the editors of these accounts have excerpted details from various interviews with the veterans which put certain aspects of their stories into sharper focus. We can also be grateful for the footnotes which explain the sometimes arcane lexicon of armies and theaters of war. The editor's hand is invisible which is the sure sign that it is deft, and its work is at once minimal to the alteration of the story and maximal in its art to present it smoothly.

So long as men are prone to fight battles, veterans will be morally responsible for telling stories which both frankly acknowledge the fascination of war and, at the same time, confess its utter evil. We can be grateful to the veterans who participated in this effort. They succeed to inspire and even to entertain, but in the larger cause, they also succeed in making us sober about the realities which war brings and the meaning it bears.

DER KRIEG IST VERLOREN

Die alliierten Armeen rollen unaufhaltsam gegen das Herz Deutschlands. Sie haben die Wehrmacht in jedem Gefecht geschlagen.

Deutschland hat in 5 kostbaren Kriegsjahren seine Stärke verausgabt und hat der alliierten Übermacht nichts mehr entgegenzustellen...

Du bist bis jetzt noch mit dem Leben davongekommen...

Du hast deine Aufgabe im Krieg erfüllt und eine neue Aufgabe erwächst für dich und alle anderen Deutschen: Am Wiederaufbau Deutschlands mitzuwirken!

Falls du dich für die Mithilfe entscheidest, ist für Deutschland

EIN LEBEN GEWONNEN!

Leaflet dropped by Allies to German troops encouraging them to surrender.

Dulce et Decorum ...

— Charles McGeever
University of Maryland, Asian Division (Japan)

The war was over," Harry Bee explained. "There was no reason to have maneuvers then.... but every once in awhile it still haunts me. Seeing that kid with his chest blown open. But I just went on with my life." So, too, did the other veterans whose stories appear in this book.

At some level of their consciousness, these Depression-era teens seemed to understand the timing of war. Therefore, these men had a straightforward mission: get home intact and leave dogma, politics, religion and love to poets, priests, and politicians. Indeed, there are only traces in the narratives in this book that any of the men cared for the larger issues of global combat.

The Long Road reifies the poignant reminiscences of America's military youth who cannily outwit the exhausted German enemy and the sometimes stupifyingly inefficient command structure of the Allied upper echelon. In fact, *The Long Road* is sometimes so comically vulgar and filled with such outrageous exploits of young men at war, the collection might generously be retitled, "A Romp Across Europe." The volume is, by turns, a serious testimonial about the savagery of war, the bitterness men feel toward other races and religions when forced to live together, and the transcendence of the human spirit over life's greatest adversity.

Then narrators share remarkably similar backgrounds. Predominantly first-generation immigrant children who work hard and value wit and intelligence, the interviewees lack the refined sensibilities they ably promote within their own middle-class offspring.

Each man boarded a train or bus in his home town and eventually entered into the mysterious geography of Texas, Georgia, Louisiana, Alabama, or Mississippi, their own homeland in some ways more alien than the places they had been asked to defend in Europe. William David King left in winter on an unheated Pullman whose toilets, bowls frozen throughout the long journey, thawed in Mississippi heat filling some cars with an odor many of these men will recall later.

Rocco Catalfamo, a daring storyteller, tells us of climbing a hill toward a concentration camp. At the rise he beheld the skeletonized and decaying inmates of Buchenwald whose feet and clothing were covered with encrusted grime and putrid-smelling feces. At one point places Catalfamo and his friend, Augie Placido, in a liberated Paris. In three days, these teens spend $4,000. Later, Catalfamo is promoted to tech sergeant and flies to Norway with another soldier to bring in a notorious quisling. After a fierce gun battle in which the quisling is captured, the two Americans prowl the local entertainment centers for a few days, and then return the quisling to the Allies who try and, then, hang the man. "Kid" is an endearing tale whose dark humor tones its comedic slant.

Also of interest is how this collection reveals an America struggling with its own racial and religious differences as it attempts to reconcile similar problems in Europe. James Coletti believes that different ethnic groups in western Pennsylvania "got along ... because in those days everybody was living together. They were ... a society who helped one another." John Dudek shares the same view, once offering to champion a Jewish comrade who was insulted by a another soldier of Dudek's own ethnic extraction. Mario DiPaul, conversely, recalls his own father's staunchly conservative politics which allowed him to applaud Roosevelt's death. "He's dead in the morning and will be in the ground at night," DiPaul's father exclaimed. DiPaul's father believed Roosevelt was "of Jewish extraction." Who else but a Jew would energize the New Deal? The son betrays his own bias: "They [DiPaul's brothers' teachers] took a beautiful Italian name and made it a pedestrian French name, [DePaul]."

Asked to relate his impressions about basic training, John DiBattista recalls that " ... anti-Semitism was rampant. It wasn't covert. It was overt." DiBattista allows that such sentiment saddened him " ... because as an Italian, I had a lot of that here in Greensburg. 'Dago' this and 'Dago' that so I knew what [the Jew] was going through. I had a teacher call me goddamn Dago right in front of the whole class in 1939."

English staging areas were cells of racial animus, DiBattista recalls. A captain spoke to the troops: " ... if any of you [white soldiers] get in an altercation with a black, we don't care what the provocation is, you're the one that's going to suffer." DiBattista felt that the men overseas were expressing their stateside attitudes.

On D-Day, Anonymous, a tall lanky boy with size-fifteen shoes, floated onto Omaha Beach in a safety vest. From that Beach and beyond, he saw the Germans and the Americans at their most tenacious and their most pathetic. He told the interviewer that he respected the German soldiers " ... because they trained more than we did .... " but wanted to "kill them all" as word of the Final Solution spread like disease across a liberated France. The moral decay was infectious. American soldiers shot German prisoners. American officers abandoned their men. "It was like we were on our own," he recalls. Venereal disease, rape, and adultery were common and men tried vainly to conceal their disease since it meant a soldier had to spend an additional six-months in a European hospital. None seemed able to find the moral center as western culture revealed a shameless primitivism.

This book presents one of this century's defining experiences. Many who read *The Long Road* and the Center's companion pieces[1] might not unhesitatingly support our country's summons, though the majority of narrators would. Herein are moments of strong and unhindered emotional experiences now recollected for audiences in the tranquility of a half-century's reflection. In life's twilight, these

---

[1] To date, *Reluctant Valor, Men of the 704, Mission Number Three, A Mile in Their Shoes.*

men all regard life as good. To squander this miracle on alien ground has to be the great contradiction of global diplomacy. And the travesty of war is surely revealed by western Pennsylvania's saving remnants as preserved herein. One can only conclude that these men survived as harbingers. As counsel. To remind all who read their words that Wilfred Owen spoke a lamenting truth when he wrote about The Great War:

> My friend, you would not tell with such high zest
> To children ardent for some desperate glory
> The old lie: *Dulce et decorum est,*
> *Pro patria mori.*

Photos: Courtesy of
Richard R. Buchanan

A German postcard, originally in pastel, ca. 1942, entitled "Men of the Western Front. One of our successful reconnaissance troop leaders in a hooded, winter camouflage." The card was produced by a German youth/military society.

Ghosts Along the Way

...the unreturning army that was youth
the legions who have suffered and are dust
—Siegfried Sasson, "Prelude: The Troops"

—David J. Wilmes
December 14, 1998

I met Joe Kasperik only once. It was August of 1996. I was going to interview him about his experiences in World War II. I was new to interviewing, and I was nervous. Joe met me in his front yard. We walked into his house and began talking. My nervousness passed as Joe described his life to me. The interview lasted only an hour or so. Joe looked me in the eye the whole time. He struck me as a man who had nothing to hide; who wanted to tell his story honestly but simply. I am still amazed at the matter-of-fact way he described an instance of bloody street fighting in Belgium. Joe constantly referred to his uniform. It hung on a coatrack next to him like a soldier standing at attention, a beacon from the past directing his memory. I felt Joe's thirty-eight months in one of the Army's most blooded divisions of World War II could turn out to be a book in itself. Things didn't turn out that way. I never got to see Joe again.

One day, soon after that first interview with Joe, I bumped into Sam Folby, one of Joe's old army buddies, whom I had interviewed earlier. Sam told me the sad news that Joe had died. I began thinking about Joe's final, prophetic statements. He mentioned soldiers' funerals and how old all the World War II vets were becoming. He told me how every year fewer World War II vets marched in the Memorial Day parade in Blairsville. He was right. I went to the parade that year, and there were only a few men who looked like they were of that generation of young men who would now be in their seventies and eighties. Their white hairs peeking out from under their parade caps and a lifetime of knowledge etched on their faces told me that these men were the last of their kind. Behind their thinning ranks came a larger contingent of the more recent past. This part of the parade was made up of younger generations of veterans with their own unique scars and memories of bloodshed. These passing rows of khaki and olive drab uniforms had the firmer step that comes with youth. Many of these men and women were still on active duty.

For those in this book, the World War II days of marching in formation, snapping salutes to superiors and doing "KP" are over. For most their long road has wound its way to a peaceful old age. Grandkids, traveling and retirement are uppermost on these men's minds, and their old uniforms, medals and memories are brought out of closets and attics only occasionally for parades or the curious like me.

I'm a stranger to war, and was a stranger to all these men that I interviewed before they graciously invited me into their homes or decided to meet with me at some other location convenient for both of us. Their hospitality never ceased to amaze me, nor did their willingness to part with some of their most treasured memories, many of which had never been spoken to a living soul before, not even their wives. Consequently, I feel as if I have been entrusted with something vital to the understanding of these men and World War II. What is it that I feel I have been entrusted with?

It has nothing to do with conveying the horrors of war. That has already been attempted countless times, and a lot of good that has done! There are still wars despite impassioned pleas for peace and compromise. No, it is an obligation to remember the sacrifice, courage and comradeship that these men achieved. That is what this volume attempts to do. Preserved here are the oral histories of men who enlisted or were drafted into the United States Army and who fought in North Africa and Europe. Their stories shape a picture of this area during the war years by focusing on who these men were, what they experienced overseas and how it affected the rest of their lives. These are old soldiers' tales from a past that is not as distant as we think. We see it march down our small-town streets every November 11th and on Memorial Day. But they are our last link with an incredible time period. It slips away every day, and that is what makes this book so important.

When I see all the American flags displayed on Veterans Day or Memorial Day, I realize just how revealing these stories are. When I saw the flag in the past, I could appreciate it only in a vague way. *Duty, honor* and *country* were words that popped into my head. But I couldn't put a face on those words. Men like Harry Bee, John DiBattista, Jim Herrington and Mario DiPaul helped me with that. They were some of the first to share their stories with me. In their accounts I began to realize what all those images the flag can summon up mean on a more personal level. It is not something as confusing as patriotism. It's comradeship. "You couldn't let your buddies down," "We were more than brothers," "Closer than brothers," "You had to have good buddies," "The best buddies you'll ever have," are statements made more than once by all the men I interviewed. Duty, honor and country seen in this light takes on an aspect of the sacred that defies and belittles the verbose exhortations of generals and politicians. It is a discipleship that spans decades and the vast distances of our country. Many of these men gather yearly with their wartime comrades to remember the past and renew relationships that were fashioned in training camps across the USA. Others speak of phone calls out of the blue and on the line is a voice they had not heard for fifty years. These men can pick up where they left off years ago with their buddies as if time and place were suddenly altered.

The time and the place were the same for all of these men. The roads that sprawled through their lives all began in different homes but led them in the same direction. They were born into small-town America. Their parents, mostly immigrants escaping the appalling poverty of Italy or Eastern Europe, were able to assimilate into the backbone of this country and form a growing middle-class society that would give so much blood during World War II. They grew up during the Depression. It hardened many of them with strenuous manual labor, the knowledge of conservation and the development of "Yankee-Know-How." They emerged from those difficult times instilled with a sense of worth and disciplined by a profound work ethic. These same qualities were sharpened on December 7, 1941 when the Japanese bombed Pearl Harbor.

The long road began for them with a voluntary trip to the recruiter's office or with official greetings from Uncle Sam. They left for the training camps that were popping up all across the United States. Small towns in the south that hardly had a hundred residents exploded over night into virtual cities as droves of young men flooded the nearby camps. The training these men received was grueling, often demeaning and in some cases fatal. But what emerged from this forge was a brotherhood that would outlast the rest of the long road ahead.

The long road would take them to North Africa, Sicily, Italy, France and Germany. They would see buddies die in corners of desert or forest that they never even knew existed before the war. These patches of ground are now speckled with stark, white crosses and Stars of David. It is not a glorious sight. It is sad and painful to see such overwhelming sacrifice and know that this is the end result of all that training, brotherhood and eagerness to serve. One begins to realize that it really doesn't matter whose dead these are either. The grave markers all stand silent and the men beneath them were all young. The danger, suffering and fellowship of violence described in this book are doors that remain closed to me. I have taken only a peek behind each door. The full view belongs to these men and their dead comrades.

I am just a young historian who has hardly lived through my own history, but the past of these men persistently beckons and haunts me. I have not been to Europe to experience first hand the places these men describe. Nor have I seen the countless graves standing sentries for the future. I have only begun understanding this past through the eyes of the men I interviewed. Jack McDaniel, Joe Kay, Al Kormas, Enrico D'Angelo and Jim Coletti have allowed me to recognize what courage and freedom are and what patriotism isn't. By listening to these men and examining the occasional diary and numerous photographs buried away for fifty years in their homes, I am appreciating this past and reaping the benefits of its future. It is a future that hasn't lived up to all of the expectations these men had when they returned home, but it is certainly better than living in fear, something they did for a good part of their youth. When I look at myself in comparison to what they did at my age, I realize I have it good and always will have it good because they traveled the long road before me. Only a few remnants are left from their journey, but I continue to retrace their steps into the past meeting their ghosts along the way.

The Old-Timer

Joseph Kasperik, Jr.

United States Fifth Army
1st Infantry Division ("The Big Red One")
26th Infantry Regiment
Company B

Smithton, Pennsylvania, 13 April 1916

"Then you get hard-nosed and you just don't care for nothing except your buddies. If you saw some dead Germans or even some Americans that you didn't know laying on the side of the road or half-buried in a ditch, it was almost like looking at dead animals. It was like that through every campaign, every invasion."

Sam Folby[2] and the whole gang went into the Army. Some were going in when they were seventeen. I wasn't like most of the fellas because I was a little older. The Army wasn't too bad, though, because you were with fellas you knew. You were with these guys so much you got to know them better than your own brothers!

Leaving my family wasn't tough for me, because I had been away at school for a while. Don't get me wrong. We had a close-knit family. My dad was a hard worker. During the Depression he went from coal mine to coal mine looking for work. He never went on welfare or relief. Both of us worked on a farm picking cherries for three cents a pound, just to make ends meet. My dad always made sure we had something on the dinner table.

I was drafted in December 1941, but they did not call me until a month later. I spent thirty-eight months overseas and almost four years in active service. We lived in holes or tents or under vehicles. Everybody was behind the war against Germany and Japan, soldiers and civilians alike. We went over there so they wouldn't come over here.

We left the States in spring of 1942. We got to England and trained in Scotland for the invasion of North Africa (Operation TORCH).[3] Before we left from

---

[2]Mr. Folby's history appears in this volume.
[3]8 November 1942.

Joseph J. Kasperik, Jr.

England, we insulted the British. They fed us a lot of fish in Landbury Castle.[4] We unloaded seventy tons of fish at sea, with salutes and bugles blowing! The British were very serious types, but they had a good sense of humor, and they were good soldiers!

I went into a regular Army division. It was just as strict as could be. In the end, you knew it was all necessary, but at the time you thought otherwise. We took a lot from the Old-Timers. If we were at mess, just sitting there, some career man might be sitting across from you. When they passed the food around, if you grabbed a plate before he did, you were in trouble. The Old-Timers ran the place. To them, we were just filling in. The Old-Timers made it rough until we got overseas, then they got aches and pains. They were experienced enough to know that the youngsters would do whatever they were told. Tell them to take a town, and they'd charge right in! When I got to be an Old-Timer myself, I'd say, "Sure, I'll take it, but I'll go around and take it from the rear!" After awhile, I was experienced enough to disobey an order when I knew it would be suicide.

In North Africa, we landed at Oran. That's where Sam Folby got hit. He didn't make it past the first day. I went through the whole war with only a few cuts and bruises. That's what they call luck, I guess. We moved inland and fought at Kasserine Pass.[5] It was every man for himself. Rommel clobbered us!

At Kasserine, I didn't know much. I volunteered to go back with a lieutenant into the valley to destroy some vehicles that we left behind when we retreated. The Germans were still there and it got hot! The lieutenant ran off and left me. I had to make my own way back. A day later, I found our regiment and reported in. It crossed my mind to shoot that lieutenant, but I didn't.

We were in North Africa until the summer of 1943. By that time, the Italians were finished, and we took them prisoners by the thousands! The Germans were still powerful. Their planes were everywhere, and they bombed and strafed us. All we had were our pea-shooter rifles. All you could do was duck down into your hole. Guys who were caught in the open just got cut in half by the planes' machine-guns. They'd drop 500-pound bombs and leave craters thirty-feet across! I'd jump into those craters, thinking that they wouldn't hit the same place twice. By that summer, we had enough strength to push the Germans out. Then we got ready to invade Sicily (Operation HUSKY).[6]

In Sicily, there were lots of Italians giving up. They were disorganized. So were we. We had lots of planes by then, but some guys thought of the strafing in North Africa and thought the Germans were still at it. Some guys in our outfit shot some of our own planes down.

---

[4]Complaints against the "fishy" diet provided American troops by the British were common.
[5]Site of first defeat of American troops at the hands of Erwin Rommel's Afrika Korps. February 1943.
[6]10 July 1943.

Thirteen days after we got to Sicily, Patton was up front mugging for the cameras. He had his two polished pistols out. Someone said he was looking for snipers! He shouldn't have been there, and you don't go looking for snipers with a pistol. You go with a cannon! If any of us found a sniper in a church steeple, we'd just blast the thing off! Anyway, Patton was a publicity hound.

In Sicily, we bombed the Hell out of some places. Our planes would go in and flatten towns. Then we'd go in with tanks and artillery. You wondered how people survived. Not the soldiers, but the civilians.

After Sicily, we went back to England and prepared for the invasion of France (Operation OVERLORD). We landed on Omaha Beach.[7] I remember the shell fire coming from the hills above the beaches. Landing craft filled with guys were blown to pieces. The tide was so rough that we didn't get in until evening. On the beach, some guy was yelling, "Keep moving! Keep moving! Don't die on the beaches!"

Then we moved into the hedgerows,[8] and that's where we really didn't know where anyone was. There'd be fighting going on all around, but we couldn't see it. Even in the middle of all that noise, I felt alone. I guess things looked pretty good on paper to the generals, but to me it looked like I was fighting the war by myself.

After the breakout at St. Lô,[9] we moved quickly. When we had to get somewhere, we walked. We were foot soldiers. Maybe, if we were lucky, we bummed rides on jeeps or tanks. We never got a chance to shave or clean up. We wore the same filthy uniforms all the time. I got a chance to get out of the infantry. They came along and picked so many guys for these half-track companies. They put me in one that had a 75mm gun and 50-caliber machine-guns. I didn't have to walk anymore!

Once, when I was in the half-track, we got some Germans held up in a house in Belgium. This was around the time of the Battle of the Bulge.[10] No one wanted to go down and see if these Germans would surrender. I volunteered to go with this lieutenant, a 90-Day Wonder![11] Like, I didn't learn my lesson the first time, in North Africa! He told us that there were only a few Germans down there. Five of us went down in the half-track.

I told my lieutenant to watch the treeline around this house with his .50, and I would take care of the doors with mine. There were thirty Germans in there.

---

[7] 6 June 1944.

[8] Hedgerows were barriers that divided the fields of Normandy. They were sometimes four feet thick and five feet high, and formed an almost impenetrable barrier of trees, shrubs, roots and rocks. Each hedgerow became a fortress for the Germans.

[9] After Operation COBRA and the carpet bombing of German positions. 25 July 1944.

[10] December to February 1944. German forces invaded through the Ardennes in Belgium in Operation HERBSTNEBEL 'Autumn Mist'.

[11] A term of disparagement for officers who were trained for leadership in ninety-days.

Some odds! Five against thirty. I wondered where the lieutenant got his information. The Germans surrendered, but only after we shot the Hell out of the place. I kept yelling at the lieutenant, "Don't use up all of your ammunition. Just fire in short bursts!" He was holding that trigger down, BZZZZZZZZ! I was knocking out doors and windows. I hit some German captain. I blew his leg off. He was in a bad state! We bandaged him up as good as we could, threw him up on the half-track, and kept going. I got a Bronze Star for that house job.

I got a Purple Heart soon after. It was still during the Bulge. The Germans sent over some planes and bombed the Hell out of us. I jumped into the O-ring mount of the .50 on our half-track. Some shrapnel grazed my back. It was nothing serious, compared to what some other guys got. I saw a lot get crippled, maimed, killed. It made things pretty bad. Then you get hard-nosed, and you just don't care for nothing except your buddies. If you saw some dead Germans or even some Americans that you didn't know laying on the side of the road or half-buried in a ditch, it was almost like looking at dead animals. It was like that through every campaign, every invasion. As far as the killing went, you just plowed the bodies off the road to keep the traffic moving. That happened a lot in the Hurtgen Forest and during the Bulge. Some bodies were frozen solid, and had been there who knows how long. You'd get them by the head and feet and throw them up into the three-tonners. That was Death!

When the war ended, I was in Czechoslovakia. It was the end of a long road! My buddies passed around Cognac and wine when we heard it was all over. We got drunk as Hell! I was the flag-bearer for the peace treaty in Czechoslovakia, and I had to borrow the captain's pants because mine had patches and holes, and stunk like Hell! I had to give the pants back to the captain, and I went home still wearing the same uniform I had worn since North Africa. I used to wash it in gasoline. When I arrived at Indiantown Gap, I saw this fella with nice, new, clean khakis. I said to him, "I'll fight you for your uniform!"

I still wear a uniform, once in a while. *[Mr. Kasperik takes his dress uniform from a closet and shows it to the interviewer]*. Whenever there's an Old-Timer's funeral, me and some of my buddies wear our uniforms. Whenever there's a parade, people ask us to march. We're all old-timers now.[12]

---

[12]Mr. Kasperik died shortly after this, his initial interview. The editors have placed his brief narrative here because it serves well as a distillation of events and feelings American troops experienced during World War II, at home and in the European Theater of Operations.

English Channel

Cotentin Peninsula

First Army (Omar Bradley)
V Corps
20th Infantry Division
1st Infantry Division

Ste Mere Eglise   Utah Beach

82nd Airborne

Omaha Beach

101st Airborne   Grandcamp   Vierville

Port-en-
Bessin   Arromanches

Carentan•
(Purple Heart Corners)

Normandy

St. Lo .
(Operation Cobra and
Breakout)

The Invasion of Normandy
June 6, 1944
Showing Points Appropriate
to the Text

Sherman's March

Harry Thomas Bee

United States Seventh Army
63rd Infantry Division ("Blood and Fire")
253rd Infantry Regiment
2nd Battalion
Company D

Hunker, Pennsylvania
Swissvale, Pennsylvania, 7 August 1922

"All of a sudden, a woman came running down the street hollering in German. I couldn't understand her. She's pointing up the hill. I jump in the jeep, and I'm the first one up there. There were kids scattered all over the place. Some were dead. Some had their arms off and their legs off! One was laying there with his chest all open. You could see his lungs moving up and down. I took sulfa powder and poured it in there. For the first time since I got to Europe, I got out my emergency bandage. I pulled it apart and put the pad on his chest. I got him in the jeep. The kids had found that live round and it exploded when they banged it with a rock."

They called me "Bumble Bee." I tried to join the Marines the day after Pearl Harbor, but my one eye was bad and I didn't make it. I'm glad. Most of my buddies ended up on Guadalcanal! I could have been killed there.

My father, Dennis, a machinist, was born in 1899 in Clearfield County. For most of his life he worked in Pittsburgh, at the Homewood Pittsburgh Meter Works. My mother, Margaret Campbell, was born in 1905 in Braddock, Pennsylvania. She worked mostly as a waitress. During the war she worked in a factory. Her family had a lot of children and, as the oldest daughter, she had to help raise them. I went to Connolly Vocational High School in Pittsburgh, but quit in 1939. There were lots of jobs around, and I needed the money. My education was in the mill. I joined the Army in November 1942. The Army took you if you were at least breathing. I left from Pittsburgh for Fort Meade, Maryland. I left my wife and mother crying at the station.

I decided to go into the 12th Armored Division, for the glory of it! They were stationed at Camp Campbell, Kentucky. I went on maneuvers in Tennessee.

Harry Bee: 26 May 1945. Tauberbischofscheim, Germany

I was in the Blue Army and fought the Red Army. Referees came around and said "You're dead, you're captured, you're surrounded," whatever. I was in Headquarters Company and got captured with a colonel and several other officers. They took us to a POW camp. Just like war, except the colonel laughed when he got captured.

After basic training, I went to Fort Knox and trained 90-Day Wonders to drive Shermans and fire 75mm guns. *They* dirtied the Shermans, but *we* had to clean them! The tanks were painted white inside. We weren't supposed to smoke in them, but people chewed tobacco and spit it around. Those tanks never stopped! We'd take out light tanks, medium tanks, the diesel and the gasoline ones. We'd drive them for eight hours, go into the motor pool, and another crew would take over and drive them again, report anything wrong, overhaul them and see what parts needed to be replaced. We drove everything—two-and-a-half ton trucks, three-quarter tons, jeeps, half-tracks.

Once, I fell asleep at the wheel of a half-track. We were practicing driving at night, in blackout, the way we would have to do it overseas. We never got much sleep. It was dark inside the vehicles, and I kept nodding off. We were moving really slow, watching the small lights on the rear of the front vehicle. When you were the right distance away, the two red lights would merge into one. The lights kept fading away, not because I was too far back, but because I kept dozing off. At one point the convoy must have stopped, and I fell totally asleep. I woke up and there were no red lights! The whole convoy in front of me was gone! The rest of it was backed up behind my half-track. A lieutenant came running up, cussing all the way. I told him I fell asleep. He and I walked out ahead with a flashlight to see where the road turned. We finally caught up with the rest of the convoy. The lieutenant got in the half-track with me and I'm thinking, "Boy, I'm gonna get it for this!" Thank God we weren't in combat! I got chewed out. I never fell asleep behind the wheel again.

Guys got killed in training, especially messengers on motorcycles. They would race in and out of vehicles in convoys. Tanks kicked up a lot of dust, and sometimes the drivers wouldn't see the motorcyclists. They would just get crushed under the treads.

Eventually, I got out of the tanks. I was glad I did. When I got into combat I saw inside tanks that were hit. It was like hamburger. The Shermans also used gasoline engines, and would catch on fire easily. We called them "Ronsons" [cigarette lighters]! I didn't want to get trapped in one of them. There was only one way out, through the bottom, and then small arms could knock you out when you came out from under. Tanks drew all the big fire. I was glad to be able to just jump into a hole.

Me and this other guy got fed up with it all. One day they asked for volunteers for the infantry and we said, "Let's get out of these tanks! We're going into the infantry!" First we went to the repo depo[13] at Fort Meade, Maryland. I got to go home long enough to get my wife pregnant. Then I went to the 100th Infantry Division at Fort Bragg, North Carolina. Then they wanted replacements to fill the 63rd. So I went to the repo depo again. I got more basic training in the 100th, and then more in the 63rd. We also got advanced training. Finally, they shipped me to Camp Van Dorn, Mississippi. That's the worst place that ever was. Mosquitoes as big as your finger! There were swamps and snakes! From there we went to Camp Shanks, New York.

We went overseas in a big old tub, a converted pleasure cruiser.[14] It was full of bunks, and loaded with soldiers. I was sick the whole way over. Whenever we went through Gibraltar, the water got calm, and you could see porpoises jumping. After we disembarked in Marseilles, they took us up by truck to a camp. We weren't allowed to go into Marseilles unless we went as a group. It was a rough town anyway, but at this time they had some Senegalese troops.[15] They were a bad bunch and weren't queasy about slitting throats of lone soldiers. They were good at sneaking up on Germans at night and... [*runs his finger across his neck*]. In a big field outside Marseilles, we got geared up and moved north to Nancy.

My first experience in combat was actually funny. It happened on a dark night, when I was on guard duty. Whoever was on guard would have to go under a porch and get coal for the stove. When I got into the coal bin, BOOM! Somebody started shooting at me! Bullets were whacking all around that porch! I'm in there scared to death! I took a chance and ran out. Our own boys were shooting at me. They must have thought I was a German!

A few days later was not so funny. I answered the phone and somebody told me some Germans got shot. The lieutenant and I went up and ran into Sergeant Black, 3rd Squad, from South Carolina. The cellar had one of those sloping doors, where we had machine-guns set up. Two Germans dressed in bed sheets had come up.[16] They looked like they were wearing wedding gowns. The password was "zombie/white" or "white/zombie." Sergeant Black had halted them. They stopped. He said, "Zombie!" They repeated, "Zombie!" That was it. BOOM! Black shot one of them right between the eyes! That was the first German I saw shot. They dragged him into the cellar. The other guy got away. They went through the dead man's clothes. He had pictures of his wife and kids. That sickened me!

We sent out night patrols to get prisoners. A guy in our outfit, Berstrich, could speak German and he would question them. He'd make the Germans dig a hole and told them the hole would be their graves if they didn't talk. We did all kinds of tricks, like stick guns in their face.

---

[13]Sometime "repple depple" or "replacement depot."
[14]The 63rd departed New York 5 January 1945.
[15]French colonial troops from Senegal, West Africa.
[16]Both sides used bed sheets for winter camouflage.

We stayed in a defensive position for a while. In February[17] we moved out to Sarreguemines. That's when we started to get a lot of casualties. One guy in my squad wouldn't carry the machine-gun because his feet hurt. He was a goof-off. That's all I have to say about him. *I* picked the gun up and carried it. He eventually shot himself in the foot–in front of everyone–to get out of the war. They took him away. We never saw him again.[18]

The Germans were all around us, but things were quiet. We just probed each other. After Sarreguemines we started on the offensive and crossed the Saar River. I saw a lot of guys get crippled by Schu mines. They were the worst, just little things that were *meant* to cripple. Schu mines could rip off a leg off, or the bottom half of your body. The enemy knew it took more men to take care of a wounded man than a dead one.

At night, on the Siegfried Line, we sent sappers up to the pillboxes to plant explosives. We had 60mm mortars behind us shooting over our heads. There were bigger ones behind them and even bigger ones behind those. They were constantly firing and softening up that Siegfried Line until we pierced through it. Our artillery was so intense it drove us crazy. You can imagine what it was like on the receiving end. At night you could actually see the shells flashing through the air.

We crossed the Rhine River on pontoon bridges.[19] We got to Heidelberg.[20] All night we're waiting and wondering, "What's going on?" We're sitting in our vehicles and laying on the ground. Trucks were loaded with soldiers. Then they came up with the word, "Move out! The Germans gave us the city." Hitler wanted Heidelberg destroyed, but the general commanding Heidelberg disobeyed him. He came out with a white flag. We set up Seventh Army headquarters in Heidelberg. We spent all day looking around and talking to people. I gave the kids candy. Then we got orders to move out to the next town. That's where we got it! The Germans were up there waiting for us.[21] We set up a defense along the Rhine. We could see the Germans, and they could see us. We didn't fire, but we'd draw fire. This colonel came up to me and my buddy West, "Who's that over there?"

"Those are Germans."

The colonel said, "I'm getting out of here!"

He turned around and took off!

---

[17]Task Force Harris of the 63rd defended the Vosges and Maginot Line area 22–30 December 1944 and met the German offensive south of Bitche 1–19 January 1945. Task Force Harris was discontinued when the rest of the division assembled at Willerwald on 2 February 1945.

[18]Mr. Ciavarra, whose history appears in this volume, witnessed a similar, if not the same, incident.

[19]The 63rd crossed the Rhine at Neuschloss on 28 March 1945 and relieved the 44th Infantry Division.

[20]Around 28 March 1945.

[21]On 30 March 1945, the 63rd expanded the Rhine bridgehead by attacking south through Heidelberg and Mannheim and turning east. On 8 April 1945, the 253rd was confronted by the 17th SS Panzer Grenadier Division *Gotz von Berlichingen*.

We had our machine-guns pointed at the Germans. The infantry was behind us. Our artillery would fire all night. Big searchlights lit up that whole German side. We could see everything. The Germans knew our outfit as the "Blood and Fire," and they respected us. One of my platoon sergeants was killed. His wife had just given birth to twins. We took a town and were walking up the street. The sergeant was in a squad across from us. A German stepped out of a doorway with a burp gun and cut the sergeant down. Another sergeant, an Irishman, O'Hara, just went berserk. He screamed and hollered. We all hit the ground, but the squad took care of the German pretty quick.

We took a hill just outside the town. There were a lot of dead Germans and GIs laying around. The sergeant asked me to take a couple men and pick up bloated German bodies. I got three brand-new guys who had never been in action before. We started picking bodies up and throwing them in the trailer. This one guy went down into a sniper's nest. He grabbed a corpse by the leg and it came off! That guy started throwing up and he couldn't stop! We filled that trailer! The sergeant told me to take the bodies to a big barn. There were Germans piled in there like cord wood. I had to wash that trailer out! A lot of the dead Germans had a bottle of champagne in their pockets. We did too! We were half loaded! In Heidelberg we got all that French wine and French Champagne that the Germans stole from the French.

A young fella came up. I was in the jeep. He said, "Could you take us back to the aid station?"

He had a wound in his chest, and had some blood coming from his mouth. I had to get that boy to the aid station fast! Then he said, "I have two prisoners to take back with me."

I made the Germans trot along in front of the jeep. They had the SS lightning bolts on their uniforms. When we got to this little dorf, a rear-echelon soldier stepped out of a doorway, raised his Thompson, and shot them! We hollered that they were our prisoners, but it really didn't bother me too much that he shot them. Anyway, it was just two more dead Germans.

Another time, the lieutenant of 2nd Platoon lost a lot of men. He was going crazy! He got about ten or twelve SS into a gully. You could see fear on their faces. They knew what was going to happen. So did we. He manned the machine-gun himself and he killed them. Nobody else wanted do it. A lot of people went berserk. Everybody knew it.

Up near Bubingen the Germans pinned down our troops in a stone quarry. They needed ammunition, and I took it up. Worst battle I was in. It was a rat race! There was all this shell fire. I drove up the road. There was a big field to my right. All at once, a German with an automatic weapon started firing at me. The bullets were spattering all around the jeep. One hit the windshield, right beside my head. The corporal with me said, "Stop! Let's bail out!" So we ran down to a ditch and left the jeep set up there on the road. We waited for a while and it got quiet. I said, "Well, we'd better do something."

I was a little guy, so I snuck up in the jeep, and started it. The corporal came in beside me, and we took off. The firing started again. We stopped and "hit the ditch!" Bullets were tearing through the trees and bushes. We got showered with leaves and branches. The lieutenant said, "Get those jeeps back!"

You drive a jeep backwards with a trailer attached to it, it's tricky! You never seen trailers back up so fast in your life! I didn't jackknife. I just went straight back as fast as I could, because the trailer had a load of ammunition in it! Once I got up to where the outfit was, we started to unload the stuff into a cellar. All at once—BOOM! BOOM! We got some incoming. I hit the ground and the other guys flew into the cellar. I'm laying on the ground beside the jeep! Then they started with phosphorous shells. You get hit with phosphorous you can't put it out. If it gets on your clothes, you might as well take your clothes off, because it will burn right through.

The next morning the Germans were gone. We found three of our infantry scouts lying dead. There were German dead up there, too. I'm looking the jeep over and saw that the tire valve was sheared off. The end looked like it was welded. The tire didn't leak! The valve must have deflected a shell fragment. It was still hot! I showed the guys. Thank God for the valve. I was laying on the ground right by that tire. That fragment might have been meant for me! I got a Bronze Star for getting that ammunition up there.

When we were moving across Europe there was a lot of looting and fraternization, though none of that was supposed to happen. We even "looted" our own officers' stuff. One day in Sarreguemines, I was on guard duty around the officers' quarters. They must have had a party that night. It was two or three in the morning. When I looked in the tent, there were empty whiskey bottles. One bottle was almost full and I snatched it. I thought, "They'll never know. They're all drunk and will probably figure that they drank it themselves."

I took a Nazi flag and an officer's saber from a house. I also got a German pilot's helmet, and big air pistol, and a Luger. I took the Luger from a German officer who was a prisoner. When we were on patrol, we'd poach deer. We fished in the rivers, using grenades. The concussion generated would kill the fish causing them to float up. Then the German civilians would gather them. The fish fed them, too.

It was just like Sherman going through Georgia. We lived off the land. I never liked turnips, but I dug some up in a field and ate them raw. Steal everything! We'd go up to a farmer and say, *Haben Sie Eier* ("Do you have any eggs?")

He would say, *Nichts! Nichts!* ("Nothing! Nothing!")

"The Hell you don't!" We'd look and we'd find a whole bunch. Ten or twelve eggs at a time! They were great! All we got from the Army were powdered eggs.

"Someone stole my chickens!"

In Bubingen, we robbed a bank. We stuffed German Marks in our pockets. They had practically no value. We shot out all the light fixtures in that bank! I used that money after the war. You could buy a beer for five pfennings. I could have bought the whole brewery with what I had, if it had been worth what it should have been. I gave it to civilians by the handful for washing my clothes. I bought bread from them with the money.

In one little town, my buddy and I, Bird Dog, took over a house. We found a wall safe while we were on guard. We had visions of jewelry in there. Our shift was only for two hours, but we stayed up all night chiseling into that wall safe. We finally got it open. It was empty!

We took over one house for the jeep drivers and the squad corporal. We went out scouting around for food. We found a barn full of chickens. We brought them to the barn. We got rabbits and put them in cages. We were there for three days, and every morning I'd go out and gather eggs, and green onions. Then we'd kill a rabbit and fry it. I was down in the cellar one day digging coal out for the fire and I ran into canned pork chops. I was the one who did all the cooking.

Behind a loose stone in a house I found a stamp collection. It was probably worth a lot of money. I sent it home but it never got there. Somebody stole it! I went out one day and all my chickens were gone. I said, "Somebody stole my chickens!" I stole stuff to begin with and someone stole it off me! Maybe the officers took the chickens. We found an Opal car, made by General Motors. I thought we were going to have a car to run around in. We got it running and these officers came by and took it!

As soon as the Germans took off, we would ransack. In France we didn't do too much of that because of the French people, but in Germany we took over. We weren't too sensitive to the German population when it came to food.

Not many obeyed the rule against fraternization. Even the officers were doing it. I was on patrol with my buddy, after the war. He saw this woman who worked in a barn. He said, "Pull over, I'm going to go up and get her."

I waited in the jeep for roughly fifteen minutes. He comes down and says, "Man!"

He was beat up and had straw all over him.

"She threw me all over that barn!"

Everybody was happy when the war was over. My brother-in-law, who was in the 28th Division,[22] was in Bremen. West and some other guys had relatives near there. We got a pass and took the jeep. I dropped one guy off in Triers. I

---

[22]The Pennsylvania National Guard, the "Keystone Division" from the "Keystone State." The division wore red keystone patches. The division's 110th Infantry Regiment was and still is stationed in Greensburg, Pennsylvania. The Germans called the 28th "The Bloody Bucket." Nearly every frontline soldier in the division became a casualty in the Hurtgen Forest. At the request of General Charles de Gaulle the 28th, along with the 4th Division, paraded down the Champs Elysée following the liberation of Paris.

dropped a couple more off at different towns. When I got to Bremen, I found out that the 28th had moved north to Bremerhaven. I didn't have enough time to go there. I went back and picked the other guys up. On the way back I hit a shell hole and busted the axle. By luck there was an ordinance outfit nearby. We went over there and said, "We hit a shell hole and busted an axle so we're going to be late getting back unless you fix this up?"

They towed it over and they fixed it up, but it was too late anyway. When they were finished, I said "Wait a minute, write us out an excuse."

I got back and told the lieutenant what happened. We were a day late, but the lieutenant checked the excuse and let us go.

Then I went to Camp Lucky Strike[23] in France. They had shifted me all a-round. When I was in the chow line, somebody said, "They dropped an atomic bomb on Japan."

I said, "What on earth? An atomic bomb?"

We didn't even know what he was talking about. Then we heard on the news that they dropped a second. Finally, the Japs gave up. I was glad, because they would have fought to the death! I might have gotten killed over there. The Japs were fanatics!

I came home on the cruiser *USS Boise* from Le Havre, December 1945. We raced another cruiser across. Our ship won the race to the Brooklyn Navy Yard! There were still some sea mines left from the war and we watched the sailors shooting them out of the water. In Brooklyn we got on buses for Fort Dix. When we got there, they asked us what we wanted to eat. I got steak and ice cream, stuff I hadn't had for a long time. At Fort Indiantown Gap, they asked if I wanted to stay in. I said, "NO WAY!"

I took a train to Greensburg. At the station, they were playing the *Star-Spangled Banner.* Tears came to my eyes. My mother and wife were there. We went out to Bloomfield, where my wife was living, and I saw my boy. He was six months old. I got him in my arms. I went to sit down, but I was so excited that I missed the chair! The house was all decorated!

There were a lot of good and bad things happening fifty-some years ago. When I think about the war, I remember the guys that got killed. We got the job done, but it was slaughter! I was young when I went in, and I thought there would be glory in it. Today, I tell people "War is Hell," just like General Sherman did. A lot of us might have been patriotic, but, really, we didn't think about much except staying alive and coming home. It was bad enough for soldiers on both sides. But the civilian people in Europe suffered worse.

Once I was driving along at night and saw this burning barn. The whole sky was lit up, and I heard these horrible screams of the cows in the barn that were being burned to death. Another time, a German farmer came up to me. He was

---

[23]The Army named various "mustering out" camps after various brands of cigarettes.

crying. His horse had been badly wounded from shellfire. He begged me to shoot the horse. I took my rifle and put it out of its misery.

I saw a terrible thing in a German town called Boxtal, along the Main River just below Wertheim, where there were farms. We were maneuvering in the pastures. Someone left a bazooka[24] shell behind. Our squad took over this house. I'm living in the basement. There were signs posted all around. *Verboten* (Warning! Forbidden!'). All of a sudden, a woman came running down the street hollering in German. I couldn't understand her. She's pointing up the hill. I jump in the jeep, and I'm the first one up there. There were kids scattered all over the place. Some were dead. Some had their arms off and their legs off! One was laying there with his chest all open. You could see his lungs moving up and down. I took sulfa powder and poured it in there. For the first time since I got to Europe, I got out my emergency bandage. I pulled it apart and put the pad on his chest. I got him in the jeep. The kids had found that live round and it exploded when they banged it with a rock.

More guys, some in a light tank, came up. They started hauling the kids. I had the kid I was helping in the back seat. I came down the street and all the women were screaming and hollering. I took him back to the medical station and all these vehicles were going back and forth getting the other kids. An ambulance finally went up. The ones closest to the explosion were dead. I'd see these women riding back and forth to visit the hospital. I asked this one woman how her boy was and she said he lost an arm. Just when I think those memories are gone, I see that kid with his chest blown open...

But I just keep going on with my life.

---

[24]Antitank rocket launcher.

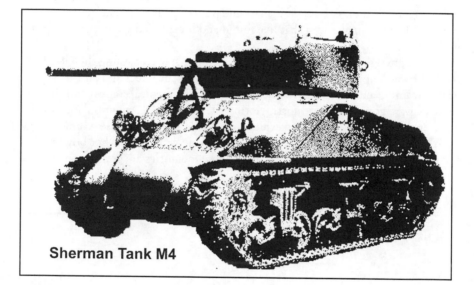

Sherman Tank M4

The Jeep, the Colonel, and I

Robert F. Black

1261st Combat Engineer Battalion

Jeannette, Pennsylvania, April, 1921

"In the south, where we had the same quotas that we had in the north, we were dealing with backward country situations. Men living in the mountains, swamps, and woods were largely uneducated. Going strictly by numbers alone, men were taken into the service who could not read nor write, nor handle themselves physically. They were absolutely frightened when they left their environment. Most of them had never been to a city. A good many didn't know what a car or what electricity was! They came into the service and got scattered all over the country in camps. Camp commanders went crying, "What are we going to do?"

My father, Milo, had a meat market which catered to the wealthy people of Greensburg. Then he worked for the Pennsylvania Railroad in Jeannette as an advertising manager. From there he opened a store on Main St. in Greensburg. That was his last place of employment before the Depression. After that everything went—the store, house, car, bank account, all the money. He slowly died in 1933. My mother always thought he died because of all those losses. She worked six days a week for ten dollars a week.

Not many escaped the wrath of the Depression. At ten I started working minor jobs cutting grass, washing cars, shoveling snow. Nickels, dimes, and quarters helped. In those days coal trucks would run coal down a chute into the cellars. They would always spill some coal. A local hauler gave me a nickel to clean up the coal after he left. When I was fifteen, during the summer, I tried to sell siding for people's houses door to door. That didn't work too well, but I did have several newspaper routes. In those days advertising was handled a lot by what they called "bills," sheets of paper that they delivered to the front door. I passed those around town for a number of stores. I would make forty cents delivering 200 newspapers.

After high school, there was no money for further education. In my senior year, however, I took classes that would help me become a CPA. I found work with an insurance company and began night school at Robert Morris Business School in Pittsburgh. Tuition was twenty-five dollars a month. For two years, I

Robert Black: Antwerp, Belgium, May 1945.

used half my fifty dollar monthly salary to pay for it. Then the war started to intensify, and in 1942 I enlisted.

When the war came, things changed. Cars and tires were limited to priority cases. There was rationing. Bomb shelters, which we never even thought of before, were now being built. There were blackouts throughout the country. People bought black curtains so that no light would shine from inside the house. Each neighborhood had a civilian defense warden who walked through the streets checking to see if everyone was complying. Names like *dog faces, non-coms, buck privates, 90-Day Wonders, ROTC, Stage Door Canteens, USO*[25] became familiar. Factory production shifted from peace to war in quick time. There were war bonds and rallies to sell them. Kids collected foil, newspapers, pots and pans, bacon grease, and all kinds of other stuff for the war effort.[26]

I was a recruiter for a while, and had the use of a car. In thirteen months I put 32,000 miles on it! Recruiting in World War II is one subject I don't think has been studied much. World War I veterans were called back. Military retirees were called back. The college ROTC trained officers. Every young man between eighteen and forty-five had to register with the local draft board, which had a monthly quota to fill.

In the South, where we had the same quotas that we had in the North, we were dealing with backward country boys whose homes were in the mountains, swamps, and woods. They were largely uneducated. The Army was interested in numbers alone. It took men who could neither read nor write, nor handle themselves physically. Out of their environment, they were absolutely frightened. Most of them had never been to a city. A good many didn't know what a car or electricity was! They came into the service and got scattered all over the country in camps. Camp commanders came crying, "What are we going to do?

It was too late to start trying to teach these men. Most of them were just uncooperative in as many ways as you could think of. It was a terrible, terrible, approach that the government used. Ultimately, many of these men caused problems. Many of them became Section Eights, the sorriest group of men that I have ever seen. They had to be treated as uneducated, insane, frightened, yet physically powerful. Never for a moment could you leave them alone or let down your guard.

In November 1942, the Army decided to use Camp Wallace, Texas as its Section-Eight Discharge Center. There was a backlog of such men past due for

---

[25]Stage Door Canteens were originally started by the British. They were founded by actress Beatrice Lillie, and were open to all ranks and services. They were places of entertainment where servicemen could associate with various members of the entertainment profession. American equivalents were the Hollywood Canteen and USO clubs.

[26]An excellent book concerning the United States home front in World War II is Stan Cohen's *V for Victory: America's Home Front in World War II*, Pictorial Histories Publishing Company, Missoula, Montana, 1991.

discharge. They came by train from scattered camps to converge at Camp Wallace. At Wallace, we had four barracks next to my headquarters office. This would be their home until discharge. Nobody in the Army knew much about procedures because the situation was new. Consequently, I had the freedom to set up my own procedures without interference from others. I got the camp hospital and the finance office to cooperate with me. When necessary, they called upon the chaplain for special help. The colonel in charge of the office gave me use of his command car and sergeant driver any time I needed it. The sergeant-major in charge of the office was sympathetic to my every need and wish.

There was a special cadre of big, tough non-coms available to me to handle special cases who couldn't care for themselves, and who had to be escorted home under guard, right to their front doors. The same corporals and sergeants watched over the barracks where they housed the special cases. The Army offered bus and train tickets for all those who could care for themselves. We had to judge what was best for each individual. We also considered notifying relatives of these men to see if they could come and pick up a family member. Houston was a starting point for those going by train. Our bus took care of that. Sometimes we had trains leaving from the camp site.

At first, the escort duty was considered to be a plum by dreamers waiting for work at the cadre pool. They soon learned that it was a twenty-four-hour responsibility, and not the luxury trip that they had in mind. The old train coaches were crowded. They had to eat boxed lunches provided by the Army. The schedule was tight and they had to immediately return to base. There was no time for sightseeing.

Each Friday I had my "graduates," about forty a week, parade down to the front gate. This was a regular ceremony that lasted from 1:00 to 3:00 p.m. The sergeants watched them as they made the one-mile trek. After they got tickets, individual orders, and instructions, they went one by one out the front gate and waited for transportation. Some of these guys had tried to shoot themselves, stab themselves, or break their own bones. In a lot of cases they did this to officers. In training, you couldn't give them live ammunition. They would try to get the bayonets off the rifles.

This was a very desperate group. Even after discharge, it was hard to believe that, even under escort, some were still able to escape. When the escorts would take them to the rest room, they would smash out the small ventilator window on the train and try to crawl out. If they weren't too big, they could make it. There was one that did go out that way, but he was killed along the tracks. Some would start terrible fights on the coaches. The officers had to be with them all the time because there were regular passengers on the train, also. Sometimes the guys lived as far away as New York, but most of them were southern boys. Today, they would put them into mental hospitals. Back then, the Army felt that it could wash its hands of the matter if it merely got these Section Eights home.

Not everyone was a Section Eight. Others were older men of good minds, but their bodies could not tolerate Army life. Otherwise, they were wonderful and capable of much. They had been placed in company with some sad characters. It was hard to believe how blind the Army classification process was, especially in letting so much usable talent go to waste. A prime example was a man I got to know. This is what happened.

The men soon learned that I was their sympathetic counselor. I worked a lot of the evenings, Saturdays, and some Sunday afternoons. Texas had little to offer me, and I poured my life into my work. When I would go back to the office Saturday and Sunday afternoon, I would find a gathering of men waiting to see me. I soon became known in camp as "Doctor." I listened to their stories. I also read letters from home to them and wrote quick postcards home for them. I tried to help them and let them know that I was a friend who was going to get them home. One afternoon, a frail, forty-five-year-old man came to see me. He felt dejected and terribly out of place. He needed a friend probably as much or more than anyone that I had worked with so far. I discovered that he was a well-edu-cated gentleman from New Orleans who worked at a plant that belonged to him and his sister, who ran the business. He was drafted and placed in a training situa-tion which he couldn't physically adjust to. He put in much time waiting to get out, but got no help from the Army. He had to endure quite a transition. He was frustrated because he thought that he really would be able to do his part in the service. Now he needed my attention and help. Of course, I placed him on the list for the next week's "graduation."

Later that week, he came back and thanked me and told me that his chauffeur would meet him at the gate. He also asked me to visit New Orleans as his and his sister's guest for the weekend. That Friday he marched with the group to the gate. A long, seven-passenger Cadillac stopped, a driver opened the door, he got in, and was whisked away. Later, I took three days and went to New Orleans. On the evening of the second day, I joined him and his sister for dinner at Antoine's Restaurant. I was treated to an unforgettable dining experience. When I got ready to leave, he asked me to get in touch with him after I got discharged. He wanted me to be a part of his business. I could have had the good life if I had done it!

Everyday in camp I saw mattresses on the fence surrounding the barracks. Mattresses also hung out of windows. These were the homes of the bedwetters! Most of these men were on a level even lower than the lowest. They had lived their lifetime with this problem because they were uneducated and didn't really realize that they had a problem. I asked one of these guys how long he had been wetting the bed. "A lifetime," he answered.

I asked about his father and mother. He responded, "The same."

I asked whether he was married. He responded, "Yes."

I asked him what his wife thought. He answered, "She does it, too."

I felt sorry for the corporals and sergeants who had to live in these buildings and daily go through this ordeal.

I spent almost a whole year on this job, and enjoyed it. Even so, I decided to take a quick change. I went to Fort Meade, where I did the same work, but at least it was a different place.

I got to England in 1944. I went in advance of my unit to set up a 1,000-man camp at Crew. The place was full of 1,000-man camps. For three months in 1944–1945, when I lived in downtown London, bombing took place on a consistent basis between 4:00 p.m. and 6:00 a.m. The Germans sending over buzz-bombs and V-2 rockets, Hitler's vengeance weapons. In downtown London there were underground railroad stations, home to hundreds of bombed-out people. They slept in bunk beds stacked right on the loading platforms. Trains would pull in six feet away from where they were encamped. I lived in South Kensington about three blocks from an underground station. I was in and out of there quite often. People carried teapots, if nothing else. They slept in eight-hour shifts, without so much as the luxury of a change of clean clothes. They moved out when the next shift came in. It was cold and damp in the underground, but a big improvement over the street. The British evacuated most of the children to the north to stay with relatives, friends or in institutions. I rarely saw a child in London.

The Colonel and I were out in the Jeep preparing to make a trip to Harrod's Department Store on Kensington High Street. I was sitting in the Jeep. He was somewhere down the street. Suddenly, about 4:30 p.m., a V-2 hit the middle of the street where two buses loaded with commuters were passing each other. Everyone was ripped to bits. The Colonel immediately came back and we got out of there! They had fire brigades, usually made up of old men. One of the departments within this group came and cleaned up the right of way. Then things got back to normal. We really wouldn't have been welcomed as helpers. They had their own ways of doing things. We found out later that sixty people had been killed.

Our three combat engineer outfits, roughly 3,000 men, were all billeted in townhouses near a devastated area in South Kensington called Cranley Place. This was the winter of 1944. We were there to construct villages for the bombed-out people. We had six weeks to finish. It was a job in itself to clear out the rubble. Then we built a series of cement pads throughout the village, and put Quonset huts on top of them. Inside there was a sleeping room, a small bathroom, with a washstand and a commode, a very simple kitchen, and a sitting area with a pot-belly stove for heating. My outfit finished the first and went onto the second in Croydon, a popular spot in London.

We finished on a Saturday afternoon, after running late on the job. A ribbon-cutting ceremony had been planned for the following Monday to mark the turning over of the gift from the United States Army to the British people. General Eisenhower was to present a symbolic key to the villages to Winston Churchill.

Plans called for me to drive them the two blocks that led into the village center where each leader was to give a brief speech. The Jeep was specially decorated for the occasion! The event never happened. On Sunday afternoon a V-2 came over and landed right square in the center of our project, wiping it out completely. That was the end of our work. It was almost biblical. The village had come from dust and rubble and returned to dust and rubble.

We moved and went to Henley-on-Thames, where we taught bridge-building to engineers going over to Europe. One morning the Colonel told me, "Tonight, you be at my house at 10:00 p.m. We're leaving."

It was a typical black night filled with lots of rain. We led a convoy of 110 trucks to Southhampton, where we boarded two-decked landing boats. There were no cabins, no luxuries. I had big trucks on both sides of me on the top deck, with the jeeps in the center. We were the ballast. All that we wanted to do was to cross the Channel and get it over with. Men were in every possible place. Some were in trucks trying to make as much space as they could find, and some were just huddled along the sides. Fortunately, I was in the Jeep and had a little floor space on which to sleep.

We left about 1:30 a.m. The Jeep, the trucks beside me, and everything on the boat were supposed to be lashed tight with heavy chains. If anything was left unlashed in the front or back it would fall off. The Channel was vicious that night. Everybody was flipping and flopping, but I was so dog-tired that I slept the night through. When we got into the harbor in the morning, I looked out and saw that number one truck on my right and number one truck on my left were gone. Everything else was there, except those two trucks. They had been pitched overboard during the night. Why I didn't go over I'll never know!

It was March 1945. We crossed France in about two days. We arrived at Aachen, Germany, and passed through the remains of the Siegfried Line. About 11:00 p.m. we reached what was left of a former luxury girl's school. Any billet in those days had to have a capacity of 1,000 men. It was a monstrous building, but there wasn't much left of it. The roof was gone, the windows were out, and there was nothing inside. We had to be careful of any holes in the floor. Despite its problems, it was better than no place at all. We got settled.

The Colonel's office consisted of a small room with a map on the wall and one chair. We don't know where he found the chair, but he found one. Meanwhile, the rest of us laid down sleeping bags. A friend in supply gave me ten blankets. I slept as comfortably as anybody could on the floor. About 1:00 a.m. the Colonel came in and said, "I've got a job for you. We have to deliver two truckloads of men into the outskirts of Cologne. We took an underground ammunition plant there. We need to relieve our guard there and put in some men who can do some work."

It was nightime and hopeless. We had nothing by which to go. The Colonel showed me an old map. I hoped the roads were still there. The Colonel told me, "Here's where you have to go. There's one turn that you have to make."

The Army must have known about the plant, but deliberately didn't destroy it. On the way, there was no sign of activity. The Colonel said, "The Germans are still within a half mile of the place. If you stay with the route, they won't bother you."

We turned off the road onto a street. The Colonel said, "Access to the munitions plant is between two houses. A door will open out of the ground for you to reach the plant. You deliver the men in there and come back with the trucks. The men will be safe there."

We used the plant to supply us with ammunition. This was a perfect example of the Army deciding ahead of time what not to destroy. There was trouble all around, except on this one street. We got back from the trip at 3:00 a.m.

While we were still billeted at the girl's school, I took the Colonel and a young lieutenant on a quick inspection tour across the German border into Holland. It was a warm, sunny day in March 1945. Compared to what was happening elsewhere, the scene in Holland was tranquil. There was no traffic on the road and no bombers in the sky. We cruised the Jeep along a white, crushed-stone road. What a target from the air! We didn't see it and we didn't hear it, but a lone German bomber dropped a bomb that came close to being a direct hit. It exploded right in front of the Jeep! Stones flew and shrapnel whizzed around us. Visibility dropped to zero. The shock from the bomb shot the Jeep a half-dozen feet straight up. The Jeep spun around in mid-air, dropped to the bottom of the bomb crater, then bounced back out onto the road, headed in the opposite direction! We were lucky to have landed upright when we hit the bottom of the crater. The wheels were still spinning at forty m.p.h., and that's what shot us straight back up and out.

When we came to a stop, the lieutenant was up through the cloth roof, the Colonel was on the front floor, and I was gripping the steering wheel. We pulled the lieutenant back inside. We were badly shaken, but nothing worse. The front wheels were splayed; one headed east, the other west. We scraped and slid the whole way back to headquarters. Within five minutes we got another jeep from the motor pool. The Jeep was "hospitalized" for a two-day cure. And the war continued.

Selective destruction by our Army was common. I was out driving by myself through our district on the Rhine River. There was nothing but rubble. Normally, the roads were cleared wide enough for one vehicle to get through. Eventually, I came to a street that had been fully cleared. I went back in there very cautiously and saw steel all over the place. I found out that it was a Krupp plant, undamaged. Everything around the plant was destroyed. Since there was no way we could requisition the ironworks we needed, I went back and told the sergeant at the motor pool that he could go and get all the iron and steel he needed for repairing bridgework. We got two of the biggest trucks we had and went out and got enough steel and iron to keep the Army going for a long time.

Our billets along the Rhine were also spared from bombing. There were double houses stretched along the river, just enough for 1,000 men. We placed cots all over the inside. There were no facilities in the houses. They were merely places to keep us out of the cold. Two miles down the road was the bathhouse a local coal company had constructed for its workers. The Army destroyed the company, but left the bathhouse intact. It was the first chance in months that we had to bathe. We got two showers a week. We would go back and forth by truckloads. The sergeant would check us in and out to make sure that we were not doubling up.

There were four German women hanging around the place. None of us ever found out from where they had come. They took care of the place, and lived in one little side office. We weren't allowed to talk to them, nor be anywhere near them. One day, the Colonel needed to talk to one of them about something pertaining to business. One of the women had a young boy about seven years old. Apparently, he sneaked out when the Colonel went in, and I didn't notice him. Suddenly I heard a noise. I looked out of the side of the Jeep, but couldn't see anything. I leaned and literally threw my body down so I could look under the Jeep. Here was the little fellow using his Hitler Youth[27] knife to cut through some lines. He probably would have started on the tires next. I took one hand and pulled him off. I took him straight to his mother. The Colonel took over from there. I was taught never to let my guard down, even with a small child. I still have the kid's knife!

I was out one day in the Jeep, on kind of a reconnaissance mission. As usual, there was a lot of rubble. One building was destroyed from the top, but a solid heavy floor remained. I stopped and went into the basement where I found a collection of radios. I went back and told the sergeant of the motor pool, "If you get a truck out there with a couple good men, I think that we can all have some radios."

Within minutes they were on their way. They carried off forty beautiful, expensive, German radios. We never saw anything so big for a table model. Unfortunately, we had no electricity. I took my radio back to my billet where some ingenious men rigged up electricity for us. At night we would have one light in our big room and a slot to plug in for the radio. We enjoyed that!

Around 9:00 a.m., on our second day in Germany, the Colonel called me in and told me, "I have another job for you. I want you to take two loads of mine

---

[27] *Hitler Jugend*, an organization set up by Adolf Hitler in 1933 for educating and training male youth in Nazi principles. Under the leadership of Baldur von Schirach, head of all German youth programs, the Hitler Youth included by 1935 almost 60 percent of German boys.

sweepers and go to the far side of the Rhine, to a small village. You will see a lot of rubble, but there will also be a path there. Go through it and when you get to the other side, drop off the men so they can start sweeping for mines. Pick the men up later."

Everything went fine as we crossed the Rhine. When we got to the village, we came under heavy small-arms fire. Bullets peppered the lower sides of the Jeep and both trucks. We pulled clear and stopped. Two truckloads of men, armed with rifles and grenades, were with us. I stopped when we were clear and told the fellows in the back, "You know what to do. Just be careful."

The usual procedure was to fan out and bring your troops to the point. The whole contingent went in. This was unnecessary, but they all wanted to be a part of it. When they got there, they found two German stragglers crouching behind a pile of bricks. They were fighting their own private war. We tossed in grenades and "removed" both of them. I took the soldiers to where they had to work, and returned perfectly safe, my mission accomplished!

After the war was over, they sent us to Antwerp to build a camp for troops slated to return home. The first thing we did was send minesweepers out to clean the area. They did a good day's work. They declared the area clean. We went to work with heavy equipment. We leveled the ground, then put up wooden bases on which we attached large tents. They were nice places to live, actually.

The Colonel and I drove to the area we were going to use for headquarters. About 100 feet in front of us was a truck. One of the passengers was riding on the front fender. BOOM! The right-front wheel of the truck hit a mine. The soldier on the fender was killed. The guys inside were banged up. That was the one and only box-mine that our sweepers missed. Whoever was responsible must have felt bad. No one was ever investigated. We just moved on.

Mines were treacherous. Once, near our base on the Rhine River, the Colonel and I saw a PFC standing alongside the road waving to us. We stopped, and I asked the GI what he wanted. He told me, "My buddy and I are back here in the truck and we're stuck."

They were back on a lane that hadn't been swept. We always cleared about five or six feet off the paved roads, but this lane hadn't been touched. The fellows were medics with only minor training. They had a three-quarter-ton Dodge truck loaded with medical supplies. They had driven down the lane to a place they could turn around, then settled down for a nap! As they prepared to leave, the rear of the truck got stuck in soft ground. We couldn't do a thing even with our four-wheel drive. I told them, "I'll back in up to your bumper and connect my hitch. When I give you the signal, you put it in low-range, four-wheel drive and feed in gas. I'll be doing the same thing. If we can do this simultaneously then maybe this will work."

It worked! I told him, "Drive straight out to the road without getting out, and don't deviate one bit from the tracks that you're following."

I went out on the road and they followed. I walked back to where they had been stuck. They had been so far down with that back bumper that they dragged the dirt right off a box-mine. Had they spun wheels anymore that mine would have blown them to bits. I brought them back and showed them what they got into.

I said, "This better be a lesson. That's why we put the markers along the road. Don't go on the other side of them!"

After the war, I made some trips to Mannheim. On my first one I saw some engineers working on a bridge. There was only one lane going through. George Patton was standing to the right of the Jeep, watching the work. His great days were over and he was now commanding non-combatants. It was a minor post for him! On my second trip to Mannheim, I entered the city on a beautiful, wide street that had a park-like setting between the lanes. At a narrow street on an intersection, I saw a khaki-colored Cadillac, an Army commander's car. There was an old truck there, too. I got out of the Jeep and walked over. As I neared, I noticed that they had taken the Army identification off the car. When I got there a sergeant said, "This is a mess. They're taking General Patton to the hospital."

What I was looking at was General Patton's fatal accident! He had been in the back seat. Those 1937 Cadillacs left a lot of room and floor space between the back seat and the back of the front seat. If he had had seat belts then he would not have been hurt, but back in those days we never heard of seat belts. So when this truck pulled across the intersection, the driver just slammed on his brakes and barely hit the Cadillac. The car was undamaged. They built them like tanks back then. Patton was thrown from his seat up against the front seat. In so doing he broke his back or neck. I didn't know which. Over the years, I've seen all kinds of stories in books and on TV about what really happened to Patton. I know. I was there!

After the war, I got to Rheims, where Eisenhower used to have a little, red schoolhouse for a headquarters. I parked out in the street and saw an officer and a sergeant coming out of a beautiful, castle-like building surrounded by a fence the Army put up. Each was carrying a case of champagne. They found it in the wine cellar of the building. At the time it was worth about twenty-five dollars a bottle. You just never saw it during the war because they safely guarded it somewhere. They did not allow me in, though. Only an officer could go down and make a selection of what he wanted. They didn't "cater" to enlisted men's "needs." I stopped them and asked him how could I get some.

The officer said, "Only an officer can get some. Don't you have an officer with you?"

I said, "No."

He said, "Then you can't, but I'll tell you what. I'll get it for you."

I went into the lobby area, which was as far as I could go. He got me two cases, which I took back to camp. A tall master sergeant saw the cases and started

"...master sergeant saw the cases and started yelling and running after me!"

yelling and running after me! I gave him a pretty good run, but I finally stopped and sold him a bottle for twenty dollars. In camp I went to the Officers' Club and offered an officer a case for twenty-five-dollars per bottle. He paid for it and thanked me. He was very happy with it. I took the rest of it to the enlisted men's tents and yelled, "One bottle per tent." I gave it to them. I never even had a taste of it. That night the fellows got looped. The next morning we were scheduled for our first day trip to Paris. When I got up in the morning, none of them were fit to drive. They missed the trip!

In early August 1945, our outfit was marking time when we received orders to move our heavy equipment to Marseilles and load it aboard ships. Men from the motor pool made the delivery. By the time they returned, everybody knew that we were scheduled to join our equipment on a Pacific island, thousands of miles away. Our orders were to build an airfield, hangars, office buildings and permanent military housing there. The Jeep, the Colonel, and I were scheduled for one last trip. We went to Rheims, to the headquarters in the Little Red School-house. The Jeep and I (by this time the Jeep could read my mind) waited outside the main entrance, knowing that the Colonel would come back out carrying written orders calling for the immediate transfer of our unit. We were wrong! Instead, a sergeant came out yelling, "It's over! The war is over! Japan's over! They've surrendered! It's over! The war is over!"

Four weeks later, most of us were moved to Epernay, France. We ended the way we started, billeted in another barebones but fashionable school for young ladies!

I got home in 1946, on the *USS George Washington*. Halfway across, one of the turbines broke down. In New York we were to march in a parade as an honor group, but we were too late because it took so long to fix the turbine. Our official welcome was two-feet of snow and the coldest winter in years. We were just as pleased that we didn't go marching down the streets of New York City on a day like that!

I got discharged at Indiantown Gap, where they gave us lectures on re-enlist-ment! Greyhound buses, destined for various cities, were parked outside. I was the last one out, and made my way toward the bus marked for Pittsburgh. The major in charge of the group hadn't talked to anyone, but he singled me out before I left and called me over. I began to think, "What in the world is going on now."

He told me, "I would like to give you a special invitation to reenlist. If you do, you can go to Officer's Training School."

If they had made me a general and had given me the rest of the year off, I would not have gone back in! I got a kick out of it because he didn't stop anybody except me. All I wanted to do was get home and start living again!

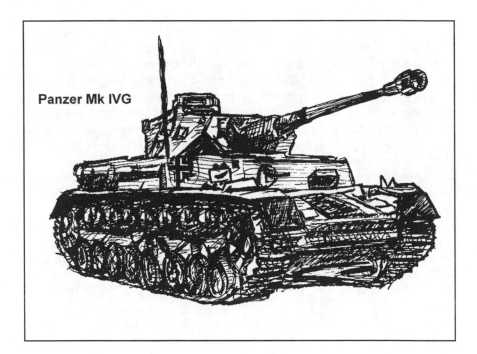

Panzer Mk IVG

"You Had to Go Like Crazy!"

Richard Brown

United States Third Army
5th Armored Division ("Victory Division," "Patton's
Ghost Division")
85th Cavalry Reconnaissance Squadron
Headquarters Troop

Stoystown, Pennsylvania, 12 June 1920

"One time, in Hofen, I went down over a hill and found a dead guy. He was our mailman. He was just laying there, still holding the mail. His blue eyes were wide open, staring at the sky. I didn't know whether to pick up the mail or what. Sometimes the Krauts booby trapped the corpses. I went back to the outfit and told them about the mailman. Some of the guys went down and gathered him up. Even after fifty years, I still see that pair of blue eyes, staring up at the sky."

There were Willman, White, Fagan, and Waggenfohr. Waggenfohr was one of the loosest people I'd ever seen in my life. If the hood or windshield flew off his vehicle, he kept on driving. He drove his peep to death. You *had* to go like crazy. We all worked together. The guy who drove the "Whore's Dream"[28] was Blaylock. Detchen drove the armored car. When you're a messenger, a lot of the guys get to know you, but you don't know them. Everywhere I went there was always somebody hollering at me.

My father, Lester, was a coal miner. Bessie Pile was my mother. My granddad came from the Black Forest in Germany. I grew up during the Depression. We walked every place we went until we finally got a 1932 Ford in 1934. Wherever we lived we never locked the doors. Nobody bothered anything. You found things just the way you left them. We also visited people more often, back then.

I only went to the seventh grade, to a country, one-room school house, Bowman School, the same one my parents went to. We didn't have any electricity. The first one that got to school in the morning built a fire, dumped the ice out of the water bucket, and filled it with water.

---

[28]Mr. Brown's armored message center.

Richard Brown; Upen, Belgium, 1944

We all drank from the same tin cup. Half the day would be gone before the place warmed up! There was only one teacher, and she was fantastic! It took some kind of teacher to wade through deep snow to get to work. There might have been thirty kids in that school. We brought a lunch. Some kids, when the snow got really deep, rode their horses to school. Then they just turned them loose and the horses went home.

I was thirteen when I started in the mines. My dad and I worked together. We loaded sixteen, two-ton mine cars a day. We did a lot of work for eighty-seven cents a ton!

Everyone was disgusted about the bombing of Pearl Harbor, and most people were willing to join the Service. They drafted me, but I would have joined up, anyway. A doctor said to me, "Do you think you'll like it in the service?" I said, "If the rest can handle it, I can handle it, too!"

When I got drafted, I was in the hospital with acute appendicitis. I went in right after I recovered. After my physical, I went to Fort Meade, Maryland. They asked me what I'd like to do. Since I rode an Indian Chief at home I said, "I'd like to ride motorcycles." They said OK! I did armor infantry first, then the rest of the vehicles, the tanks, and half-tracks—all of it.

At Fort Knox Armor School we trained hard. We had guys getting their feet smashed by tanks. My neighbor got run over by a tracked, ammunition hauler. It cut his leg off. Vehicles had to be clean at all times! Every time we stopped, and had any time at all, we had better be cleaning our vehicles, getting them ready for inspection. Motorcycles, especially, had to be ship-shape because we were escorts for the visiting big-wigs.

On Tennessee Maneuvers, I was almost run over by a half-track that swung out of convoy to avoid a hole. He ran me right into another hole. I was thrown off and rolled down the road. The motorcycle kept going and wound up in a fence row. The guys stopped the half-track, got out and said, "Are you hurt?"

I said, "No, I'm not hurt. I'm just disgusted that you ran me into a hole!"

The lieutenant came over and said, "You just sit here for a while."

They went down and got my motorcycle and brought it back to me. The handle bars were bent a little bit. I got on and took off again.

The worst place to ride a motorcycle was in the Mojave Desert, California. If there was a little weed growing in the sand you knew it was a soft spot. If your wheel hit that, you'd sink in. It was so hot in the Mojave the motor wouldn't shut off. You had to put it in high gear, hold the brake and push the clutch down. That stopped the motor!

Maneuvers were combat between Reds and Blues. If you came to a bridge and there was a white flag on it, forget it. That didn't mean surrender. It meant the bridge was blown out. So you went right across the creek! I taped up the spark-plug end wires so I could ride through water. One of our guys figured he had to do something different by using a rubber raft. He laid his motorcycle on the raft and started across, but the exhaust pipe burned a hole through the rubber and everything sank. The engineers dragged the cycle back out. The engineers had graded a road and built a pontoon bridge across the Cumberland River. This cook wanted to be a motorcycle rider. He went barreling out of control down a ramp and went flying into the river. That was his last ride. He went back to cooking.

In March 1943, while traveling by train from California to Tennessee, we hit head on with another train. I was in the sleeper and all my gear came crashing down on me from the sudden stop. I looked out the window and all I could see was steam. The engineers got killed, but all the troops survived. Some of the cars were jack-knifed. Another train came to pull ours back onto the tracks. When we got to camp there was a corn field, just stubs of stalks and snow and mud. The first sergeant said to us, "Here's your home! Put your tent up in this mud hole!"

And it *was* a mud hole. Water every place. Two days later someone came up and said, "We need all the motorcycle riders. President Roosevelt is going from Washington to Warm Springs, Georgia."

We were assigned to guard the railroad from Tennessee to Georgia. The Army thought there might be sabotage.

In February 1944, we left New York on the *USS Alexandria*. It was rougher than a cob! When we got on the boat, I went into the kitchen the first morning for breakfast. They served some kind of cooked fish and hard-boiled eggs. Can you imagine?! British cooking! I took an orange and slipped out of the place! They had a canteen set up. I bought two boxes of candy bars and went back to my bunk. While I was laying there, the first sergeant came in and said, "I want two volunteers."

I said to my buddy, "I wonder what that's about? It couldn't be all that bad, as long as it's not in that kitchen."

I figured it wasn't for KP, so I and my buddy volunteered. They took us up to help the Merchant Marines. We ate good meals with them. They fed us at least five times a day. We stocked life boats, we checked all the flashlights, put new fishing equipment in and so forth.

They told us not to go up on deck when the sea was rough, because they wouldn't stop to pick anyone up if he got washed overboard. The waves would come clear across the ship. An aircraft carrier ahead of us bobbed up and down. Sometimes you would see the propeller going around in the air. Ahead of that was a big battleship. Sometimes you'd see it and sometimes you didn't. There were 7,000 of us on our ship, including our General.[29] We knew we were going into combat, but we had to blank that out. We felt like cattle going to the slaughter-house. We were on that ship for nearly two weeks. We went up to the North Atlantic, Greenland, Iceland, and came down and landed in Liverpool, England.[30]

---

[29]Major General Jack W. Heard.
[30]24 February 1944.

Liverpool was dark. The air-raid whistle was blowing. We went up the street carrying everything we had. You could see people's heads sticking out of basement windows. The buildings were all blown down. We got on a train and went to Tidworth, where we set up camp. I got a new peep[31] packed in cosmoline. I cleaned it off. There were fifty peeps lined up for our division. We signed up for them and then we started driving on the "wrong" side of the road. I got to like it because I sat on the berm side. I wasn't on the side next to where I could get hit!

I was still a messenger. I got picked to go to Plymouth to drive for an S-4 officer and another colonel. They were getting all the supplies ready. I drove this colonel back and forth to Bournemouth, right on the English Channel. I'd take him over at night and come back at night. No lights. I had this great, big, old Chrysler with the three seats. I never cared for that colonel. He'd sit in the back seat and he'd say something real low and you'd turn your head sideways to hear what he said and he said, "Look straight ahead!"

I didn't like England because of the fog and all the barrage balloons, but I never had any problem with the people. I took officers different places where they had friends in the British army. I'd visit with British troops while the officer did his thing.

Almost every night you'd hear Bed-Check Charlie.[32] One night in Plymouth the whistles started blowing, then all the search lights came on. I went outside and looked up and I saw this plane, shining in the searchlights like a silver dollar. Charlie dropped a flare and it lit our building up like daylight. I thought for sure we were going to get clobbered. Instead, Charlie's bomb went right through the roof of a garage down the street. It was a delayed action bomb, and went clean down through the cement floor before it blew up. English girls of the ATS[33] were firing anti-aircraft like crazy. They were good at it, too. The sky was red with tracers. I'll tell you they were the best fireworks I ever saw. When the lights came on and anti-aircraft fire stopped, we knew a British plane was going up after Charlie.

We left for France from Southampton.[34] The sky was black with planes. I couldn't imagine that anyone could have that many airplanes! We landed around Omaha Beach in the daytime. It was a pretty rough-looking place with sunken boats and blown-up bunkers. We knew someone had a rough time when they landed there. We saw a lot of wooden bullets the Germans used laying around,

---

[31]Armored troops' name for "jeep."

[32]German bomber or patrol aircraft who usually arrived over the front at precisely 10:00 p.m. This was the universal name, but there were variants.

[33]Auxiliary Territorial Service. See Elizabeth Slaney's history in the Center's *Out of the Kitchen: Women in the Armed Services and on the Home Front. The Oral Histories of Pennsylvania Veterans-World War II*, 1995.

[34]25 July 1944.

purple ones and red ones.[35] We spent a day there before we took off. Immediately, the Air Force caught a German horse-drawn artillery outfit and blew them to pieces. Horses and men were laying all over the place. There were Frenchmen who collecting horses that survived. Some of them were leading three or four horses.

After St. Lô, we moved through the hedgerows pretty fast, especially after our tanks got rigged up with these plowshares somebody welded onto their fronts.[36] They tore right through the hedgerows. I ran messages. They gave us a map with an overlay of the section we were to travel in. My buddy took care of the map reading and I did the driving.

It wasn't until the Falaise Gap that I saw combat.[37] We went in there and got right in the middle of it. The Germans were on both sides and we lost two messengers. One of them was named Locke. I never saw anyone worry so much about going into combat as Locke did. He always asked, "I wonder who's gonna get it first?" He was!

We were on the road and the Germans got in front of us. Everyone except the guys in the armored cars got out onto the banks of the roads. I and my buddy had a bazooka.[38] We got it out and got it all ready, but nobody came our way. After it got quiet, we went down the road and ran into Lieutenant Chase, who was in an armored car. His unit had been ambushed! The Germans had blown big trees across the road. Chase's armored car went off the side. His car commander had his head shot off, and he was laying alongside the vehicle. They dumped him out because he was in the way of the gun. The car was at an angle and Chase was sitting in there firing a 37mm until he got his arm cut on the recoil. Our fighters came in and strafed. German anti-aircraft was firing. I got pretty serious about what I was thinking and doing. It was gonna be me or them! They buried the headless man there. They just dug a hole, wrapped him in a mattress cover, and put him in. The hole filled with water. They covered him up, and we left the area. I've often wondered if they found any of the guys we buried along the road. People missing in action? I think that was mostly guys who got buried somewhere.

Another guy by the name of Tilly got his legs shot off. He rolled himself out of the peep and dragged himself over to the bank. He was trying to walk on his stumps. I sort of expected some of this from training. I never worried about getting killed because I wouldn't know if it happened anyway.

---

[35]These bullets splintered in contact with human flesh.

[36]This was the Rhino invented by an American tanker, Sergeant Curtis G. Culin, Jr. The Rhino was considered to be on of the major contributions to the breakout at Normandy. Culin was awarded the Legion of Merit for his invention. He later lost a leg in the Hurtgen Forest.

[37]August 1944.

[38]The bazooka was designed so that individual infantrymen could defend against armor. It could penetrate three inches of steel. The weapon was given its name in 1943 by Major Zeb Hastings, who likened it to radio comedian Bob "Arkansas Traveler" Burn's musical instrument.

My days as a messenger were pretty typical. Usually we'd be in the message center. There was a half-track there with a radio operator inside. Headquarters would get a message ready, and we'd have to take it right away. Sometimes they sent us out at night, when we couldn't use headlights. We could have used radios, but there were some messages they didn't want to let go out over the air. We had an armored message car built. We called it the "Whore's Dream." They placed a higher keel roof on it. We had maps on the walls and everything else in there. We took our turns. As messengers we didn't have any protection. We were on our own. Since there were only two of us at a time together we had to be careful. If we were caught then we had to run it out or whatever. We drove like crazy! They had to be pretty good shots to hit us. In fact, I wore two motors out in my peep during my time in Europe. I often wish that I would have kept track of the miles that I put on my peep.

After Falaise we headed for Paris.[39] We stopped in a park outside the city because the higher-ups agreed that the French troops should be allowed to liberate the place.[40] I don't know how much liberating the French really did because the Germans were already gone. The next morning we took off, traveled through the city, past the Eiffel Tower, through to the other side of Paris. As we moved through some of the French towns, the peasants gave us everything they had. One woman gave us some sugar lumps. They acted in a Christian way.

The Germans had snipers and spotters in church steeples. As soon as we got to a town, we'd put 37mm rounds into the steeples. Not far outside Paris we went through a small town, then over a hill, and made a curve. That's where our colonel got killed. Four or five of our armored cars were in a field. The colonel said that he was going to lead the cars on through. Once he got out in the field, he was killed by 88mm[41] fire. We realized that we were sitting ducks because the road was narrow and we couldn't get turned around. We had to stay there. Our tank with a 76mm gun[42] came up and knocked out the 88 positions.

I went on top of a hill. A Frenchman up there said, "Boche! Boche! Boche," which was their word for the Krauts. Raymond Manning and I took off over to a barn, where we found a Kraut. Raymond Manning told him to put his hands over his head, but the German soldier wouldn't do it, so I belted him one. That straightened him up! Then I lowered him on the front of my peep. He held onto the wire catcher. I took him back over the hill.

By that time, the tank column was catching up to us. In the meantime, the Krauts started firing mortars. They were exploding all around in the field. I made

---

[39] The division moved through the city of Paris on 30 August 1944.
[40] The Free French 2nd Armored Division under Major General Philippe LeClerc (1902–1947).
[41] The most feared of German artillery pieces. It was a triple threat weapon because it could be used as an anti-aircraft, anti-personnel, or anti-tank cannon.
[42] Probably an M18 Tank Destroyer.

that Kraut sit on the hood of the peep. I made him watch his own artillery coming in!

The outfit had pulled out to the other side of town where they bivouacked for the night. The next morning Risenger and I came back up through. Some Frenchmen stopped us. They had the colonel. Sergeant Seals had been killed also. John Berry was burned, and Stetson the driver was captured. Stetson came back to us later, but they finally sent him home. John Berry got better and came back later on. He said that one of the Frenchmen had hidden him in his sugar barrel overnight. Risenger and I got treated mattress covers, and used them to wrap the colonel. I picked him up by the shoulders and all the bones went together because he was crushed. We laid him on the hood of the peep and took him over the hill to another outfit. I didn't notify my outfit that he was dead until I came back. I told them, "I just took the colonel back. He was killed."

Later, we were going up the road and saw a German truck pull into a garage near a house. The Krauts took off. We weren't supposed to, but after talking it over we decided to go and see what was in the truck. It was loaded with bread. I told my buddy, "If we get this truck running, I'll drive it and you drive the peep. We can take this back to some of the hungry people."

I never before drove a vehicle that had as much clutch slippage, but I managed to back it out of the garage. I followed my buddy back to our squad. They thought we were nuts. They asked, "What in the world are you driving that German truck for?"

I said, "It has a load of bread."

Somebody else took it back to the Frenchman. We took a loaf of it. It was sourbread.

We went through France, then crossed into Belgium[43] and Luxembourg.[44] One night, on the Siegfried Line near Hofen,[45] I and my buddy killed a bunch of chickens and were frying them in a skillet. We heard this noise in a house. I told my buddy to go in through the rear while I entered at the front. This was a stupid plan that could have gotten us both killed, but we followed it anyway. When I came to the door, I listened for a few seconds, trying to make out the sound, but I couldn't. I kicked the door open and saw two pigs eating a dead German. All that was left of him were his ribs. His insides were all out. We left. There was nothing we could do about it. The pigs probably finished him. I never knew that pigs ate people.

---

[43]5 October.

[44]2–10 September.

[45] 85th Recon entered Germany with a dismounted patrol near Stalzenburg on 11 September, thus becoming the first Allied unit to enter the German Reich from the west. Combat Command R crossed the Sauer River on 14 September and cleared Wallendorf. The division moved to defensive lines in Monschau-Hofen on 20 September.

There were pillboxes everywhere. There was a barn in Hofen without doors. There was a pillbox inside. There were bunk beds similar to the kind onboard ships. They had acoustical pipes set up so that you could hear any noise from outside, but you couldn't shoot through them. One of our tank destroyers had fired a lot of rounds into that bunker, but couldn't destroy it. There were dead Krauts all over the place. There was one tank load of them. Our guys just dropped a rope around their necks and dragged them all out, then dug a hole along the road and threw them all in. I often wondered if they ever came across those Germans when they started to rebuild Hofen. They had to have.

We got moving fast on the main drags so we didn't have time to watch all the flanks. You had to contend with that and the Germans. There were a lot of Germans spotters who scouted for artillery. Certain roads were pre-sighted. They blasted the road to Wallendorf all the time, making huge holes, just to deprive us of a place to go. If you could get through, then you got through. If there was a rail line then you'd go around it, but you had to watch because they laid a lot of mines.

The Wallendorf road took us about a week to travel and cost us many lives. One day, coming back down the road from Wallendorf, Sergeant Redford's D Troop got hit with a *Panzerfaust*. The round split him and his buddy in half. They were lying along the road. At the same time, four guys were coming up from a field. Two of them were dragging another guy by the arms. We just got around the curve when an artillery shell exploded over their heads. Everything was covered with black smoke. I figured that they were all killed. But, when the smoke cleared, I saw them still coming. I couldn't believe that they made it through that blast! We weren't allowed to stop for anything, but I often thought to myself later that I should have stopped, picked that guy up and taken him to the medics. But messengers didn't do that kind of stuff. When we saw somebody dead, we put the gas pedal to the floor. If we hung around, we could get the same thing. There was a farmer near Wallendorf who would drive his cows across the road every time he saw us. He would make us slow down, and that would make us vulnerable. Finally, my buddy said, "The next time we come through here, and he drives them cows across the road, he's getting it and same with the cows." We would have killed them all because our lives were on the line.

The first time we got any rest was after the colonel got killed and Colonel Benjamin took command. We pulled back into Belgium to a rest camp set up by the 28th Infantry Division and 102nd Cavalry. When we got there, we showered and washed our clothes. We were supposed to spend two days with them. I drove my peep around. I found Manning. He told me, "The food isn't worth anything back here. The fish down in the lake swim with their backs out of water. I fried some trout last night. Let's go down this evening."

We went down to the lake and shot at the fish. We had no luck. We started to prepare some dynamite to blast the water with. A voice on the hill yelled, "COME UP HERE! COME UP HERE!"

It was a captain from the 102nd Calvary. He took us all in a building and gave us a big lecture, but it all went in one ear and out the other. One corporal named Charlie Gonzalez had his stripes taken off of him. The captain told us, "Do you want to shoot? I'll send you somewhere where you'll get some shooting."

I looked him straight in the eye and told him, "You won't be sending me anyplace new!"

He didn't say anymore. I went back to where we were sleeping and told my buddy, "Let's go!"

We loaded everything up and went to headquarters, where I met Colonel Benjamin for the first time. The guys asked, "What are you guys doing back here?"

"They didn't like people who shoot fish. They were going to send us to some-place that got a lot of shooting."

Colonel Benjamin got a big bang out of that! Everybody stuck together in my outfit. If they had taken our stripes, we would have gotten them right back. I think Charlie Gonzalez got his back.

We were in action so much that I didn't have time to write home. I did once, but Captain Anderson took a pair of scissors and just cut everything up. When I saw that I said, "That's it."

My mother got in touch with the Red Cross because she never heard from me. Anderson came to me and said, "Hey, you better start writing home."

I said, "What's the use. You cut everything out that I put in it. Just forget about it."

Anderson was something else. He was the only officer in our outfit I didn't care for. Everytime we made something to eat, he sent us out with messages. In the Hurtgen Forest we had some bacon frying over a gasoline burner. Anderson came along and said, "Take a message back."

One of my buddies mouthed off to Anderson. I think Anderson was a little bit leery of him. I was, too, because my buddy was the kind of guy who didn't care about rank or much else. We went, but we finished our bacon first. A bunch of dead Krauts were laying around. We pulled off at the side of a dirt road. Tanks came up from the 34th Armored as replacements. One tank pulled off the road and drove onto a tree stump and got hung up. Another tank came up and made a right turn. His rear track caught a frozen Kraut corpse and shot it up into a tree that had survived the shelling. The other tanks just ran over Kraut corpses and smashed them. They just seemed like road kill. Our dead gave me a totally differ-ent feeling.

One time, in Hofen, I went down over a hill and found a dead guy. He was our mailman. He was just laying there, still holding the mail. His blue eyes were wide open, staring at the sky. I didn't know whether to pick up the mail or what. Sometimes the Krauts booby trapped the corpses. I went back to the outfit and told them about the mailman. Some of the guys went down and gathered him up. Even after fifty years, I still see that pair of blue eyes, staring up at the sky.

In combat, you slept when you could. The Army passed out Benzedrine, but I never needed anything to stay awake. We got chocolate D-Bars that had a high caffeine content. One bar would last all day. They were so hard that you could hardly cut them with a pocket knife. We also got Nescafe in little packs. We would heat it in aluminum canteen cups. The Nescafe would burn on the inside of the cups so badly you could hardly scour it off. I hated to eat out of something that looked like that, but you couldn't help it. Helmets were for protection and washing. I never put mine over the fire.

When Holland was taken it got more quiet. We went in there and stayed overnight in a one-room schoolhouse. The next day we took off again and went through Aachen,[46] where we got instructions. When we got to the Rhine River,[47] the engineers had a pontoon bridge built. There was a burning town on the other side. We followed a medium tank across. When we got over, we found a lot of our paratroopers and glider troops hung up in trees.[48] After we got through that mess, we took off on our own again.

We pulled back into a town, where it seemed like we were surrounded. They brought a bunch of these tank destroyers up. It was there that a Messerschmitt strafed us, and I got hit. My finger was nearly blown off, so a medic patched it up, stuck a drainage tube in, and told me to soak it in salt water. After a couple days my finger swelled up like a balloon. The medic pulled the tube out. I kept soaking it in salt water until it was healed. I also got a fragment in the chest. Today, every time I go for a chest X-ray they ask me, "Do you know you have a piece of metal in your chest?"

Like a lot of guys, I didn't want to leave the line when I got wounded because the Army might return us to another outfit when we came back, to a bunch of strangers. I saw guys get wounded three times in one day, but they wouldn't leave.[49]

Somewhere along the way, I picked up a German camera and took pictures when we got to Buchenwald. Woolslayer, one of the guys from D Troop, knew something about developing pictures. We had a Luftwaffe developing kit and

---

[46]25 February 1945.

[47]The division crossed the Rhine River at Wesel on 30 March.

[48]Mr. Brown witnesses the aftermath of Operation PLUNDER which was commanded by Field Marshall Bernard Montgomery. At 10 a.m. on 24 March 1945 an airborne Rhine crossing was undertaken northwest of Wesel by the American 17th Airborne and British 6th Airborne.

[49]The American replacement process was thoughtless, inefficient and detrimental to morale. It was a piecemeal system. Recovered wounded, except on rare occasions, would be returned to units other than those with which they trained.

made a darkroom. After I saw Buchenwald, I hated those Nazis even more. It was pretty hard for me to believe why more people didn't know about what the Nazis were doing. The people who lived around the area said that they didn't know anything about it, but I could hardly believe that. The smell was terrible! They had to know!

By the time we got to the Elbe River, we were moving fast. The Germans wanted to give up to Americans, and they surrendered in masses because they didn't want to get caught by the Russians. We had so many prisoners that they built a fence around this field close to a salt mine. There were maybe some 100,000 German prisoners in that place. We were relieved by an infantry outfit[50] after we got to the Elbe.

After going full steam every day, pretty much on our own, everything stopped dead for us. The war ended. We were relieved, but bored. The Army put us back into the old discipline. I didn't have a careless feeling, but there were some people who did. My buddy and I were returning from a hunting trip and some drunk used his Thompson to spray a fence row. We were on the other side and nearly got wiped out. There were also a lot of people who got killed by mines after the war was over. The Germans had dug holes in the hard roads to put mines in. Then they started putting mines in the berms to trap those who tried to bypass the hard roads. I saw a lot of vehicles that hit these mines. We put sandbags inside our peeps. There was just enough room to get your foot in there to push the brake and clutch.

On occupation duty I met a pair of German twins whose dad was in Berlin. I didn't know if he was still alive or not. They were the nicest kids that you ever saw in your life. We'd sit and talk. They were just starting to understand some of the things I said. I treated the German people well, because they treated me well. I left no enemies behind. There was an old lady who washed my clothes for me. She didn't have soap. I knew the guys in the mess hall, and they gave me soap which I gave to her to wash my clothes. She washed some of the other guys' clothes, also. Then, when I caught fish, she baked them in her oven.

I finished in Muhlhausen, where there was an airstrip. Our pilots were taking guys up for rides, and they rode in our armored cars and half-tracks.

I finally went to Camp Lucky Strike in France. I came home on the USS *Alexandria*, the same ship I went over on.

---

[50] 29th Infantry Division.

"To Hell With the Germans! Drive on, Garrison!"

Dr. Richard R. Buchanan, M.D.

United States Third Army
4th Armored Division
Battalion Surgeon
704th Tank Destroyer Battalion[51]

Cincinnati, Ohio, 28 May 1914

"There was a time soon after I came home that Emily and I would get a baby sitter and we'd go to the movies. One time it happened to be a war movie. There came a cry, 'Medics, medics!' I began to cry, and I had to get up and leave! I can remember the other time I cried, it was after the bombardment of Lunéville. We had evacuated all the casualties, we had done our job as best we knew how, we were evacuating the area, we were moving out in the dark with the battalion to Arracourt to face the German tanks there, and all of the sudden I began to sob. In between sobs I said, 'Now, men! I'm not going combat-fatigued! I'm all right!'"

Throughout the war, I was always the same. The first death was just as bad as the last, and the last as bad as the first. There was no way I could become innured to some man being badly hurt. I never developed a tough skin toward casualties.

We were the combat medics, and because of that we got to wear the Combat Medical Badge, something only the doctors and the aid men who were on the front lines were privileged to wear. I'm prouder of that badge than I am of my Bronze Star with the Oak Leaf Cluster or my two Purple Hearts. I got one Purple Heart when our truck hit a mine, close to the Saar River. My driver, Garrison, and I would have certainly been killed except for the fact that we had sand bags on the floor of the truck. The other Purple Heart was from a mortar. I got blown into a crater by a near miss that tore up my left knee. Altogether I broke my arm, hurt my back, my knee and got fragments in my legs. We ran over that mine in

---

[51]A complete history of the 704th and its medics appears in *Men of the 704: The Pictorial and Spoken History of the 704th Tank Destroyer Battalion in World War II*, Publications of the Saint Vincent College Center for Northern Appalachian Studies, 1998.

Captain Richard M. Buchanan, M.D.: at Stonehenge

December 1944. That made me miss the first part of the 4th Armored Division's march to Bastogne.

I don't know how I got the Bronze Stars. The citation says all kinds of wonderful things. It says, "Meritorious achievement in ground combat against the armed enemy during World War II!" Oh, gracious! Just general statements. I don't think they knew what the heck I did! They were just being nice. They must have said, "Poor old Doc, we'll give him something!" Anyhow, each Bronze Star was worth five points toward my discharge points. I got to come home fairly soon after the war!

My father, Carl, was a chemist. My mother, Ethel Gwen Rowlands, was a school teacher. I was an only child. I wasn't much of a student in elementary school. I was more interested in fun and games. It was only in high school that I got interested in science and began to think about pre-med. My formal education, pre-med, medical school was at the University of Cincinnati. I was in residency in the Cincinnati area when the war started. I really didn't know much about what was going on in the world until Pearl Harbor, when suddenly I became alarmingly aware of how critical everything was. I called my fiancee, Emily, who was a resident at another hospital. We had graduated in the same class together. "This is going to change our lives," she said. And it certainly did.

I volunteered to go because I thought I could be of greater use to America in the service than at home. Besides, things were going from bad to worse for us overseas. I applied to the Navy on 29 December 1941, but they turned me down because I had a problem with color perception. Then I applied for the Army, and they took me immediately. By April, I was a first lieutenant and by May, I was the Battalion Surgeon of the 704th Tank Destroyer Battalion with no basic training and with no indoctrination as to the duties and functions of the job. I was not alone in my lack of knowledge. Many of the young line officers in the 704th were just as unsure of their jobs as I was of mine. Even the basic concept of how tank destroyers were to be used in battle was undecided. It was a learning experience for all of us, and we bonded together as we became more knowledgeable.

Three months before we were to go overseas, the adjutant looked through my 201 file. He said, "Hey, Doc! You've never had basic!" So they sent me to Carlisle Barracks in Pennsylvania for my basic training. This was three months before we went overseas! I had been developing the medical detachment for almost two years, and at the end of 1943 they decided to give me basic. Crazy!

As battalion surgeon, I was entrusted with the medical care of roughly 650 enlisted men and thirty-five officers. In combat I would share that responsibility with sixteen first-aid men who would have to be trained in the recovery and treatment of casualties from the front lines. Skills in care of bleeding, burns, fractures, shock, open chest and abdominal wounds, pain relief and proper wound dressing to prevent further infection, all had to be ingrained in our combat medics through repeated instruction and practice, practice, practice.

I assisted other officers in eliminating from the battalion those men who were either mentally or physically unfit. We called all those who didn't meet the full criteria of a good soldier "Eight-Balls" because they were classified as Section Eights by the Army. We got rid of them during our stateside training in Pine Camp, New York, Camp Hood, Texas, and in the Mojave Desert. Some of the things that disqualified a person for service in the battalion were social ineptitude, insubordination, and mental and learning deficiency. There were some instances where men tried to get out on purpose. Anyone who deliberately tried to fool us didn't, and we were perfectly willing to see them leave the battalion because they could never be trusted in combat. We probably eliminated fifty or sixty men.

The basic training I received before going overseas was fun! We were at Carlisle Barracks for six weeks. There wasn't anything that they were telling me that I didn't already know. Emily and I were married by then, and had a little apartment in Carlisle. Every morning I would trudge out to the barracks and go through everything from close-order drill to kitchen inspection. When they found out I had been in the Army since April 1942 they made me the drill sergeant. We had drill, map reading, night marches and lectures on everything. These poor, young doctors, they didn't know how to read a compass. They couldn't take an azimuth if their life depended on it. It was fun to get them oriented and straightened out. It was quite a nice change from what I had been doing at Camp Maxey.

After Carlisle, I went back to Camp Maxey, Texas where we were having our last shakedown on the T70, the technical name for the M18 Tank Destroyer.[52] We felt proud of ourselves because our battalion was designated to do the first field testing of the T70. The boys really ran it through the paces. All improvements we suggested were in the vehicle by the time we were assigned them on the Salisbury Plain in England. By then they were officially M18s.

After Maxey we moved into a camp near Boston. We boarded the *HMS Britannic* in late February 1944, and arrived in England in March. The trip over was boring. There were masses of soldiers aboard. The crowding was unbelievable. We moved at the rate of the slowest of the freighters in the convoy. We went up near Iceland to avoid the submarines and then down into the Irish Sea and then to Liverpool. After we got off the ship, the British transported us by train to the Salisbury Plain where we prepared for D-Day.

In England we did dry runs, went over and over again the procedures for the evacuation of casualties, and thought of what it was going to be like. We really had very little to go on. In World War I it was always a progressive, slow march forward, with battalion aid stations being established in one spot and maybe not moving for a month or two. But our battalion aid station would be in a truck

---

[52]The Hellcat. The 704th was assigned thirty-six M18s. The vehicles were lightly armored and had torsion-bar suspension. The 76mm was mounted on a Sherman tank chassis. The M18 was the only purpose-designed American self-propelled gun produced during the war.

following the tanks! We didn't know how we were going to get casualties brought from the tanks to us, and when we were going to be in motion, we didn't know what we were going to do with casualties when we were ready to evacuate them! We tried to think of every possible complication and plan for it.

Once in Europe, the first step back from the Battalion Aid Station was the 4th Armored Division Medical Battalion, 46th Medics. They evacuated casualties to field and evacuation hospitals, then to general hospitals, and then to base hospitals in England. The most critical step in the whole chain was to get wounded men out of the tanks, to the truck, give them some form of pain relief and sterile care, fight shock, stabilize them, get them ready and maybe move them five, six, eight, or ten miles back to the medical battalion. We were so dependent on the skill, character and moral fortitude of our aides, because they were the guys who crawled out on their bellies and dragged wounded men back to a protected area. Our stock as medics went sky high in combat. When the combat soldiers were in trouble, the cry for medics came through loud and clear. All of us tried to do what needed to be done. But there were times when it got pretty hairy and we were sure we were going to die.

We had so many problems. For example, we had planned all this medical evacuation of casualties on the basis of medical peeps out in the field bringing them to the aid station from the tanks. Then after stabilization, transferring them to our ambulance, which would then take them back to the 46th Medics. But then the word came down from higher headquarters that we would not have ambulances because of their high silhouette, something which would draw enemy fire. We had to unload our medical supplies from the three-quarter-ton weapons carrier we used for a battalion aid station and use that to carry wounded to the rear. This order came down while we were still on the Salisbury Plain. At least we had time to construct a frame to fit into the medical truck that would support four litters. But having to unload all the medical chests, blankets, litters, etc. when the truck was making a trip to the rear, meant that the aid station would be left behind as the battalion moved forward. This concept gave me nightmares. One ray of hope was that a captured enemy vehicle might be given to us. This actually happened several times.

I don't know for certain if we ever lost any men specifically because of the lack of an ambulance. When we were at Lunéville, France, an artillery barrage fell on the aid station, HQ Company and Recon Company. We had casualties all over the place! We were trying to get them evacuated with our truck. The recon peep had taken a direct hit. Our recon medic was killed and his partner was hurt. In desperation we radioed back to the 46th Medics, "Send us some ambulances!" They did. It seemed to us poor thinking on the part of the brass to give us no transportation and make us unload our aid station during an attack! Only when we were just ready to cross the Rhine River in March 1944 did we get our own ambulance from the Army.

We got the first hint that we were going to France in late May 1944. We were on the Salisbury Plain when we got orders to fill the radio waves with garbled messages in order to confuse the enemy. We boarded our LSTs on 24 July and debarked on the 25th. We went to France one month and six days after D-Day because the 4th Armored Division consisted of some 2700 vehicles and some 10,000 men. An armored division needed a lot of room for the deployment of that many tanks and men. We were told that we were going to have to wait until the front line was moved back at least ten miles before there'd be space for us. That took about a month. I had some worries as we crossed the Channel. For some unbelievable reason, my medical unit was detached from the battalion and sent over as an individual unit on another LST! We hit the beaches before the battalion did and my worry was, "Will I ever find my battalion!?" Remarkable as it may seem in all that melee of people and vehicles, and with the help of the division MPs, we got to the right place at the right time.

We set up a battalion aid station by the time that the gun companies began to roll into the bivouac. A captain[53] had gone over ahead of time to reconnoiter, and bitterly complained that the area that was to be assigned for the battalion wasn't big enough. He got things straightened out, and he brought them in. It was awesome to see the power of the whole movement—bringing these ships in and unloading all this stuff, ammunition and men and casualties going back again on the empty ships. Suddenly we were aware, "Boy, we're in it now! We're in it for sure and God help us! What are we gonna do when we have to face the enemy? Are we gonna have the guts to stand up and be counted?"

There was a lot of calling upon God for help. This was the first time a real enemy was ready to kill us. Some of us were more gun shy than others. I have to admit that I was a little bit appalled by the fact that some of our high-ranking officers were the first to hit the slit-trenches when a round of artillery came in. I'm not holding myself up as a hero, but I really wasn't all that concerned by the danger of it and I kind of wanted to see how my men were taking it. I wouldn't walk around if the rounds came close; I would take cover. But, boy! The apprehension that became apparent by the activities of some of the officers gave me concern.

As time went on, we became a little more knowledgeable about incoming artillery. We could tell by the sound if the shells were going to be close and dangerous. It was astonishing how we picked up the auditory variances from our stuff going out to their stuff coming in. When we saw a burst to the right and then to the left of our position we thought, "Uh, oh! They're ranging in on us." The next business would be a fire for effect!

---

[53]Thomas J. Evans of Greensburg, Pennsylvania. See *Reluctant Valor*, Captain (later Major) Thomas J. Evans' oral history. Publications of the Saint Vincent College Center for Northern Appalachian Studies, 1995-1996.

After the breakout at St. Lô we started direct fire against their tanks and likewise our tanks were targets for the Germans. Then it wasn't long until we lost our first tank destroyer.[54] The M18 we lost was misused. Its crew was directed to make a frontal attack by a full colonel, an infantry commander who didn't realize that M18s couldn't attack a dug-in anti-tank gun head on because our armor wasn't sufficient. The correct procedure was for an M18 to attack a target from a covered position. This colonel, who outranked our colonel, directed the tank to march up the road and blast that anti-tank gun. And the result was that A13 was demolished with three of the crew killed instantly. The commander of the tank, Sergeant Turcan, survived and was able to continue firing the gun until he used up the ammunition. He got the German gun. The driver, the assistant driver, and the loader were all killed. When the battle moved on, and the tank could be reached, I felt responsible to remove the three bodies. It was my first experience with what part of the human body withstands fire. It's mostly the pelvis and lower back. I had to remove what I could in bags for proper disposal, and label them according to position in the tank because there were no longer any dogtags. That was pretty awful, but I just couldn't ask my men to do that.

After the hedgerows we were moving, moving and moving. My aid men began to realize that any port in a storm would do and they did not hesitate to take our casualties to another aid station to get care for the guys they couldn't get back to us. We took care of other units' casualties in return. We became more resigned to the fact that even if it looked impossible, somehow or other we'd get our casualties back to safety and care.

Later on, we started taking care of a lot of Germans, too. Some of our guys didn't like that. Hatreds would surface, especially after the Battle of the Bulge when our troops became aware of the massacre of American prisoners. When we got into Germany, discovering the death camps further intensified the hatred. When the war started to wind down I felt there was going to come a time when we were all going to have to live together again as human beings. I didn't think it would hurt to start giving some care to the enemy, even though it caused resentment on the part of some of our guys who had lost buddies or had been wounded themselves.

Some of the Germans we treated were still resentful of our help. We took in a wounded but cocky SS colonel named Fritz Hofmann. He thought that was about the most degrading thing that could happen to him! He wasn't really the run-of-the-mill German soldier. Most of them were glad to see anyone give them some care. If they were in bad pain, they were really glad when we got out the morphine syrettes. "Danke! Danke! Danke!" they would say.

---

[54]No. A13.

I had college German, but it was laughable. When I tried to tell Germans what to do I usually got nowhere. Once, while I was taking care of a wounded German, six armed Germans came into the room and I said, "Hande Hoch!"

And they did! I thought for a minute that they had come to capture us! I pointed them back up the road toward the MPs. I said, "Gehen Sie! Gehen Sie Schnell!"

These guys wouldn't leave us! I think they were afraid to because if they got with combat troops they thought they might get shot. Finally, after we had loaded up the casualty, and the Germans still refused to leave, I said to my driver, "To Hell with the Germans. Drive on, Garrison!" And we took off. This got to be a saying in the battalion, "To Hell with the Germans! Drive on, Garrison!"

We had a way of evacuating Germans. They were segregated back at the 46th Medics, and then captured German doctors were given supplies and given an area to take care of their own. Eventually they would be evacuated to German hospitals that had survived or were being reorganized.

We had red crosses on our vehicles, and I don't think the Germans ever fired on us directly, but we were in lots of crossfires and had trouble with indirect fire on occasion. I think the Germans respected the red cross. Once I had a strong desire to strike one of my superiors over the use of the red cross on one of our vehicles. We had evacuated a number of 704th casualties from our aid station to a medical facility at Nancy, France. These men had been injured in the big tank battle at Arracourt[55], which was now in a lull, and I was using this time to have Garrison drive me back to Nancy in the medical truck. I wanted to know how the men were doing. As we neared the hospital, a peep bearing several officers pulled ahead of us and flagged us over. I jumped out and gave them all a snappy salute, noting that the ranking officer was a medical bird-colonel. It went through my mind that perhaps he was going to say some nice things about how well we combat medics were doing our job, but was I ever wrong!

"Captain," he yelled "What do you mean by having those red crosses painted on that truck!? That truck is a weapons carrier. Don't you know that's against the Geneva Convention! Red crosses are only to be painted on ambulances. Remove them immediately!"

I was speechless, but finally managed to stutter out that this truck was indeed our medical evacuation vehicle as our ambulance had been taken from us in England.

"I don't give a bleep-bleep, get those red crosses off!"

---

[55]For detailed personal accounts of the Arracourt and Lorraine tank engagements (September/October 1944) see the Center's (Thomas J. Evans) *Reluctant Valor* and the 704th Combat Diary by Mullen and Macomber contained in the appendices. See also the history of John DiBattista in the present volume. See the Center's (Richard R. Buchanan, M.D.) *Men of the 704.*

I wanted to say in effect, "Look, Sir, you're a doctor and I'm a doctor. Let's just step back behind the truck and talk this over sensibly."

But that was a ridiculous thought. Instead, I told Garrison to smear mud all over the crosses, and we left before I gave the colonel a chance to court-martial me. On the way back to the front we washed the mud off.

Many of our boys who came to the aid station suffered from small-arms fire, penetrating wounds of the abdomen, penetrating wounds of the chest. If we had a penetrating wound of the head we usually had death. One of the medics was killed by a tiny piece shrapnel that hit him behind the ear. He was gone like that! Even minor wounds were dangerous because of infection. Because the Germans used so many horses, tetanus was a worry. Penicillin was just beginning to be available in the hospitals, but all we had to prevent infection were sterile bandages and wound-powder, a sulfanilamide we scattered on the wound. If the casualty did not have a penetrating wound of the abdomen, we had wound-tablets. Every soldier carried a wound kit. Our medics were taught to always use the casualty's dressing first. We had plasma, not whole blood. We hooked up the dried plasma with sterile water, shook it up to reconstitute it, and then gave it intravenously for hemorrhage and shock. The men were taught to use pressure dressings to control bleeding. We did the best we could with what we had. We were just front line first-aid men.

Sometimes the frontline was a mile or so ahead, but sometimes the enemy was as close as the next hedgerow. Since we were involved in mobile warfare, we were often behind enemy lines. It was a very fluid situation. The Germans never knew where we might materialize, nor did we know where we might confront them. Usually, though, the aid station was back from the front by several thousand yards. Such was the case when General Patton came up to view the Battle of Arracourt from a hill called Les Jumelles. The battle was on one side of this hill and my aid station was in the lee on the other. Patton with two or three of his staff parked their peep, marched on up through my aid station past us. We were breaking our backs giving him the biggest salute we could! I don't think he even saw us! The 4th Armored was fighting against the 11th Panzer Division. He wanted to see how his best tank division was doing against Hitler's best tank division. That 11th Panzer was supposed to be the *creme de le creme*, and their mission was to stop Patton. The 4th Armored chewed them up with the help of the 704th. On 19 and 20 September 1944, the 704th alone knocked out twenty-nine Mark Vs and VIs.

The Battle of Arracourt was the big one for the 704th. It was the biggest Allied tank engagement of the ETO. We were there for almost a month in that one muddy field. The boys were bringing the casualties in with their peeps. We were in a wall tent that could be blacked-out at night. We had all the medical supplies unloaded so the truck was empty and readily available to take the casualties on back. Once in a while the boys would call back and have me come forward to one of the gun companies because they had something to handle that they weren't sure of. I remember going forward one time and I missed out on roast pig. The boys had found a suckling pig. One of our medics was a butcher in civilian life. That suckling pig was soon turned into pork. They were almost finished roasting it when I had to go forward and visit my medics in B Company who were having a Hell of a time. They were running on pure nerve. Their adrenaline was wearing out, so they needed some encouragement. They were all doing very good work and deserved to be told. By the time I got back, the pork had all been eaten. That's the way it goes!

I was sympathetic to men whose nerves got frayed. In spite of what General Patton wanted to believe, combat fatigue was very real. I'm not sure how many men we evacuated from the 704th because of it, but I know it was a sizable number. Most of the cases occurred early in the war when we were in France. I had occasion to go back to the Combat-Fatigue Treatment Center where a rest-sedation technique was being tried. This program had been developed by a former teacher of mine, a neuro-psychiatrist named Dr. Howard Fabing. The program consisted of three days of relatively deep sleep induced by healthy doses of Nembutal. After this period of withdrawal from reality the men were sent back to combat. While checking on the progress of some of our own men, I talked at length with the psychiatrist in charge. I was quite shocked to discover that he was nearly a combat-fatigue case himself because of the personal struggle he went through when he sent men back to the front, knowing their pleas not to be sent back to the line were justified. He was under orders to do so. He had tears in his eyes as we talked. I wondered how long he would last.

Our medical clerk, Corporal Morelli, developed a case of combat fatigue right under my nose. We got caught in a surprise artillery attack. We had no time to seek foxholes. Morelli and I dove under the medical trailer. As the shells landed and burst, a fragment hit the tire just above my head. There was this loud hissing sound. Morelli shouted into my ear, "Captain, I'm hit! I've been shot!" I yelled back, "Bleep-bleep it Morelli! You're not hit! That's just the bleeping tire going down!" But Morelli had had it, and he was no good from then on. We evacuated him. He never came back. He was assigned as a clerk/typist to a unit in the rear. General Patton just didn't understand that sort of thing. It just wasn't in his character to appreciate the fact that we can't all be perfect at all times.

In December 1944 our division got orders to go to the relief of Bastogne. I missed the first part because of my encounter with the mine. By the time I got there, the aid station was to the south of the town. It wasn't so bad at our aid station. We could even help the Belgians. One time in the middle of one of the coldest nights I ever had to go out in, I was hauled out of the sack by the people in whose house we had the aid station. They said they had a person come to them and ask, "Would the doctor please come and help my friend who was suffering so terribly."

So I got up and got my boots on. My driver that night was Sergeant Bennett. He was scared because the roads were treacherous, covered in snow and ice. Also, we had no idea of where enemy patrols might be active. We got to this primitive little house, where I found a Belgian screaming in agony. It didn't take me long to discover that he was passing a kidney stone. I gave him some morphine and some relaxant. I made him push fluids and he soon passed the stone. That was the end of that! Bennett said that was the worst experience he had in the Battle of Bastogne, getting Doc to the Belgian peasant's to take care of the kidney stone!

The men suffered a lot from frostbite at Bastogne. Really serious cases. We didn't do amputations. Those were done in the rear-echelon. To the north, the effects were terrible because casualties couldn't be evacuated. They would get a wound, go into hypothermia and die. When the 4th Armored broke through to Bastogne, evacuation became possible. The ambulances went into town the day after its liberation.

The American casualties most memorable to me were those who died, especially when it fell upon us to evacuate bodies. Captain Burkett from Headquarters Company, Battalion Maintenance, had gone forward because he had heard of a knocked out M18 whose engine was still functioning and could perhaps be driven back for repair or used parts. He found the M18 and began to drive it out of what was called the Bannholz, a thick woods north of the town of Sinz. He was driving down a lane toward the town where he would hit another road, which would take him back to the battalion. The Germans had laid a dead GI half way across the road and Burkett, trying to not run over the body, took the tank off onto the shoulder of the road where the Germans had buried four or five 105mm howitzer shells, nose up, and on top of that a Teller mine. As soon as Burkett's tank track hit that Teller mine it exploded all those shells and blew the whole side of the tank off, flipping it upside down. The concussion must certainly have killed Burkett instantly. We had to get the wrecker up into that area and winch the tank right side up so we could open the driver's hatch and remove the body, which was intact. Burkett had tried not to disfigure the GI and had lost his own life. There was another officer riding on the back of that tank who was thrown into the surrounding brush. We evacuated him, and he got home safely, after transfer to England.

I took pictures all across Europe. I also "liberated" a movie and still camera from a German house.[56] Film was so hard to get because my little folding Kodak camera shot size 127. The only way I could get it was from my brother-in-law who was an artist back home and was doing all kinds of war work. He would plead with his good friends at a drug store to save rolls of 127, which he would send to me. I would then use them cautiously to get what I thought were significant pictures. I only got about eight pictures to a roll because the negatives were a pretty good size. My camera was among the first at the death camp at Ohrdruf. This was the first time I became aware of the mass killings going on. Man's inhu-

---

[56] All of Dr. Buchanan's photos have been published in the Center's *Men of the 704.*

manity to man shocked me to the point of speechlessness. Dead inmates were lying half-clothed, their necks awry from pistol bullets to the spine. Colonel Clark, the commander of Combat Command A, made the civilians of the town, including the mayor, march through this horror. The mayor later committed suicide. We asked them, "How could you support a regime that would do this!"

"Well, we didn't know it," they would say.

I thought, "This is something that people *should* know about."

Ohrdruf was just the tip of the iceberg. Buchenwald, just north of us, Dachau, Auschwitz and Treblinka were so much worse! But the shock of the first one was overwhelming! Our guys took one look at the burned bodies and turned away. I took a picture of two survivors. I was reluctant to question them. I wasn't sure I could speak their language, and they had been through so much I just felt loath to put them through anything more by making them talk about it. Their care was immediately taken over by the 46th Medics, who did what they could to help the survivors. There weren't many. I don't know what happened to the ones who were marched off to the east before our arrival. I'm sure most of them died somewhere along the line.

The method of extermination at Ohrdruf was starvation, inhumane care and overwork. The *coup de grace*, when these slave laborers were so weak that they couldn't do anything, was a shot in the neck. We saw the bodies piled up. We saw them stacked up on railroad ties. The Nazis had poured some sort of crude oil on them and tried to burn them, but the burning was poor. We saw the pits where the Nazi guard would shovel the remains. This was not the production line management of the bodies like those developed at other camps, the wetting down, then the gassing and then the ovens. It was mass cremation. We who saw it still can't believe that there exist today persons who deny that the Holocaust happened.

When we heard the war was over, we started counting points! I got into really big trouble. My wife at home was hearing about the war being over in Europe and that the boys would be coming home. Then came an offer for an officer of the 4th Armored Division to go to London for two weeks to take a course in tropical medicine. I told them, "I'd love to go to London!"

I did, and I took a wonderful, two-week course at the London School of Tropical Medicine listening to the British officers of World War I who had done monumental work in the understanding of tropical diseases in their colonies. The British knew more about tropical medicine than anybody. One of the wonderful lecturers was Sir Manson Barr. He was the one who discovered the fact that the anopheles mosquito transmitted malaria. When I wrote to my wife and told her that I had gone to the School of Tropical Medicine, she was ready to divorce me. She figured that now it was a sure thing for me to go to the Pacific, instead of coming home, at least on leave. Her letters were pretty hostile for awhile. But it wasn't long after that that the Bomb dropped and everything settled down. All of us who were medical officers were pulled out and sent to big areas to get troops ready to go home. We went home with them.

I got home 28 September 1945, my son's first birthday. I had never seen him. I was joyful. Then the reality set in. I thought it was all gonna be love and kisses and "Oh, Daddy, aren't you a wonderful guy!" It wasn't that way. Suddenly there was a threat on the horizon that challenged this little guy for the attention of his mother, and that had to all be ironed out.

I went back to the hospital where I had taken all my training and took a refresher for three months as a resident and worked there while I tried to figure out what to do. All my plans were shot to pieces. Everything I had hoped to become in Cincinnati went down the drain. There were so many doctors returning to Cincinnati from the service that there were no openings. I had to go and break new ground somewhere else. I went to see Colonel Conard in his office in Wilmington, Ohio. Conard had been the medical officer in charge of the procurement of Ohio doctors for the Army in World War II. We spent an afternoon together and he outlined a number of places that needed doctors and at the end of that time, being an old Army officer himself, having been a regimental surgeon in World War I, we discovered a lot of common ground. Finally he said to me, "Dr. Buchanan, why don't you go into practice with me."

So that's how it happened. I went into practice with Doctor Conard and settled in Wilmington where he introduced me to some of the finest people I have ever known. We worked together until he retired and I progressed to the point where I could buy my own building, develop my own practice, and help build a hospital (we had no hospital in Clinton County). We opened the doors in 1952. I've practiced medicine here for more than fifty years.

There was a time soon after I came home that Emily and I would get a baby sitter and we'd go to the movies. One time it happened to be a war movie. There came a cry, "Medics, medics!" I began to cry, and I had to get up and leave! I remembered another time I cried, after the bombardment of Lunéville. We had evacuated all the casualties, we had done our job as best we knew how, we were evacuating the area, we were moving out in the dark with the battalion to Arracourt to face the German tanks. All of a sudden I began to sob. In between sobs I said, "Now, men! I'm not going combat-fatigued! I'm all right!"

I got it out of my system and that was that. It was tension. It was so horrible. I hate to even mention it. We were so tired and finally the column stopped and they said, "Okay, we're gonna be here for a couple of hours."

We just laid down there on the ground. We were there for more than a couple of hours because when we woke up it was dawn. I looked at myself and I was soaked with blood from my elbows all the way down. I hadn't washed off the blood of the wounded. I didn't even know it was there!

I'm sure we medics saved lives, but we didn't think about it too much. It was our job. After I was home, a very busy doctor trying to build a family practice, I got a letter from a sergeant. I wasn't going to many 4th Armored reunions because

I was so busy. The letter said, "Hey, Doc. Are you the one that saved my life at Lunéville? If you are would you please come to Columbus, Ohio to the 4th Armored Convention."

I went and there he was! My we had a real reunion! But his recovery was still not 100%. He could not walk very well, but well enough to lead a satisfactory life. We know that a lot of guys will say, "If it hadn't been for you, or if it hadn't been for Antel, if it hadn't been for this guy or that guy!"

Sergeant Antel! He was my first sergeant. He was the backbone of my enlisted men's strength in that detachment. After the war he continued to be affiliated with medical care of veterans. He went to Oklahoma General Hospital, and became a very skilled physical therapist and devoted his life to the rehabilitation of Korean and Vietnam veterans. He is still alive, we still correspond, but he's quite feeble. He's older than I. I'm 83, and he must be about 85 or 86.

I had a lot of remarkable men in my outfit. Bennett, who is the president of the 704th, is a Ph.D. and a psychologist specializing in criminal psychology in the California Penal Psychological Evaluation Program. Dick Bowman was a professor of English in Long Island. These two are the editors of our battalion paper *The Five Star Review* which they continue to publish. It was begun in Landshut, Germany in June, 1945.

There are good things that happened, too! My bad knee finally gave out and in 1957 I had to have it operated on. I was out of circulation for six weeks. And it was in that time that I decided to put the battalion record together. I began to get out all the maps, all the negatives, all the little snap shots and all the letters and began to think, "I really have something here that the kids should know something about."

I had a great-grandfather who was a captain in the Civil War and who fought in the Battle of Look-Out Mountain and didn't survive. We haven't the slightest idea about him. I thought, "My gosh. My kids are going to know about my participation."

Then I began to get active and started going to 704th reunions and took stuff along and the guys said, "Boy, I've gotta have a copy!" So, I began to think in terms of the battalion rather than my family, and it began to take on the shape that it is now, which is quite extensive, extensive enough that I wrote to the National Archives in Washington and got everything they had with the name 704 on it. I got 400 pages of material in which the S-2 reports and S-3 reports and the after-action reports are recorded. The Patton Museum has all of that. It presents to anyone really interested in looking at archival material, pertinent to the 704th, a pretty darn good cross-section of what went on!

1. The Fighting Second Squad. Somewhere in Germany. (Left to Right): Sgt. Paul Pellitier, Corp. Boza, Harry Bee (driver), Ed Wolf, C. Stone, Jesse Dyer, Bill West, Charles Body.

2. Private Robert ("Bird Dog") Sheffield.

3. On Patrol in Tauberbischofsheim. West, Bee, Pellitier, "Bird Dog."

4. In Bavaria near Boxtal, May 1945. Bee (kneeling), Private Engle (left), Private Mann.

1. Robert Black as Recruiter and his friend, Mr. Ford.

2. Orsoy Bridge (Bailey) prepared for the Rhine Crossing, April 1945. A previous bridge was destroyed in a spring flood. *(Courtesy Robert Black).*

3. Robert Black in Henley on Thames, England. His jeep is named after his girl friend, whom he would later marry.

1. Richard Brown in a German uniform. Muhlshausen, Germany.

2. Richard Brown (left) and his fishing buddy, Raymond Manning, pose with their jeep mounted with a wire-cutter.

3. Richard Brown with his catch of the day. A certain captain was not too happy with Brown's piscatorial endeavors.

4. Richard Brown stands on the cowling of a German Ju87 dive bomber (Stuka). The plane has 37mm anti-tank cannon mounted under the wings.

1. The dead at Buchenwald on the day of liberation.

2. The gallows at Buchenwald.

3. The crematoria at Buchenwald.

(Photos: Courtesy of Richard Brown)

1. The front of M18, No. 13, the first tank destroyer lost by the 704th TDB. Three crewmen were killed. Roger Turcan won the Silver Star in the action.

2. Camouflaged battalion aid station.

3. The Last of the Mohicans. The medical detachment, 704th TDB. **Top row, from the left:** Danzeisen, Bennett, Carlson, Miller, Walker, Hester. **Middle row, from the left:** Scholnick, Barresi. **Bottom row, from the left:** Garrison, Antel, Myer, Shelton, Bowman.

704th Tank Destroyer Battalion combat medics proudly pose with a captured German Schwimmwagen. Steve Antel is the driver. Left to right are John Meyer, Harlow Garrison, Clarence Leeman, and Thelis Deslauriers.

Photos: Courtesy of Richard R. Buchanan

Two 704th Tank Destroyer Battalion medics, Dick Shelton, above, and Marv Carlson want to take this German tank home for a souvenir.

While defending against counter-attack at Sinz, Germany, Rollins, in an M18, gets mail from
704th Tank Destroyer Batallion Mail Clerk Masirovits.

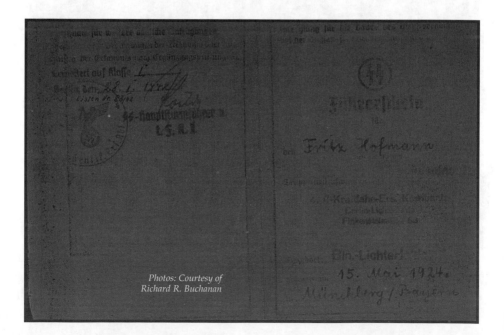

An especially cocky SS man, left these ID papers at the 704th Tank Destroyer Battalion aid station after being treated and evacuated.

Photos: Courtesy of Richard R. Buchanan

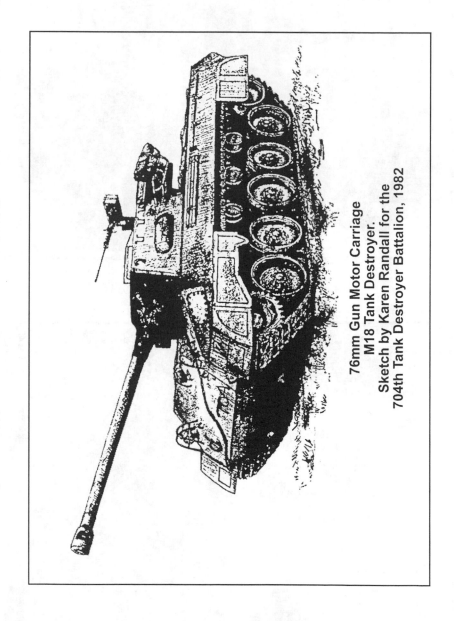

76mm Gun Motor Carriage
M18 Tank Destroyer.
Sketch by Karen Randall for the
704th Tank Destroyer Battalion, 1982

1 Typical layout of German tank

Pz.Kw. III
(models E, F, G)

These collages are taken from the scrapbooks of Doc Buchanan

German Medium tank Pz.Kw. IV

Armour, thickest plate	50 mm
Weight, laden	23 tons
Crew	5
Armament, turret	One 7·5 cm gun, one MG
Armament, hull	One MG
Overall length (without gun)	19 ft 4 in
Overall width	9 ft 7 in
Overall height	8 ft 6 in
Engine	300 bhp petrol
Speed, road	22 mph
Radius of action road	100 miles
Trench crossing	9 ft 0 in
Step	2 ft 0 in
Fording	2 ft 9 in

29

The famous and much respected German General Rommel

"I'm Alright, Ma!"

Amerigo John Casini

United States Fifth Army
13th Field Artillery Brigade
36th Field Artillery Battalion

Scottdale, Pennsylvania, 7 September 1915

"I had some close shaves at Anzio. Once, down in my foxhole, I had loosened the top of my boots. They shouted 'Red Alert' and I jumped up to get to my machine-gun. The Germans began to shoot artillery at us and a piece of shrapnel hit the side of my machine-gun and went down into my boot. That shrapnel is red hot. It just blistered the Hell out of my foot! Another time a piece of shrapnel hit the dirt in front of me, caught my shirt and just scratched my side by my rib cage. It didn't bother me at all. This guy said to me, 'If you go to the hospital you might get a Purple Heart for that!' I said to him, 'Jim, you can shove that Purple Heart up your ass!' That's the way we felt! I mean, you get the old GIs, they're like that!"

I grew up in Kifertown, in Scottdale, Pennsylvania. I grew up like Tom Sawyer and Huckleberry Finn. In Kifertown, a lot depended on who lived on one side of the tracks and who lived on the other. I couldn't join the Boy Scouts because I was Italian! I couldn't join the YMCA for the same reason. In sympathy, some people decided that they weren't going to let their children join, either. They used to burn crosses up on Pigeon Hill in Scottdale.

One of my names is "Mid." My mother used to yell for me when I was outside, "Ameri! Ameri!" It finally got down to "Middy," and then to "Mid!" In the service I was "AJ," which was an easy way to say my first name, and "Bee-Bee Eyes," because I could see better in the dark than anyone else in my outfit. Also, I could distinguish sounds in the dark more accurately. One time, in France, close to the old Maginot Line, sounds were coming from somewhere in front of us. Right away you start thinking about a German patrol. I kept listening. The sound would go a little way and stop. I told my buddy, "It's either a cow that's got loose from a farm or it's a deer." He said, "You can't see 'em!" I said, "I can't see 'em but I can hear 'em!" It turned out they were deer!

**Amerigo Casini and Best Buddy Earl Lamey:
Maddaloni, Italy November 1944**

My father was Pietro Casini. He was a millwright, and repaired heavy machinery. He was born in the town of Porte de Abbe. My mother, Amalia Amichi, was born in the town of Cole about a mile away from my dad's village. They came to America around 1910. For hours and hours my parents told me little fables and tales from the mountains of Italy.

Everybody had it bad in the 1930s. Daddy never wanted to go on relief. He would do anything! Odd jobs here and there. Digging coal for people for a couple cents a bushel! He had some property in the old country and he finally sold all of it and got the money back here. Finally the Works Progress Administration came in and he worked a while for it. He drew around sixty dollars of relief and the money was held against him. When the borough had jobs, they'd get relief workers and they could work that amount off. When my dad went to pay off the debt on the house, they had this lien against it in the Greensburg court house for sixty dollars! My dad went to the borough and said, "Hey, I worked that sixty dollars off!"

Well, they had no records. He asked the bank president what he should do and he said, "Mr. Casini, if I were you I'd just pay it off and forget about it. By the time you hire a lawyer it's going to cost you five times as much."

My first job was in a greenhouse, for one dollar a day. I had to spend a quarter a day for streetcar fare. Then I went to the steel mill and worked there about a year. Then they shut all the mills and started the Irwin Works. I didn't get a job in Irwin, so I went to Detroit and I got a job there in a factory that made carbonizers that hardened steel for automobiles.

While I was in Detroit I got drafted. This was before Pearl Harbor. I didn't want to go. I was young and full of piss and sowing oats! I went to the draft board, and appealed. They turned me down. I accepted things and told them I wanted to get drafted from Scottdale, figuring there would be somebody I knew there who was also drafted. I got to come back home. A couple weeks later I had to report to Pittsburgh for the Army physical. They gave me a real going over! There was a major with these old, bronze maple leaves on his shoulders. He said to me, "You'll do, son!" And he tapped me on the back. A year later I would have whacked him!

There were thirteen of us from Scottdale. Four passed! But they were more strict in the beginning. Later on, the Army took anybody who could move. I had a guy come in as a replacement when I was overseas and my God, it was pitiful! I looked at him through his glasses and all I saw were these two big, blue blobs for eyes! I said, "My God, you can't stay up here!"

I told the top sergeant about the kid and he told the captain, "That guy can't stay up here! He can't see!"

You get worn down in combat. You get to look old. You get to feel old. We were up in the Vosges Mountains in France when the 100th Division came in to

"My God, they're sending kids over here!"

relieve us. I said to my buddies, "My God, they're sending kids over here! Look at those guys!" I went up to one of them and asked "How old are you?"

"Twenty-four."

I couldn't believe it. Babies! They had clean uniforms on and were clean shaven! They were as old as we were. But we'd already been through North Africa, Sicily, Italy, and France.

Anyway, back to the beginning. They tried to kill us in training. The old Army guys training us called us [*Mr. Casini says this in a snarling voice full of contempt*] "Draftees!" We took it! You can imagine what it was like on that parade ground in North Carolina in July! Guys would drop like flies! They'd get up the next day and they'd do it again. I never fell out once!

When I first got into the artillery, we only had sidearms. Then they decided to give rifles to the artillery crews. The CO also called for each battery to have four heavy machine-guns. A hillbilly pal of mine from the National Guard (God bless him, wherever he is!) knew all about those machine-guns. He wouldn't say, "I can't do it." That wasn't in his vocabulary. He put a blindfold around our eyes and had us break down the machine-gun and put it back together. Then he said, "You know just as much as I do about it now!" They put *me* in charge of all four of the guns.

When the Japanese attacked Pearl Harbor, we were in the day room at Fort Bragg, listening to the radio. Everybody thought it was a joke. All at once whistles went off. The top sergeant and the officers yelled, "Fall out! Fall out!" In two hours we were on our way with our guns to the East Coast. We ended up near Myrtle Beach. We placed our artillery out along the beach, waiting for an attack. We stayed there for two days. I guess they figured that it was useless us just staying there. They gave us ten-day furloughs for ten or twelve guys at a time.

Finally, on 13 August 1942, we boarded the *Argentina*, crossed the Atlantic, and landed at Grenock, Scotland on the 26th. We went on a train from there to an Army barracks in Parnem Downs. The whole brigade was there. We kept training on our howitzers. We also hiked to death. One night we were woke up and told to pack for Liverpool. In Liverpool, we boarded the *Monarch of Bermuda*. We landed in North Africa in LSTs. We were attached to the British 1st Division. I was ready to puke from seasickness, but when that first shell came over I forgot everything! I just wanted off that damn boat! Ju-87 Stuka dive-bombers came straight down at us. That scared the shit out of me!

When we were at El Getar, Ju-88s were giving us a lot of trouble. They were bombing us two and three times a day. Finally, our P-38s came and shot down one after the other. I was in my foxhole screaming up a storm at them! When we got to the Tunisian front German planes hunted us like dogs hunt rabbits! The British were supposed to have planes guarding everything, but we never saw one! The British didn't care about us, and we didn't care about them, I hate to tell you!

When we went over the Atlas Mountains, there was a foot of snow. Naturally, our vehicles were all four-wheel drive. Even our GMCs and jeeps and weapons carriers were all four-wheel drive. The British were trying to get up over the mountain, and they were blocking the road. We'd yell, "Get that goddamn thing off the road or we'll knock it off!"

The Germans broke through at Kasserine Pass. Our 2nd Battalion of the 17th Field was there. My battalion was along the coast at the time, and when the Germans broke through Kasserine we got our march orders. We marched all night and the part of the next day. When we pulled up, it wasn't quite dark. We started firing as soon as we hit the front. When the Germans came through Faïd Pass[57] our barrels were leveled so low we had to bore-sight[58] them, but we stopped the Germans! The 2nd Battalion of the 17th Field got wiped out, though. They spiked[59] their guns and the Germans caught them. Our outfit was supposed to get a Unit Citation for our actions in Faïd Pass, but we didn't. After the fighting in Tunisia, the Army stopped us and let the British go into Tunis. The Army did this all the time. They'd let the British take the final objective. We didn't care! We just sat there.

After the North African campaign, we left Bizerte for Sicily on an LST. It took three days to go seventy miles. The Mediterranean was like glass, not even a little ripple in the water. We landed at La Cata, Sicily with the 3rd Division. We went in easy, but the 1st Division took a bunch of crap about ten miles down the coast.

"Old Blood and Guts" Patton and our captain came down and said for us to take off and don't stop. We had to get into Palermo[60] as quick as we could. We made it in three days. They pulled us out and we went down through the desert center of Sicily with the 1st and 9th Divisions. We got into a bad battle. I lost two good buddies in Troina, on the other side of a mountain.[61] They were taking cover in a ditch and an artillery shell hit close to them and killed them. We stopped at Randazzo, at the foot of Mount Etna.[62] We didn't get anything to eat for three days. We had to eat our chocolate bars, our D-rations. They couldn't get food to us. After Sicily, we invaded Italy. We went into Salerno[63] and it was rough as Hell for about a week! The German tanks were behind and in front of us.[64] We had planes and shells shooting the Hell out of us! They were sending combat patrols through.

---

[57]In Tunisia. This engagement took place in the same week as the American defeat at Kasserine Pass (February 14, 1942). Rommel sought to cut off Allied supply lines by breaking through the Faïd Pass, which was guarded by inexperienced American troops.

[58]To look directly through the barrel.

[59]To render them useless, most often with an explosive charge that "banana peeled" the barrel or blew out the breech.

[60]Port on the Tyrrhenian Sea.

[61]30 July 1943.

[62]14 August 1943.

[63]9 September 1943.

[64]16th Panzer Division and the Herman Goering Panzer Division.

Anzio[65] was terrible! I went in D+2 with the 45th Division. It was ten o'clock. At first it was easy, then we got shelled with big guns.[66] The 45th was getting off on the beach and one of them big shells hit right off one of the LSTs. I don't know how many of those guys got killed. Anzio was flat land, and we were in the open. The Germans were on the hills. We lived inside a smoke screen for I don't know how many weeks. It was like a fog all the time.

When we hit Anzio, I immediately got my weapons ready. We moved out on a weapons carrier, and the Germans started throwing shells at us. We were told to pull into the woods. There were some 2nd Battalion Rangers there, and we dug our holes in along side them. We stayed there and they went on. They were just regular guys. They got wiped out, and I think we did it to them! I was set up by some railroad tracks. The Rangers got surrounded by German tanks.[67] There was nothing the Rangers could do, so they surrendered. We called fire down on the German tanks, but the Rangers were there, too. They kept telling us, "You're shooting good! You're shooting good!" But you sometimes didn't see where your rounds were falling.

I had some close shaves at Anzio. Once, down in my foxhole, I had loosened the top of my boots. They shouted "Red Alert" and I jumped up to get to my machine-gun. The Germans fired some shells at us and a piece of shrapnel hit the side of my machine-gun and went down into my boot. The red-hot shrapnel blistered the Hell out of my foot! Another time a piece of shrapnel hit the dirt in front of me, caught my shirt and just scratched my side by my rib cage. It didn't bother me at all. This guy said to me, "If you go to the hospital you might get a Purple Heart for that!"

I said to him, "Jim, you can shove that Purple Heart up your ass!" That's the way we felt! I mean, you get the old GIs, they're like that!

I used the .50 caliber at Anzio against enemy planes, day or night, for about three weeks. They brought a colored squadron in flying P-51s. They made the airstrip along the ocean and they put the hospital right next to it! Well, the Germans started shooting the air field. The hospital got all the short rounds, and that's why so many nurses got killed at Anzio. They finally moved the air field.

The German pilots were afraid of that .50! If one bullet from that .50 hit their gas tank or motor it would wreck them. That didn't stop them from strafing every damn thing that moved. We had the machine-gun dug in on the beach, and I was watching this plane coming in from maybe a quarter mile away. He was strafing and my buddy hit me in the back of the head and yelled, "There's another one coming straight at us!"

---

[65]Landings at Anzio began 22 January 1944.
[66]These were, among others, "Anzio Annie" and "The Anzio Express," German railway guns that hurled 562-pound projectiles then withdrew into railroad tunnels for protection.
[67]On 30 January, the Ranger battalion had all but six men killed or captured.

We could almost touch him! I switched that machine-gun around, but he was going so damn fast that by the time I was ready to fire he was gone! Then about an hour or two afterwards here comes two of them in formation. I started shooting at the one, but missed. I did shoot the top off a telegraph pole! Incendiary bullets exploded all over it.

You never really knew if it was you who made hits on the German planes. There was so much of our ack-ack around, that every time a plane went down in flames, this outfit said they hit it, and this outfit said they hit it! At night, at first, we only had orders to shoot if we saw the plane. Sometimes you could, especially if it was a bright moonlit night. I told my machine-gunners, "Don't shoot at any of them. They're only looking for a target!" Then we started to call area fire like the British did. We divided the sky into squares. If a plane came into a square, everybody assigned to that area would fire. If the plane got into the next square, everyone assigned to that area would fire. It kept the damn planes away, and they dropped their bombs inaccurately after that. Sometimes, we got a little confused. One night a plane came over. I yelled, "Spitfire!"

We wanted to know what the Hell a British Spitfire was doing there! The Spitfire knocked out two trucks and a jeep. We found out later that it had a German pilot. The plane probably had crash-landed somewhere, and the Germans fixed it up.

Because Anzio was so flat, you saw a lot of planes go down, especially after we lifted the smoke screen. Most of the ack-ack came from the ships. One day, nine Ju-88s came over the beach. You've never seen firepower like what went up at those nine German planes. By the time they got to that beachhead there wasn't one of them left. They all went down.

We could also see our B-24s when they went to bomb the German lines.[68] There were ten or twelve and one of the German 88s got a direct hit on one. All you saw was pieces of the plane coming down. It was obliterated! One plane was all crippled up, and was trying to make the beachhead. The pilot made it, but he hit an embankment, flipped up, came crashing down and caught on fire. There was flame everywhere! The captain was hanging out of the cockpit, still alive. We ran onboard and dragged him out. He was badly burned. All the others were killed. They were all on fire.

I don't know how many American planes went down around Anzio! The pilots would try to crash land on the beach, or they bailed out. There were ten guys on a bomber. The chutes would get to seven and we'd yell for the last three guys to get out. Sometimes they did, sometimes they didn't. Sometimes we only saw a few bail out. We saw German pilots bail out, too. We caught two of them one time. They bailed out behind our lines, and we sent them down to the MPs

---

[68]After 22 January, 11,000 tons of bombs are dropped in support of the Anzio operation. The Fifteenth Air Force B-24s flew out of Grottaglie, Italy.

for interrogation. I hated the Germans! Especially those haughty SS guys. They were sonofabitches. That's what I thought of them then, and that's what I think of them now.

One day we were up on the line and this lieutenant told me, "Run these two prisoners down to the CP."

I said, "All right!"

So I started down with them. This one guy was lagging behind so I got out my bayonet and I shoved it at him and said, "Move goddammit, or it's gonna go the whole way through!"

He started yelling, "*Nein! Nein!*"

I was angry! In those days, when you were in combat, you had no real sense of the value of life. I stuck my bayonet in him and said, "Halt! Put your hands up over your head!"

He had his hands in his pockets, so I hit him. I thought he had a weapon or something, but it was his wallet. I looked in his wallet and here he had a picture of a woman and a couple of kids. I picked up that picture and tore it in half in front of him! He started yelling, "*Nein! Nein!*"

That was kinda rotten, but back then it was different. Combat was a different world. Today, I laugh at a lot of things, but they weren't so funny at the time, because we were always so scared shitless!

That whole Italian campaign was one disaster after another. Muddy, dirty weather. One hill to take after another. Sometimes I wonder how we came out alive. I had so many close calls you wouldn't believe it! I had a shell hit at my feet! It would have blown me to bits. I think it was a three-inch shell. It landed right in front of me and the shrapnel blew backwards. Not one piece came toward me. I said, "Hey, guys come and take a look!" I was in a grape vineyard, and the plants were half the height of an average man. That shrapnel just cut them off like a scythe! I never got a scratch!

Another time I was sitting on my helmet outside my hole. It was a beautiful morning. At Anzio the ground was really soft. You could go six or seven-feet down and it was all sand. The Germans knew it and they'd shoot these big shells and make them detonate underground with the delayed fuse and cave your fox-hole in. One of them came right over my head and hit about ten feet away. It made a hole you could put a house in! I must have got blown back about twenty or thirty feet from the concussion!

After Italy we went into Europe through southern France. That was nothing like the Italian campaign. We were moving all the time. We had taken a town. My buddy Andy and I were in an outpost on 100% alert for a German counterattack. It was colder than Hell, and it was snowing like Hell! Andy was the best in the world! We'd take a town and it wouldn't be ten minutes that Andy would get back to us and say, "There's chickens in this town!" Anything that was going on in town, Andy knew! He knew where all the good food was and where all the booze was! He even got to know the gossip. He found out one time that the

French were cutting hair off women who collaborated with the Germans. Anyway, we were on our post and out in the darkness we saw this guy come out of a house and go over a high-board fence. He was gone for about ten minutes, and then he came back again. Pretty soon he's there again. My buddy Andy says, "Kill that sonofabitch!"

I say, "No! Hell no! It's just some little old man. Let's go see what he's doing."

Next time he comes out we grab him. Over there every farm had its own still to make whiskey or *grappa* or whatever you want to call it! That was what he was getting. He offered some to Andy. Not only could Andy find anything, he would also drink any damned thing! I said, "I ain't drinking none of that stuff!"

He said, "Go on drink it! It won't hurt ya! Drink it!"

He took a drink and I took a drink. After about the second or third drink, why it tasted good! Then I got sick! I was puking green!

Andy said, "You'd better go down to the CP."

I said, "We'll wait till daylight."

Andy takes me down to the CP. Oh, God was I sick! They asked me, "What'd you do?"

I said, "I drank some damn whiskey or something."

The captain said, "You know you shouldn't drink like that! You can't tell whether that stuff is poisoned or not!"

So I said, "There's nothing wrong with Andy!"

It turned out that I wasn't that sick after all and I was back on my feet pretty quick.

It was so damn cold in France in December 1944 I froze my feet. We were about 300 yards from the main road. There was a little cluster of buildings by the road. We were up on a hill by a little building. We had dug a hole there and that's where we had our observation post. The lieutenant did all the talking, all the time, on the radio. The lieutenant said, "Well, fellas it's time for my whiskey ration. I'm going down to get it."

All officers got a fifth of whiskey every month. He was going to bring his back for us. We said, "Okay, lieutenant."

The infantry outfit with us was moving out because the Seventh Army withdrew, voluntarily, during the Battle of the Bulge, to straighten their lines. When the lieutenant tried to get back, he was told he couldn't because the Germans were there. Consequently, we stayed up there for three days. On the fourth night I said, "We gotta get back! We can't stay here any longer."

I hadn't had feeling in my feet for two days. I said, "We can't stay here and we can't surrender."

We couldn't surrender because there were SS guys around us. We saw them going down the road in their tanks and half-tracks. I told the guy with me, "You know that creek down there? I bet that's the creek that goes through headquarters battery."

He was scared. Don't get me wrong, I was scared too! I was scared as Hell!

I said to him, "Our only chance is to get along the bank of the creek and follow it south. Something's bound to happen."

We walked all night. We went around a German roadblock about 100 yards away from the creek; we could hear them talking. We never knew when we went through our own lines. It was daylight now. There was a field with a patch of woods next to it, then another field and above it the mountains and forest. I said, "We're going to go into that patch of woods across the field, and we'll see what happens."

We started up and we heard a rattling in the hedges. I looked up and I said, "Hey, look! Is that a star on the side of that truck?"

He said, "Yeah! That's our truck!"

So I said, "Listen. When we start up there, if anyone yells at ya just hit the ground and yell, 'I'm a GI! I'm a GI!'"

English-speaking Germans were behind our lines dressed in American uniforms. Fortunately, the truck belonged to a service company of the 79th Infantry Division. Boy, you've never seen two happier guys! They talked to us for a while and some major came and interrogated us about what we had seen. He said, "Did you see a lot of troops?"

I said, "There seemed to be a lot. Tanks, too! There were Tiger tanks up there!"

We told him what we found and the name of the town. He got a map out and found out where our unit was. He said, "That's not far from here. We'll take you back to your outfit."

They brought me back to the headquarters of my outfit and I told the lieutenant, "I haven't felt my feet for a couple of days."

He said, "You'd better go down to the dispensary and see what's wrong."

I went down and told the doctor what happened. He said, "Take your shoes off."

I took my boots off and you could see where the threads of the old woolen socks meshed into my feet. I said to the captain, "Look at my feet!"

He said, "You gotta go to the hospital!"

I had to grin when he said I had to go to the hospital! I ended up in the 78th Evacuation Hospital. I stayed there two weeks. Then this captain came by and said, "I'm sorry. We can't keep you here any longer."

I thought I was going to go back to a convalescent center and then shipped back to my unit. He said, "I gotta send you over to the general hospital."

I said, "The general hospital!"

He said, "It has just arrived from overseas. There's white sheets, and the nurses are nice, fresh girls!"

When I got there, I told the nurse, "I can't get into that bed!"

She said, "Oh, stop your kidd'n and get in there!"

After living like a rat for how long!? Even at the evacuation hospital there were only brown GI blankets. I climbed into those soft, white sheets and it felt good!

The doctor at the evacuation hospital was sweating over my feet for the first two weeks. My feet weren't black. If they're really frostbit they get blacker than a piece of coal! I could see the skin start to wrinkle. That meant the swelling was starting to go down! I never used a bed pan in the hospital. Every time no one was around I snuck into the toilet.

They didn't know what to do about frozen feet. They tried all these different things. They went out and got a bucket full of snow and rubbed your feet with snow! The worst things I saw tried were on this one kid from Maryland. They were sending him to Walter Reed because half his feet were frozen black. He never saw combat, the poor boy. He was going to be a replacement up at the front. He said, "They gave me shoes that were so tight that I had a Hell of a time putting them on." If he would have grabbed some newspapers or something and wrapped them around his feet he would have been better off than having those tight boots. They baked a cake for him and brought it to him. He ended up getting his feet amputated. Poor kid! He was a good-looking kid!

They ZI-ed me![69] They took us to Marseilles and we stayed down there about a week. Then we got on the hospital ship *Acadia*. The trip back was something! There was one guy who had his jaw shot off and they were feeding him with a tube in his mouth. They asked him what he wanted, but of course he couldn't talk. His mouth was sewed shut and his chin was gone. Another guy had both his eyes missing. He got shot in the side of his head and the bullet went across his face and tore off part of his nose and took out both his eyes! There was another kid, just nineteen years old, from Bradford, Pennsylvania. He was a good-looking, blond-headed kid, and his leg was taken off near the hip.

We landed at Charleston, South Carolina. They sent us to Stark General Hospital. I stayed there for two days. Then I went to Camp Butner General Hospital up near Durham, North Carolina. From there they sent me to Dix to get redistributed. I had enough points to discharge two guys!

When I got home, my mother said, "Thank God!"

I felt that way too. I had been gone a long time.

She said, "How are you?"

I said, "I'm all right, Ma!"

I was one of the first GIs to get back home. They really respected you. We were talking about the war in general after I came back and one guy said, "I suppose you were never scared?"

I said to him, "Buddy, I've got calluses on both the sides of my knees from them knocking together. That's how many times I was scared!"

---

[69]Sent to the Zone of the Interior or the United States.

I didn't have that much trouble adjusting. I had good friends. Everyone made you feel at home. As a matter of fact we were allowed to draw one year unemployment compensation. I think I withdrew one check of that and then I went to work. At that time I did the jobs that nobody wanted. That's what was left for us GIs. All the good jobs belonged to the 4F guys or somebody else.

I went down to the Overholt Whiskey and they said, "Are you looking for a job?"

I said, "If you've got a good one I'll take it!"

I started shoveling coal for eight hours a day! Finally, I went back to the greenhouse. I made a living with it.

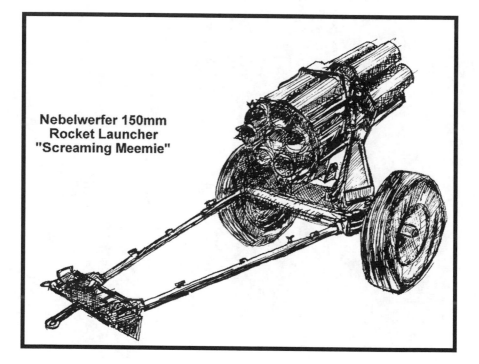

Nebelwerfer 150mm
Rocket Launcher
"Screaming Meemie"

"What the Hell's Cannon Fodder?"

Rocco James Catalfamo

83rd Infantry Division
330th Infantry Regiment
Company C

Pittsburgh, Pennsylvania
Candandaigua, New York, 10 May 1926

"The war made a man out of me. I was full of piss and vinegar and a little wild. I never got involved in anything criminal, but was rough around the edges. I think it straightened me out for the rest of my life. But I wouldn't do it again. Period! I just learned too much about killing. I found that you couldn't have any good buddies, because you don't know what's going to happen to them. I found out, also, that you *need* good buddies, so they can protect you while you're sleeping, and you can protect them while they're sleeping."

When the Army was drafting older men, I enlisted. Most of my old Army buddies today call me "The Kid." When I was in the service they called me "Cat." Many have passed away, or are too feeble to come to reunions. I met one of my platoon sergeants last year at a reunion in Daytona Beach, Florida. He was wounded early in the war and missed most of the action. He asked me how I survived. I told him I was just lucky.

My father, Joseph, a gandy dancer[70] all his life, came from Reggio Calabria, Italy. He went to the sixth grade, then went to work. My mother was Josephine Maria Sofo, also from Reggio Calabria. Both my parents were proud of their US citizenship.

I worked on the railroad when I was young. We needed the money. I did the same thing as my dad, only less. My uncle was foreman. I worked with the "puppy gang," a group of young fellows who had parents or relatives working on the railroad. When I came back from the service, I went into insurance, owned a restaurant, and did work for a local service company. I was a business agent for

---

[70] A railroad section-gang worker.

fifteen years for the International Brotherhood of Electrical Workers. I've been in security and police work for almost forty years.

I first volunteered for the Air Corps in September 1943. I went to Fort Dix, New Jersey and had all of my shots and got my clothes. The Army put me on a train headed south. I slept through the trip. When I woke up, we had pulled into a siding where a sign said: "Welcome to Camp Croft, South Carolina. Home of the Infantry Replacement Center." I thought, "Well, that must be for some of these other guys, that's not for me, because I'm going to the Air Corps!"

As soon as I got off the train, I told them I was supposed to be going to the Air Corps. They said, "Get in line, you're going to be cannon fodder."

I said, "What the Hell's cannon fodder?"

I was a toughie from a small town, so I got along in training pretty well. The only thing I didn't like was the regimentation. And I wasn't alone. I was a little bitter, because I was in the infantry instead of the Army Air Corps, but I made the thirty-mile hikes with blisters on my feet, like everybody else. I was chosen to be a scout. A scout was trained to be the eyes and ears of the company, and was always out in front. I was told not to worry too much, because the enemy never shoots the first scout. If they shoot the first guy, then the they would miss a chance to get everyone else. That made me feel a little bit better. Later they said that scouts had a fifteen second survival rate on the front lines. I got scared shitless. Then I took Ranger training, which was the ways and means of efficient killing.

After training, I went to Camp Shanks, New York, boarded the *Queen Elizabeth*, and in six days was in Scotland. From there I went to Wales and took more Ranger training with the British Commandos, survivors of the Dieppe Raid,[71] a real bunch of bastards. They taught us more about killing. They were very jealous of us, because we had better food, American cigarettes, clothing, and money, more money than they ever had. We chased their women and we caught them! The British Commandos were very good at sneaking up and killing the enemy. Two scouts were assigned to each platoon. From those, the Army selected a first and second scout for the company. I happened to be one of them, because I was small, was able to maneuver a bit, and had the training.

We went over to France on D+12. When I stepped off the boat, I hit a hole and went straight under. On the way down I said, "Oh, my God, I came all the way over here to drown!"

I hit real hard and shot myself back up, and somebody grabbed me and said, "Hey, Cat, you can't die here; you've got to die on the beach!"

---

[71] 19 August 1942. A major raid by the 2nd Canadian Division and Nos. 3 and 4 Commando accompanied by some American and Free French troops. Designed to provide intelligence of German coastal defenses for use in the future, the raid was a disaster. The raid was designed by Field Marshall Bernard Law Montgomery. Montgomery washed his hands of the event, which was typical of him.

The beaches were secure, but not for long, because we went right into combat a couple days later, at most.[72] For my first assignment a redheaded Sergeant Dooley from Chicago, Illinois said, "Cat, get those bodies and cover them up so no one can see them."

They were American dead. That was quite traumatic for me, because I was only a young kid. I was full of piss and vinegar, but not enough to do that. But, I did, and other guys did the same.

We were at St. Malo and Dinard. They were holding this castle,[73] or a fortress, I should say, out on an island in the ocean. It was our job to attack that. For some reason or another, the German colonel in there wouldn't surrender. We brought up artillery and there was a lot of shooting. Planes came in and blew the place up. The Germans finally surrendered.

That day at the Citadel and at Dinard and St. Malo was my first combat experience. I used up a lot of ammunition. It was the greatest experience I ever had. I couldn't see the Germans any more than they could see me, but it was just something we were taught, keep moving forward, keep shooting, keep their heads down. We kept moving until we hit the hedgerows. They were all over the place. You could be on one side of a hedgerow that was twenty-feet wide, and the Germans could be on the other side. You could sneak through one and look up and see a German tank sitting there, and you never knew it was there. The Germans lobbed shells over and we lobbed shells back. We took a lot of casualties. Sometimes the mortars would shoot so many feet in front of us and try to make an opening for us. Other times we used what was called "marching fire," when everybody put their rifles down to their hips and, at the command to move out, start shooting, without aiming. Maybe you'd hit somebody and maybe you wouldn't. After the artillery would bombard a place, we'd move in to clean out whatever was left. In towns and villages I would trade my M-1 for a .45-caliber submachinegun, which was more effective in those close places. The .45 sprayed a lot of ammunition and it gave me a lot of confidence. I was still afraid, but kept moving. There were people behind telling us, "Keep going, keep going."

The older combat officers would lead from the front. If we went out in an open setting, in what we called a diamond formation, the officer would be near the BAR[74] man. At other times the officer might be in the back giving orders to a sergeant. I think a lot of the war was really won by sergeants. We had a lot of officer replacements, what we called "90-Day Wonders." They didn't last too long because they'd come up with shiny brass buckles, perfect targets! The ones that

---

[72] The 83rd landed at Omaha Beach, France, 19 June 1944, and attacked strong enemy positions toward Périers on 4 July. The division was part of the Operation COBRA breakout 26 July 1944 and crossed the Taute River the next day. With the 6th Armored Division, they reached the fortified city of St. Malo 4 August 1944.

[73] The Citadel, which capitulated 17 August 1944.

[74] Browning Automatic Rifle, the .30 caliber M1918A1, an 18.5 lb squad light machine-gun.

were smart talked to the sergeants and got as much information from them as they could. Many of the lieutenants that came up wanted to be leaders, but they didn't know how to lead because they didn't have any combat experience.

After the hedgerows, we moved pretty fast, most of the time in trucks. We didn't know it at the time, but the Air Force had been bombing quite far in front of us. This opened things up, until we got to the Battle of the Bulge.[75] We were pulled out of our salient, which was on the right side of the Bulge, and brought in to help on the Bulge itself, where the 106th and 99th Divisions got the Hell beat out of them.[76]

I was at Aachen when it was liberated. I was at Dusseldorf and Hamm, Germany[77] on Easter Sunday. We blew the safe in the post office. We didn't find anything but worthless German money. Twenty-five of us went on combat patrol across the river at Dusseldorf, Germany, to blow up an ammunition dump. The other scout was Robert Haff, a full-blooded Indian. It was pitch dark. All we could see was just a small piece of tape on the backs of our helmets. We completed our mission, and then had to get our butts back. I never had too much trouble getting back, but I lost the second scout and the second scout lost the platoon, and so on. I got to the boats and waited for what seemed like hours, but was only minutes! I kept muttering, "C'mon, c'mon, c'mon," because I knew that as soon as we blew our objective, the Krauts were going to come after us. Eventually, the rest of the platoon came in and I said, "Where the Hell have you been? What did you do?" We started arguing back and forth. We jumped into the boats and got back to our base. We went in and had a critique. They asked, "You mean you lost them?"

And I said, "No, I didn't lose them, they lost me!"

In the Harz Mountains, we encountered what they called the Hitler Youth. They were young kids, twelve or thirteen years old, who were taught how to use a *Panzerfaust*, which was like our bazooka. One time we were being shot at from behind and we couldn't figure out where it was coming from. All we saw was a woman pushing a carriage. Inside the carriage was a Hitler Youth. He had a Schmeisser machine-gun, and he'd been shooting our guys up. One of our boys saw this and blew them both to Hell.

A guy by the name of Sergeant Gruber, one of the older guys who had children back home, was a little more lenient. We captured a number of Hitler Youth in the Harz Mountains and some of the guys wanted to shoot them. Gruber said in German, "Come here." He asked them how old they were and they told him. Gruber said, "You're about as old as my kid," and he kicked them in the ass good and hard and told them to take off. I thought that was nice on his part.

---

[75] December 1944.
[76] See King's account in this collection and Whiting *Death of a Division.*
[77] 1-2 April 1945.

In the Harz Mountains, I was on top of a tank with a .50 caliber machine-gun. I loved that .50 because it could knock over trees. Some of our guys came back with some German panzer prisoners. There was a lieutenant inside the tank I was on. He said, "Shoot those bastards. They're tankers. They're sonofabitches."

I told him, "I'm not shooting anybody. They're prisoners."

He said, "You'd better."

I said, "I'm not going to shoot them."

The tank started to move. The lieutenant told the GIs to get out of the way. The GIs ran to the side and the lieutenant mowed down about twelve of those German prisoners. I got off the tank. I couldn't handle that. A prisoner was a prisoner, as far as I was concerned. We weren't innocent and the Germans weren't either. But I just couldn't see shooting unarmed prisoners.

I almost got it in Gosler, Germany. I was helping another kid who had a bazooka. Out on the road there was a tank and a half-track. I was told to make sure to knock them out. A lieutenant came over with us and he said, "Line 'em up."

I put the missile in the bazooka, wired it up and tapped the kid on the head. The lieutenant told us when to fire. We knocked out a tank and a half-track with men in it. We took turns. Then the lieutenant said, "You guys did a good job tonight. You're going to get an award."

When the tank exploded metal flew all over the place. I jumped into a hole right on top of somebody. Neither one of us dared move. I reached down into my boot for the Bowie knife my mother bought me. It was either him going to make a move, or me going to make a move. Finally, somebody yelled, "All right, let's move out."

I got up and he got up, and I said, "You know what? You almost got killed."

And he said, "Yeah, you almost got killed, too. I had a .45 pointed at you!"

We never got the award we were promised. We did nothing heroic, because everybody was doing it anyway. It was just the idea that the lieutenant said we'd end up with a medal. I especially wanted it because it gave you extra points when it came time to get discharged. I asked about our medal and they said they didn't know anything about it. They said the lieutenant got a medal. I asked them what he did. They told me about the tank and the half-track. I said, "That sonofabitch didn't do anything. All he did was stand back and tell us when to shoot. We did all the work." I never saw the other kid again. That's the only time I got mad enough at an officer that I could have shot him.

The war started to wind down. We went to a place called Ziebest[78] and Marburg, where the 83rd Infantry Division put up the Truman Bridge across the Elbe River. We crossed and dug in and set up booby traps. The Russians were advanc-

---

[78] 28 April 1945. From this point the 125th Cavalry Squadron moved east to contact advancing Soviet forces.

ing from the east and pushing the Germans toward us. We put up safe areas through the minefields with yellow ribbons. Then we went out and they told us to post these signs that said, in German, "If you wish to surrender, stack your rifles here and follow the yellow ribbons. You will be taken prisoner." I thought that was awfully stupid. It was a good way to tell the enemy where we were. It worked, though, and they came in and surrendered.

I got pneumonia when we got to the Roer River.[79] I was cared for by a Belgian family who put me in the straw with their cows. Those Belgian people took exceptionally good care of me. Our medics approved. Then one of the medics came in and found out that my temperature was a little over 103, so they rushed me to the hospital. I was taken to the hospital in Maastricht, Holland.

When I got back I got to Paderborn and then finally ended up in Brunswick, Germany, at Burgermasterson, where there was an Italian prisoner of war camp. I was put in charge there, because I could speak Italian. I was there when the war ended.

The Italian camp was funny as Hell. The officers in my unit asked, "Does anybody here speak Italian?"

"I do."

"Okay, c'mon, you're going to go."

We went into the headquarters of this Italian group and my colonel said, "Don't tell them you can speak Italian. Just listen to what they say."

A lieutenant and I went in and he told the Italians we were taking over the camp and that we were going to make an inspection. These Italian officers were giving us a bad time in Italian, but they didn't know I could understand what they were saying. The next day, we went in early to make the inspection and half of these guys were asleep. We got them all up and spoke to them in German and they kept saying in Italian, "I don't understand German." But they understood enough to get by with.

The Italian general came in and said, in Italian, "What do these SOBs want from us, anyway?"

When he called me a SOB, I answered him in Italian, "I'm no SOB."

From that moment forward, things changed drastically. They cooperated fully with us. We went through the camp, which was filthy. We made them clean it up. Each Italian officer had at least one mistress with him. Some of them had their own children there. I got treated royally. I can't complain. I got everything within reason. I got my hair cut and my shoes polished, my clothes tailored. Then the order came for them to move out. They all boarded the train, just the men, not the children and women. The prisoners who wanted to take their women along snuck them aboard. The rest of the women and children didn't get on. They

---

[79] Around 7-14 December 1944.

shipped the prisoners off to Italy and shipped me off to the CID. I was very happy about it.

The CID was the Criminal Investigating Department of the Army. What we did was to investigate criminal acts of our own troops and atrocities. I was involved mostly in investigating atrocities. I was sent to Bremerhaven with a Captain Corner. I was a tech sergeant at the time. We were sent there to infiltrate, to find out what was happening. They'd gotten a complaint back in the States that packages were being opened and emptied in Bremerhaven. He stayed with the officers and I stayed with the enlisted men. We did find out what was going on. There was a colonel and some enlisted men taking stuff out of packages, selling it, and sending the money home. We caught them and brought them back to Frankfurt, Germany, our headquarters, for prosecution. I saw that colonel about three months later. He saw me and called me over.

I said, "Yes, sir?" and threw him a high ball.[80]

He said, "Do you remember me?"

"Yes, sir, I do."

"You and your captain thought you were pretty smart."

"We were just doing our job."

"You forgot one thing. You see that?"

He held out the flat of his hand and showed me his West Point class ring. They had broken him down one grade, fined him and gave him a different assignment.

One case was reported to us by a Lutheran minister who also told us where to find the person involved, who was now in Norway. His story concerned some American fliers who were captured and paraded through a German town. One of the airmen was limping badly and his buddy was helping him. As they walked through the streets, the bystanders threw stones and battered them. There was a Norwegian, a quisling,[81] who went up to these two and told the one airman to leave the wounded man alone. He did, and the guy who was injured fell behind and the bystanders started to beat him. His buddy went back and started carrying him. This Norwegian had a sickle and he hit him across the head, killing him. The airman who was injured lunged for the Norwegian and dug his nails into the guy's throat. The other people pulled the airman off and killed him. Captain Corner and I were assigned the case and we flew to Norway, where we met our counterparts in the Norwegian police, who agreed to help. They discovered this guy high up in the mountains. The captain and I went up there and we captured him without too much of a fuss, just a little gunfight. We handcuffed the guy and put him in jail.

---

[80]Slang for "salute."

[81]After Vidkun Quisling (1887–1945), a Norwegian collaborator. Quisling was a general and Norwegian Minister of War from 1931 to 1933. He was captured at war's end, held prisoner in Oslo, and executed.

We still had a few days left, so we went out and had a ball. The Norwegian people really treated us like we were saviors. We could've had anything we wanted. The captain was a little older, and he took care of me. We stayed our limit of fifteen days, the time limit we had to finish a case, picked up our prisoner from the jail and went back and turned him over to Colonel Brown. They gave him a trial and then hanged him.

After these trips, we took some rest and then would be given another case. Usually, most of the cases were already advanced, and people had things ready for us, or had prisoners waiting for us. We traveled around quite a bit. The Colonel used to tell us, "Don't forget to come back home." He knew what we were doing, he wasn't stupid. We were eighteen and twenty years old, and had $800.00 expense money for each case.

There were many other teams like Captain Corner and me. We operated until enough of the war criminals were picked up. Most of them were hung, because they'd committed outright atrocities. Some of them were given prison sentences. But they were all given a trial. The people who supplied us with the information testified against them.

I put in an extra six months after the war. I had been corresponding with my mother and she wanted me to come home. The Army said if I stayed, they'd promote me to lieutenant. That wasn't enough. I told them I wanted to go and I came home, 10 October 1945, the *Lewiston Victory*. That was an adventure by itself.

As one of the ranking noncoms, I was given charge of the kitchen. I had some friends with me. I went into the freezer and, my God, I've never seen so much good food in all my life! We ate like pigs. I took care of my people. They all got seasick except me. They were throwing up all over the place.

There were nurses berthed in the upper decks. We saw officers going up there, coming in and out. We couldn't figure out what the Hell was going on. We tried to get up there, but couldn't get in. Well, the nurses were hustling themselves and charging the officers money. We were a little disgusted with it, but I'm sure if we could've come up with the money we could've gone up there, too.

We landed in New Jersey, and went to Camp Dix to get discharged. They gave us the Ruptured Duck[82] pin and we put it on our uniform jackets. We didn't have any other clothes. We went into New York City and everybody looked at us like we were a bunch of bums. The attitude was "You just got discharged, when are you going to find a job? You're going to be sorry you got out. There're no jobs around here. You should have stayed in the service."

---

[82] A lapel pin awarded to veterans for honorable service between 8 September 1938 and 31 December 1946. Designed by a German, Franz Sales Meyer, it was modeled after the eagle used by the Roman legions.

I heard any number of cracks like that. I came home and joined the 52/20 Club,[83] until I went to school.

I wouldn't trade my war experience, good, bad or indifferent, for a million dollars! I saw Patton once, somewhere in Germany. I was in one of his honor guards. We had to polish our helmets until we could see ourselves in them. They gave us clean clothes and dressed us up. They even gave us some medals. I don't know what the medals were, but we all looked good anyway. Patton came down on a review and he gave us a salute and we went to "present arms." It was just one of those things that happened really fast. After that, they gave us our rifles and they shipped us right back to the company! They didn't even give us a good meal. They took our helmet liners away.

In the field we did what we had to do, plus a lot of screwing around. They didn't really want us to get to know each other exceptionally well, because tomorrow we might be killed. We were different people, from different towns and cities. They mixed us all up. We had a little bit of everything. The only way they could improve morale was when they'd send some good food. When they brought the mail up, everybody shared what they had. When we went back to take baths, we saw movies. We saw Ingrid Bergman and Jack Benny in a USO show in France. Another time some girls from the Red Cross came and brought donuts up. The next thing I knew, they were with the officers and that was the end of that.

Mail came not often enough. Sometimes it took months to get to you. Other times you'd get two or three letters at a time. My mother sent me a Christmas package. She mailed it just before Thanksgiving and I didn't get it until long after Christmas. The food in it was still good, because it was Italian salami, which had all that crud on it. Some of the guys said it was spoiled. I said, "It's not spoiled, don't worry about it." I cleaned the stuff off of it and cut it and it was just as fresh as could be. Pepperoni was another thing she packed. Of course, the crackers and cookies were all crumbled up into little pieces! Sometimes there were cigarettes and little cans of food.

I got a leave to go to Paris, where I met a buddy of mine, Augie Placido. I picked up two or three Lugers and a few souvenirs for us to sell. Whenever anybody got leave, everybody else would pitch in something for them to sell. Of course, *we* only had a few bucks. I was sending home an allotment, so there wasn't very much left. We sold the stuff. Augie asked how much money we had. I told him $4000.00.

He said, "Oh, my God, we can have a ball."

And we did. We blew it all in Paris in three days!

I sent loot home that never got here. I picked up as many silver plates from a castle as I could and hid them. Later, I gave them to the kitchen and they put

---

[83]Veterans could receive twenty dollars for a period of fifty-two weeks.

them away for me. Then I found a German that would make a box strong enough to pack them in and send them home.

My lieutenant said, "Cat, they're not going to get there, because we have to tell the Army Post Office what's in there."

"Tell them it's something else."

"Well, they'll open it."

So, somebody opened it, found what was in it, and it never got here. They were very valuable, those plates. I sent home an 8mm Mauser, which my wife later "sporterized." I hunt with it. I have a few other small souvenirs that I picked up here and there.

A lot of people shot themselves in the leg. The Army found out because of powder burns. When they were found out, the men started shooting *each other* in the leg just to get out of it. It was too close to the end of the war and nobody wanted to get killed. Now, neither did I, but I don't think I had the guts to shoot myself. I was willing to do what I had to do, just like everybody else.

I wish we would have had more food and bedding. We slept in holes and trenches. We had nothing to cover ourselves with. We had heavy overcoats, but most of us threw them away.

We ate a lot of K-rations. I thought the K-rations were OK myself, because I used to put them inside my shirt. I figured that if a German would shoot, the bullet wouldn't get through the K-ration and hit me! That wasn't true. Shrapnel and bullets would get through. It was just something I felt much safer doing. The K-Rations were cans packed in a four-by-six cardboard box sealed with wax. There were eggs and bacon, a chocolate bar and some crackers, packets of Raleigh cigarettes, with five or six cigarettes in them. The chocolate bar was about two-inches square. Whenever the armored guys would come by, we'd distract them and steal their C-Rations, which were much better than K-rations. Other K-rations had SPAM. Lots of SPAM.[84] We got to the point where we didn't want to eat any more SPAM. We'd shoot a cow every now and then.

I had some concern about the four grenades I always carried. I was afraid that one of them would be shot and explode on me. One of them happened to be a white phosphorus grenade and I didn't want to die that way! When you threw two grenades, you picked up two more. When you fired off a bandolier of ammo, you'd pick up another bandolier. My pants were half-dropping down on me from the weight. I carried two canteens of water. That's a lie. Only one canteen was water. The other was booze. We got hold of plenty of whiskey.

---

[84] An American invention, still popular today. Spam consisted of chopped ham and pork shoulders and was first introduced in 1937 by the Hormel Meat Company. The advertising campaign featured George Burns and Gracie Allen in an early singing commercial. The product gained worldwide recognition because of its distribution to American servicemen overseas, and no less so for its widespread use through Lend Lease in England, nicknamed "Spamland." The British called it "Escallope of Spam." In reality, the "Spam" given to the American soldiers was a wretched invention of the U.S. Army Quartermaster Corps.

I remember this young kid, about the same age as me, eighteen, nineteen years old. He must have been about fifteen or twenty yards from me. We were going through the woods and an 88 came in and obliterated him. I never saw him again. It just blew him all to Hell. I couldn't figure out what had happened to him. I went over and looked in the hole and I just saw some blood. That's all. It was as close to a direct hit as possible. He wasn't really my buddy; we weren't close. I thought, "I wonder if he felt anything?" I tried to put it out of my mind, because I felt that if I didn't, it would have a direct effect on my ability as a scout. I didn't even know what his full name was.

I was involved in the liberation of Buchenwald. I was on a night patrol sometime in April 1945. We were supposed to go out and meet the 4th Infantry Division. We walked on a roadway until the full moon came up, then we moved into the woods, to get cover from the trees. There was this terrible stench. We thought it was from rotting horses or cattle. The German army used a lot of horses. We climbed a hill. Near the top we saw what looked like a bunch of zombies, skeletons. They were full of sores. They were wearing these zebra-striped suits. They came up to hug us and rub against us. It made me queasy. I wanted to throw up. We handed out cigarettes and candy bars. When they saw us coming, they hollered, "Amerikanskie! Amerikanskie!"

I said, "Where the Hell are we? What did we get into now?"

We were on the high-side of Buchenwald, near a barbed-wire fence. The 4th Infantry Division came in from the other side and had actually gotten inside Buchenwald. The skeletons knew that more Americans were coming. We stayed there for one night. We made contact with the 4th, then moved out. There were dead all over the place. The worst thing about the whole deal was the stench and the liquids oozing from the bodies. I can still smell it!

I came across other camps in the Harz Mountains. When we got closer, the Nazis would eliminate the workers, so they wouldn't have to transport and feed them. There was one camp where people were treated "decently." The Nazis weren't killing them as fast as in other camps. They were feeding them beet juice and turnip juice with potatoes mixed in. It gave everybody diarrhea. You could smell that on the wind a half mile away.

We heard about these camps, earlier. When we went into some of these smaller camps, at first we couldn't figure out what was going on, because there were so many displaced persons from so many countries. When the Allies made their big advances and the Germans started to move back, they had to make a decision about what to do with all of these people. Well, two, three, four or five, here and there, escaped and were picked up by our military intelligence and explained what was going on. So we were told that there were big camps somewhere around our area. We knew about Buchenwald, but we never thought we were going to reach that far when we went out on that night patrol.

The war made a man out of me. I was full of piss and vinegar and a little wild. I never got involved in anything criminal, but I was rough around the edges. I think it straightened me out for the rest of my life. But I wouldn't do it again. Period! I just learned too much about killing. I found that you couldn't have any good buddies, because you don't know what's going to happen to them. I found out, also, that you *need* good buddies, so they can protect you while you're sleeping, and you can protect them while they're sleeping.

[*The following are written comments provided by Mr. Catalfamo following his interviews*]

A Machine-gun Nest

Once I passed up a German machine-gun nest. When they opened up, I went down and tried to hide myself. I could hear the second scout saying, "Cat, where are they? Cat, where are they?" I heard the lieutenant behind him say, "Point your rifle at the enemy, point your rifle." I said, "Point my rifle up your ass! If I point my rifle, they're going to kill me!" So I stayed there. Then my buddy, Rosie Casper, who was a BAR man, made a flanking movement and wiped out the nest. He came up to me and asked, "Are you all right, Cat?" I said, "Yeah. Jesus Christ, what took you so long?!" A few minutes is an eternity when you're under fire. If they'd thrown a grenade, they could have killed me. Sometimes you just laugh about little things like that happening.

Close Calls in Hamm, Germany

Shrapnel from an 88 fell about two feet from where I was standing. I heard the metal burn into the ground. Two feet more and I would have been gone. Later on I was chased up and down a hill by a small scout car with tracks. I ran for the nearest cover I could find and the scout car did not fire at me. To this day I don't know why. One of our BAR team and a bazooka team stepped out from one of the streets and destroyed the scout car. I told them, "You bastards, why didn't you knock them off before?" They just laughed at me and said, "We wanted to see how fast you could run." I told them, "Thanks for nothing."

Another German Machine-gun Nest

Rosie Casper and I were part of a team moving from house to house searching for snipers and machine-gunners. In the distance we heard machine-guns chattering away. We hurried to a huge house and busted in. We heard a machine-gun firing on the second floor. We crept up the steps. I opened the door and threw in a hand grenade. Rosie sprayed the room with his BAR. We killed six Germans. We continued into Germany.

"...there were millions and millions of Marks floating through the air."

Boxing Match

At the war's end I was in this little town and I had made the boxing team with Rob Chatlow, Jimmy Lawski and another guy. We fought our way to the finals in Freyoung, Germany. The next step was the Championship in Passaua River. I lost the final match to a black soldier who was about six-feet, three-inches tall and whose arms stretched all over me. (I'm only five-feet, three-inches.) But I got my licks in. Somehow, I fouled him—I hit him in the nuts—and we had a three-minute break. My lieutenant said, "Do you want me to throw in the towel? He's killing you. You can't reach him." Anyway, I lost the bout. Our reward for being on the boxing team was five days at the Oberhaus in Passaua, Germany. We had a wonderful time there and then we returned to our base.

Getting Rich in Hamm, Germany

While going through the city, we happened upon a huge postal office. We entered cautiously and looked around, went in behind the cashier's cages, but found no one at all. Just then, a bazooka team entered and one guy said, "What's up? What is that big safe?" We decided to try and open it. There had to be something in it. The bazooka team fired two shells at it and the door opened. As we entered the safe, there were millions and millions of Marks floating through the air. We looked for other things that might have been valuable and found only some food packages being sent to German soldiers.

We then searched for more money and found zillions of Marks all over the place. We loaded them into our musette bags and screamed that we would be millionaires. We took as much as we could carry. Other soldiers came in behind us and loaded up. I then figured I had to live through the war because I would be a millionaire. We found out later that the money was not as valuable as we had thought. The German Mark, without gold to back it up, had depreciated into nothing. We used it for toilet paper.

Cherries in France

Somewhere on the French-German border our troops discovered a mountain with a huge cave. In the cave were German tanks, guns, ammunition and food and wine, like champagne. As soon as we secured the cave, our vehicles drove in and we took out many cases of wine, champagne and boxes and boxes of cherries. It lasted forever. For the next two weeks we ate cherries jubilee, cherry pie, cherry-everything. And we were probably the drunkest soldiers in the ETO.

Hot Shots

William Louis Ciavarra

63rd Infantry Division
253rd Infantry Regiment
3rd Battalion Company M

Fayette City, Pennsylvania, 1925

"I had never been away from home before I went into the service. I wondered what it was going to be like. A lot of the men were ashamed when we went for our physical in Greensburg, because they had to stand naked. I went in with two men from Fayette City, Neal Marshall and Ralph Gill, and we tried to get into the paratroopers, because they had really great boots! We figured we could pick up a girl really quick with good boots and wings! We weren't thinking about having to jump out of an airplane. We thought that we would be hot-shot soldiers. When I tried out, they told me, 'Ciavarra, you're not heavy enough.' 'What do you mean, I'm not heavy enough! I can carry an eighty-pound pack!' 'If you jump out of the plane you won't come down! You'll stay up there!' I raised some Hell about it, but they still didn't take me. Only Ralph made it, but he didn't see much of the war. On his first jump, just as he hit the ground, shrapnel took off half his leg. Before we shipped out of New York, the Army gave us combat boots. If you wanted to see a bunch of smart-ass guys going down the street we were it! There we were with our pants up showing off the boots. We were just like paratroopers, only their boots had laces whereas ours had buckles."

My father was Joseph W. Ciavarra, from Italy. When he was younger, he studied for the priesthood, but he couldn't fulfill the commitment, so he dropped out and went into the tailoring business. He worked till he was ninety-three. He passed away a week short of ninety-five. My dad was a World War I vet and raised Hell when they stopped the veterans' pension. He was married to my mother for more than fifty years. My mother's maiden name was Edna Ellian. She was born in a little town south of here called Gilespi. My father spoke three languages. English, Italian and Polish, and he could write in Italian and English. I don't even know my heritage language.

I learned the tailoring trade from my father in the family shop. I started working for my dad when I was in the ninth grade. After school I'd be in the shop learning how to be a tailor. I hated it because I wanted to be out with the boys.

William Ciavarra; Somewhere in Europe

There wasn't a large Italian community. There were mostly eastern Europeans. There were never any blacks. They said this town was in sympathy with the South. There were cross burnings here a long time ago. Picket boats used to dock down at the wharf. Some of the guys on the boat were black and used to come into town. Some people in town would stop these black guys and tell them that they had better be out of town before dark. I guess there were some fights at night. Minstrel boats used to dock here and they had both black and white workers. I went in with the minstrels after high school. I suppose that if a black were to see a minstrel they would think that we were making fun of them, but we really weren't. I think that it was a boost to the blacks in a sense that we were trying to be like them. There were six of us minstrels who would blacken our faces and give performances.

My dad had a black customer from Arnold City. One guy, the head of the Dragon Club, came into my dad's shop and told him, "Since you didn't get rid of that man we are going to boycott you."

My dad knew this town and he was a little shook up. The next time the black man came into the shop, my dad overcharged him, hoping he wouldn't come back, but he did. My dad told him, "I'm sorry, but I wish that you would not come anymore because they are going to boycott me if you return to my shop again."

He never came back after that. This wasn't the Klan that did this. It was just a club formed by a bunch of the guys here. Today, if any blacks come in my shop, I treat them like any other customer, and I won't hear nothing about it.

We were mad when we heard about Pearl Harbor. But, when you're young you don't understand politics too well. I was drafted straight out of high school. We realized that it was only proper that we go and do our share. I guess that's what they would describe as "waving the flag." Well, I've been waving the flag for a long time. When Desert Storm started, I wanted to enlist because I was ticked off about it. The recruiter said, "You're too darn old! Get out of here!"

I guess I waved the flag in other ways, too. I buried every veteran from around here who had been killed in World War II. They brought them back to the States for two years after the war, from Europe and the Pacific. I blew taps at the funerals. The last burial, which was for a captain, put me in the hospital. We were remodeling the store at the time and pulling the wall paper off. We had been working till about 3:00 a.m. and waking up at 8:00 a.m. for the past couple of days and I collected some congestion in my lungs from the old wall paper. They told us that they were bringing a captain in next morning, and we were expected to report early at the cemetery. I told them that I didn't think I would attend because I didn't feel very good. The guys said, "Come on, Ciavarra quit your horsing around!"

I went. We lined up with the color guard and I started on the bugle. I got through it, but afterwards I passed out. They called the local physician and rushed me to the hospital. I collapsed my right lung. I was there for everyone, because I felt that it was my duty.

I had never been away from home before I went into the service. I wondered what it was going to be like. A lot of the men were ashamed when we went for our physical in Greensburg, because they had to stand naked. I went in with two men from Fayette City, Neal Marshall and Ralph Gill, and we tried to get into the paratroopers, because they had really great boots! We figured we could pick up a girl really quick with good boots and wings! We weren't thinking about having to jump out of an airplane. We thought that we would be hot-shot soldiers. When I tried out, they told me, "Ciavarra, you're not heavy enough."

"What do you mean, I'm not heavy enough! I can carry an eighty-pound pack!"

"If you jump out of the plane you won't come down! You'll stay up there!"

I raised some Hell about it, but they still didn't take me. Only Ralph made it, but he didn't see much of the war. On his first jump, just as he hit the ground, shrapnel took off half his leg.

Before we shipped out of New York, the Army gave us combat boots. If you wanted to see a bunch of smart-ass guys going down the street we were it! There we were with our pants up showing off the boots. We were just like paratroopers, only their boots had laces whereas ours had buckles.

In training we had a great captain named Jewell, whom we all hoped would go overseas with us. Unfortunately he had malaria, so he couldn't go overseas. He treated us like human beings. He wouldn't put up with any BS though. When he would call out orders, we obeyed them to please him. We all looked up to him. He told us, "Remember when you go overseas, protect your jewels."

I took to basic training. I was determined to work and earn my stripes. It wasn't long before I got to be corporal. I had a lot of trouble with some of the guys who said that they would whip my backside. I said, "Sure you can, but when it's all done I'll have the last say because the stripes will come off of your shirt."

They didn't like to see a little guy barking orders to the big guys. We had to come to fists a couple of times. I held my own. There was a guy in my squad from Pittsburgh named Omar. We used to get into it a lot, but he was a good gunner. I recognized his talent when we were training in the swamps, and that son of a gun knew how to put that mortar base plate in the swamps so that it didn't move around too much. Even though he was a good soldier, I broke him once or twice by taking his stripes. He would threaten me, but never carried it out. I got along well with the mortar crews that I had overseas because I took care of the men the best way that I knew how.

We did a lot of things that others might have looked down on, but you do these things to keep up morale. On a twenty-five-mile hike in Camp Van Dorn a couple of the men fell out. This nutty guy ran up to them and talked real effeminately at them. This made them madder than heck, and they jumped up and started walking again. Their feet were bleeding. When we came back into camp General Ben Lear was there to inspect us. Word went around that this general was an SOB. He made us stand inspection in a horrible downpour. Another time a soldier, who had just finished a twenty-five-mile hike, whistled at one of the girls in the PX. When Lear heard that, he ordered the company out for another twenty-five miles!

They sent us into the Okeefeenokee Swamp on a night compass mission. As squad leader, I had the compass. I was to shoot the "back azimuth," that is I would go from point A to point B in a semicircular route, and end up at point B as if I had followed a straight line. I wasn't too swift on a back azimuth. I asked some of the guys what they thought, but they didn't know what to tell me. I said, "Let's head out and see if we can get through this swamp."

We tried to go straight through. A couple of the guys went in a few feet and came right back out again. They were nervous because of water moccasins and huge white snakes about ten to twelve feet long. We got lost. I said, "We might as well sit down and wait for the trucks to come looking for us in the morning."

When we were in Camp Van Dorn, we were training specifically for the 63rd Division. We saw General Louis Hibbs there. They used to call him "Mess-Kit Louie" because when he took over our group he removed the dishes from our camp and had us eating out of our mess kits. He would tell us, "Now you're hot shots and when I see you, you had better have that overseas cap at an angle touching your ear."

Near the end of our training, we were told that everyone was supposed to get a fourteen-day furlough before going overseas. I got my furlough and went home. That's when I heard about D-Day. I helped ring some of the church bells in town, and two days later I was called back to camp with orders to go overseas. We got into camp to check in and this one guy who was on duty said, "What the heck are you guys doing back in camp?"

"We got orders to come back."

"For what?

"We are going overseas."

"You're not going overseas, yet," he told us.

"What are you talking about."

"There are no orders for you to go overseas. I'm in the order room so I would know something about the papers."

What actually happened was Captain O[85] had orders for us to ship, but instead of letting us continue our furlough, he called us back to camp just to be an SOB. So we were at camp for the rest of our furloughs, even though we didn't have to return until afterwards. One guy remarked, "That SOB! He better watch out when we get into combat!"

---

[85]The Captain's full name has been omitted here.

Captain O was killed in battle very quickly in an area of the Black Forest. A lot of people were suspicious. We think one of his own men killed him. His company did a lot of hand-to-hand fighting in the Black Forest, and half the company was nearly wiped out.

When we boarded the ship to go over, I was in pretty good spirits. We were on a Liberty Ship made in Mississippi. The ship had a strong odor. While we were making the crossing, we encountered a heck of a storm one morning when we went to breakfast. The storm caused dishes to break, oatmeal to fall on the floor, and soldiers to stumble. We were lucky that nobody got seriously hurt. We had to laugh, since we were all on our behinds. We were really worried about getting there. After getting over to the Straits of Gibraltar, they told us, "If you'll all be very quiet, then you'll be able to hear the people of Casablanca talking."

So everybody got very quiet. We *could* hear people on shore. It was the eeriest thing!

Our ship landed in Marseilles around December without any problems. We got off and walked through a compound that had a stockade. I tapped the guy next to me and said, "Look at the guys in the stockades. I wonder who they are?"

He said, "Look at the size of them!"

The only thing that I could think of was that they looked like Russian-Mongolians. Some of them had great fur coats on them and they were very huge. One guy asked me, "What do you think?"

"If those are the guys that we are going to fight, then I'm turning around and getting back on the ship!"

We moved north and they put us on this plateau where they told us to get our two-man tents up. The ground was so frozen it looked impenetrable, but we finally got the tent pegs in. We dug in pretty well and remained there for about three days. They warned us about German observation planes. We couldn't build any fires, except once in a while when they let us have a small one. This plane came over one night, so we tried to douse our fires. Gas cans were made with a specific type of cap that was different from water caps, but they both were the same size and had the same grip. One guy grabbed the wrong can and threw gas on the fire, which lit the whole darn place up. That pilot must have gotten really good pictures of how many troops were there.

Then they sent us into an area where we spent an evening and night listening to all the types of firing going on from artillery, machine-guns, and rifles. They used this exercise to get us used to explosions. In the morning we started our forced march and stopped outside of a town called Gros-Rederching.[86] They had to use dynamite to make holes for the base plate of our mortar because the ground was so frozen. They sent scouts out to find out what was going on near a ridge in front of us. News came back to us that there was a panzer division coming our

---

[86]This is January 1945, the first real battle for the 63rd, around Sarreguemines.

way. One guy pulled up his foot, took out his rifle and shot his whole foot off in an attempt to keep from facing combat.[87] We found out that it was the 17th SS Panzer Division that was coming toward us, so we retreated and left almost everything that we couldn't carry.[88] We loaded our jeeps to capacity. Most of us got into a half-run and left a lot of brand-new equipment. That was what they referred to as a "strategic withdrawal."[89]

We got reassembled when we got back into town. Most of the men didn't have their mess kits so they had to use some of the old, empty, K-ration cans. They had just set up the kitchen when we started getting strafed by a German plane. I ran into a barn that had about thirty men in it. We were all screwed up and didn't know what the heck to do. We designated an area outside of the barn as a latrine. We would run outside in between the strafing and try to do our business. Some of our guys were running with their pants half-down! I never saw a mess like that in my life!

That was a rough start for us. We withdrew because an infantry outfit fighting against a panzer division seemed like sure slaughter. We got reorganized and moved out to another town. We were sent down to a railroad station near a big, empty field. Our job was to put fire on the forest beyond the field. I was at the railroad station with the lieutenant, who was the forward observer for the 105mm. I asked the lieutenant if he wanted to fire first since he had the big gun. He said, "You go first and then I'll come after you with the 105."

About that time my radioman said, "Hey, Ciavarra, you're wanted on the radio."

Then the guys said, "Ciavarra, we have 4.2 back here."

I asked, "What is a 4.2?"

"Never mind what it is," they said. "The captain said to fire it just like you would fire an 81."[90]

"Are you sure?" I was a little bit leery about calling down fire from a weapon that I didn't know much about.

"Yes," he said.

So I sent the smoke round out and when that thing hit the lieutenant hollered over at me, "Ciavarra, what are you firing?"

I told him, "I don't know. It's a 4.2 they told me."

---

[87] Harry Bee describes the same incident. Mr. Ciavarra describes the man as having black, curly hair. "I was right near this guy," Ciavarra stated in a telephone conversation with the Center.

[88] The 63rd would meet the 17th Panzer again in April, when the outcome would be the opposite.

[89] Mr. Ciavarra added in an aside: "I often wondered where our tanks were that day. Very seldom did I see any of our tanks with us. We saw a good many German tanks. One time we had a Sherman with us and we were trying to get the commander to take his tank down the road to wipe out a machine-gun nest. He said, 'Hell, no! There's a Tiger tank down that road.' They said the Sherman was too easy to knock off in a frontal attack with a Tiger. We had a Hell of a time with some of those tankers."

[90] 81mm mortar. Sergeant Ciavarra was a section leader in charge of two eight-man mortar crews. He was responsible for laying down mortar fire as a forward observer.

The 4.2 shell turned out to be just a little bit smaller than the 105 round. It had a heck of a punch.

"Holy Shit," he yelled!

So we fired up the woods pretty good. I thought, "I'll never use a 4.2 again. Let another outfit do it."

Meanwhile, the Germans had set up a heavy-machine gun at this railroad station in the town. There were supposedly three or four Germans on the machine-gun. We turned our mortars on them and pounded them for a good while. Suddenly, I realized that one of my men was missing. One of my guys told me he saw him go into a barn with a woman. I got mad and went looking for him. I found him and ordered him to get back to his mortar crew. By the time I got back to my crew the German machine-gunners had a white flag out. One of our captains stood up and motioned for the Germans to come out and surrender. The Germans shot him. Some of our infantry rushed the machine gunners and got them. We saw the soldiers bringing the Germans through the town. There were three of them. The guards marched them right past us. When they reached my squad the guards said that they would take the prisoners back to a POW camp. A little further out of town, those guards pulled up their guns and shot the Germans. Our guys took revenge for the captain. I didn't blame them. Those Germans must have known that they were going to get shot. I knew what was going happen.

When we crossed the Sarre River,[91] which was on another nasty night, the coldest I ever knew, the Army sent up a change of underwear. We were in our foxhole trying to get a little bit of rest. One of the guys said, "Come on, Ciavarra, you are going with us."

"Heck no!" I said, "I'm keeping my dirty underwear on."

Some of those guys stood naked in the cold changing into their long-johns or two-piece outfits.

We slept in holes. That's how we survived. Alton was my foxhole buddy. We held each other to keep warm. We left the hole only when we had to, and that was usually to move our bowels. We urinated in the hole. You learned to live with the filth. We went through misery with our feet and hands. We never did find anything that was good for the feet. A lot of men who had to walk a long distance would get sweaty feet which eventually froze. I never got frozen feet, but I did get trench mouth, a disease that attacks your gums. My gums bled and my teeth loosened. The whole outfit had trench mouth. None of us could brush our teeth properly. How much hygiene could you expect on the line? They brought up peroxide for us to use. We ended up using every bit of peroxide that we had.[92]

---

[91]February 1945.

[92]Mr. Ciavarra added as an aside: "Later, we couldn't get any help from the Army. After the war I went to the VA. They wanted signed affidavits from three soldiers who were with me during that time. I said, 'You have to be kidding me!' We went round and round about this. I said, 'The heck with it then.'"

On the line morale was vital. Some guys got Dear John letters. There was a time when my girlfriend stopped writing to me. There were some problems with her family. They didn't want her marrying an Italian, but that's another story. I saw some of my men get Dear John letters. It took the fight out of them. I talked to a couple of guys who got letters and tried to encourage them the best that I could. I was close to my men, so I could feel for them.

Some of the men were in a bad state of mind when we were going through this wooded area one day. They were tired, depressed, thinking about their girls. Then we passed by a dead German. His head and a good bit of his torso was blown away, but the lower half of his body was just sitting on a tree stump, like he was resting. He had been there a good while and one of his legs was nearly severed. I picked up the leg and chased my men around with it. It got their spirits up. It wasn't proper to do that, I guess, but the guy was dead. He wasn't going to miss his leg.

There was the time that my buddy George Gialas got killed. He was a rifleman and radio man. I was the forward observer and I was getting orders to lay down some fast mortar fire right in front of us. One landed short. That happened sometime. George's back was blown away. One of my men was hollering at me, "Come on, Ciavarra!"

"I have Gialas here! He's hit," I said.

"Put him down, he's dead," he yelled back!

I guessed George was dead, but I didn't realize it. I held onto him for a long time. I go to his grave every so often. I feel bad that I never went down to see his parents after the war. That's one of the many mistakes that I've made in life. I didn't go because I knew that they were going to ask me all these questions, and I didn't want to answer them.[93]

Eventually, I got leave to go to Dijon, where I was treated for combat fatigue. We had been on line for 124 days without any relief. We did our share. That's why we complained that the 253rd, 254th, and 255th didn't get the credit that they deserved. My officers knew me pretty well, and we got along, so maybe they noticed me doing some bizarre things that I didn't recognize myself, and realized that I needed a break. I guess in time you draw everything within yourself. The accident with my buddy might have caused some problems. It stayed with me. My wife has often told me, "You have never forgotten your past."

I was in Dijon for three days and got drunk in the outside cafes. Some guys and I got mixed up with a bunch of French people. There was a little bit of a fight. We caught heck for that when we got back to camp, but we had to get it out of our system.

---

[93] It was later discovered that George Gialas was killed by friendly fire from a short round of artillery, probably a 105mm, not from Mr. Ciavarra's mortar round.

After the war there were a couple of GIs killed in Heidelberg. We were bil-leted in what would today be considered a hotel, with the kitchen being set up in the lobby. Everyone had weapons in their field jackets, even though there were orders that we were not to have weapons in town. Then we heard this story about two guys who were crossing a makeshift bridge who got killed by some Germans. After hearing that we thought, "The heck with this. We are going to carry our 45's."

Heidelberg was nasty. We knew that if any German girls were seen with GIs, they'd cut all their hair off. Some were shot. One girl came to the chow line a couple of times. I told my soldiers to give some food to some of the people if they looked bad. When this girl found out I was the one responsible for the food she came over to me and we got pretty friendly. She wanted so spend the night, but I refused. We did go to a GI dance in Heidelberg. The guys would kid me saying that when I danced with her my nose was right between her breasts. She didn't mind it, though. Whatever happened to her, I don't know.

When the fighting was over, I got transferred to a heavy-ordnance outfit. It was located right on the Autobahn between Heidelberg and Mannheim. I was there a short time when I heard about the accident that killed General Patton. They brought his car into the ordnance garage. There was very little damage. The crash, however, was enough to break his neck. Some people thought that it wasn't an accident at all, but that it was deliberate. I don't know. There are some things you can't know for sure.

Some officers attached to Patton's headquarters came in and wanted us to prepare two half-tracks for the General's funeral. They wanted to transport his body on one of the half-tracks. They wanted us to clean two of them, and they would pick the best-looking one. We stayed up all night preparing the vehicles. Why they picked one over the other, I don't know. They both looked good to me.

I get to thinking about some of the boys who were killed. Some of them were so young. They never knew what it was like to be with a woman. They were just kids, what did they know about life, or get a chance to know about it? They were eighteen years old and then they were dead. They went from high school straight into the war. That's a pretty short life.

"It Made A Man Out Of You"

James J. Coletti, Sr.

United States Seventh Army
71st Infantry Division
66th Infantry Regiment
1st Battalion
Headquarters Company

Greensburg, Pennsylvania, 5 March 1919

"I remember when Steinmetz got hit. He was about an arm's length away from me. We were on the ground in this wooded area. He didn't even know he was hit, but I saw his field jacket started to get all red on his shoulder where he was bleeding. The bullet went clean through. It never hit a bone. But, still, since I was there, he wasn't alone. You have to depend on one another."

My parents, Joseph and Victoria were both born in the 1880s in Italy, in Abruzzi, just northeast of Rome. Her maiden name, Muzi, always sounded funny to me because it was like the first part of Mussolini's. My mother came from the "lower town" or Campobasso. Like most immigrants in those days, my parents gravitated to the mining towns where there were jobs. It was like Tennessee Ernie Ford's recording "Sixteen Tons." They worked hard and bought all their goods at the company stores. The company always made sure it got paid. It got the money in advance by attaching paychecks.

We survived the Depression on a farm at Hannastown. My dad smoked hams and sausages, mainly with sassafras wood. We had a spare bedroom we called the "refrigerator." In there we had poles strung along with sausage and hams. They hung there all winter.

On Sundays my father would go to different coal-mining towns with a couple of his friends to play good old Italian games of *more* and *bocci*. It got pretty loud. He would come home on Sunday nights hoarse. The losers paid with wine or beer they brewed at home. The Italians were a close group, but they got along well with people of other ethnic backgrounds. Neighbors helped each other. In those days, respect (*respetta*) was the word.

James J. Coletti, Sr.

I graduated from Greensburg High School in 1937, in the commercial program, then went to work for Robertshaw Company. I also helped found the Young Voters' Club in town. We were playing cards in the club when news of Pearl Harbor came over the radio. We were dumbfounded. I said, "They're stupid. In three or four weeks, once we get the military over there, we'll take care of them.!" I underestimated the ability of the Japanese. Soon, a hatred built up within me that made me want to blow them off of the map.

I was drafted in August 1942, and inducted in a town just on the other side of Harrisburg, PA. We were shipped to infantry training at Camp Wheeler, Georgia. If I had had a choice, I would have stayed home, but in those days the country was very patriotic so we felt it was our duty to go.

I wound up in the Specialist Training Battalion, a thirteen-week basic-training course, seven weeks in basic training and six in the technical/clerical school, basically a repeat of my high school courses. Instead of bookkeeping, I learned how to complete all the Army forms, and there were millions of them, in triplicate or quadruplicate!

I got out of bivouac training because camp headquarters called the school and wanted someone to process Section Eight cases. There was one case in particular concerning a young fellow from Harrisburg. He cried during his questioning, and expressed his fear of all types of weapons. When it came time for bayonet training, he just went bananas. I often said to myself, "If this was his natural reaction then I felt sorry for him, but if it wasn't then he was a doggone good actor and could have won an academy award in Hollywood."

We also dealt with bedwetters. As soon as the first one got discharged, other men started to throw their mattresses over the banisters outside their barracks. Whether these guys were actually wetting the bed on purpose, or just pouring water on them, I didn't know.

I stayed at Wheeler a little over a year, and was in charge of the payroll section for approximately eight months. Then we got some WACS[94] in to replace us. Finally, I was shipped to Fort Benning, Georgia, to the 71st Infantry Division, which was making preparations to go overseas. We left the States 26 January 1945, from New Brunswick, New Jersey, and landed in Europe 6 February 1945. The trip over reminded me of my mother's stories about her journey to the New World. It took her fourteen days in what they called "banana boats." She had four little girls in tow. I can't understand how she did it.

We went into Europe through Le Havre, where we boarded a train for the Saar Basin. We were there for about two weeks of training, quartered in pyramidal tents. I practically froze. All they had were cots, and the ground was so muddy that sometimes they had to bring bulldozers in to scrape off the top layer of mud

---

[94]United States Women's Army Corps, established 30 September 1943. The WACS grew out of the WAACS (Women's Army Auxiliary Corps).

to get to a drier level of ground. We weren't allowed to cut trees for firewood. They gave us sleeping bags that were extremely thin. You could see through them! One morning we heard chopping. We looked and some guys from a black regiment were chopping down two-by-four tent supports for firewood.

In the Saar Basin, a young lieutenant from California just out of a college ROTC program, got killed in the first week of combat. The 100th Infantry Division in the Seventh Army had an ideal defense set up in the Saar Basin. They had big search lights they would aim up into the sky and the light would reflect off of the clouds, so that would give us pretty good light to watch the enemy. The Germans had the area mined, and two American boys from the 100th were lying dead in the mine field. Our assistant regimental commander, a colonel, ordered the lieutenant and a couple of medics to retrieve the bodies. It was a useless order. You hated to see them out there, but they were already dead, and not worth more casualties. But that's exactly the way it wound up. The lieutenant got killed. I heard some officers say that if they were ever in a convenient combat situation, they would shoot that colonel! We discovered sometime later that the colonel had never been in charge of a combat unit. He was always in Army administration. You could never get near him because he had taken some members of our regiment and formed them into a jeep patrol. He was always hidden in the middle of about six jeeps!

The biggest fight our outfit had was Holy Week of 1945.[95] We encountered some SS troops that we did not realize were so close to us. We were guarding the east exit of a forest. It was Good Friday and we were all set up to have a nice quiet weekend, but it didn't turn out that way. We were contacted through division headquarters that our regiment had to move to an area that was captured by the SS troops. We got into our convoy and our whole division left for this town. The terrain in there was so rough that the dirt road went through the mountain area as just one lane, so if you got off into the ruts you would just tumble down over a cliff. At that place, an American motorized cavalry unit had been completely annihilated by the SS troops. Two officers and two enlisted men in weapons carriers came down to meet us. There was no way for them to turn around, so they had to back up. We followed them out. As they came to a T in the road the SS attacked. We had a Hell of a battle there which lasted all afternoon of Good Friday into Holy Saturday. Steinmetz was hit. He was to my left. I looked over and saw his field jacket starting to seep blood. He had a flesh wound and I guess with the excitement, he didn't realize that he was hit. He survived, but it was a deep flesh wound.

That night a German, who had captured a jeep from the motorized cavalry earlier that day, broke through a check point at one end of town. He had the jeep

---

[95] 1 April 1945 was Easter Sunday. Mr. Coletti's units would have been in the area of the Budingen Forest in Germany.

in low gear and it was making an awfully big roar. They radioed to the check point on the opposite side of town. When he got there the guys at the checkpoint opened fire, hit the jeep and exploded a five-gallon gasoline can. I still see that German. Part of his skull was burned down to the bone. Some of his brains oozed out. The rest of him was charcoal.

During the Easter week fight we were in the woods and took cover among the trees. My own particular part in the battle was to provide cover fire. You shoot to kill, but nine times out of ten you shoot to give cover, just like in the movies. My part in the fight was small, for even though I was in the convoy that was hit we were told to pull out shortly after the fighting started to let the infantry troops take over.

As we pushed deeper across Germany toward Czechoslovakia's border, we were suddenly ordered back west, then south into Austria.[96] That's where we ended the war. There was a town in Austria that had been hit by our division artillery's phosphorous shells, and some of the buildings were burning. We got there about eleven o'clock in the morning and stayed there till about two or three o'clock in the afternoon, and allowed nobody in or out of the town.

We were told that Hermann Goering had a castle there.[97] We were ordered to go inside the castle to see if he was still there. He wasn't. He had left that morning on a special train about an hour before our unit had arrived. His train was just an engine and a coach which hauled all of his stolen treasures further south into Austria. The castle wasn't exceptionally big, but it had a big stone wall around it and the stone had a bluish color to it that was really pretty. We weren't allowed to loot the place. I was looking in a drawer in the pantry and he had a ton of silverware that was monogrammed "HG," Hermann Goering. I would have liked to have had that, but somebody else got it. I don't know who.

There were strict rules against fraternization and looting, but I don't think they were honored much. I know that when we got into some of the towns, there were camera shops and weapons shops. I found a .32 caliber semiautomatic pistol which was brand new. Naturally I took it, and came home with it. A lot of the soldiers took cameras. The only type of camera that I got was a box-type one, which I didn't bother with. I had heard that some of the big brass had truckloads of loot, but you couldn't prove it by me. Our assistant commander, a major from Mississippi and a West Point graduate, jumped on us and our company commander, a captain from one of the Carolinas, Captain Graham. The major made us leave all the loot there. The regiment had a motorized MP platoon set up. He put the MPs in there to guard the place. We figured that when the MPs got there, if they didn't get it, then the others would get it before them. So we left the castle without anything.

---

[96] 2 May 1945.
[97] In Neuhaus.

We got to Wels, Austria. Near the city airport was a POW camp the Germans set up for Russian troops. It was pathetic. They looked like they were in gray and white striped pajamas. Some of them came running towards us. They would collapse because they were skin and bone. They were covered with lice. They had been deliberately starved. I noticed the swollen joints. We had the quartermaster corps come up with food and other needs.

We came to the town of Steyr, where we stayed for about a month.[98] Then we went back into Germany proper for occupation. A good many other fellows were being transferred home, under the point system. We replaced the guys from our unit. Once we became a full force again, we started Pacific warfare training. Patton came down once or twice a week just to make sure everyone was alert. They made fun of his shiny helmet, which had a high-gloss lacquer sprayed over it. We didn't have to use our Pacific training, because the Japanese surrendered.

Occupation duty was fairly routine. They lifted the anti-fraternization rule, and we got along real well with the German civilians. They didn't appear to be bitter. They never talked well about Adolf Hitler, and they didn't talk bad about him either. A lot of our soldiers in our unit, and those I've talked to after coming home, felt that the German civilians treated us better than the French did. We never spoke well of the French. The Germans were human beings. If they were millionaires it meant nothing because there was nothing to buy. The only food they had was domesticated rabbits, geese, chickens, and ducks. In the town of Murnow there were a couple of families that would invite me to dinner, but I would refuse because I knew they didn't have much in the way of food.

In the town of Murnow, we cooperated with the Burgermeister. For about a week we didn't get any beef from the quartermaster, so we decided to go out into the wooded areas to shoot some of the little roebuck. If we got a deer or two more than we needed we took it down to the Burgermeister's office and let him distribute it to whomever he wished. We did our best to cooperate with them and they did their best to cooperate with us.

Also in Murnow, the company commander assigned one of the first lieutenants to keep the troops occupied. There was this nice building in the town where we established a club. We got a five-piece orchestra down from Munich and we found living quarters for them. We also supplied them with rations and paid them with the German Invasion Mark. The guys would come to this club, bringing some of the local ladies. We had beer and wine, which we would sell for practically nothing, just so we could raise enough to pay the orchestra.

During the whole time we were fighting and moving across Europe, we were lucky to have had Father Guinovin as chaplain. We would always have Mass, if it was possible. He felt it was his duty to be there to administer to the wounded and the dead. He was persistent about being right up front with the troops the night

---

[98]5 May 1945.

before the final push into Germany, but the battalion commander wouldn't allow that. He said, "You follow us up with the troops." The chaplain would come up when things were actually cleared. When he did, it was a guarantee that things were pretty safe for anyone else to come up.

We always had fun scrambling for food that would supplement what we got from the Army. The battalion commander once sent word up to have the cook set up a hot meal for the troops. What he did was heat up some C-Ration cans in thirty-gallon garbage cans filled with water. The colonel blew his cork. The next day the mess sergeant was demoted to private and assigned to a heavy-weapons outfit. He ended up carrying a heavy mortar base. As the convoy passed him, guys hollered, "Hot chow! Hot chow!" I could see him burning up.

In a basement in Austria I found eggs in big vats of some solution which looked like clear water.[99] In another part of the cellar there were potatoes and onions. I whipped up a batch of eggs and put the potatoes and onions in with them. The captain came in with the battalion commander, the lieutenant colonel and his assistant. He said, "What's that cooking?" They got to the food before we did, and ate it up. They told me if we got into another little town, make sure that we find the eggs, potatoes, and onions. It was an awful good meal. I learned it from my mother.

I was transferred to a cavalry outfit and came back to the States with them after Christmas 1945. I was discharged through Indiantown Gap 6 January 1946, and then I came home from there. At Indiantown Gap they did everything but twist our arms to join the Reserves. I refused. I had my mind made up that when the war was over and I was discharged, I wanted no part of the service unless there was another war. I've kicked myself in the pants since then for not getting into it because with my promotion to first-sergeant I could be drawing an Army pension along with Social Security today. But that's water over the dam!

When I came home, my father was pretty outspoken. He didn't like to see us go over there in the first place, because we would be fighting Italians. But like all families, when their sons and daughters come home from war, mine was pretty happy. I can understand now how worried they must have been.

The war helped mature me. When I got out of high school I was eighteen. I thought I knew everything! When I went into the service, I was around twenty-one, still not yet a man. The service puts a lot of sense in your head. In other words, it makes a man out of you! You work and live with other people. You depend on them and they depend on you, because you aren't doing a regular job. If you don't depend on them and they don't depend on you then your chances of surviving are not going to be great. In other words it's teamwork.

---

[99] A practice called "water glass." Many GIs would become familiar with this process of preserving eggs, and would look for such vats in the basements of houses.

I remember when Steinmetz got hit. He was about an arm's length away from me. We were on the ground in this wooded area. He didn't even know he was hit, but I saw his field jacket started to get all red on his shoulder where he was bleeding. The bullet went clean through. It never hit a bone. But, still, since I was there, he wasn't alone. You have to depend on one another.

"I Guess I'm Gonna Make It!"

Enrico D'Angelo

United States First Army
69th Infantry Division
880th Field Artillery
C Battery

Saltsburg, Pennsylvania, 8 April 1918

"My dad lived down by the railroad. I was coming home about eleven-thirty one night from seeing my girl and there was an oncoming train. They used to put what we called torpedoes on the tracks, dynamite caps, to warn a train to be careful because another train was ahead. They went off. I stopped the car, jumped out, and laid flat along the road side. I thought for a minute that I was over there again!"

When I was little, I couldn't speak English, just Italian, because that's all they spoke at home. When I went to school my first-grade teacher said something to me and I didn't understand her. I didn't finish at Saltsburg High School, because I had to help out at home. The mines weren't working too good. I joined the Works Progress Administration for fifty-two dollars a month. We worked on the roads, shoveled snow in the winter. We went out and picked wild apples, made gardens, and put up preserves. Then I started in the mines. When I got my draft notice,[100] I went to my superintendent and told him I was leaving. He said, "You don't have to go if you don't want to. We'll keep you. We need you here."

I said, "Nah! One year ain't gonna hurt me!"

When I was at Fort Meade for about twelve days, one of the guys from my town brought in the *Indiana Gazette* and showed me an article that told of an explosion in the McIntyre Mine. Nine men were killed. Two of the dead guys used to ride to work with me and my dad and my uncle. If I hadn't left for the service, I might have been one of the mine casualties. When I read that I thought, "I guess I'm gonna make it!"

At Fort Meade they asked us what outfit we'd like to join. This one guy said, "Tell 'em you want the coast artillery."

---

[100] 26 June 1941.

Enrico D'Angelo; Camp Wallace, Texas

That's what I did. We were sent to Camp Wallace, Texas, between Houston and Galveston. They didn't have enough guns to give us, so they gave us the old World War I helmets and broom sticks to do the manual of arms! That lasted about three weeks, until we got the old Springfield rifles. Then we trained on 40mm anti-aircraft guns and the new 90mm guns.

One day we were out for reveille and the first sergeant looked at me because I was smiling. He said, "Wipe that smile off your face!"

I couldn't do it and he said, "You're on KP! Report to the mess sergeant!"

When I got there the mess sergeant said, "What are you doing here?"

"The first sergeant said I was supposed to do KP because I couldn't wipe the smile off my face."

"I don't need anybody for KP. I need a carpenter who can build me a rack to put my dishes in."

"I can do that for you."

"Go to the first sergeant and tell him what you're gonna do for me."

"No, you want me to build that rack, you go tell the first sergeant."

So he went to the first sergeant and told him that he had a fella that could build the rack. I had to go to the supply room to draw the tools and the first sergeant was there and said, "Oh no, not you again!"

I built the rack for the kitchen and the first thing you know the captain came to me and said, "Where'd you learn the carpentry?"

"At home."

"Well, the officers' quarters needs coat racks. Can you build them?"

"I'll come up and have a look and see what I can do." I was three weeks building coat racks and cupboards for the officers' quarters!

After that they made me an acting corporal on the drill field. They gave me an orange arm band. So we had what they called "open ranks, stack rifles." Well, I did it the right way and the lieutenant comes to me and says, "Were you in the service before?"

"No."

"Where did you learn that?"

"Out of my manual."

They called me into the office and said, "You did a good job out there. How about we make you a PFC?"

I was only in there three months and they made me a PFC! Then I got to be permanent corporal. And I was still carpenter for A Battery. C Battery had a carpenter who was a Swede who talked broken English. They were making him paint the bannister outside the barracks and he said to the sergeant, "Can you make me a sign that says 'Vet Paint?'"

That's the way the sergeant made the sign, "Vet Paint!" We had a good time over that!

Then I got to be platoon sergeant and was training recruits. We even trained ROTC officers on the 90mms. When the camp broke up they sent me to Camp

Shelby, Mississippi. When I got there, they wanted to make me a gun sergeant. I said, "You've got men on there already that are qualified for it. I don't want to take somebody else's job."

The lieutenant asked, "What do you know about the guns?"

"I worked with 90mm guns."

"Let's go down to the gun section."

We went down there and he showed me the guns. "Do you know the nomenclature of that gun?"

The first thing I did was I kicked the tire. I said, "That's a tire."

He looked down and he grinned. I started naming different parts of the gun, described the recoil, explained when to check it for oil.

One day I went to the first sergeant and I said, "My brother's home on furlough. Can I get a furlough?"

"All I can give you is a ten-day pass."

So I came home and met my brother. When I went back, they took my buck sergeant rating away and made me a T-4 with the same pay. I became an artillery mechanic, and remained that until I went overseas. I was supposed to go to artillery school, but the lieutenant said, "I already saw that you know enough about the guns. You don't have to go."

At first we trained as a provisional platoon in Texas. We trained on the beach at Galveston without ammunition. That's when we got the news about Pearl Harbor. I said to myself, "Holy heck! I'll never get outta this Army now!" Then they brought in live ammunition to us to practice with. We were expecting the Germans or Japs to attack us! Some of the guys cried. A couple of fellas committed suicide on the firing range. One fella in my platoon hung himself from the second story coming down the steps. I guess it was a combination of heavy training and homesickness. They must have hated where they were.

We would go through infiltration courses. There was barbed-wire and fox holes. I led the recruits through there. We crawled through, with our rifles, while they fired live ammunition and played explosions and gunfire over a loudspeaker. One guy raised himself up a little bit and got wounded. Every so often a real dynamite blast would go off during an infiltration course. One guy who climbed into a hole and there was a rattle snake in there. He got out of there in a hurry, but he was lucky he didn't get hit by the firing when he jumped outta there! He didn't get bit either!

When I went to Camp Shelby, they wanted to send me through the infiltration course. I told the captain, "I trained recruits every three months. I've already been through it." They agreed, and I didn't have to go through it again.

At Camp Shelby we got on boats out on these lagoons on the edge of the Gulf of Mexico.[101] They put these rope ladders on the boats and made you climb

---

[101] Actually stretches of shallow sea water separated from the Gulf by sand dunes.

up. That was pretty rough. We had guys bouncing back and forth against the boats and guys falling off. They were training us to go on the boat and off the boat for invasion or in case of abandon ship. We got chemical training, too. We had to go into a gas chamber with a gas mask, and they let loose tear gas. They put a piece of mustard gas on my hand. It took a long time for it to heal up. That was just to let us know what it would feel like in case we came across it.

During maneuvers we camped in these little pup tents. This one guy bugged me all the time. I was sleeping on one side of the pup tent in what was called a shelter-half. I had half a pup tent and he had a half. It was raining like Hell. This guy started bugging me, so I rubbed his side of the pup tent and all this water came down on him. After that we was all right.

When Italy joined up with Hitler the captain called me in and said, "Sergeant, what do you think of the Italians going in with the Germans?"

"Captain, I'm fighting for the United States. Whoever I have to fight against, that's who I'll fight."

"That's the best answer I've gotten yet."

That's the way I felt. When I lived in this mining town, the Italians lived in one area, the English people in another area and the Polish in yet another area. Then we had a few blacks there, but they lived in one area too. We got along with all of them, but the roughest people were the English. They were bosses in the mines and all that stuff. When we went overseas, it didn't make any difference. My friends were Protestants, or Presbyterians. We mixed in the service. Especially overseas. Except the Army was segregated. Blacks had their own units. At Camp Wallace, Texas we had a battalion of blacks. A bunch of us was going for a walk through the camp and we said, "Let's go into this colored PX."

We walked in there and these blacks didn't know what to say. We went up to the bar and ordered a beer. They didn't know if they should give it to us or not. This one black sergeant comes up to me and said, "You guys ain't allowed in here. You know that."

"Why?"

"Because the whites don't like the blacks."

"I'm gonna tell you something, sergeant. Where I came from, we had blacks in our town. I went to school with the blacks, we got along. There was no problem."

"Well, before you guys get into trouble, I wish you would leave, for your own good."

A couple days later we had chemical warfare training and our captain told me, "Sergeant you ride in the jeep with this gas canister of tear gas. I want you to ride up to that column of niggers. I want you to pull this pin and hold that out and see how many of those guys put gas masks on and run."

The black troops were singing while they were marching. Some of them carried their rifles over their shoulders or by the sling like they were carrying a suit case. I hated to do it but the captain was watching. He said, "Okay, sergeant! Do it!"

So I did it. Boy, they scrambled. Some of them tried to put the gas masks on, some of them run away. I hated to do it! Then this black sergeant recognized me later, at military parade. He shook his finger at me. I asked, "What's the matter, sergeant?"

"You pulled that gas raid on us."

"Yeah, I was ordered to. I couldn't help it."

"I know. I know."

That's all the further it went.

We had one kid in basic training. He was a troublemaker, but I liked the kid. He went AWOL one day. When he came back, the first sergeant said, "Take a pick and shovel, take that kid up to the other side of the parade ground, and make him dig a six-by-six hole!"

I helped him dig the hole. We got done and I went to the first sergeant and said, "The kid dug that hole. What do you want me to do now?"

He gave me a box of matches and said, "I want you to light a match and throw it in that hole and tell that kid to cover it up."

That's how rotten that first sergeant was. That kid filled that hole, but he never forgot me. When he got shipped out, he used to write me a note every now and then, thanking me for the training I gave him. He became an officer.

In basic training the officers were tough, but at Camp Shelby we had a General Bolte, who had been in North Africa. They sent him back to train our division. He was tough. We were out on maneuvers three to four days out of the week. He would ride a horse, him and his aid, and they would come and visit all the outfits. One day he came in there on his horse and one of the guys in my outfit shouted "High-Ho, Silver!"

Bolte never found out who it was. Bolte trained us hard, but it served us well when we went overseas. *Everyone* knew what he was doing.[102]

We thought we were going to go to the Pacific. We were worried about the Japanese more than anything else. We thought that we'd stand a better chance in Europe. It wasn't until we headed east and to Camp Kilmer that we knew we were going to Europe. We went over on the *USS Lejeune*.[103] The boat had 6,000 of us on it. There were also 2,000 Navy men and 600 Marines. The Marines were supposed to keep us from getting into fights with the Navy!

---

[102]Mr. D'Angelo added as an aside, "We got to be real marksmen with those guns. Overseas, an executive officer set up the gun positions. He called out the firing order. Our battery fired about thirty or forty rounds and then he said, 'Cease fire!' He didn't say anything for a long time, then he hollered again, so many degrees right and up. Germans started coming out of their pillboxes, waving their blankets. He ignored it. 'Fire for effect!' We did. Then he yelled, 'Cease fire!' He was quiet for a minute, then said, 'They'll shake their blankets no more.'"

[103]1 December 1944.

The weather was good going over. We were in an eighty-ship convoy. It took twelve days to cross. They had one ship with nurses and WACS on it and the Germans were in the area, the U-boats, so they put us on the outside and the women in the center of the convoy. The Navy destroyers were out there dropping depth charges around us. We had these life vests that had three gas cylinders each. You had to activate these in order to inflate the vests. When we landed in England we said, "Let's see if these things really work?" Mine didn't! A lot of them didn't!

We docked in Southampton, England on 12 December 1944. We stayed at Berkshire Barracks in Reading, until right after Christmas.[104] We invited the kids from Reading, and shared what we had with them, sang Christmas songs. Then we boarded LSTs[105] and left for France. We thought that we were going in to relieve the guys from the Bulge, but it was pretty much over by the time we got there. We went past Malmédy.[106] They were sweeping the snow off the bodies and picking them up. They were the first dead we saw. As we went up this muddy road, we saw more bodies wrapped up in blankets. We knew they were GIs.

We relieved the 99th Infantry Division.[107] They took their artillery out of their positions and we put ours in. It was snowy and cold. Mud clear up to your knees! We got a firing mission. My battery fired the first round of our division. We pulled the guns with a six-by-six truck. I drove what was called a weapons carrier, a four-wheel-drive truck that had a .50 caliber machine-gun on it. It was me, the lieutenant, the radio operator and another guy who helped the lieutenant set up the gun position. Sometimes we traveled in the day, sometimes at night. One night we were blacked out because there was still a danger of the Germans attacking us from the air. The captain was in a jeep ahead of us and my lieutenant had a luminous watch on. He got out and walked in front of the truck and that was the only way we could keep on the road that night! I had to follow the light in his watch!

We usually knew what we were firing at. Whenever a position was taken, they told us to cease fire and we wouldn't fire for a long time. If there wasn't another target to fire on then we had to load up and move closer to the front. We

---

[104]Beginning 13 December 1944.

[105]Mr. D'Angelo's diary reads: "20 January 1945, left Reading, England for marshalling area. 21 January, Weymouth, England. Left Weymouth 0710. Arrived Portland 0810. Boarded LST #317 at 0900. Sailed 1600. Arrived Le Havre, France 0430. Debarked 1200. Proceeded to La Fuillie, arrived 2130. Roads snow covered. Weather cold. Morale Excellent. No changes from 23 January to 1 February.

[106]Arrived 9 February 1945. Site of a massacre of over 100 American troops killed by an SS unit, under the orders of Joachim Peiper.

[107]Mr. D'Angelo's diary reads: "10 February, Mirfeld, Belgium. Traveled 175 miles. Roads muddy. Weather fair. Morale excellent. 11 February, Mirringen, Belgium. Took combat position 1030. In combat. Activity light. Weather fair. Morale excellent. 27 February. Hollerath, Germany. In direct support of 1st Battalion 271st Infantry in attack on Hill 630 and high ground running north to within 880 yards of Dickerscheid, Germany. Beginning with fifteen minutes preparation fire at 0630. Objective taken and consolidated.

saw the towns we destroyed. At Eilenburg, the Germans just wouldn't give up. Our officer told us we weren't going to lose any more ground troops. We fired 15,000 rounds of artillery and leveled that town. The infantry went in, and there wasn't much left for them to do. Near Eilenburg, there was a wrecked German airplane. I saw a glove next to the plane. I picked it up and there was still a hand in it! I threw it away and got out of there.

One time at night I was on watch with this corporal. We heard something coming up close to us. He said, "Someone's coming."

"I didn't hear anything."

So we listened again. We both heard it. We hollered, "Halt!" Three times like we generally do.

I fired three rounds from my hip with my carbine. I heard something flop and the next morning we went out to have a look. We thought it was a German, but it was a horse. I thought I had killed somebody!

Once I took a prisoner. I went up into a hay loft. When I got up there this fourteen-year-old kid threw his hands up and said, "I surrender!" He had hand grenades stuck in his belt and he had a rifle. He could have shot me as I came up. We took him with us, fed him, and finally turned him over to headquarters. We had one kid who could speak a little German and he spoke to him. He didn't say too much. We saw a lot of older men taken prisoner. They gave up easily, but the Nazis and SS were strong-hearted. They wouldn't give up. There were two SS men we took prisoner. They were dressed in civilian clothes. They said they left their uniforms under a woodpile. We made them put them back on. Most of the guys we took prisoner were glad to be out of it. A lot of them said that we were fighting the wrong people, that we should have been helping them fight the Russians. We didn't know what to think of that. The Russians were our Allies.

We probably took what little food the German civilians had. We took souvenirs, too. I took a Luger off a German observer who was in a church steeple. We fired a machine-gun into this church steeple, and then me and this lieutenant went up and I told the lieutenant, "You have your Luger, but you can take the wrist watch off the guy and I'll take the Luger." That's what we did. There was a German colonel and a sergeant. They gave up really quickly. When we fired the machine-gun into the church steeple, we thought we killed them. It didn't feel right shooting at a church, but we had to do it.

When we met the Russians they had accordions and they started singing and dancing and passing the bottle around. That was the first and last time I drank vodka. It made me sick! Another time we were taking a load of GIs to a movie. We were going to take a short cut and the Russians stopped us, wouldn't let us go through. They had submachine-guns. So we had to turn around and go the long way to see the movie. They acted like they were superior to us. They were cocky.

"We were goose-stepping."

When we heard the Germans surrendered, we had two men from our outfit go into this church and ring the bell. The local preacher said that was the first time that bell was rung since the war started. There was an officers' camp in this town. Some of the guys donned German uniforms and we took these instruments and formed a band. Hardly anyone knew how to play anything but we made a lot of noise. We had a ball. We were goose-stepping. I could play the clarinet and another guy from Ohio could, too, and a couple guys played the sax. Some guys found wine and whiskey cellars. We drank, played and danced.

When the outfit broke up, I got shipped to the 29th Division[108] and was sent to Camp Lucky Strike.[109] We were waiting for the first ship to go to Japan. Luckily we weren't put on that ship. We dropped the Bomb on Japan.

Coming home felt real good. One of the guys from our outfit spotted some of his family at the train station, but he wasn't allowed to get off. He opened up the window and hollered out.

I got discharged December 7, 1945. I went to Pittsburgh, but it was so late at night there was no way I could come home. I slept at the YMCA and the next morning hopped a bus home. My family didn't know I was coming. When I got off the bus there, an automobile salesman I worked for part-time before the war was at the station. He had been a pilot in World War I. He come rushing to me and said, "Rico, do you have two dollars?"

"Why?"

"You're joining the American Legion right now!"

And I've belonged to the American Legion ever since.

I was walking up the street with my barracks bag over my shoulder and one of the fellas who had come home sooner came out, grabbed my barracks bag and carried it for me. The town dentist came out and he took pictures of me walking up the street. When I got to the house my mom and dad came out and we hugged each other. That evening I got my dad's car and went up to see my girlfriend! My dad lived down by the railroad. I was coming home about eleven-thirty from seeing my girl and there was an oncoming train. They used to put what we called torpedoes on the tracks, dynamite caps, to warn a train to be careful of another train ahead. They went off. I stopped the car, jumped out, and laid flat along the road side. I thought for a minute that I was over there again!

My dad came home from work one day and said, "The superintendent wants to see you, you've got a job."

So I went to work at the coal mines with my dad. I stayed there for forty-five years.

I never thought about being killed or wounded when I was over there. Now, when I see some of the vets who were wounded in our wars, I think about wheth-

---

[108] 29 June 1945.
[109] Arriving in Bremen 3 August 1945.

er I would rather have been killed or wounded. Not too long ago my American Legion post sponsored a dinner for the disabled veterans of Aspinwall Hospital. We had thirty veterans come up, from World War II, Korea and Vietnam. There were nine of us. We helped them with their wheelchairs. We asked them what outfits they were with and that brought back memories. Out of thirty people we had there, twenty were in wheelchairs. I couldn't have lived that way.

They don't teach this stuff in schools, and that makes me mad! I was at a gas station one day, and they were advertising the fiftieth anniversary of the war on television. We asked some of these young fellas who came in, "What do you think of that battle of Normandy." They said, "I seen that. That's just a movie." A lot of them don't believe it! They think it's a movie!

1. Amerigo Casini sits in the cockpit of an American P40 fighter plane, downed over Anzio.

2. Amerigo Casini's 155mm gun emplacement.

3. A "Chicago Piano." An American anti-aircraft emplacement at Anzio, four .50 caliber machine guns and one 37mm cannon.

4. The "Anzio Express," A massive German railway gun captured at Civitavecchia (Leghorn). It fired from 26 miles away into the Anzio beachead.

5. An LST converted into a "flattop." The ship was used by Piper Cub artillery-spotter planes

6. Amerigo Casini's buddies at Fort Bragg, 1942.

1. Middle-aged German prisoner of war near Pirmasens, Germany.

2. Concrete tank traps and pillboxes on the Siegfried Line.

3. Vehicles of the 71st Division cross the Rhine River in a smokescreen. Pontoon bridge was built courtesy of the Third Army Engineers.

4. The dining room in Herman Gocring's castle near Neuhaus.

Photos courtesy of the 71st division

1. Enrico D'Angelo's battery mates.

2. Bayonet "practice" at Camp Wallace, Texas. Enrico D'Angelo is on the far left.

3. Enrico D'Angelo (center) with his buddies Don McPherson (top) and Stanley Halo.

1. 37mm anti-aircraft gun and crew at Camp Wallace, Texas, before Pearl Harbor. Enrico D'Angelo said, "We didn't even have live ammunition!"

2. The Carpenters. Enrico D'Angelo (left) and Corporal Martin.

3. Clockwise: Al Dewey, Enrico D'Angelo, Corporal Martin, and Sergeant Miles before the war started. The helmets are World War I vintage.

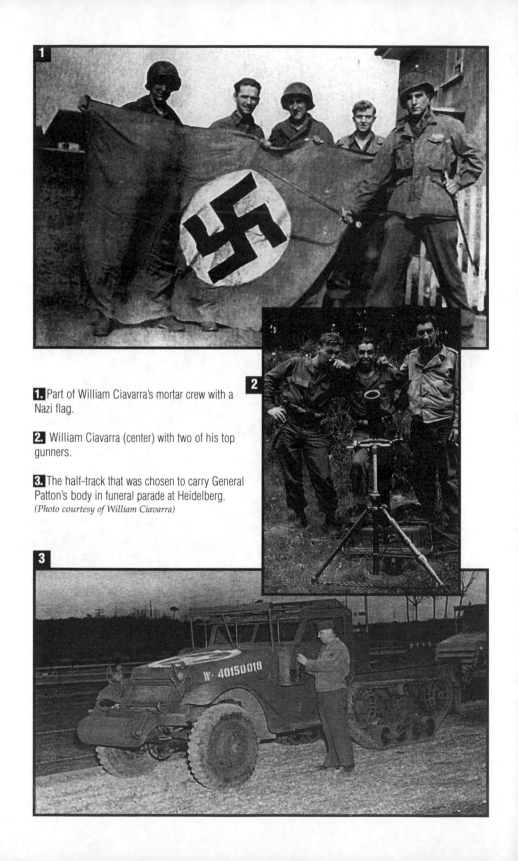

1. Part of William Ciavarra's mortar crew with a Nazi flag.

2. William Ciavarra (center) with two of his top gunners.

3. The half-track that was chosen to carry General Patton's body in funeral parade at Heidelberg.
(Photo courtesy of William Ciavarra)

Cowboys and Germans

John J. DiBattista

United States Third Army
4th Armored Division ("Olympic")
25th Cavalry Reconnaissance Battalion

Greensburg, Pennsylvania, 4 January 1925

"It was like playing tag. It was like those old John Wayne cavalry movies. Ben Johnson used to play the ex-Confederate and he'd be the scout. John Wayne would be like, 'Whadda we got here?' Then Johnson would get down and look. 'Kiowas. See this little chip. This is their trade mark. This deep chip here that's Kiowas. I'd say a war party of ten braves!' Mayforth was our Ben Johnson. He used to do the same thing with tire marks. On a dirt road (and we were on dirt roads a lot) Mayforth would halt the column like John Wayne. He'd walk out, and as blind as he was without his glasses, he would look down and say, 'Yeah. A Kraut armored car and a Volkswagen.'"

One day I was coming out of the Strand Theater in Greensburg with a friend, Henry Marconi. Somebody said something to a cop and the cop answered, "Yeah, you'd better go get your gun now!"

We didn't think anything of it. On the way home we bumped into other friends of ours, who said that the Japanese had bombed one of our oil tankers. When I got home, I found out that it was Pearl Harbor that had been bombed. This was about three-thirty or four o'clock in the afternoon. I was astounded! My first reaction was, "Where's Pearl Harbor!?"

Next day at school they suspended classes, put one chair on the stage, put a radio on it, and turned it up full volume. We sat in the auditorium all day. We listened to Roosevelt's speech, "The Day of Infamy." We were getting flash reports—"The battleship *Pennsylvania*, damaged," and so on. There were a lot of racial remarks from the people in town like, "Those slant-eyed bastards!" You'd hear nice old ladies saying things you wouldn't expect! Some of the older guys got up, went down town and enlisted. I was only seventeen, and my mother was determined that I would finish high school because she wasn't able to. So my parents weren't going to sign for me.

Everybody else was leaving. When I turned eighteen, a bunch of us decided to go up to the Draft Board and volunteer. Recruiters didn't have a problem getting

John J. DiBattista: Landshut, Germany, Fall 1945.

recruits. Each branch of the service was set up at the 110th Infantry armory on Pennsylvania Avenue. At first I was rejected because I had tachycardia, an excessive heart beat. "Skinny" Ribosky was standing in front of me at the Armory. This was "Skinny's" second time. He turned to me and said, "If I don't make it this time I'm 4F." Then he said, "It's going to happen to you."

I said, "What are you talking about?"

He said, "You're going to get turned down because of the same thing. You watch!" Sonofagun if that didn't happen. He had the same problem as me. One of the first stops was the heart test. I was nervous because I was thinking about what he had told me. They said, "Go to the last stop."

At the last stop there was a medical officer who had Army, Navy, Marine, and Coast Guard rubber stamps. He picks one up and, boom, REJECTED! That was it! I go home and tell my mother. She liked the idea that I wasn't going, but she didn't like the idea that I had heart trouble. My father, who was selling insurance at the time, had a doctor on West Otterman Street who did the physicals for his applicants. So about six o'clock that night my father took me up to this doctor. He said, "Hey, they told my boy he had something wrong with his heart."

The doctor had me jump up and down and run in place. Then he'd listen and listen and listen to my heart. He said to my father, "John, I can't find anything wrong!"

Despite the late hour my dad said, "Let's go up to the Armory." He wanted to talk to the guy who rejected me. He wasn't there, but my dad said to this other guy, "I took my son to another doctor and that doctor thinks he's OK"

The medical officer said, "Well, the man who rejected your boy is coming in the next couple of weeks. So he still has a chance."

I went back in a couple of weeks and the same thing happens. I go to the fella there with all the stamps. He was sitting behind the desk reading the paper. The headlines were about fighting in North Africa. I'm sitting in a chair. He looks at me and says, "What the Hell is the matter with you, DiBattista?"

I said, "I get in that room and I get a little nervous."

So he said, "You just sit there for a while."

He just sat there and read the paper. He's reading and reading. Then he reaches over and takes my pulse. He takes one of the stamps and, boom, ARMY!

I left a week later. The Draft Board at the court house gave us our records, we came out of the door, took a left, marched up Main Street. Crowds were on both sides of the street. This late in the war, too! People cheered us! We marched to the train station where there was another crowd. My mother didn't go to the train station, just some aunts and cousins. I said goodbye to my mother at home.

We got to New Cumberland, Pennsylvania, around four in the morning. They unhooked our car and put it on a siding. We had no heat and no lights. We sat there for an hour or two. It was cold. We were waiting for the station people to wake up. There were no lights in the depot. About five o'clock or five-thirty some MPs came down and said, "OK, girls, let's go!"

The Army's first official act was to check us for venereal disease. We were all clean. They issued us clothes and then put me on KP. I worked on a huge dish-washer shoving aluminum trays through this big thing. I wasn't taught how to make a bed or put on leggings like the other guys were.

That night we get on a train, not knowing where we were going. Everybody was speculating. All we knew was we were going west. I bunked with Joe Falcone, who graduated with me. We stayed up so we could see Greensburg as we passed through it. We got to St. Louis, then turned south. We ended in Camp Polk, Louisiana. They received us very nicely. The first thing they did when we got off the train was to take us into the mess hall and give us a steak breakfast. Sergeants waited on us! What's that they say about the condemned man? The last meal!

The first morning I put my leggings on backwards, and I didn't know how to make my bed. So then here comes Sergeant Battle. He had an appropriate name, but he was the easiest NCO in the whole company. I'm trying to make my bed and he comes up and said, "Don't you know how to make your bed?"

"No, nobody showed me."

"What the Hell were you doing back at the reception station!? They should have taught you that when you got there!"

"Hey, I was on KP and then shipped out that night! The only thing they did with me at the reception station was give me a uniform and then put me on KP!"

He showed me. Sergeant Battle later got busted to private. One time we went to the dentist and we're lining up and they're getting information. The girl says, "Rank?" Battle said, "Used to!"

Once, after formation, I fell out and this young second lieutenant comes by and says, "Hey, soldier your leggings are on backwards. Didn't anyone ever show you how to put them on?"

I said, "No, sir." So I went through the whole thing again about doing KP. He was very nice about it and he showed me right there. Then it got tough.

I found I was in an armored division. I felt that a lot of the guys were elated about it. They drove tractors on family farms and they knew how to drive. I didn't even know how to drive a car. I thought, "I'm not going to start out on the same level as these guys!"

I was unaware of the structure. Me and Tony Carolli,[110] a guy who always found out things, always knew what was going on, went into this large room and there were warrant officers sitting at a large table. They had signs hanging down the table. "AR." "AIR" we thought! "Hey, they must have planes!"

So I go up to this officer and I said, "Hey, do you have any infantry in this outfit?" Like I was a veteran or something.

He said, "Oh, yeah!"

---

[110] Tony was killed in action.

I said, "I'd rather be an infantry man. I'm not mechanically inclined. I don't have any driving ability."

"Yeah, we have mounted, armored infantry. They ride in half-tracks with machine-guns on them."

"Yeah, that's what I want."

So he gets a tag and writes "AR." He put it on the button on my blouse and I walk out with the rest of the guys. So Tony comes over and he said, "Let me see that tag. Where are you going?"

"I'm going into the infantry."

He looks at the tag and said, "No, you're not!"

"What do you mean? That guy told me..."

"Do you know what AR is?"

"The infantry."

"It isn't! You're going into a tank regiment like I am!"

In training we were constantly in the field. We'd get up at about five o'clock, stand reveille, have a head count, go back in the barracks, make our beds, mop up, and then shave, whether we had to or not, like me. Platoon Sergeant Peach made us shave. My father, who had a really heavy beard, had given me an electric razor. He thought that if I started out with an electric razor, I wouldn't acquire the same kind of big heavy beard he had. We'd go down on the range and Peach would come up to me and say, "You didn't shave!"

"I don't have to shave, sergeant. I've got peach fuzz."

"By God, I don't want to see any more fuzzy cheeks!"

If Peach didn't like the way you went down the steps, he'd make you go back up and do it again. He would start, "When I say fall out, I MEAN FALL OUT! I want to see you guys storming down these steps! NOT FAST ENOUGH! DO IT AGAIN!"

We, 3rd Platoon, were on the second floor. The first guy who went down hit that screen door and tore it off the hinges. That was fast enough! Back to the bunks, mop up, make the bed, shave. We didn't have time to shower. We did that in the evening.

Sergeant Peach was maybe five-foot-one, and we were scared of him. If it got noisy he'd come out of his room and he'd shout, "WHAT THE HELL DO YOU THINK THIS IS!? GRAND CENTRAL STATION!? PIPE DOWN!"

Peach was in the latrine one night which was under the steps. I came down on my wooden shower shoes. This was after lights-out. He said, "YOU GO BACK UPSTAIRS AND COME DOWN QUIETLY!"

Peach made me do it wearing wooden shower shoes. He had me going up and down those steps about ten times!

Discipline was generally harsh. The old timers would call you a sonofabitch and everything else. Guys would have to stand outside all night with kerosene lanterns, while other guys dug up tree stumps. Guys would have to run up and down the company street carrying their shoulder arms or their Thompsons, which were heavier. God, I got KP!

After breakfast, we'd fall out and march to the motor pool. We'd get lessons on tanks. No driving yet. These guys were horse-cavalry thrust into the mechanized age. We'd go through the old cavalry drill. "TANK CREW FALL IN!" We'd fall in. "TANK CREW SOUND OFF!" "TANK COMMANDER! DRIVER! GUNNER..."

We had to do it fast. If it wasn't fast enough he'd say, "DO IT AGAIN!" "TANK COMMANDER! DRIVER! GUNNER!"

Then came, "PREPARE TO MOUNT!"

You scrambled up that tank, over and over and over again! Then we got into weapons training. At that time the tank crews' sidearm was a big, old cavalry revolver. "MODEL 1905 BLAH, BLAH, BLAH, HAND-HELD WEAPON, .45 CALIBER!"

The tank commander had a Thompson submachine-gun. Later they gave the whole crew Thompson submachine-guns. We didn't get to fire the 75mm for a long time. We'd have dry runs over and over again! We went out to fire it for the first time and one guy didn't have the cannon bore-sighted. He put a HE (high explosive) round right in front of the tank! They canceled the target practice that day. There was a .30 caliber air-cooled mounted on a steel ball that you fired from the hip. You didn't aim. You just watched the tracers. I got pretty good at that, and got commended for it.

Even though I was inept, they forced me to drive a tank. I knocked down a tree! When you did something like that, the Army had to pay. I got KP for that. Another time I hit a jeep with three MPs in it! I thought I was going to get court-martialed for that! I'm coming down this hill about thirty-five mph on a secondary road on a highway between Shreveport and Louisville, Louisiana. They had halted a convoy of Army trucks. The MP unit was right on the road. They had a lot of confidence in us! I closed my eyes! I was scared. I couldn't shift down. My tank commander said over the radio, "Shift her down, John! Shift her down!"

I pulled the left lateral and heard a blood-curdling scream over all the noise of that Wright-Cyclone airplane engine sitting behind us! I thought I ran over somebody. The commander said, "John, you hit that jeep! Kick her in the ass!"

I sped up. We went down the highway and I had all kinds of visions in my head. There's Colonel Goodrich standing there with his staff! We stopped. The tank commander came down. He was laughing about it. First he was stern then he broke out laughing! Goodrich didn't say a word.

On marches they'd double time you. You'd come up a slight hill, you'd have to run up it. Sweat! We didn't have time to shower. We had to go in and put on our class A uniform and stand retreat. Our shirts would be ringed with sweat! Then we'd eat.

On Monday nights, after dinner, we'd go to the division bowl on the other side of camp, a three-mile march. We never knew what was going to happen. We'd ask, "What are we going to do there, Sergeant?"

He'd snap back, "You'll see!"

The first time we did it they had an Army Air Corps major who gave us a class in aircraft identification. He'd say, "In about thirty seconds you're going to see a fighter plane. The P-40 Curtis known as the Tomahawk. Note the leading edge of the wing is straight and the following edges are elliptical! Blah, blah, blah! Look up in that direction!"

Zoom! A P-40!

Then he'd say, "Okay! In about forty-five seconds you're going to see a B-26 Martin Marauder which is a light, two-engine bomber! It has very short wings. It's known as the 'Flying Prostitute' because it has no visible means of support!"

Zoom! A B-26!

One Monday there was a Special Services officer on stage. He said, "We have some visitors here this evening!"

This light tank comes roaring in, kicking up dust. It does a quick turn at the stage. Bob Hope jumps out wearing our coverall uniform! Then comes Jerry Colonna, his side kick, and Frances Langford, the singer. Now we're hearing jokes that you didn't hear on the radio, where it was clean. Now we heard and saw another side of Bob Hope. He'd tell these dirty jokes. It was a nice surprise.

We would go out in the field on Wednesday afternoon and come back Sunday night. We'd spend Monday and Tuesday cleaning the leaves out of the tanks. Grease would build up over the transmission. We'd clean the bogie wheels. Wednesday came, back out! We'd get up at maybe three or four o'clock, go down to the motor pool. The drivers would do what they had to do. They'd fire up their Wright-Cyclone engines. It was eerie. You had all these tanks in a row with their 75s elevated!

About the thirteenth month we finished. For the D Series of basic training we were on the Louisiana-Texas border, preparing for multi-divisional maneuvers. One day, we were in an administrative bivouac waiting to move back to the garrison at the south camp. Right after lunch the first sergeant blows the whistle. We fall in and he said, "The following men will..." (Every thing was "you will") The following men will go on leave tomorrow!" He read off a lot of names and I was one of them. I thought it was great! We only had one leave up to that point. We went back to work and about thirty-minutes later he sounded his whistle again and we fall in. He said, "Those names that I read off earlier. You will not go on leave tomorrow. You will go on leave tonight!"

We were all privates and PFCs. We frantically got our dress uniforms together. They were a mess! Mine was moldy! We were told it was a pre-embarkation leave. We were told that failure to return would be avoiding hazardous duty punishable by court-martial, and in time of war we could be sentenced to death! They always said this before we went away.

We came home. One of the tank crew was Salvador Orlando from Belle Vernon, PA. Sal was a Penn State graduate, a big guy, and an honorable mention in football at Penn State. He could have got a commission but he wanted combat. He had married after he got in the Army to a girl from Belle Vernon. He came into Greensburg with his wife. He said, "Don't you mention that we are going overseas!"

We're in the Chrome Room in the Penn Albert Hotel having a drink, and I let it slip. He kicked me in the shin!

When we went back, our first sergeant, a mean son of a gun, talked to us. He was big and husky with broad shoulders and no neck. He comes out and says, "All I can say is they're taking the best damn men out of this company!"

And he started to cry! We were so dumbstruck! Here was this guy who threw us on KP at the slightest infraction, chew us out and every thing else! And he's standing there crying! His name was Barker. How appropriate for a first sergeant! As good a name as Sergeant Battle! I guess Barker developed an affection for us over the months, but he never showed it until then.

In training, prejudice was overt, from the platoon sergeant down, and the men picked it up. There was a Jewish guy in the next bunk, a New York fella named Katz. He caught it all the time. I don't know how the Hell he could stand it. Peach would constantly pick on Katz. In inspection Katz always got gigged.[111] Then the guys would pick on him. He was out one night and the guys cocked the bed. Those bunks folded up on the ends. They tied it to all his equipment on his shelf. He comes in after lights out, sits on his bed and every thing falls on the floor. Everybody laughing. That was sad because, as an Italian, I had a lot of that here in Greensburg. Dago this and Dago that. I knew what he was going through. I had a teacher call me "goddamn Dago" right in front of the whole class back in 1939. But there were so many Italians in the Army that there was strength in numbers!

On our way to embarkation we stopped at Fort Meade, Maryland. They took all our old clothing and issued new stuff. We were greeted by a captain who stood at the top of the steps. He said, "In six months, sixty or seventy percent of you will be dead!" Thanks!

I don't know why he said that. Maybe shock. A lot of us never thought we'd see combat, especially after they kicked Rommel out of North Africa and they took Sicily in a few weeks, and they landed in Italy. So through training they would say, "When we get in combat..."

We used to go, "Nah! Won't happen."

After Meade we went to Fort Kilmer, New Jersey. A friend of mine, Al Diamonte, was from White Plains, New York. His father was a gardener. They lived on the estate. Beautiful house with flag stones. Al was a talented accordion player.

---

[111]Cited for punishment.

He had a fifteen-minute, local radio show. Very confident young man. Handsome. Girls would gravitate to this guy. Spoke classical Italian fluently. When we were at Fort Kilmer he said, "I'm going home."

I said, "You can't! They're not giving any passes!"

"I'll go over the fence!"

"Al! You heard what they said! Avoiding hazardous duty! You could get shot!"

"I don't care."

"How do you know we won't be here when you get back!?"

"I ain't coming back."

"Come on! Don't talk like that!"

Well, he did go and he did get back.

We went over on the *Queen Elizabeth*. She was very fast and changed course every few minutes. They said it took a submarine so many minutes to get ready to fire. We made it in five-and-a-half days. We were going thirty-some knots. It was spooky. You wanted to get out of the hold and get up on deck and you look out on the ocean and you fantasize about all these submarines out there!

We ate two meals a day. We were constantly in the line to eat. No sooner you got done with breakfast, it seemed like you only had an hour or two before they'd announce dinner. We ate in a huge, beautiful dining room. The floor of the dining room was all scuffed up. In the wood of the railings guys carved their initials. When they refit the ship, they did not replace all those initials carved. They just lacquered over it. We ate British food. Fish for breakfast. Mutton for dinner. We ate a lot of Milky Ways going over. We just couldn't take that other stuff! When I went to England in later years, I lived in an apartment and the landlord had fish for breakfast. That smell would remind me of that trip over.

We were in D Deck. There were 17,000 people on that ship. They had us stacked by priority. The paratroopers slept on the open deck. The 600 WACS and nurses were in the upper structures, in first class. You hardly would see them. The paratroopers were on the deck because they were to be the first ones off. We pulled into Greenwich. Greenwich didn't have a pier. We anchored and went in on a ferry. It was 5 June. Next day would be D-Day! Up to that time, the only two armored divisions that saw combat were the 1st Armored in Africa and the 2nd Armored Division. Later they brought the 2nd to England so there was no immediate need for us. Then the next priorities were the infantry, artillery, and bomber crews on C Deck. We didn't get along with the bomber crews, because they were flyboys! The paratroopers didn't like us because we were armored.

We didn't get off the ship until 6 June. So it was D-Day for me, too. Thank God, it wasn't Omaha or Utah Beach! We got up in the morning. We're on the promenade deck having a smoke and over the PA system comes, "NOW HEAR THIS! NOW HEAR THIS! NOW HEAR THIS! THE SUPREME COMMANDER HAS AN ANNOUNCEMENT!"

Eisenhower came on and said, "AS OF BLAH, BLAH, BLAH, WE LAND-ED ON THE COAST OF FRANCE."

We knew it wasn't going to be long for us. As soon as the armored divisions were committed, we would be the first replacements. We got set up in a town called Welles, in the city park. There wasn't an open place in England that didn't have storage facilities, vehicles lined up, replacement vehicles, replacement tanks, big stacks of ammunition, all in this small country! Three-and-a-half million Americans! At first we couldn't understand the English! We thought, "Gee, we thought we spoke the same language!"

Prejudice was still with us. Up to that time there was only one black infantry division in existence, the 92nd. They came down to Louisiana from Wisconsin. That was the first time they saw tanks. They maneuvered with us, but they ended up in Italy. They went out with some of the white girls, and this enraged the southerners. A lot of the northerners didn't like them going out with white girls either. They had to keep them segregated from the camp dances because it would just end in a brawl. Every day the same captain would give us the same lecture about the relations between the whites and the blacks. He said, "I'm telling you right now, if you get in an altercation with a black, we don't care what the provocation is, you're the one that's going to suffer!"

Our group didn't have any trouble. We had an all-black quartermaster battalion, which weren't organic to an armored division, but they were attached to us all the way through. When we got the Presidential Unit Citation, they got one, too. They were very proud of the fact that they were attached to us. They even called themselves the "Armored Quartermaster Battalion."

We'd stay up and talk at night. They had this triple-daylight-savings time. We'd stay up talking and talking and, "Hey! It's still daylight! It's 11:30!" By the time it got dark it was after midnight. Then the German buzz-bombs would come over. We'd watch the fireworks! All that ack-ack! So we'd hardly get any sleep. The routine was all messed up.

We moved to Warminster. We were an armored, replacement package. We were told we were in package X-24A. We never heard a designation like that before. The 3rd Armored Division was there. So we thought, "Oh! We're going to end up in the 3rd Armored Division."

We were occupying pyramidal tents. An infantry packet would come in, would be there about three hours and be gone! Over to Normandy! Armored was just sitting there, uncommitted. The camp commander said to our Major Butler, "Major, move up on that hill and pitch pup tents. We need this space for infantry."

Butler said, "My men aren't going to sleep in pup tents!"

"Well, that's your problem! Get them out of here!"

It's June, and in England June is cold and rainy. Butler said, "Sit tight, guys! Don't pitch any pup tents."

So he takes off. He's gone three or four hours and then here comes a convoy of trucks with pyramidal tents. We pitched them and named the place, "Camp Butler!"

The food was terrible. This time we're eating American rations. Major Butler during every meal time would walk around us and say, "Hi, how's it going?"

We'd say, "Gee, Major this food's terrible."

"I know. I'm eating the same thing. If there's anything I can do about it I'll do it."

We had canned meat. It was stringy! It was SPAM.

Butler told us, "I'm going to give you guys passes. I'll tell you what. I'll give you passes from six to midnight, but if you're in a pub and someone comes in there and says, 'X-24A!' You get your asses back here because you know the consequences!"

We sat in that camp for a couple of weeks. Then we got our orders to move. Butler had already gone over with a separate battalion. Now we had this captain. We went to Southampton. The place gets hit with a V-1 buzz-bomb. All it did was blow up a latrine! Huge camouflage nets over everything. Who do you think was there? The 3rd Armored Division. Now we're starting to think. "We go to Warminster and here's the 3rd Armored. We go to Southampton and there's the 3rd Armored. We're going to cross the Channel at the same time. As soon as they lose a couple of guys we're going."

We didn't spend the night, but headed right for the ships. We got the best Army food, up to that time. They had six chow lines. If you didn't like what they had in one chow line you could go to another. Everyone said, "They're fattening us up for the kill!"

We got on the *Princess Margaret*, a pleasure ship. They put us down in the hold. No bunks, nothing! We're only supposed to be in there a few hours. So we got out to rendezvous with the convoy. We missed the rendezvous. We come back in. I don't know how many rendezvous we missed, but we were on that damn thing for about three days with no mess facilities! The ship had canned British rations. What was unique about theirs is they had a tube that ran down through the middle of the can. You struck a flint thing on the surface and it would ignite whatever was in that tube and immediately heat the food. If we had American C-rations we had to eat them cold, which was what you did most of the time. We found huge boxes of hammocks in the hold. We strung them up.

Finally, we made a connection with a convoy and we went to Utah Beach. It was flat. It wasn't like Omaha, with that cliff. We get into an LCM, like a huge baking pan. We went into the beach. Who's unloading? The 3rd Armored Division![112] It was eight o'clock at night, but the sun was shining because of the weird daylight savings time. We were loaded down. The armored units had single cover-

---

[112] The 3rd Armored landed in France 23 June 1944.

alls. We were issued an impregnated coverall which went on top. It was supposed to protect you from chemical agents. We had gas masks. Our leggings were leggings on top of leggings. We were carrying the Thompson submachine-gun. We get off and here's a captain with a little M1 carbine. He said, "Okay, men! Follow me!"

There was still debris around from the invasion. I saw a mine. We went by it. I thought I saw a body floating out there. So we start off, and this guy's walking fast! He's not doing the 120 steps a minute. He's almost double timing. This goes on and he's getting way ahead of us. He'd come back and say, "Come on, guys! Keep up!"

Discipline started to break.

"Slow down, you sonofabitch!" someone somewhere in the middle of the pack was hollering him. He'd ignore it. Now it's dark and we're still marching. Men started throwing away equipment. First the gas mask. That was always the first. Then the impregnated clothing. There were even rare instances where they threw away the Thompson. All night they were throwing stuff away. Cussing. I didn't throw away a thing. Where we were supposed to rendezvous with the truck convoy, the captain had orders, "Don't mount up in the trucks unless you have the correct percentage of men you started out with."

Apparently they anticipated guys getting lost, straggling. I don't know why this captain took off at such a pace unless there was a strict schedule. After about a six-hour march we got to where the truck rendevous was supposed to be. They're not there! It was dark. I went down on my back and fell asleep. It must have rained, because I was soaked when I woke up. The trucks were there!

The captain didn't have the required percentage to mount up. So we're waiting, one or two guys straggling in. One guy had nothing. He was dragging a blanket. All he had on was his coverall and shoes. We had some guys in that packet that didn't have the training we had. They may have just been plucked out of a division that had just been formed. Maybe they had basic training, but our guys were pretty fit. Finally we got quota, mounted up, and rode.

We got into the *Bocage* (hedgerow) country. Each packet was confined to one hedgerow square. We had an infantry packet next to us, then there was an empty field. Almost every hedgerow compartment was occupied with something, but this one was empty. There was a .50 caliber machine-gun for anti-aircraft purposes in each field. The oldest captain I've ever seen in the Army, all silvery-haired, maybe a World War I veteran, maybe sixty years old, commanded the complement that was supposed to take care of us, maybe five or six guys. They had a field kitchen there and they fed us. So we moved in there and were told to dig in. We said, "What the Hell are we digging in for!? We're not up there yet!"

They said, "Well, you'll see tonight!"

We were told if that if a .50 caliber sounds off we had to hit our holes. Everything flying after eleven o'clock at night was considered to be the enemy. What we called Bed-Check Charlie would come in just after eleven o'clock. The German aircraft had a distinct, undulating sound. They were looking for an airstrip in the hedgerows. I think Charlie got the heaviest concentration of anti-aircraft in the history of the United States Army. Anything after eleven was up for grabs!

They told us to dig the holes because a lot of that anti-aircraft crap was coming back down. We'd get up in the morning and we'd see the graduations on the metal where artillery men had set the timing. One night, a truck company was moving in the empty section between us and the infantry guys. Here comes Bed-Check Charlie. The pilot must have seen a light or something. He hit that company with two bombs, one regular and (we soon discovered) one delayed action. All the guns started firing. We got in our holes. Big explosion! They put one right in the middle of that place. We got out of our holes and the trucks were on fire. Rescue operations were going on. We're watching this from maybe 200-yards away. The infantry guys' tents were all blown down from the blast. We watched for a while then we went back to sleep.

I don't know how long I was asleep, but what woke me up was my head bouncing against the ground just like a basket ball. BOOM! BOOM! BOOM! Huge explosion! I don't remember my feet hitting the ground. I just remember going through the air like Superman, down into the hole with the guy I shared the tent with. That's when we found out about the second bomb, calculated to explode when the medics got in to help the wounded. Delayed action bombs dig in, and when they explode they kick up a lot of dirt. A big hunk of clay killed one guy. They said there were forty killed there. I didn't see that again in combat, so many men dying in one instant! It was a black company. We went over there the next day and it was ghastly. Body parts and clothing were hanging all over the trees. We were told to stay away.

A little later we witnessed the carpet bombing at St. Lô. That's where General McNair was killed.[113] It was a sunny day. We had no idea what the Hell was happening. Strips of tin foil came falling out of the sky.[114] I thought, "What the Hell is this!" We hear this drone. Thousands of planes![115] We started counting. We counted about 800 and thought the Hell with it because you had the bombers and

---

[113] This was Operation COBRA. Lieutenant General Lesley J. McNair (1883-1944), the highest-ranking US officer to be killed in the war.

[114] Called "Window," which the British used to confuse German radar.

[115] 500 fighter-bombers of the American 9th Air Force, followed by 2,000 heavy and medium bombers (B-17s and B-24s). Over 4000 tons of standard and high explosive bombs and napalm pounded the German positions, supplemented by 125,000 rounds of artillery. Popular correspondent Ernie Pyle wrote: "[The bombs] began like the crackle of popcorn and almost instantly swelled into a monstrous fury of noise that seemed surely to destroy all the world ahead of us." (Blumenson, *Liberation*, 54 – 55). Initially, a last-minute postponement resulted in American casualties, and confusion on the following day caused by obscured target markers resulted in more American casualties (600+). General Fritz Bayerlein, commander of the Panzer Lehr Division later said: " ... my front lines looked like the face of the moon (*Mondlandschaft*), and at least 70% of my troops were out of action — dead, wounded, crazed or numbed. All my forward tanks were knocked out, and the roads were practically impassable." (Blumenson, *Liberation*, 56). The commander of the German Army Group B, Field Marshall Günther von Kluge, was discredited by Hitler. On his way home to meet Hitler, Kluge committed suicide.

then the fighters below and fighters on top. Then the ground started to shake like it was an earthquake. We're standing there like we were wearing electric exercise belts. The planes also dropped smoke streamers. The streamers showed the pilots where the target was. What happened was the wind blew them back and confused the pilots. Hundreds of our troops were killed.

A day after the breakthrough we mounted up on trucks, still thinking we were going with the 3rd Armored Division, especially since the 3rd had many casualties in Normandy. Instead we went with the 4th Armored. We got on trucks and we traveled and traveled. The French were greeting us and handing us bottles of booze. You'd think we were the liberators, but the guys who liberated them were up at the front. We got to just past Coutances which the 4th Armored had captured.[116] Finally, they deposited us division forward because it was out in the field. There's a division forward and a division rear. The nickname for division headquarters forward was "Lucky Forward." That was the code name for the 4th Armored Division, "Lucky."[117] We got our assignments. This captain said, "Dale! You're going to the 8th Tank Battalion! Diamonte, (I forget the tank battalion), DiBattista! 25th Cavalry!"

What! About three or four of us go to this captain and said, "Gee, Captain we're medium tank crewmen. Why are we going to the cavalry?"

"Don't worry about it fellas! They have a light tank company!"

"We're not light tank crew men!"

"Well, a tank's a tank!"[118]

The population of our truck became less and less. It was down to about five guys, because the cavalry units had to go further. Now we're all by ourselves. We're not seeing any troops or vehicles. Nothing! We're getting a little apprehensive. "What the Hell's going on? What are we, lost? Are we going to bump into a German down here?"

We're going down the road and there's two guys in the ditch with an air-cooled machine-gun. They stopped us. The driver said, "Where's B troop?" They told us where to go. So we get into this grove of trees. We were trained that way,

---

[116]29 July 1944

[117]In combat the 4th Armored's code name was Olympic.

[118]Mr. DiBattista added as an aside: "I ended up in a point jeep not realizing that nobody wanted that job because it's usually the first vehicle to hit a mine, and the first to get shot at. You wished you had four sets of eyes on your head so that you could check the roads for mines or defended roadblocks. The other guys knew when the point vehicle got hit. They knew. The 4th Armored took off and captured Avranches, and Coutances. We replaced a cavalry jeep unit that was in Coutances. They had hit a mine. I don't remember whether they all were killed or wounded. The division went west to Lorient, did a 180 and came back. We went to headquarters troop and got our combat uniform. Only armored troops have them, but you didn't get it until you went into combat. The infantry would steal them. We got a tanker jacket, tan with the elastic cuffs and collar. We got a helmet like the old pilots had. Very seldom would guys wear that. It had a long neck that we could tuck under our jackets. Then we got a bib overalls, with two straps that snapped on the bottom. They were warm. Blanket lined. When they told us about these uniforms in the States we looked forward to getting them. "When you get into combat, the first day they'll give you these!"

get under the trees, get under cover. They split us up again, "Okay, so and so you're going to 1st Platoon. DiBattista 3rd Platoon!"

So we got in a jeep and traveled some more. We got to an orchard and there's 3rd Platoon commanded by Lieutenant Wiley from Texas. We used to cuss him out because if they gave him a hairy mission and we accomplished it he'd want to do another one. He'd volunteer. We didn't like that. Hey, we survived one, what the Hell do you want to do? We'd be driving along and there'd be an infantry unit that would stop us and ask us to do something, and the lieutenant would be like, "Okay, we'll take care of it!"[119]

So Wiley's talking to us: "Who can handle a .30 caliber machine-gun?"

At least I knew what that weapon was. I knew it blindfolded. I raised my hand.

He said to me, "Okay, you go with Sergeant Mayforth."

Mayforth was the scout sergeant. He was incredible. Without his glasses, he was as blind as a bat. He was also the bravest man I ever met. A little reckless, at times. His father was a colonel in the despised Air Corps, and that was held against him. He was a maintenance clerk in the motor pool, then when a jeep unit was lost, they made him a scout sergeant. None of those corporals who were scout corporals came running. It was automatic promotion, but nobody wanted that job. I was assigned as his machine-gunner and radio operator. What did Patton always say, "L'audace, l'audace, tujours l'audace."[120] Well, Mayforth had that personified. He was daring. He was cultured. Spoke a smattering of French. A nice guy.

Just before Arracourt, when we were pinned down by mortar fire, Mayforth showed he was fascinated with explosives. There was a small mortar round, a dud. The fins were sticking up out of the ground. Mayforth goes over to it. Here's a highly intelligent guy who's so inquisitive about this thing! We're all standing around saying, "Don't touch it!"

"It takes nerves of steel!" he said. And he touched the thing! We talked him out of picking it up. Maybe he was just pulling our chain!

---

[119]Mr. DiBattista later added: "That's what we felt then. I now realize that Lieutenant Wiley was a highly motivated platoon leader fighting a war."
[120]"Audacity, always!"

"...Volkswagen and an armored car."

Another time, near Orleans, the road was clear but you had all these Teller mines on the surface, almost as far as the eye could see. They weren't buried but they were booby trapped with the S mine. The S mine came out of the ground. It had three little prongs that protruded above the surface. It was also called "Bouncing Betty."[121] The road was clear to Orleans, but NO!—we had to stop. Mayforth's admiring these mines!

Our dash across France was cowboyish. We often worked alone. As recon, we saw a lot of stuff and heard a lot of stuff over earphones that ordinary units didn't see or hear. We did a lot of stuff that other units didn't do. Sometimes the whole 4th Armored was like that. I think Patton was the only army commander in Europe who really understood the mobility and firepower of armor and deep thrusts into the enemy rear.

Our tank battalions truly went with the sound of the guns! It had to be automatic. Patton called it "reconnaissance in force." You had your reconnaissance but immediately behind that last vehicle of the recon troop was the first tank of the tank battalion. They saved us a lot of times. General "Tiger" Jack Wood, the division commander, understood it as well. We didn't see headquarters platoon, we didn't see the other platoons. Maybe a guy would come up and drop off rations and then scoot back. When we did run into the Germans a lot of it was small-arms action. We'd go down one road and ten-minutes later the Germans would come down the road. It was like playing tag. It was like those old John Wayne cavalry movies. Ben Johnson used to play the ex-Confederate and he'd be the scout. John Wayne would be like, "Whadda we got here?" Then Johnson would get down and look. "Kiowas. See this little chip. This is their trade mark. This deep chip here that's Kiowas. I'd say a war party of ten braves!"

Mayforth was our Ben Johnson. He used to do the same thing with tire marks. On a dirt road (and we were on dirt roads a lot) Mayforth would halt the column like John Wayne. He'd walk out, and as blind as he was without his glasses, he would look down and say, "Yeah. A Kraut armored car and a Volkswagen."

We had three jobs. The first was leading a combat command. Recon troops would be out front, and immediately behind the last vehicle was the first tank of a tank battalion. We had four recon troops, A, B, C and D. We were on the point of the combat command and we screened the flanks. That is, we covered the flanks, gave them security. We provided early warning if the enemy tried to cut the column off. We didn't seize and hold ground. In a static situation we would go out in front of the infantry. In the Civil War they called them pickets. At

---

[121]Filled with steel pellets and detonated by three prongs that protruded above ground, the "Bouncing Betty" shot four feet into the air, hurling the pellets to a radius of 150 feet. It was designed to wound, rather than kill. Castration by this mine was common, and feared. The prongs could also be activated by a trip wire. American and British equivalents were the M2A3 and the Shrapnel Mk 1. Teller mines held eleven pounds of TNT. It was designed to disable tanks.

night, we would be a listening post and in the day time we would be early warning. Then on rare occasions, very rare, we would plug a hole in the line, but we weren't structured to do that.

The first time we encountered the enemy on the ground was along a river. We started firing across it. I had the Thompson submachine-gun from my tank days, but it didn't have the range to get across the river. They gave me an old, rusty M-1 rifle they picked up somewhere. No butt-plate. It was already loaded. I fired it, but I didn't know at what. I just aimed it across the river. When the clip flew out I got startled because I had absolutely no training on the M-1 rifle.

So I told Sergeant Mayforth, "How do you load this thing?"

"For crying out loud, didn't you have any training!?"

"No! I'm a tank guy! We don't have M-1 rifles!"

So he gave me a quick lesson on how to put a clip in and later he showed me how to break it down and how to clean it.

The next incident was at Orleans.[122] The bridge was blown over the Loire River and the Germans were digging in on the other side. We were sent in there to help a regiment of the 35th Division, Harry Truman's old National Guard outfit. We contacted the regimental commander and at first we didn't know that the town was even taken. We were in a screening process and they expected eight to ten-thousand Germans to surrender. So we had a German prisoner go out to what was left of that stone bridge.[123] He spoke to his comrades on the other side, "Hey! It's all over!"

Only eight swam over! We were called back since there wasn't going to be any mass surrender. Then we were made point for combat command. Combat commands were flexible. You had three—A, B, and the reserve. That would change almost daily. Strictly tactical. No administrative unit. So I don't know which one we were leading then. The day that we had the point was uneventful. We may have gone thirty or forty miles. Practically every bridge we encountered was blown. The following day 1st Platoon took over. We rotated the point daily. The next day the order of march was 1st Platoon, then our platoon. I was in the first vehicle of our platoon. Headquarters Platoon and 2nd Platoon were in reserve, and we had a tank battalion.

We're coming into the town of Blainville.[124] We were on the side of a valley. Down in the valley was a railroad and then a bridge. I'm listening on the earphones. Lieutenant Whiting of 1st Platoon was stopped at the bridge. He called

---

[122] Around 16 August 1944.

[123] Two columns of Combat Command A, one led by Lieutenant Colonel Bill Bailey of Danville, Virginia, then commander of the 35th Tank Battalion, and the other commanded by Colonel Delk M. Oden, then of the 704th Tank Destroyer Battalion, attacked Orleans at dawn. Three hours later, they turned the town over to the 7th Combat Team of the 35th Infantry Division.

[124] Around 11 September, in the Moselle River area.

the troop commander, Captain Fred Sklar. Whiting said, "Fred, this bridge is intact. There's a dirt road that goes straight on into town."

Whiting was suspicious of the bridge. Sklar was an oil man from Louisiana. Very coarse. Very profane. Brave man. He said to Whiting, "Go ahead and see what happens."

A minute later Whiting was dead, shot right through the neck. He had his head out of the turret. They had an ambush there. They *wanted* us to cross that bridge. We didn't. It was a good thing. The Germans were in an orchard. So we fired back and I happened to look back and here comes this whole tank battalion.[125] This may have been Colonel Abrams.[126] It was like a thundering steel wall coming at you. The 35th Infantry dismounted from the tanks and marched alongside. They just rolled right through our position with infantry. Germans were running all over the place! The tanks were firing at any possible target, even haystacks. If one had a vehicle hidden, it would go up in black smoke and flame. During the fight we went off to the right of a dirt road. I fired one belt from the .30. Mayforth went out one side of the jeep, the driver went out the other side and I flipped out over the back. I stood up and did not reload. I just fired into the orchard, not aiming at anything. This whole thing took less than ten minutes! I was in awe of it! We were in the city, to the river—all these knocked out vehicles and prisoners. The guys from the 35th Division complained, "Hey, you guys didn't leave anything for us!"

You'd think they'd be happy! That tank battalion deployed in line. They never asked questions. I noticed in other units if you ran into something they would give the recon the third degree!

We were ordered to reconnoiter a ford over the river. That tank unit didn't wait for us to find one. There was a little sandbar in the middle of the river, and a tanker volunteered to try to make it to that sand bar. He went down to the river and the water started to go into the hatch. He made it to the sandbar though. Sat there a minute until the water drained out. Then he made it to the far shore and that was it. Once they lost contact we went back to the point. That was our job. That was one experience leading a combat command. My first experience.

Then we went to a town called Troyes. I'm not sure of the sequence.[127] We screened it. I'm listening on the radio. It was like listening to a radio adventure back home. The town held 3,000 SS troops, their best. Intelligence said maybe there was a few hundred! It was supposed to be a breeze. We were in a tree line. We had two armored infantry companies and a company of tanks. There was an open field with a big antitank ditch. They went in desert formation and charged.

---

[125]See Koyen, *The 4th Armored Division: From the Beach to Bavaria*, 36.
[126]Probably medium tanks of the 8th Tank Battalion, under Lieutenant Colonel Edgar T. Conley. See Koyen, 36.
[127]The action just described probably took place after Troyes, since elements of Koyen's account corroborate DiBattista's. Action around Troyes occurred around 25 August.

They hurdled the antitank ditch.[128] They went over and there was a drop and a tank would hit the wall on the other side. So they got beyond that and the ditch was full of SS troops. They were climbing up the sides of the tanks and half tracks. It was hand-to-hand. The armored infantry would knock them off. They took the tree-line. Sergeant Riley, in the point section, got surrounded. They ran into a German armored unit that was last seen in Italy. It disappeared in the intelligence's order of battle. It disappeared from the Italian front.[129] What they did was they came up through southern France and we bumped into them. So Riley's trapped.

Corporal Gezicky sets up a mortar and gets this kid Fabregas over there. Fabregas said, "I don't know a damn thing!" Gezicky gave him instructions on the mortar right in the middle of combat.

He said, "You see that button there. Put your finger on that, ease it into the tube, and when I say, 'fire' drop that thing, but don't let that thing fly out. That flies out when the thing leaves the tube!"

They got the aiming stake out and lined the thing up. Riley said, "I'll tell you when to fire and when they land we're going to make a break through it!" They were desperate. But Riley was cool over the radio. Gezicky is talking really fast. I looked over there and I said, "My God! Fabregas is firing the mortar!"

Right after that a German tank zeroes in on our armored car. The tank fires a round short of the car, and then got one in beyond it. Sergeant Couches was in the armored car. They get a short and they get an over, and it's in line. So he knew the next one would get the car. So he jumps out and guides the car out of that thicket, and as soon as he gets the car out a round lands right where the car was! He got shrapnel in the back. He was a big strapping guy with broad shoulders. He walked by our jeep and we didn't know he was hit until he passed us and his shirt was all bloody and chewed up. He came back a few months later.

We moved across France, liberating these little villages. The French people went crazy! We had a Hell of an experience in Neufchâteau, France. The lieutenant was told not to go into the town. Neufchâteau was a big town. We had a platoon of thirty guys and a French paratrooper with us named Tony.[130] His

---

[128]See Koyen, 31.

[129]This would account for German prisoners in Italian khaki uniforms who were taken in the action around the Moselle River.

[130]At this point, Mr. DiBattista adds the following aside: "Great guy. We gave him parts of uniforms. Tony spoke good English. He was fearless. Tony's family suffered under the Nazi occupation. His sister was raped by them. The war was very personal with him. He didn't take any prisoners. He rode with us for a good while. Tony would dress in his American uniform and talk to the people. They would say, 'Boy! You speak very good French for an American!' He said, 'Well, my parents immigrated to the United States. I'm a coal miner from Pennsylvania.' He took all the stereotypes. In the next town he was a cowboy from Texas. In the next town he was a gangster from Chicago. The girls would ask him, 'Hey, how do you say, 'Kiss me.'' Tony would say some obscene thing. And he'd tell them, 'Kiss me quick, you sonofabitch!' And these girls would come up to you with their arms open and smiling saying, 'Kiss me quick, you sonofabitch!'"

commander was a one-armed major. His unit jumped a month before D-Day in Brittany.[131] Their mission was to do all the damage they could to the German Army and then be relieved by Third Army. They were there a long time wondering where in the Hell the tanks were.

Anyway, the lieutenant decides to go into Neufchâteau, against orders! Mayforth says, "Hey, Captain Sklar says, 'No!'"

Lieutenant Wiley says, "Well, we'll go in anyway."

So we go into town. A big difference now. There's no welcoming committee. The mayor wasn't there. There were no crowds shouting, "Vive, Americains! Vive, le France!" Empty baby buggies in the street. Windows shuttered.

Mayforth says, "Something's up."

So here comes the postman. He had a stack of letters in his hands. He's looking through the letters keeping his eyes down. He went over to the postman, "Bonjour! Le Boche? Ici?"

The postman nods his head. Still wouldn't look up. "Oui."

"Combien?"

"Several. They have a tank, but something's wrong with it. But there's nothing wrong with the gun."

The street doglegged. You'd think we'd have the presence of mind to look around that corner. The lieutenant says, "Mount up!"

We go down around the corner and start down the street and there's a whole bunch of Germans at this bridge! They had no idea we were that close. It's just starting to go into dusk. They had a wooden barrier over the left lane. The right lane was open. Parallel to this bridge was a railroad bridge. Several rail lines converged in the town. There was a big roundhouse and repair shops. We stopped.

"Germans! Germans!

"Wait a minute!" Mayforth says, very calm. He didn't have his glasses on. He says, "They might be FFI."[132]

We could see the piping on the sergeant. "Hell no! Those guys are Germans!"

"No, goddamnit, those are Germans!"

Mayforth gets out of the jeep and he starts down the road toward them. It was like *High Noon*! Now they see us. He used to tell me, "You never have a round in that chamber. You keep that machine-gun at half-load and you don't put a round in that chamber until I tell you!"

So I'm sitting there at half-load. This is a factor in the story. He starts walking down and the German sergeant starts walking up. He has a potato-masher grenade in his hand. Me and Simms are jumping up and down in the vehicle trying not to shout.

---

[131]Near Vannes, where the 4th Armored found them in August 1945. Led by the one-armed major, the units had been fighting in small bands for nearly two months. See Koyen, 24.

[132]French Forces of the Interior, part of the French Resistance movement.

"For crissake, he's a German!"

So then Mayforth turns to us and said, "What the Hell are you guys waiting for?" So I took that as a command to put a round into the chamber and start shooting.

When the Germans heard that bolt slam forth, they scattered. We got a few shots at them. We hit one who was going around the corner of a building, but we didn't kill him. We later saw blood there. There was a scene in a Cagney movie where he was ambushed by a machine-gun. He was a gangster and the opposing gang had a World War I air-cooled machine-gun and Cagney ducks behind this brick building and they shoot the corner off. You thought crazy things sometimes. I thought, "Gee, it's just like in the movies!"

Mayforth runs up on the railroad bridge and there was a viaduct under there. He runs across the bridge, and the Germans had a vehicle under that viaduct. Mayforth's standing on the edge of that bridge and he's bouncing grenades down on them. Then he goes, "Get over the bridge!"

We went as fast as we could. It was a really short bridge, but I thought we'd never get over it. I visualized some German with a plunger ready to blow that thing right out from under us! The armored car crossed and engaged the viaduct at very close range. It blew the Hell out of the Germans.

Simms and I went up to the next block. There was a T-intersection. We parked the jeep at the head of the T, and I aimed the gun down the street. Simms dismounted and ran across the street to watch the building above me, and I watched the building above him. So the platoon gets over.

Now it's dark. We're in the middle of town. We stop at this intersection. The lieutenant consults the map. While this was going on we heard a tremendous explosion! We assumed the Krauts came back and blew that bridge up. Now we're on the wrong side of the river! Now the lieutenant's worried. He calls Fred Sklar, the troop commander. "Fred!"

"Where the Hell are you, Wiley!?"

"I'm in Neufchâteau."

Boy, Sklar started to cuss out Wiley!

"Goddamnit. I told you to stay out of that town! It's too big for you guys!"

"They blew that bridge behind us!"

We found out later it was really the Germans blowing up their tank.

"Wiley. You got yourself in that goddamn mess, you get yourself out! I'm not doing a thing! I'm not sending anybody up there or nothing! That's your problem!"

I can hear both sides of the conversation over the headphones. I'm keeping Mayforth informed. Mayforth consults his map, and while he's doing that a vehicle comes out of the alley. There's no lights in town, but you could make out the vehicle. It turned left and came straight for the jeep. I could see people on the running boards. I could see figures against the sky. The guys start screaming for me to fire. I said, "Jesus! Maybe they're French!"

I thought maybe it was the welcome committee.

Mayforth yelled, "Shoot, goddamn it, shoot!"

So I fired. The vehicle made a left turn about forty-feet away, then the occupants surrendered.

"Kamerad! Kamerad!" they kept saying.[133]

Meanwhile, the armored car comes up. Tony's in the turret. He yells in English, "I'll comrade you, you sonofabitches!" And he mowed them down with the machine-gun! There we are!

Wiley looks at the map. The next town was Coucy, then Domremy. So we go into Coucy, four-point-eight miles from Neufchâteau. It was a nice, balmy night. We cross over this creek, on a little bridge there. Wiley booby-traps the bridge with a quarter pound of TNT. He said, "We'll sleep on this side. Anybody tries to get across the bridge we'll know it."

We laid down by the banks of the stream. Sleep was rare. You learned to sleep sitting up. Suddenly—BOOM! Turns out this cow crossed the bridge, hit the trip wire and the booby trap blew up! The cow went mooing off. A quarter pound wasn't going to do that much. It was just to alert us.

We go back to Coucy and put our jeep on the Neufchâteau road, gun toward the direction of the enemy and the front of the jeep pointed the other way, in case we had to make a quick getaway. I looked down the highway and I see this civilian coming from Neufchâteau. I alert Mayforth, Mayforth alerts the lieutenant. The lieutenant comes over. As he gets closer, we can see that this civilian has an old overseas hat on with captain's bars, a World War I overseas hat!

He gets closer and sees us and yells, "Hey, guys! Come on, goddamnit, the whole town's waiting for ya!"

It was an American who either stayed over there after World War I or went home and then came back. He had a car dealership there. They had an American Legion Post there and everything. Of course, I guess he didn't sell too many cars during the war.

Wiley's suspicious. He comes closer and introduces himself. The guy says, "The whole town's open!"

What happened the night before was, the Germans ran out of one end, we took out of the other. Nobody had the town that night! Then the FFI and the Maquis[134] came in. So we decided to go in with two jeeps. Wiley had the guy sit on the hood of one of the jeeps like we do with prisoners. His head's about eight inches away from the muzzle of the .30.

---

[133]The same as "friend" or "comrade."

[134]French resistance, named after the thick, impenetrable bush country of Corsica.

"Everytime I took a swig the crowd would yell."

Wiley takes me aside and says, "If we get ambushed the first thing you do is blow that sonofabitch's head off!"

"Okay."

Seven of us get into town. Three in our jeep and four in the lieutenant's. homemade American flags are hanging out the windows. Just mobs of people! They didn't stand on the side like they were watching a parade. It was wall to wall people! The jeep was like a snow plow! Instead of snow it was people! There must have been 10,000 people in that square. They were grabbing and tearing at us! I'm sitting up high on some ammo boxes. I almost got pulled out of the jeep a couple of times! What did Andy Warhol say? "Your fifteen minutes of fame!"

We get to the town square and the mayor comes out. The lieutenant goes up and introduces himself. The mayor made a speech and I'm standing there on the front of the jeep. Somebody hands up a bottle of champagne to me! Every time I took a swig from it they'd cheer! Every thing you did they'd cheer! It was an exhilarating moment! I passed the champagne around.

In Southwest Junior High we learned the *Marseillaise* in English. So I started singing *Les Marseillaise* in English. Boy, that whole crowd started into it. We get done with the singing of the *Marseillaise* and they break in, it surprised me, singing "It's a Long Way to Tipperary!" It stunned me. I guess they remembered that from World War I! Imagine all these Frenchmen out there singing, "It's a Long Way to Tipperary!"

We meet this guy who says he is a British airman. I still wonder if he was really British. We wondered then, but we accepted him for face value. He was in civilian clothes. Blonde, blue-eyed. He said he had been shot down, and his crew-mates were dead. He might have been on the level. We did decorate some graves of airmen who were shot down in the area and buried in Neufchâteau. They gave the lieutenant a wreath. We had all these formalities just because seven guys came into town! The rest of the platoon was back in Coucy with three armored cars and four jeeps. Then here comes the FFI. The commandant in riding breeches, a chest full of medals and a beret! We decide that we would be a mobile reserve, our section, just our two jeeps and an armored car. We'd bring the armored car in, and the FFI would guard the town. All the approaches and everything. Anywhere we were needed, we'd go.

The armored car comes in and now we're ready to have a nice night. All this adulation! Absolutely crazy! We were so assured of ourselves. We took the machine-guns off of the jeeps, off of the armored car! That's how confident we were! We were going to bed down for the night, do a little celebrating. Then we get a call on the radio: "Get out of town! There's a convoy with four armored cars and twenty trucks with an estimated 800 Germans headed for Neufchâteau!"

Mayforth goes back and informs the commandant, who blows his stack! He says, "You sonofabitches! Now you're going to abandon us!"

Mayforth says, "Hey, those are my orders!

The Commandant didn't care. We were cowards, we were this, we were that! Mayforth says, "I'll tell you what. We'll go to that road they're coming in on. We'll put a mine field on the road, we'll cover the mine field. When they hit the mine field, we'll open up on them for a few minutes, but I gotta get outta here!"

Mayforth took a big chance! We go to the road they're coming in on, put the mines down that we carried on the sides of the armored cars. The CO calls, "What's your position! Where in the Hell are you at, Mayforth!? Are you at your new position?"

"Well, we're on the way, sir!"

We hadn't left yet. So this goes on I don't know how long. A couple of hours. Sklar keeps calling, "WHERE THE HELL ARE YOU!? Why aren't you in position yet? You should have been there a long time ago!"

Finally we tell that commandant, "We're sorry. We gotta go!"

We go back to Coucy and join the rest of the platoon. They gave us a patrol, me, Mayforth and the driver. By ourselves! We had to drive back to Neufchâteau! We get up on the high ground around the town. We could hear all this noise. Rumbling vehicles, Germans shouting orders. Mayforth says, "John, you stay here. Stay on that radio!"

It was pitch black out and raining like Hell. It was one of the most terrifying nights I had! "You're not going to leave me here!?"

"Yeah! You stay here! When we get back, you'd better be here!"

They put GI blankets over their heads and took off up the road. I don't know how long I was there. It seemed like an eternity! I'd hear a noise. The fence posts started to move. Scared to death! They warned me, "Hey when we come back don't open up on us!"

They may have been gone a half hour, but it seemed like five hours. Pretty soon I see this blob coming down the road. It said, "Hey, John! Take it easy! Take it easy!"

I'm a nineteen-year-old kid. Those guys were old guys. They were nearly thirty years old! They got back in the jeep and we went back. They confirmed the Germans were there. We came back the next day with our section. There's shooting going on, there's hollering going on, and the French are running out of the city. We stopped them, and they said, "Well, they're grabbing all the Frenchmen and making them work! Putting in tank traps and slit trenches."

So all this hubbub is going on down below us. On top of this, here's this British guy, here's Tony! It was like the Foreign Legion!

At every railroad crossing, there was a little house for the guy who lets down the barrier for the trains. This guy had a telephone and he was connected with Neufchâteau. The phones were still working. Tony said to him, "Call in there and let's find out what's going on!"

So they called the mayor. "What's going on!?"

The mayor was screaming on the other end. "Ohh! Le Boche! Beaucoup! Beaucoup!"

So we're getting all this intelligence. So the British guy volunteers to go into town to get to the mayor and to give him a message. Even today, I think about this. We didn't suspect him. He gave us his address and he said, "If I don't come back..."

It was daylight when he went in. He had a beret on. He looked like a typical Frenchman. We gave him a P-38 German pistol. You get caught with that damn thing! But he was in civilian clothes, anyway. They'd shoot him as a spy. We figured, "Gee, if he didn't get to that mayor's house..." We never heard anything. He just gave his name and said, "Tell my mother..."

Actually, we did Neufchâteau a disservice. People in Neufchâteau asked us, "Where's your army?"

We didn't know. We'd tell them, "Neufchâteau, ici. American Army." [*Mr. DiBattista gestures to a point on the table being Neufchâteau and then moves his hands around that point demonstrating how the American Army bypassed Neufchâteau much like water in a river flowing around a rock*] We did that! I don't blame them for being wary! Eventually, it took an entire regiment of the 79th Infantry Division to take the town.[135]

Then came the Battle of Arracourt. Big tank battle. We were up against the 11th Panzer Division. The Battle of Arracourt was my first experience where sizable units faced each other.[136] This was static warfare. Artillery duels. Tank battles. We were almost out of gas. A lot of our gas went to the British who were doing Operation MARKET GARDEN. Patton wasn't too happy about that. We captured some German gasoline, but that ran out. We were on a ridge and we couldn't go any more. The guys were working repairing vehicles and tanks and welding. It was very quiet for several days. Our job during the day was on a forward slope of a ridge doing early warning. At night we were out there listening. One day we're out there in this pasture about 500 yards in front of the line. Everybody else is up on that ridge defiladed. When we turned around and looked we couldn't see anything. The Germans were on the reverse slope. So we're there with two jeeps. There were six of us. We're in a big bush, and there were barbed wire fences. And here comes a German Volkswagen and an armored car. A recon unit just like ours. There was a road right in front of us about 300-yards away. A crossroads to our left front. I picked up my binoculars and looked right down that German officer's binoculars! He's standing up in the Volkswagen looking in our direction! I don't know if he saw us. So we called in, "German jeep and an armored car!"

---

[135]The 315th Infantry took the town 13 September 1944.

[136]On 22 September 1944 the German commander Balck ordered a resumption of the attack around Arracourt. The heaviest blow fell upon the 25th Cavalry which was screening Combat Command A's left flank northeast of Arracourt itself. 25th light tanks and armored vehicles were hard hit until a platoon of the 704th Tank Destroyer's C Company, waiting in hull *defilade*, destroyed three German tanks near Juvalize (Gill, I-8).

So off to our left rear we saw three of our light tanks. They fired on the Germans. The Volkswagen rolled down the side of the road. I don't think they took any prisoners. All Hell broke loose! *Now* they knew where we were. They probably surmised for some reason we weren't moving and they brought up troops. We would sustain a tank, infantry, tank attack in the morning and the tank, infantry attack in the evening. That went on a couple of days, heavy shelling. A lot of stuff went over us and landed in the middle of the ordnance battalion. Those poor guys were trying to work, and they were getting the Hell knocked out of them.

We changed positions. Apparently the division figured that if we're not going anywhere we'd better go into division defense. So we were assigned to dig in in front of A Company, 10th Armored Infantry Battalion. They had a platoon out there that was really getting beat up bad.[137]

We sent an armored car up. Here comes a huge Panther tank. Heavy armament. That 37mm pop gun we had on that armored car was useless! I'd watch them fire high explosive shells out of there and I never saw an explosion. Then we had armored-piercing, but you'd fire them at the front of that tank, forget it! They had better guns than we had on the tanks then. The Shermans had the old, short, French 75. Our M18 Tank Destroyers had a high velocity 76 which eventually they put on our tanks. The first Sherman I saw with a 76 was in the Battle of the Bulge. Hell, the war was five months from being over!

Our crew just abandoned the vehicle. What could they do? The radio operator's name was Lehman. The British had given us some sweaters. They were blue and white knitted, and Lehman had one of those on. He got picked up by one of our units, and he looked like a German. They thought he was a prisoner of war, because when we got back we listed Lehmen as missing in action. A couple days later Lehman came back after he convinced them he was an American soldier! I was sure he had his dogtags on. Maybe they suspected that he picked them off somebody. We always thought those radio operators were a little eccentric.

There was a high knoll which we used as an artillery observing post. There were four units represented with artillery forward observers. There was an infantry heavy weapons platoon or antitank platoon and down behind us were some 704th tank destroyers, M18s, with 76mm guns. We had to dig in. We built a roof over the hole because they were hitting us with small-caliber mortars. We could hear them take off, that's how close we were. It sounded like a cough. There were four of them and they'd fire six rounds each. They did that for a while, and what they'd do is get you used to a routine and then switch it around. We were all crammed in this place. We couldn't speak. Everybody had to whisper. Their forward observers were directing their fire and when we first got up there Mayforth said, "Come with me. I want to show you something."

---

[137]This was on 27 September 1944 on Hill 265 at Rechicourt, France, at the height of the Lorraine tank battles. See Koyen, 43.

So we go with him and he says, "See that little bump out there?"

He gave me the binoculars. We could see them digging in. Occasionally you could see a shovel come up into view with dirt flying out of it. We were up there for about five days. I don't know how many times a day they'd let us have it with those mortars.

Out comes a tank. There were rolling hills and he sort of came out between this draw that was perpendicular to it. The Germans get out and start chatting. I'd say they were 600 or 700 yards away. A 704th M18 came up. We showed them the target. Everybody got down in their holes. Just the muzzle blast of that thing! BOOM! BOOM! Maybe two or three rounds went off, but I don't think our TD hit it. At least we didn't see it after that, so apparently that crew jumped back in and got out of there.

We went back to our troop and we got 88mm fire. There was a guy grazing sheep way off to our left. Maybe about a mile away. There was no foliage, just pasture. The Germans were laying down some pretty accurate fire. We knew somewhere someone who had a good view of our area was directing that fire. Usually observers would be in tall chimneys or church steeples, but there were none around!

It turned out that the "shepherd" had a cape with a radio under it. When the 26th Infantry Division, a brand-new, New England National Guard division (Yankee Division) came up to relieve us, they went right by this shepherd. They got a real baptism of fire? They were told by Axis Sally, "Welcome 26th Division. You're going up against the veterans of the desert..." and all that.[138]

Colonel Abrams[139] came up with the 37th Tank Battalion. When he entered the area it was electric. You'd hear these guys cheering. We were up on the slope and he was coming up this little road. He went right up in there and we watched his tank firing. In the Civil War there was a lot of that happening. Sheridan, or Jackson, or Lee would ride down waving their hats and the men would cheer. But to see this! This was an unusual phenomenon in modern war. These guys cheering, "Hooray for the Colonel!" He had his crash helmet on and a big cigar in his mouth.

After Arracourt our vehicles needed maintenance and replacement because we had done a 700-mile stint. Our jeeps only had a couple thousand miles on them but they were wrecks! We were in this village in Alsace-Lorraine and Patton drove through. I heard this Greyhound bus horn. In the 1930s and 1940s, the Greyhound bus had a distinctive sound to their horn. I was walking up to the barn where we had our mess hall set up. I thought, "My God! A Greyhound bus!" I

---

[138]The 26th relieved on 12 October 1944. See the diary entry for October 26 in Evans *Reluctant Valor*, 90.

[139]Creighton Abrams, Jr. (1914–1974), who would spearhead the tank column that broke through to Bastogne during the Battle of Bulge. Abrams later became a four-star general and commanded all US troops in Vietnam.

looked around and here comes a jeep and Patton was scrunched up in the seat. The jeep had the big red metal flag on it with the stars. I said, "My God! It's Patton!" He went right by. He was going up to the front, like always.

Then we got a mission. We thought we were going to go back to the Metz area, but they said, "There's a hole up in the line."

We went up there for two days and we had six men on one hill and six men on the other and nothing in between. The artillery gave us concentration numbers. They told us, "If they come straight at you call for concentration number 10. If they come from on your right call for this concentration." And we had all these concentrations written down. We got called off of there and we thought, "Now we're going for a rest."

Instead they told us, "No rest period. Something's happening up in the First Army area."[140]

We were, like, "Oh, come on!"

So we went on this road march. Combat Command B went first,[141] and we didn't stop. We went one-hundred-fifty-one miles in nineteen hours! Bumper to bumper. If the German air force had come out they would have had a field day, but the weather was bad. On the right lane was the 80th Infantry Division bumper to bumper.[142] If a vehicle broke down, we put a cable on it and towed it! We even had our lights on, the first time since we left England.[143] We got up into this Belgium town and it was cold.

Now the Belgium Neufchâteau comes into play! We were in this house with an old lady and four teenagers. Some of them were upstairs, sleeping. Refugees coming through kept saying the Germans were on their way. The old lady started packing, and we'd talk her out of it.

I almost killed myself there. I had an M1 rifle. Simms had borrowed my Thompson. We had a guy from Louisiana named Naff. Huge guy! He carried this little carbine. I never had any training on a carbine. One of the guys had an anti-tank rifle grenade. As if we were going to knock out a tank with this little anti-tank grenade! When we posted guard, they wanted us to have an antitank grenade on our weapon.

I said, "Hey, Naff, can I borrow your carbine?" This is like three or four in the morning.

The old lady didn't like the idea of those grenades on the end of our rifles. We told her, "See the safety pin? There's nothing to worry about."

I was walking through the kitchen and I'm fiddling with that thing and BANG! It goes off! What saved me was a shaped charge. That's where all the force

---

[140]The German breakthrough in the Ardennes, the opening of the Battle of the Bulge.
[141]From 18 December onward. The final drive to Bastogne began at 0600 on 22 December.
[142]Also the 26th Infantry Division.
[143]Compare Critchell *Four Stars of Hell*, 215: "Night had fallen and the trucks ran on. Despite the risk, headlights blazed along the whole convoy—a deliberate gamble for the sake of speed."

goes straight. It goes through the ceiling. One of the kids had his trousers hanging on the bed post. The trousers and went up through the roof! The fin came down and hit me in the chest. I heard it hit the floor. My ears are ringing. I staggered back into the dining room, where the guys were sleeping. Everybody was up with their guns. They were all on edge hearing all this stuff about the Germans being twenty-kilometers away, the next stop ten, the next five! Then they're right outside of town. The lieutenant came in with his .45 drawn saying, "What the Hell is going on here!"

I said to one of the guys, "Don't pick that grenade up!" I thought that it was still there. We were in the kitchen.

They said, "What the Hell are you talking about? That sonofabitch went off!" I thought that it didn't detonate. When the thing went off the muzzle was close to my ear. I thought it was just the blank propellant going off.

The lady of the house starts to raise Hell. Here comes Captain Sklar, "What the Hell's going on!"

The lady wanted a statement that damage was done by an American soldier. Sklar says, "Lady! We've got a goddamn war on here!"

He tells the lieutenant, "You get your butt going! Get your platoon down there!"

We were assigned to point! We mounted up and went down the highway and took off to join Combat Command B. We're going along the road, it was snowing heavily. Daylight comes. No contact. The tension mounts. You know you're going to find them sooner or later. The intervals between the vehicles start stretching out. We're driving along and a voice in a conversational tone says, "Hey, GI."

It was really quiet because the snow muffled the wheels of the vehicle. Nobody was saying anything. Then this voice, "Hey, GI."

Mayforth turns to me and says, "Did you say something?"

"No."

He turns to Simms, "Did you say something?"

"No."

So we stopped the jeep. There were pine trees heavily laden with snow and there were bushes there. We heard a rustle in the bush and out comes something that didn't look like a man, but an apparition. His hands were up. "One-Oh-One," he said. "One-Oh-One." The 101st Airborne! They were with the 324th Engineer Battalion. They were soaking wet. No helmet. Beards. They had old wool GI overcoats on that looked black. Then when we saw their buttons. We had heard stuff about Skorzeny and his commandos.[144] We gave them the routine,

---

[144]Otto Skorzeny, SS Colonel (1908-1975), head of Operation GRIEF during the Battle of the Bulge, in which English-speaking Germans (special forces called Brandenburgers) dressed in American uniforms to confuse the US Army.

"Who's Mickey Mouse's girlfriend?" and all that baloney! Then another one came out and then another one. Eight of them came out. We just told them, "Just walk toward the rear of the column. Somebody will help you out eventually."[145]

So they took off down the road. This happened two or three times. The headquarters guys fired on the first bunch. We could see the tracers going right past their heads! They're screaming, "One-Oh-One! One- Oh-One!" One of our guys was about ready to shoot the guy in headquarters platoon who was firing the .50 caliber machine-gun!

Then we got to the town of Burnhem. The Command A went up the Arlon-Bastogne highway. Combat Command B[146] and us took a secondary road. We were abreast. R was in reserve. We got to Burnhem and we made contact. Lieutenant Wiley was wounded and evacuated. He survived. We started to get harassing fire. The Germans were firing a pretty big caliber gun, but it went over us.

Somebody would shout, "Mount up!"

We'd mount up and wait a while and then they'd say, "Dismount!"

And we'd go back into the houses. Then they'd come again, "Mount up!"

This goes on and on. We had a rule. We were always told, "Don't sleep in any upper floors. If there's a cellar in the house go down into the cellar. No cellar, stay on the first floor."

Well, the houses were packed with our guys. There was a light tank unit attached to us, a rarity. They took most of the sleeping places in the houses. There was a barn next door with a loft. We go up in this loft. Every twenty minutes this artillery round would come over and land about 150 yards down the road. There was a tank down there firing across a river. Maybe that's what they were trying to hit. We're stretching our blankets out. Here comes a guy from the tank unit. He comes up the ladder and says, "Guys, I hate to tell you this, but mount up!"

We cussed. Guys are going down the ladder. I'm the last guy down. This shell comes again. It sounded different. I don't know whether I jumped off that ladder or I got blown off, but it hit the barn! I remember scrambling into the house. Of course the guys heard the explosion and I come in there and I can't talk! They said, "What's the matter, John? You hit!?"

I got all these tears in my clothes. So they're looking through all these tears, "Hey, maybe you got hit here!"

They had me in a chair looking at me with a flash light. So Mayforth said something to somebody. They go out and come back and they said, "That thing came through the roof and exploded in that hay loft!" Just a matter of seconds!

After midnight, we mounted up. 1st Platoon starts out over the bridge on point. It's freezing! We were right behind the 1st and Headquarters Platoon and

---

[145]See Koyen, 66.

[146]Combat Command B remained with Mr. DiBattista's units until Spring, 1945.

the 2nd Platoon were in reserve. We have a new lieutenant in the 1st Platoon, a sergeant who got a battlefield commission.

There was a rolling hillside, with heavy forest on both sides. We're out in the open there. The next town is Chaumont.[147] There was a German self-propelled on the outskirts of Chaumont at the base of that hill. We're talking a range of maybe less than 100 yards from this gun. The self-propelled opens up and the lieutenant gets killed. He was in a tank. We used the tank as point, the only time we did this. We just sat on the road all night. Our guns froze. We didn't strip them down and clean them. We urinated on them to thaw them out.

The next morning, A Company 10th Armored Infantry and A Company, 8th Tank Battalion attacked. We came across a Ferdinand.[148] Then the Germans had some 7th Armored Division tanks. So confusion reigned! The tankers had to make sure who they were shooting at! Then these Ferdinands came into play and they cleaned up on A Company, 8th Tank Battalion. They backed out. When they go back they don't turn tail. You keep your frontal armor to the guns. They backed up that hill! It was a vivid scene!

We were screening to protect the flanks. We spent all that night on the road, and when we got off the road the Krauts attacked. You got these whole outfits on the road. In other words, you're not moving up abreast. That morning we started to dig in. The ground was so hard! When we took out our entrenching tools, it was like hitting concrete! Luckily we carried mattocks. So we passed this pick around, because once you broke the crust you could go with your entrenching tools. They hit us with mortars. One landed about fifteen-feet away! The round hit a kid on the other side. He looked like he was fifteen. His name was Stean. He was from Missouri. Close call! When I got home they told me my mother was going to church every day and making Novenas right and left. That must have saved me! Stean was crying for *his* mother. I was just stupefied!

2nd Platoon gets ordered to go into the woods. They go in. BOOM! BOOM! BOOM! They're back out. Sklar's very distressed about this. He was wearing a pair of flying boots he picked up somewhere. He'd walk around in that frozen, plowed ground and he'd go, "Oww! Ouch!" I guess the heels of those things are soft.

He says, "I'll show you how to do it!"

He pulls out his .45 and leads the 2nd Platoon back into the woods. The same thing happened. But Sklar didn't come out. We got information from a captured German medic that they picked up a scalp-wounded captain who was wearing flying boots. 2nd Platoon went back in again. They found a helmet with a bullet

---

[147]20 December 1944. The 8th Tank Battalion (under then Major Albin F. Irzyk of Salem, Massachusetts) and the 10th Armored Battalion (under then Major Harold Cohen of Spartanburg, South Carolina) entered Chaumont on 23 December.
[148]Previously JgPz Tiger (P) "Elefant." A self-propelled 8.8cm (3.46 inch) gun mounted on a Tiger chassis. It had 200mm of armor.

hole in it. Sklar used to say, "Take the insignia off your helmet? That's a bunch of baloney!"[149] Ironically, the round hit right where the captain's bars were and opened his scalp.

Now the enormity of the Battle of the Bulge starts sinking in! My God, they're overrunning units! I'm looking around and must have gotten a startled look on my face. Mayforth says, "What's the matter?"

"Those guys, they're the 110th Infantry from the Greensburg Armory, my hometown unit! I must know some of those guys!"

But then with the attrition and the transfers and casualties and things like that a lot of those guys were in other companies or they went to OCS or they went to flight school or whatever. I probably didn't know anybody.

The day after Christmas we employed the Combat Command Reserve. Colonel Abrams, who had about twenty tanks left in the battalion, and the 54th Armored Infantry, came around our rear and attacked on our left into Bastogne. They get to this village, I forget the name.[150]

It's 3:30 in the afternoon and Abrams is talking with Colonel Jakes, the battalion commander, who was under strength about a third. They get talking and they look at the map. They see this little village, Assenois. It's only a couple kilometers from Bastogne. The company has six tanks left. Lieutenant Boggess is in command. It was getting dusk.[151] They had four artillery battalions to hit that town! That's a lot! They had one corps artillery with 155mm. But they had all three of our battalions plus this additional battalion.[152] Abrams said, "Okay fellas! Play it low and sweet!"[153]

While our shells were falling, Boggess moved out. They wanted to get as close as they could to the village while we were still pounding them. The driver said the dirt from the explosions was on his periscope! So they get in the middle of town and two tanks took the wrong turn, but they got back in line.[154] There was a gap.

Boggess was going; he's on his way. I don't know how many vehicles were ahead but they were going and the woods came up to the side of the road and there were mines and the infantry got out, picked up the mines, put them on the side of the road, remounted and kept on going. When there was a gap between vehicles the Germans came out and put the mines back out. In the meantime, a couple of our half-tracks got hit with our artillery. Killed a few guys. Then Boggess saw a pill box. He told his gunner, "Put a round in it!" BOOM![155] It

---

[149]Officers' rank designation on a helmet drew enemy fire.

[150]Possibly Clochimont.

[151]Boggess, commanding nine medium tanks from the turret of his *Cobra King*, himself describes the situation. See Koyen, 72.

[152]The units were the 94th , 22nd and 66th Armored Artillery Battalions with 105mms and a supporting battalion with 155mm howitzers.

[153]Mr. DiBattista hears this over his earphones.

[154]See Koyen, 73.

[155]The people of the area erected a monument to Boggess. It remains in the same spot today.

turned out it was an old pill box from the First World War! Then he sees a couple of GIs. He hails them and says, "I'm Lieutenant Boggess, 4th Armored."

A guy says, "Where the Hell were you guys!? It's about time!"

Soon after, they started the ambulances going to and from Bastogne.

We protected that highway. Our only job was to get into Bastogne, and then after we did that we stayed a few days to hold the main supply route open and then Patton pulled us out to get us ready for the drive into the Rhine. So we had it made.

We went to Luxembourg. I got to go to Paris. There was a lottery and my number was picked. It was next to going home! I had just turned twenty! I had my birthday in Marvy, a little village right outside of Bastogne, right off that highway. That's where we saw our first Sherman tank with a 76mm cannon. So we went down to Luxembourg and stayed with a family named Fishbock.[156]

We went back up and got ready for the drive into the Rhine. One day we didn't have an officer. Sergeant Pat Patrolli was Acting Officer.

They said, "All officers to the CP!" Patrolli comes back and says, "In twenty-four hours we'll be on the banks of the Rhine River!" This was seventy-five miles away!

I said, "What? Come on! They must be dreaming!"

Well, twenty-four hours later we were on the banks of the Rhine River![157] They punched a hole in there and that's where they said the front was twenty-six-feet wide and seventy-five-miles long. We captured Bitburg[158] and I don't know whether Koblenz and Worms, which one is north of the other.[159] But we got to Worms. They had the bridge blown. I think we turned south and ran parallel to the river. It might be the other way around. We crossed on the night of the 23rd March.[160]

Montgomery's up there with all his artillery preparations shooting across the river for about two days! Patton's sitting there and he sneaks the 5th Infantry over. He calls Bradley and says, "Brad, I'm across!" He was unopposed.

Then they put up a pontoon bridge that night and we went over and we cut northeast. Eisenoff, Orburg, Offort, and then we got on a westbound lane of the Autobahn.[161] We got to go to Germany, and Ohrdruf.[162] Patton came up and visited Ohrdruf, the infamous camp, and that's where we made the Mayor and his

---

[156]Mr. DiBattista revisited the family in 1948.

[157]It was at this time in early March that 3rd Platoon of Company A of the 704th Tank Destroyer Battalion joined the 25th Cavalry Reconnaissance. In Operation LUMBERJACK General Omar Bradley ordered Patton to head for the Rhine River, forty-four miles from Bitburg.

[158]Around 27-28 February 1945.

[159]Koblenz in early March, Worms on the 20th. Koblenz is North of Worms on the River Rhine.

[160]Actually the 24th. See Evans, Combat Diary for 22 March 1945, 110. See also Evans 42-43.

[161]The movements are described in *Reluctant Valor*.

[162]A Nazi death camp, liberated on 4 April 1945. See Evans, 44-47, and Art Goldman's account in Wissolik, *Listen to Our Words*.

family go through that place. They went home and killed themselves. I have un-censored pictures of that place. I didn't go in there though. One of our guys took the pictures and we set up a dark room after the war. A.B. Rodgers from Cleve-land. We had all these rolls of film, and he said, "Hell, I know how to develop that stuff." Later, we broke into a camera store and took the stuff we needed.

We got on the road again. We were almost at Chemnitz. After the postwar partitioning, Chemnitz was deep in the Russian zone. Then we were sent to Bay-reuth to get ready for the invasion of Czechoslovakia. It was going to be a big deal. They were going to drop paratroopers and it was our job to get in there and make contact as quick as possible because paratroopers can't hold ground for too long.

Well, they jumped, and we took off and it was nothing. Some of our units got to Pilsen. We were only there a few days and they gave it to the Russians. People there were kneeling down begging us not to leave. We had to push back people coming from Czechoslovakia to Germany. That was cruel I'll tell you! We hated that! They wanted to get away from the damn Russians. They were scared to death of the Russians. You had a lot of Sudeten Deutsch[163] there. It wasn't healthy for them around there. Then the war ended.

The German 11th Panzer was an old adversary. They faced the Russians. When their division commander found out that the 4th Armored was down there, he said, "We're going to surrender to the Americans." He turns his division a-round, surrenders to the Americans, and then he discharged his men immediately. When the inspector came around to see how they were handling the prisoners he said, "Where the Hell's your prisoners!? Where's your barbed wire!? Your POW enclosure!?"

The officer in charge said, "I don't have one, sir."

We came back to Landshut, Germany and went into the old garrison, and spit and polish. Then we got ready to go home. We had a big parade. This big general came over from the States and we had a first big division review. There's only two Army divisions that ever got the Presidential Unit Citation prior to Bastogne. The 101st was the first. Regiments, companies and even a platoon could be cited by the President. This general pinned the streamer on our division flag. We were the second full division to get it. And the black quartermasters got theirs, too.

I did casualty work in Europe after the war. That's how I found out what happened to Captain Sklar. We had all these files, and all casualties were listed on these cards. So every once in a while I'd think, "I wonder what happened to so and so." I'd go look it up. I had a Danish girl working in there. That was her job. When they would resolve an MIA, they would send the correction and we would amend the cards. I would just hand them to her. I wouldn't even look at them.

---

[163]The Sudetenland was a section of Austria awarded to Czechoslovakia after World War I. The area consisted mostly of German speakers.

One day I thought, "I wonder what happened to old Sklar?" I found a card on him. It said he died in a prison camp. I said, "Dammit, that came right across my desk and I didn't bother to read it!"

I got out of the Army. I went to college for a little bit. After two years, I went back in. I don't know why. Maybe guilt, because I got to come back home. Most of the guys who trained with me and got into tank battalions were dead.

I went to Korea. I had it easy in Korea. I was in a helicopter ambulance unit. I transferred to Seoul. There were some officers down there I had worked with in Europe. I worked in the tent taking the calls where to pick up the casualties.

I got a battle star for Korea, the last campaign. I got what we called the "Green Hornet," The Army Commendation Medal, twice. I got The Republic of Korea Unit Citation. We had a CO who had fifteen Air Medals! Fifteen! He'd get one for every twenty-minute round trip. He'd say, "Okay, today I made a flight here and a flight there. Put down here that I was under artillery fire. Put here I was under machine-gun fire!"

He was Louisiana National Guard. He'd talk on the radio like he was crawling through barbed wire and machine-gun bullets! He'd call in, "I'm coming in now! (Pant! Pant!)."

We called him "Jack the Actor." While I was putting all those Air Medals in for the captain and the other pilots, our choppers brought in 94 patients! It was a record! I composed the citation. The CO never thought of the unit. I put it right down in front of him. I said, "Hey, how about the rest of this unit?" He signed. Later on they changed it and made it like the Presidential Unit Citation. I came back to the States and I stayed in the States for the rest of my time. I stayed in the service for twenty-two years.

I had a lot of different jobs. I was zone commander of a recruiting unit in Baltimore. I used to patronize a little store in Baltimore run by a Jewish guy, a survivor of the death camps. The store was in a really bad neighborhood. I asked the guy one day, "Aren't you afraid to have your store on this street?"

He pulled up his sleeve and showed me the identity tattoo the Nazis had given him. "After this, " he said, "I'm not afraid of anything!"

One of the guys at the unit was Sergeant First Class Jimmy Gordan. He was a handsome guy. Gordon had been to Vietnam with the 1st Division, The Big Red One. He had served in the 3rd Regiment Ceremonial Unit in Washington. You had to be sharp to do that. When I retired, he came to see me at Montgomery-Ward's, where I worked. We had lunch. He called me "Top." He said, "Hey, Top! How about some lunch?! I'm going back to Vietnam." I don't know if he volunteered for it or not. He said, "I'm not coming back."

I said, "You get that out of your head! You're going to come back!" I kept saying that, "You're going to come back! Just get that notion out of your head!"

He should have been on his way home, but his application for Officers' Candidate School was accepted, and he was kept over in Nam awaiting orders. On the last day of his tour he got killed. When I went to the funeral home in Glenmurry his wife said to me, "This was the day he was supposed to be home, and this is how he came home."

And she pointed to the casket.

That's how he came home. Nice kid. That's who gets it. The nice guys.

"That Damn War!"

Mario DiPaul

Seventh Army
63rd Infantry Division ("Blood and Fire")
253rd Infantry Regiment
Company G

Ligonier, Pennsylvania
Greensburg, Pennsylvania, 16 February 1926
d. December 6, 1998

"This brave medic came by, took a look at me, cut a hole in the back of my jacket, pumped some sulfa in there, a shot and he said, 'You're OK, Tiny. You're OK!' I said, 'Yeah,' because I still couldn't feel anything. He called six guys from nearby holes, and those guys came, put me on a stretcher and ran me through a field of fire the whole way to an ambulance. That took guts! While they were running I saw people who were dead! I mean heads blown off! It took me years to get over that. Every time I'd have a slight fever my mother knew I'd have nightmares about that damn war!"

My father's name was Carmine DiPaolo. When we went to school they Anglicized the last name. My father had no objection, and neither did I. My records are always DiPaul. My two brothers, the older one and the younger one, when they went to school, the teacher said, "Your name should be spelled with a De." So they spelled it DePaul, even today.

My father was born in 1894 in a little town called Manopello. It's in Abruzzi, on the Adriatic coast about half way up the Italian boot. He was in the Italian military during World War I. He got hit in the leg with shrapnel when he was in the front line at Monfalcone, near Trieste. He didn't have much to say about the war. He hated the French, and he had a very low regard for the English.[164] Years later the Italian government sent him a little plaque and a medal, plus a stipend of

---

[164]John DePaul informed the Center, "Our father was convinced that Allied strategy and resource allocation favored the Western front, which resulted in adverse impact on Italian military operations versus Austrian (and, later, Austro-German) forces on the Italian front. He later suffered through the Italian retreat from the Isonzo River to the Piave, an action described by Ernest Hemingway in *A Farewell to Arms*."

Mario "Tiny" DiPaul

Autumn ousts Summer;
Cold Winter winds frost windows:
Nico is our Spring.

Haiku by Mario Joseph
14 November 1998

thirteen dollars. He kept that award on the wall and every three months he would wait for that little stipend of thirteen dollars, not that he was worried about the money, but because, I remember him saying, "I fought for the people and I have this coming! It's mine!"

They called him *Cavalliere* DiPaolo. He hated war. He thought it was a terrible way to settle differences between civilized people. That's why he always used to tell me, "Don't go over there. They've been killing each other for 2,000 years! They're just barbarians!"

Dad hated Communism. He hated Fascism. He hated monarchies. He hated everything except American Democracy. That was the only thing worth living for, or fighting for. But there was a fly in the ointment. He was a dyed-in-the-wool Republican-Conservative. He couldn't understand why these welfare programs were starting under Roosevelt. When he heard Roosevelt had died my father fell on his knees and said, "He's dead in the morning, and he will be in the ground at night!"

He was convinced Roosevelt was of Jewish extraction. That's why they'd bury him so quickly! My mother sat there in the corner making the sign of the cross over and over.

When I went to war, my dad changed his mind. He said, "This is a just war. They've attacked our country and we have to defend it. If you have to go, you have to go. We'll be praying for you. You just take it easy and watch out."

I know he was worried every day I was away, but he believed in the war. He thought the Germans were nothing but jack-booted barbarians, and that some day they'd be ruling Europe, as they did centuries ago. He said, "They'll do it again. They'll subjugate everybody."

When my father died, my wife sent a floral bouquet for him in the form of an American flag. It said, "To Pop, who loved America."

The first job I ever had was at the Pennsylvania Rubber Company building truck tires by hand in six-hour shifts. This was my first experience with a union. I'm going along beautifully building these tires. All of the sudden somebody is tapping me on the shoulder. I said, "Yeah?"

"You know, I'm the union steward."

"Yeah, I'm doing pretty well here. I like this!"

"You're only supposed to make five of these a night."

I had already made ten! Then I said, "What?!"

"You're only supposed to make five of these a night."

"Why!?"

"That's what the union demands. You make five. You don't make any more."

"That's crazy! I'm here for six hours I may as well do it all and I can make more money that way!"

"You do that, and we're going to fire you!"

I thought to myself that my father was absolutely right about this bullshit of unions telling you how much you can do. This is what happened to this country with its loss of labor productivity. I would sit there and I could build five tires in two-and-a-half hours. Then I sat there the rest of the night! Other guys are leaning against their machines smoking cigarettes and reading sports magazines! Do you know the impact this has on a seventeen-year-old kid? You just say, "What the Hell is going on here!?"

I had an older cousin who was teaching me to ice skate. It was December 7th, and he picked me up before lunch and said, "Come on I'm going to give you some more lessons in ice skating."

As we were driving along, he turned his radio on and there it was, the Pearl Harbor announcement. I remember being angry. I wanted to retaliate. I said, "What the Hell are they attacking us for?"

At that time I was only 14, but I was still angry. Everyone else's reaction was pretty much like mine: overwhelming anger and a desire to get even. I can remember the day after Pearl Harbor—if you drove into Greensburg, past the court house, there were lines of young people waiting to enlist or volunteer for the draft.

When I got to be eighteen, my feelings to get even were even stronger. Some of the guys who were in high school with me had already gone. Two didn't make it. One was Paul Danks. I didn't know him very well, but he was a sailor who was washed overboard the carrier *Monterey*, the same ship on which Gerald Ford was an officer. Death reports were coming back and this got everybody mad as Hell! War hysteria really got stoked up by the media. The propaganda mills got going full tilt. Everybody believed it. Also, everybody would hover around and listen to Edward R. Murrow and read Ernie Pyle.[165]

In 1944, my senior year, I was tapped for the class play, and I was terrified. At that time we had a gal in the English department named Katie Johnson, a good teacher. She ran the senior play and she asked me to try out. I said, "I can't do this! I'll just melt up there."

Rather than go to the tryouts, I thought, "What I'll do is go down and volunteer. They can take me early."

Anyway, all my friends were trooping off, and I was left all alone. I decided it wasn't right. I wound up at Greensburg Armory. I had the physicals, the exams and all that kind of stuff. I passed. I missed the senior play.

My parents were angry and upset with me that I had volunteered to be inducted early, but they had a big dinner and all the neighbors and all the relatives and all the *paesani* came over to wish me well. I remember one guy, who had been working at Robertshaw in Youngwood (an Italian, and a friend of my father),

---

[165]Edward R. Murrow (1908–1965) was chief of the CBS European News Service. His reports from London during the Blitz and his account of his visit to Buchenwald are still held as classic examples of on-the-spot reporting. Ernie Pyle (1900–1945) was a Pulitzer Prize winning correspondent who was much beloved by American troops. He reported the stories of the average GI. He was killed by a Japanese machine-gun on Ie Shima off Okinawa, 18 April, 1945.

telling me that they were working seven days a week and they were getting all kinds of money. He said to me, "I hope this war lasts a long time! We'll get rich!" Then he said to me at the train station, "Don't shoot at any Italians!"

Then my father and two of my uncles came up to me and said, "Shoot anybody that threatens you, goddamnit! Shoot 'em!" I don't think my father spoke to that guy again.

I had this big send-off. I was feeling pretty good, like a local hero going off to war. Of course, there were about a 150 other guys going on the same train! Maybe they all felt the same way, I don't know. They had drinks and sandwiches for us, but guys sitting on that train had this artificial bravado. They would sing, but I couldn't bring myself to sing. I kept thinking, "I wonder if these guys really feel that?"

I was trying to imagine what the Hell was ahead! But, when you're young and eighteen, you think you're invulnerable. It was going to happen to somebody else, not to you.

I got my first taste of the Army the next day at induction. The Army issued me all these clothes and other things. I though it was great! I was going to defend my country. I lost my idealism pretty quickly. They trundled me off to Cumberland Gap, Pennsylvania. We checked in, got up very early, and began to learn what the Army was really like. We were sworn in first, then we got our equipment.

It was at Camp Blanding, Florida, where I developed and foster to this day a great hatred for the military. Some of those in charge at camp ceased being human when they put on that khaki, especially if they were in a position of power. Once, in formation, I put my rifle down. This smartalecky corporal came up, grabbed my rifle and said, "There's sand in the butt-plate!" And he got me for that! Chickenshit! I developed a loathing for the military that you couldn't believe! I got to hate every damn minute of it, and I got to think that this was absolutely the worst thing that could ever happen to me!

Camp Blanding was not too far from Jacksonville, in a place called Stark. If they ever give the United States an enema that's where they'll plug it in! It was hot at Blanding. We were in little five-man huts. The training period there was seventeen weeks. At first, I was very interested in the Army. I said to myself, "I'm here I may as well learn something about it."

They gave us a soldier's handbook. I memorized that damn thing! This was mistake number one, because when the sergeants gave talks on the nomenclature of the M1, or the machine-gun or whatever, I would lift up my hand and tell them that the book says something else. Well, this went over like a lead balloon. I think I was the only yard-bird private who spent every day of basic training doing KP. It was a miserable experience. I could never understand why I was being penalized because I knew what I was supposed to learn, and what I assumed everyone else was supposed to know.

At Blanding one night I pulled guard duty. The guard had to know the regular and special orders. I had memorized the soldier's handbook so I knew them all. Captain Poe, the company commander, came by. He was an old southern gentleman, a really nice guy. Unfortunately, he was killed in the war. Poe was the only decent human being in that company. Poe came by with the regimental commander, a colonel. I went through the routine. "What's the password!"

The colonel advanced and said, " Do you know all the general orders!" And I rattled them off. He said, "Fine! Any special orders?"

"Yes, sir, we have special orders!" And I rattled those off.

He said, "Hmm. Thank you very much."

Captain Poe was so relieved and the colonel looked at him and said, "We've finally found a guy who knows what the Hell is going on around here!"

I found out later that not a damn guy knew any of the general orders and none of the special orders! The next morning I was called into Poe's office and he said, "The colonel wants to see you. He's at camp headquarters. He wants to see you right away."

I went over there in a jeep. I found myself facing a board of officers. They barked questions at me, trying to confuse me. I answered them all and must have done very well. Of course, I thought a chimpanzee could have answered those questions just as well. Then they called me back in again and asked me why I was fighting, what I was going to do overseas. I told them good stuff about America and freedom and defeating the enemy. After that I was sent back to camp. The next morning Captain Poe called me and said, "You've been recommended to go to Fort Benning, Georgia for Officers' Candidate School."

I said, "This is great! I'm going to be an officer!"

So I went out and was drinking this awful 3/2 beer with my friends. And they said, "What happened, Tiny?"

I was big, that's why they called me "Tiny." I said, "Hey, I'm going to go to Officers' Candidate School!"

"Oh, that's very bad!"

"What do you mean that's very bad?"

"Well, you're only eighteen years old; they can't send you overseas until you're 19. If you go to Officers' Candidate School you'll be a 90-Day Wonder, you'll be shipped out right away. You'll be a replacement. You'll be cannon-fodder!"

Stupid! I said, "Geez, you're right. Everybody *is* getting shot."

I didn't want to go over there as a shave-tail and get thrown in somewhere and have to stand up in front of everybody and get shot from the front or the back, you know! I thought it over and decided that my friends were more than reasonable. So I said to Captain Poe, "I don't want to go."

He couldn't believe it.

So I said again, "I'm sorry, I don't want to go. I want to stay where I am."

Sure enough, my trip overseas was delayed. Most of my friends went, but I was sent to the 63rd Infantry Division in Camp Van Dorn, Mississippi. Again, if the country needs another enema, that's where they'll plug it in! It was the most awful place in the world. It was barbaric, and the people who lived there were barbaric. And there was a Catch-22. I found out to my chagrin that the rule of not being sent overseas until you're nineteen didn't apply to a combat-ready outfit. It applied only to replacements, not to line outfits. That's what the 63rd was. A short time later I got orders to go overseas!

We did heavy training day and night under small-arms fire, artillery fire, and strafing airplanes. Sometimes they used live ammo. More exercises, and more obstacle courses—this time with a vengeance. We did this eighteen to twenty hours a day.

We had sessions with hand grenades. It all started out very beautifully and was well staged. A corporal was the instructor. He would say, "Now here's the hand grenade. You see this lever here? You hold it tight, and when you pull this pin out the hand grenade is armed!"

He held the pin in his hand and said, "This hand grenade is armed! You see! You don't want anything at all to happen to that!"

And it flies out of his hand and everybody starts scrambling all over the place!

And I said, "What crap is this!? High school stuff!"

Then he starts to laugh, "HA! HA! HA! HA!" And he picks it up and says, "We're lucky. This one is disarmed."

That's what we did. They told us how to sit and kneel, and how to throw the grenade. It was very simple. I think we only had one or two sessions in that. I just remembered that little ploy that guy pulled. I thought that was crazy! I never got to throw a live hand grenade in my life, except for one in training. I couldn't imagine myself using a hand grenade. I mean, what the Hell! There are people all around you and you have a rifle. What the Hell do you want to use a hand grenade for? If someone is in a machine-gun nest the best thing to do is to go around it and don't bother with it!

In training we got the usual propaganda. We listened to newscasts which were nothing but propaganda. Then they showed us the usual films about sexual disease, what Nazism and Fascism was really like compared to our ideas of democracy, and all that stuff. They made these people look really sinister and evil. They'd whip up anger in you so all you wanted to do was go out and start shooting them up and killing them all. I thought, "What the Hell, this is war. They did attack *us*. They *are* shooting at *my* friends."

Finally, we got on a train in New Orleans and wound our way all over the country. They didn't want anybody to know where we were going. One of the biggest things they did was tell us to keep our mouths shut, don't talk to anybody, which was good advice. We wound up at Camp Shanks, New York. It was a POE, a Point of Embarkation. That's where we found out we were going to Europe, and the 63rd was going to be part of the Seventh Army under General

Alexander Patch. The commander of our division was General Louis Hipps. They used to call him "Mess-Kit Louie."

We got on this little Liberty Ship, and it was awful! We were about five-deep in the hold, I don't know how many hundreds of us. People yorking all over the place, and they wouldn't let you go out on deck because they didn't want any lights there. I sneaked out one night and I just stayed out on deck and pleaded with someone who tripped over me to let me stay there, because I couldn't stand it any more down in the hold. I was going to jump over the side. We finally made our way across. We landed in Marseilles, France.

I wondered what I was getting into. I was eighteen years old. What does an eighteen year old think? I hoped I would get out alive. I hoped everything was going to be all right. We knew it wasn't going to be a bed of roses, and that we weren't going to have any time to ourselves. They told us that! There were no furloughs, nothing in those days. They gave us an occasional cigarette and beer ration, but that was about it.

We didn't stay in Marseilles long, just long enough to draw new equipment. It was late November, early December 1944. We started out and it was cold. Then we got on a train for the Ruhr Basin. The train didn't have seats. They were box cars. They had slats in the sides and it was very cold. I looked through the slats and saw dead Germans strewn all around. I think the Army left them there just to show us what it was like, and it did make an impression on everybody. It got everybody fearful and angry at the same time, and as a result I had a burning desire to just get this damn thing over with and go home. Hell, we'd only been gone just a few weeks!

We drew some snow gear, because it was getting colder. Snow gear was white camouflage suits. We put white stuff over our helmets so we could go out on patrol. If we didn't have clean whites, we had fatigues, over which we strapped white tape to break up the outlines. It was some kind of childish camouflage, I thought. Some guys used bed sheets they had picked up here and there.

In those days we had what they called "grease guns," because that's what they looked like. They were simple and were made out of pressed metal. They looked like something out of Buck Rogers. It had a little wire butt on it so you could put it up to your shoulder or else hold it in your hand and fire away. You had clips for it too. I don't know how many rounds were in the clip, but the guns were good. Then we had white tape over the little "grease guns," and so on. You would be reasonably camouflaged.

The thing that everyone hated the most was looking for mines. God, patrolling through a minefield was hairy! If anybody ever tells you that they went on patrol through a minefield and weren't frightened, you can look them in the eye and know you're talking to a real liar! We would just walk along. That's it! If somebody blew up well, hey, you knew something's around there! We didn't have any maps. We knew that we were going to use this terrain for an attack sooner or later and the Army wanted it to be clear. It was hilly and it was flat in some cases, it was wooded in some cases, and it was open in some cases. That's the one we really hated, the open ones, because you were right out in this wide open space! And we were always doing this at night.

When you got to a spot where Intelligence told you there might be mines, you got down on your hands and knees, got your bayonet out, and started probing through that crusted ice. In those days they didn't have the fancy detectors; you had to dig them out with a bayonet. You would go along carefully and stick your bayonet in the ground at a certain angle so you wouldn't trip anything. That was really frightening, and everybody would say, "God, I hope I don't have to do this again! I hope I don't have to do this again!"

We did lose some people. We were fired on several times while doing this, but maybe it was just *pro forma*. We were fairly safe because often they couldn't see us. You couldn't get hurt with a rifle shot unless they gave you a direct hit. We weren't all that upset about that. We worried about those 88s.

In two-and-a-half weeks I went on five mine patrols. This is something I've tried to block out of my mind for the past fifty years. Everybody had to do this, though. Five guys at a time and sometimes a whole squad of about ten or eleven guys would go in. Every once in a while somebody would say, "Shhh! I got a mine!"

Then they called somebody up who would disarm it right away and then get rid of it. Then they would mark the area as a minefield. Once they found where the minefields were they had a reasonable chance of getting through them OK. They had some idea of the way the Germans planted these Schu mines which were designed to blow off a leg. I never found a mine, but people I was with found them often. I'm really grateful for that because I probably would have screwed it up anyway and wound up spread out all over the place! I never saw anyone get hit by a mine, but I heard mines go off and somebody get hit. Every time it did happen I'd put my head down, close my eyes and start praying like mad. There's no atheists in the foxholes! That was true! All of a sudden, no matter how devilish a life you've led, and no matter if you were exposed to religion at all, man, you conjured up some prayers real quick! The worst thing was when your sphincter muscle lets loose, and you can't hold it out of sheer fear. You just clean out your bowels, boom! You know the expression, "Somebody had the shit scared out of them?"

The Germans would also have patrols out. One time we saw a bunch of them before they saw us. We just started to shoot. We killed all the guys in their squad. I had my BAR and I pulled the trigger on one of them. I closed my eyes and he was down. I couldn't get up to look at him. The squad leader's name was Squilicot. He went up to him and dug out his papers, but we kept right on going and the cleanup detail came behind. I did penance for that for a long time. I still think about that. At the time I thought, "If I don't do it, they're going to do it to me." It becomes almost instinctive.

Those patrols were really deadly, and we all had to take our turns. I've actually seen some big guys refuse to go. There was a big blond Italian who was the bully of the platoon. He turned to jelly one night and just couldn't go out on patrol. He showed his true colors. On the other hand, some little guys who were real timid and scared waltzed right out and did it. I was half way in between! I was too ashamed not to go!

One of the worst kind of patrols was when I went out after a battle or a skirmish, and started picking up bodies. I would find our dead guys and rip off their dog tags. Then I'd shove one part of the dog tag between a guy's teeth. Then I'd stick his rifle in the ground or some kind of a stick so that the Graves Registration Unit could find him, put him in a bag and take him back. Some of these guys had taken direct hits with mortars!

Eventually, we were sent up to a place called Sarreguemines which is right in Alsace-Lorraine in the Ruhr Valley. My company was assigned to an old insane asylum. They had a very ornate Catholic church there, and the chaplain celebrated Mass one night. During the war they gave general absolution.[166] You could be the world's biggest sinner, but with a wave of the hand you'd be OK. Get shot and you'll go to heaven!

The asylum had been evacuated. It was right on a good-sized stream, and the Germans were on the other side. They would play songs on their loud speakers like "I'll Be Glad When You're Dead You Rascal You," or "I Surrender Dear." You would think that this would be harmful to morale, but the guys got mad, laughed, or simply enjoyed the music. These were popular hits from home, after all.

We got a call one night, three days after my 19th birthday. It was a cold, cold night, 18 February.[167] We were starting the Big Push. The Battle of the Bulge was already over. We were going to come from the south and go up. We were out in full force that day. We had a whole flank going. I had my BAR. I remember saying to myself, "What in the Hell is going on here!"

We got to a hill. I was in a slit trench. We didn't have time to dig a foxhole. There were trees all around us, and we could hear the Germans down at the bottom of the hill in tanks getting ready to rumble up at us. That sound in a young mind was like the Gates of Hell rolling open. It was just after dawn. You could see little things running beside the tanks—German soldiers. Then our artillery did a good job on them. But their artillery was still firing at us. We had mortars going like crazy, BOOM! BOOM! BOOM! Just one right after the other. The mortar squads weren't really aiming. They just lobbed them over. We could see the Ger-

---

[166] General absolution meant that Catholics did not need to make an individual Confession. Mr. DiPaul's point is that the men were spared confessing "embarrassing" sins. It was also convenient for those who had avoided going to Confession for a long period of time.

[167] Across the Saare and Blies Rivers at Sarreguemines, and into the forests. The 253rd fought the battle for Auersmacher 17-19 February 1945.

mans flying in the air or dropping. Then the Germans opened up with their 88s. It seemed like every one was going to hit me right in the middle of the back.

The Germans kept coming up the hill in their tanks and all Hell broke loose. Carnage everywhere, and I thought, "Jesus, this is the Valley of Death! Look, here comes the Six Hundred!" "Into the Valley of Death Rode the Six Hundred." Oh, God, "The Charge of the Light Brigade."[168]

An 88 comes in. This kid next to me carrying my ammo said, "Boy, this is going to be close!" It was close all right! It hit the tree right over me, and the tree burst came right down and hit me in the middle of my back. I said, "I think I'm hit! I think I'm hit!"

I was numb. There was no pain. So this kid goes nuts and starts yelling, "Medic! Medic!"

Our tanks started rolling downhill firing at will at everything that moved. We finally pushed them back, but the 88s still kept coming in. This brave medic came by, took a look at me, cut a hole in the back of my jacket, pumped some sulfa in there, a shot, and he said, "You're OK, Tiny. You're OK!"

I said, "Yeah," because I still couldn't feel anything. He called six guys from nearby holes, and those guys came, put me on a stretcher and ran me through a field of fire the whole way to an ambulance. That took guts! While they were running I saw people who were dead! I mean heads blown off! It took me years to get over that. Every time I'd have a slight fever my mother knew I'd be having nightmares about that damn war!

They got me on the ambulance, patted me on the helmet, and wished me good luck and went back. Probably some of them were killed just after that. The bravery of those guys, lugging me across that field like pall bearers! They got this ambulance going and I asked this guy if I could have a drink of water. The ambulance driver said, "Sure, give him a drink."

I looked back over and the corpsman was shaking his head, "No. No water!"

At that, I knew I had been hit in the stomach. That's one of the things they taught you; don't drink any liquids at all. I got to this emergency hospital, they looked at me, and they said, "We've got to send him to an evacuation hospital." As I remember, the evac hospital was in Strasbourg. They didn't know what the Hell was wrong. I remember them talking and some guy cutting the clothes off me. Then all of the sudden I went out. They performed an exploratory laparotomy. They put a big, ten-inch hole in my stomach, took my organs out. Some of the intestines were lacerated, a kidney had been bruised, and my spleen was completely gone. They took that out.

I woke up the next day, and I was all trussed up. I had a catheter out of my mouth, a Waginstein function out of my nose, and a catheter in my penis. I was paralyzed from the waist down and couldn't move. The evac was in an old school

---

[168] Poem by Alfred Lord Tennyson (1809-1892).

building, in a classroom. They had beds all over the place, haphazard. They were moving them in and out, in and out. Every once in a while you'd see somebody come in, look down at somebody, listen to him and then pull the sheet over his head. Man, that didn't do *me* any good! I didn't know if I was going to make it, or what? I was really upset. This was three days after my birthday. Oh, boy, I was unhappy!

A young major came over. He was a short guy, very muscular. He looked at me; he was so tired. He told me he had been operating for three days. He said, "You're gonna make it. You're gonna make it. Don't worry about it. You're gonna make it! We took your spleen out. You're gonna make it! You've got a strong constitution! You're a little bit afraid, but don't worry, you're gonna make it!"

The major was from Mount Sinai Hospital in New York. They drafted some of those guys as a group. God was really taking care of me then, because here I had a bunch of really skilled physicians and surgeons taking care of me. They patched me up and I was there about a week, and going in and out in and out of consciousness. They still had me on pumps and other stuff. Finally they said, "We're going to send you to the Third General Hospital in Marseilles, out of the war zone, because you'll get better treatment there."

In Marseilles they had this wonderful hospital with a big ward. They had Italian Service Forces workers there. Some of these Italian soldiers had surrendered and had left the cause, and they were working for the Americans.[169] They had khaki uniforms, and the Italian boot on one shoulder. They treated me very well because I had this Italian name. I'd grown up in an Italian household, so I knew the language, at least part of the dialect. There was a guy there we called Clark Gable, a real handsome Italian guy. He had dark skin, pearly white teeth, curly hair. Just the kind of guy women like and guys hate! He was cutting a path through all the nurses. I think he impregnated half of them, but that's the Italian way!

He pleaded with me to help him, because I could speak to him. I said, "Well, what do you want?"

"Well, how about some prophylactics and all that stuff."

"Oh, geez!" You could get anything you wanted in the military. So I got him some and he was so grateful.

In a true Italian style, the next day he comes in and gives me a rosary and said, "For your mother!"

Can you imagine an exchange like that?!

Then he would bring me wine. All the guys knew it. I had bottles down beside my legs. They'd come over and say, "Hey, Tiny, how about some wine." They were all drinking my wine.

---

[169] Italy surrendered to the Allies on 25 July 1943.

"That's alright son, I have something for you."

One day the hospital commander, the medical officer, came in on a surprise visit. He was going up and down the ward. I said, "Oh, my God!"

He was checking on all the guys' wounds. He read out my name and said, "Well, you really got shot up. Let me take a look at you." I had the splenectomy, I was all taped up, I couldn't move. I had fifty-two stitches in my stomach! So he came up to my bed and I had this damn wine down under my sheets by my legs. And all the guys are sitting there real tense. So I pulled the sheets up close to me and I said, "Sir, I'm sorry! Please! I don't feel well!"

"That's all right, son. I have something for you," And he pinned a Purple Heart on my pajamas. And I could see all these guys around me—sweating, you know!

So then he turned around, talked to another guy and then came back to me and he said, "I'm going to send you back to the ZI (Zone of the Interior).

"I'm going home?"

"You're going home."

Some German POWs came and got me. They put me on a cot and carried me down to an ambulance, which took me to the wharf. GIs were there with rifles, and they were really mean. I could hear this one guy telling this German, "All right, Kraut! You drop this guy and you're dead!"

The MPs treated the Italians differently. They liked them.

They got me on the hospital ship *Thistle*. It was all white with big red crosses on the sides; port and starboard, one on the bow, and two on the front. It was all lit up, and it was fast! We were unescorted. Germans didn't bother hospital ships, anyway. We zoomed right across and went to Charleston, South Carolina.

I was in a bunk on the top side, and there was a guy in the middle. The only part of his body that wasn't covered in a cast was his face. God, he was in such agony! I don't know to this day whether he made it or not. You could hear other guys screaming, especially the amputees. They could still feel their legs. They didn't know how to block nerves in those days, or they just couldn't take the time to do it. It was really a gruesome experience. The only thing that was great about it was I was going home.

Halfway across we heard that Roosevelt had died, and that really got every-body depressed.[170] You know it was like "Oh, Captain! My Captain!"[171] "Where's our leader? What's happened? We're done! What's going to happen? What's going to happen?" Everybody thought that way generally. Well, after four terms, what the Hell can you expect, you know! He was an old grandfather figure! So, any-way, good old Harry Truman took over.

---

[170] 12 April 1945.

[171] Mr. DiPaul alludes to the Walt Whitman poem "O, Captain! My Captain!" about the death of Abraham Lincoln.

I got hauled off the ship and was waiting for an ambulance. This little old lady in a Salvation Army uniform came up to me and she said, "What would you like to have more than anything?"

I said, "Boy, I sure would like to have a milkshake and a hamburger."

And she said, "We have some here."

I said, "Well, I don't have any money."

She said, "You don't need any money! This is a gift from the American people. This is free!"

Previously the Red Cross had charged me for every damn thing they gave me. Decks of cards, ping-pong balls, anything! I couldn't believe this little old lady. To this day I have a low opinion of the Red Cross. I won't give the Red Cross a nickel, but the Salvation Army can have anything.

This little old lady went up to the canteen cart with Salvation Army written all over it. They were making hamburgers and milkshakes. They knew what the guys wanted anyway! She brought over a big platter. Then she said, "I have a real treat for you. We're going to give you a call home. You can call home."

I said, "I don't have any money."

She said, "No, this is a gift from the Salvation Army."

And I'll be damned if they didn't take me back to a booth and I called home. They had a set up where they hauled you in there and they had a table with phones. I was in Charleston only a week. They evaluated me, and they said, "We're going to send you up to a place closer to your home."

It turned out to be Fletcher General Hospital in Cambridge, Ohio. They sent me up there by hospital train. I had a very comfortable ride. Of course, I was sedated most of the time. It wasn't until July that I started to get around. I was paralyzed for a while from the waist down. They didn't know what was causing that. They finally got that straightened out, and everything was fine. Then they had to be sure my kidneys were OK. I got a good, clean bill of health on that, and they gave me first-class treatment at that Fletcher General Hospital. They couldn't do enough for you. Mom and Pop were going to come down to Cambridge, Ohio and I said, "No, no they're going to send me home pretty soon."

While I was there, they checked me out completely, and said, "You're recovering nicely." I remember one of the things that was going on was constipation. There was blood in my stool. I complained to the one doctor and said, "There's something wrong."

"Ahh, we gotta look."

He took me into an examining room and trussed me up. A bunch of guys were standing around. They were medical residents, I guessed. They put that damn proctoscope in me. And the surgeon said, "Take a look guys!"

They all looked and said, "Hemorrhoidectomy is indicated and advised."

I said, "Oh, Jesus! Not again!"

So they took me in and cut out these hemorrhoids.

There was another guy that went through it. They took us into this little latrine. When they cut your hemorrhoids your're red and raw! The new treatment was salt water enemas! Salt water on an open wound! Jesus! I went in there and sat down and I mean it was like broken glass, barbed wired and crumpled fenders! It felt like all of that was coming out of me! The guy in the next stall let out one scream and then passed out cold! At night little old lady volunteers would come in and put me in a *sitz* bath and I would say, "God this is the most awful thing that has ever happened to me!"

Then they gave me some other routine examinations. I had lost about thirty pounds, and I was scrawny. I hadn't eaten much for two months! They had me on IVS. I was getting penicillin shots every eight hours for I don't know how many months. They'd wake me up in the middle of the night and give me the shot. Of course, it saved my life. They put me on soft food. That's when I developed this taste for cream, because they had a lot of creamy things there. Finally, came the steaks! I remembered going for days in a foxhole, not changing my underwear, my clothes, or anything for days! I mean can you imagine what that's like, living like an animal! It's just awful! Do any people like this crap! And eating frozen C-rations. You open a can that's frozen spaghetti and meat balls, but you eat it because that's all there is! So I went to the mess hall and I said, "I don't know what I can eat."

"Your chart says you can eat anything you want."

"OK!"

They had pitchers of cream on the tables for breakfast. I'd put corn flakes in there and fill it with pure cream, douse it with sugar and eat gads of bacon and eggs and sausage! Then they said, "Boy, we gotta put you back in shape!" In about three weeks they cut me off. They said, "You're back on a diet!" Man, I was gaining weight like crazy!

Then, one beautiful day at Fletcher General Hospital, a legal officer came in. He had an Italian name. "I've got to talk to you about something. We're going to give you a medical discharge."

"Really!"

"Yes. Now, I want to make sure you understand what you've got coming so when you sign this you'll be absolutely sure."

Finally they discharged me, and they came and brought me into Pittsburgh, where I got a train into Greensburg. The family was all at the train station. I contrasted that with the send-off I had received about a year-and-a-half earlier. It was so sad then, but now it was different. Everyone was clapping and singing and raising Hell. They couldn't do enough for me. They wouldn't let me move, they wouldn't let me do this or that. They watched every move I made to make sure I was OK. That was just absolutely wonderful. It was probably one of the best days of my life. That was the end of my military career. I was in a total of fourteen months. I was given an exam about a month later in Pittsburgh and I was told that I was going to get 100% disability.

I said, "Gee this is great!"

In those days it was something like $200.00 a month, which today is nothing, but in those days it was a lotta moola. I wanted to go to the University of Pennsylvania. I didn't want to go to Pitt. I passed all the tests at Penn. The guy said, "I'm sorry we can't admit you."

"Why not? I passed all the tests!"

"I'm sorry you're from the western end of the state. People from this end of the state have priority to Penn."

So I went to Pitt. I hated Pitt as much as I hated the military. I thought it was a crappy school! There were about 22,000 people there. I learned very little. I went through in two-and-a-half years, summer sessions and everything. Then one day I went in for an exam at the VA office. The guy said, "You're doing fine! We're going to level you off at fifty-percent disability. You will get that the rest of your life. You don't have to worry."

At one time I thought my life would be shortened because I had my spleen removed, abrasions in the kidneys and some intestines taken out. I said to myself, "Boy, you can't live like that for long."

The guy said, "You're in great shape! Keep it up! You're doing fine!"

I took some graduate courses, and in the meantime I had applied for a job with the CIA. I got into the CIA, and spent the next twenty-five years working most of it overseas, mostly in the Far East. I was in a place called Hokkaido in Northern Japan, Okinawa, Hong Kong, Japan proper, Bangkok, Thailand, the Philippines, a short stint in Rangoon, and once in Cyprus in the Mediterranean. Then I went back to Japan where I was assigned to the Tokyo embassy and I stayed there four years. I retired there at age fifty, and I haven't lifted a finger since!

I wanted to work overseas because I wanted to live overseas and study overseas. I wanted a job in writing, and I wanted to retire early. I didn't want to work all my life and keel over. I was very fortunate that I got the chance to do exactly that.

When I got out of the CIA, I got a part time job with the *Tribune-Review* in Greensburg, PA. I wanted to learn a little about newspaper work. I wound up writing a weekly column for them in the Sunday editorial page. I did that for about seven years until it started to get tiresome. Then I had a chance to get syndicated, but then I would have had to do three columns a week, and I'd have to have so many ahead of time in the can. Plus there would have been some kind of control over content and subject. So I said the Hell with that, I don't need that because I'm old. If someone had offered me something like that twenty years ago I would have leaped at it like a hungry trout after a June-bug, but it was too late for me. Anyway I wanted to start moving around and traveling again. So that's what we did.

My wife, Colleen, got a job in Babenhosen, Germany. She was an education advisor. We bought an old car and toured all over the place. One day I said, "Let's retrace my steps. Lets go to Sarreguemines."

The nearer I got to Sarreguemines, the worse I felt. When we there we started to ask questions about where this place was or where that place was. Most of the old stuff was gone. I got a feeling of depression like I've never felt before or since. I just wanted to get the Hell out of there. Those memories just came roaring back. So I hopped in the car and Colleen said, "What's the matter?"

I said, "I don't know. We've just got to get the Hell out of here."

We just took off, and that's about the last time I ever had any thought about trying to relive anything that happened to me during my military years. Maybe I should have stayed in that damn senior play!

"It Was A Darn Shame."

John Dudek

VII Corps
195th Field Artillery Battalion
Battery C
4th, 90th Divisions

Mowein, Pennsylvania, 20 August 1922

"I was with a guy whose name was Harvey Farthing. We both had to dig a foxhole in the snowy, cold ground. After digging the foxholes, we had two hour shifts on guard duty. I had to go at 4:00 a.m. and he had to be on at 6:00 a.m. He said, "Hey, John, I have piles. Would you trade with me?" At the time I didn't know they were hemorrhoids. "I'm not going to trade with you!" I said. "I could get more sleep." I traded with him anyway. He was sitting on top of the foxhole. I was down there with the straw. At about 4:00 a.m. these Screaming Meemies hit us and I heard him screaming. I found out later he got hit with thirty-two pieces of shrapnel."

My dad, Walter, was a coal miner so we moved around maybe three or four times while he looked for work. My mother was Rosa Liez. I would try to talk to her about Poland, but she never would unless we were alone. I think she was part Jewish. They lived in communes[172] over there, I think. My dad's father was in the Polish army. They buried him in his uniform. We had eleven kids in the family.

We didn't have proper clothing, good housing, or good facilities, such as water or bathrooms. We always kept it inside how difficult we had it, how tough it was, and how poor we were. I would talk to the Italian boys, whom I hung around mostly. We all felt that we didn't have anything. I remember seeing the cookies, the meat, cheese, and other things at the company store. We didn't have much of that at home. The mine owned the homes, and it took a certain amount of money out of the employee's pay to cover rent. The companies would charge exorbitant prices; there was never any money. To help out, we collected copper to exchange for a few cents so that we could run and get a lollipop. There weren't

---

[172]Called *shtetls*.

John Dudek and friend at Buchenwald

many jobs around. One thing that we did was to haul coal in our bags for people or haul water for them. Sometimes we would do hoeing for the farmers, who paid us about thirty-cents for the whole day. After I got out of school I went in the mines for about a year. Oh, I hated the mines!

In our town there were eastern Europeans and quite a lot of Italians. We all had gardens and cows. My family made its own sauerkraut, which we would tramp down with our bare feet. The Italians would make wine, tramping grapes down with their bare feet. My dad made moonshine. You can't convict him now though, because he's gone. I used to stay up all night and watch the distillery. We would make a couple gallons. My dad was a generous man. If somebody would come who didn't have much money he'd charge them twenty cents or twenty-five cents for the moonshine. Not only that, but when the miners would come to our house, while we were upstairs they'd be in the kitchen drinking for free. After Prohibition, the authorities raided some Italians and smashed all their wine barrels. That shocked me, since I got a chance to see how the police force could operate.

I heard about Pearl Harbor over the radio. There were about four or five of us guys standing on the corner. The temperature was in the sixties, and for December, that was a nice day. Everybody was a little shocked, but at that age, how do you accept something like that? It was a dirty, dirty, thing that the Japs did, and we all felt patriotic about it. That's how it was. I was eighteen years old. I wanted to go in right away, but I got into a scuffle with a guy. I hurt him pretty seriously. I had to wait around for a trial. Otherwise, I would have gone in a few months earlier. I got acquitted. Before I was drafted, I worked with a group of kids who collected iron and aluminum for the war effort.

I felt good when I was drafted. I went to Apollo, PA. We all boarded a train and a band sent us off. You never saw people grow so close together and be so proud of going to war. It was the first time that I had ever taken a long train ride. We stopped in Des Moines for a couple of hours, where we had pie, cake, and coffee. In the Sierra Nevada Mountains, the snow was fifteen-feet high, and bulldozer trains were pushing the snow off the tracks. When you see that for the first time it's really a sight! We got off in Oakland, California and I was transferred over to Fort Ord.

For the first two nights I had KP, because I overslept. The sergeant came over and rolled me out of bed. I never did that again! Once the sergeant told me to dig a six-by-six hole. I thought it was ridiculous! After I started digging he said, "Come out of there, son, you don't have to do that."

I thought the military was great! At Fort Ord, we had a band come around about 5:00 a.m. playing "The Beer Barrel Polka." You wouldn't believe the food! We usually ate well at home, but in the Army there was a greater variety of food. What I didn't like was the regimentation. We had a command when to eat. I thought it was a dumb idea to get up, stand in line, then march every day. I didn't approve of the power that some of the officers assumed that they had. It went to their heads a little bit and you could see it. There was a captain I really didn't like. He demanded a table and tablecloth along with service! It wasn't so bad that he didn't eat with *us*, but to demand his own table and a tree to eat under reminded me of a monopoly or something. I don't even think that General Patton would have been that bad. This captain never talked to anyone, and he never had a smile on his face. I think that if he ever got to the Pearly Gates, they would close on him! Anyway, I was a true patriot. We had retreat every night, and would salute the flag. My chest would expand a little bit, and I was proud of my country.

We went to the Mojave Desert for training. It was a lot of heat, dirt and wind. I like to remember the good times in the Mojave. We went to the Hollywood Canteen. Imagine a kid from the coal mines getting to meet Mickey Rooney and Joan Blondel, it was fantastic! Five of us sneaked out under a fence to go into Mexicali, Mexico. We hired some guy to ride us down. Then we started drinking some Tequila. It was my first time drinking. I ended up on the other side of the town of Mexicali. I walked up to a bar. Some Mexicans with banjoes came up to me, playing. I only had a little bit of money on me, but I tossed them a handful of change. When I walked out, I saw women waving their arms. I never saw anything in my life like that!

There was a good deal of prejudice in the Army. Many of the guys were sons of immigrants. Some grew up with prejudices. I think that Jews in the Army were persecuted for reasons that they should not have been. I think that the Eastern European people were given a bad shake in that they were considered dumb people. When we got into combat, a lot of that disappeared. I had a lot of prejudices in my mind growing up until I actually got into the Army and met some of the guys. The guys I admired most in the Army were the Jewish boys. They were intelligent. They were considerate. They made time for you. I saw the goodness in them. I almost felt how they felt. They helped me grow up. They introduced me to *Time* and other magazines.

I got into a fight with a soldier of my nationality over a Jewish kid named Herman Goldberg. Herman was a proverbial Sad Sack. He was skinny and had such a dark beard. He would shave, but two hours later he would need another shave. He had unusual features, so the other guys picked on him. I visited Herman after the war. He lived just outside Los Angeles and had a chauffeur pick me up. We had dinner. I never contacted him after that.

We went to Camp Kilmer, New Jersey. From there we went to New York for one night and when we came back, we were shipped out. We landed in Swansea, Wales and from there we went to a place called Camp Hershey in England, near Winchester. That's when we had our first association with the English people. I liked the English, although a lot of GIs didn't. We called them "Limeys," but they were good to us. We would go to a bar at night or a place where there was a bunch of English people drinking a beer and we all sang. I thought that they were jolly and bright, loyal and patriotic. They shared their cake and tea with you, if you happened to be with them at 10:00 a.m. For ten days, we went to

Wales and practiced shooting at targets at sea. We were frustrated because we didn't know where we were going to go.

We landed in France about eight days after D-Day. We got to Ste. Mère-E-glise, which was still a hostile town. Neither artillery nor German soldiers would scare me as much as airplanes, especially at night. Normally we would dig fox-holes. The Germans would send what we called "Night-Time Jerries,"[173] recon-naissance planes which dropped flares. We were in our foxholes. We knew that the reconnaissance airplanes would come over around 10:00 p.m. Then fifteen minutes later the German bombers would come over and they would bomb the heck out of us. By that time the flares were out and bombs were going off all over the place. I saw guys who were so scared that they would get out of their foxhole and run. I would be shivering. Then you would get up the next day and see dead GIs and dead animals all around. One day I saw a dead German soldier, a para-trooper, who was about nineteen years old. I was alone with him. I looked at him. I thought to myself, "We look the same age. It's a darn shame."

Another time I saw a fight between tanks. German tankers were trying to get out of their tanks, burning, falling. The stench was ugly!

All that I knew was that I was with the 195th. I had no idea that the First Army was with us. We were called a "Bastard Outfit" because we would move from here to there, wherever we were needed. I could never sleep. There was always the thought in my mind that we would liberate wine barrels, which meant going into the cognac factories and taking a few shots of the stuff to settle our-selves down.

After the breakout at St. Lô, the scene was ugly and the temperature was hot. We started to get a real taste of war, a lot of burning tanks and dead bodies, de-stroyed towns. We continued our drive to Paris. Outside Versailles we took a break, which I used to get a dental checkup. They had an old-fashioned spinning-wheel drill.

In mid-August, we got to Paris and went through the city really fast. There were thousands of people with flowers, and it gave us a wonderful feeling. We thought the war would be over in no time. We could tell the way our Air Force was going that Germany wasn't going to last long.

Nights were the big thing. Not only would the enemy airplanes scare the life out of you, but the artillery was awful as well. You could hear machine-gun fire maybe a thousand yards away, but that didn't disturb you too much, because you could almost feel where things were.

We had most of our casualties at the Battle of the Bulge. I was with a guy whose name was Harvey Farthing. We both had to dig a foxhole in the snowy, cold ground. After digging the foxholes, we had two hour shifts on guard duty. I

---

[173]Or "Bed-Check Charlie."

had to go at 4:00 a.m., and he had to be on at 6:00 a.m. He said, "Hey, John, I have piles. Would you trade with me?"

At the time I didn't know they were hemorrhoids.

"I'm not going to trade with you!" I said. "I could get more sleep."

I traded with him anyway. He was sitting on top of the foxhole. I was down there with the straw. At about 4:00 a.m. these Screaming Meemies[174] hit us and I heard him screaming. I found out later he got hit with thirty-two pieces of shrapnel.

During the Bulge, we retreated. Then it started to snow a lot. I remember that we were close to Malmédy where the SS massacred our soldiers. You could see the frozen bodies. It was fearful to think that the Germans would so something like that.

When we got into places where the Russians were going to take over, the people got scared when we would pull out. Some of those Russian troops were brutal. Some didn't even know what a commode was. The Germans were afraid that they would take jewelry and anything that they could get their hands on. I felt pretty bad about it, but there was nothing that I could do.

When I saw Buchenwald, I felt for the Jewish guys in our outfit. I felt so embarrassed and ashamed about how awful humanity could be. Yet, I kept in mind that I was of Polish descent and there were a lot of Polish people there also. Later on, I heard that there were a lot of gypsies there as well.

When the war was over, everybody was quite happy and confused. We just wanted to get out of there. The first thing that I wanted to do when I got some leaves was to go to Paris, and that's what I did. At first, they sent me to Camp Phillip Morris, where I could shower. Then I went to Paris. I saw the Louvre, the Eiffel Tower, Notre Dame! I forgot all about the war because this was ancient history, packed with a lot of culture. And there were a lot of women in Place Pigalle.

After it was over, I patted myself on the back and told myself how lucky I was. I was just a green kid who wanted to see the rest of the world. We associated with a lot of the German people after the war. I used to go over to a man named Willy Schmidt's house for wine and bread.

We were all glad to see each other when I got home. I still had a nervous condition. I started drinking some beer and going out on dates and so forth. It was hard to adapt for a while. I had an awful hard time sleeping, which I believe led to my tendency to drink lots of beer. I thought that I would need psychiatric help or something. I think that's one of the reasons why I reenlisted. Once I returned to the service I went to see the doctor, but they didn't help me. I just had that nervous condition ever since. I tried to work it out.

---

[174]Nebelwerfer 41. A 15cm rocket launcher. It was a toss-up among GIs which was the most to be feared, the 88mm or the "Screaming Meemie."

My parents didn't know why I reenlisted. I just explained to them that I had a chance to go for a year and just wanted to go and see another country, but really I wanted to get some help. I went to Japan, which I don't regret, but I wasn't very happy. Still, it was an interesting and an educational time of life for me.

I landed in Yokohama and became attached to the 25th Division. I had a brother-in-law, a prisoner of the Japanese, who had been in the Bataan Death March. I went to Cochin Stadium and visited the hospital underneath where the Japanese had kept prisoners of war, and where my brother-in-law had also been kept. I traveled quite a bit around Japan. The Japanese were very nice people. We were in the process of trying to introduce free elections. They had places where geisha girls with one-string guitars played and sang for us. The kids had never seen Americans. We had no fear, nor threats. After I got acquainted and started associating with the Japanese I realized that they were just like us. I didn't understand why we were trying to kill each other, anyway.

The experience in Japan really didn't help me that much. I still kept drinking and trying to go to school when I came back. It took a long time for me to settle down. I got married about eight or nine years later, in the early 1950s. I went to a school called Business Training College in Pittsburgh to study management. Finally, I got work in a grocery store, in the meat department. I became manager and remained there for the rest of my working life.

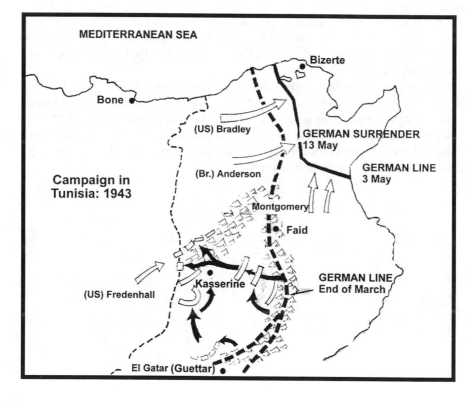

MEDITERRANEAN SEA

Bizerte

Bone

(US) Bradley

GERMAN SURRENDER
13 May

(Br.) Anderson

GERMAN LINE
3 May

Campaign in
Tunisia: 1943

Montgomery

Faid

Kasserine

GERMAN LINE
End of March

(US) Fredenhall

El Gatar (Guettar)

"Goodbye, Jack!"

John Dumnich

United States Fifth Army
36th Infantry Division
753rd Tank Battalion

Captured near Lyons, France Dec. 14, 1944
Liberated from Moosburg, Germany, April 29, 1945

Salemville, Pennsylvania, 23 July 1923

"I went to Naples with a couple buddies. We were standing around and the kids came up to us. We would give them candy, cookies, or fudge. One of their fathers came and invited us to supper. We tried to pay him for the meal, but he didn't want it. It was like an insult, me paying him. I had the feeling that we should offer it to him because he may need it. He finally took it. After that it was "Goodbye, Jack." "Goodbye, Jack" meant that we were moving out. It could also mean you were moving out, period, to the Great Beyond. They gave us a little two-day break. Then, we took off again."

My father, Stephen, was a coal miner. I was six years old when we moved from Salemville to Crabtree. I only went to primary school and began work in a Civilian Conservation Corps camp. Then I went to work at Pennsylvania Rubber in Jeannette. I was drafted while I was still working there in February 1943.

We left on a train from Latrobe, Pennsylvania. The station was packed with people. My mother bawled and my brothers wished me luck. I just took off. I couldn't wait to get on the train. When it pulled out, I couldn't find my mother. She was lost in the crowd.

From Latrobe we went to Washington, D.C. to Fort Myers. We sat there for a week or two before they decided where we were going. We ended up in Fort Hood, Texas, in the Armor Training School. I started off in an M10 Tank Destroyer, an open turret tank with a three-inch gun. We took them over to Italy with us. Then they got rid of the M10, and put us in Shermans.

We went to Virginia from Texas and then to Shenango, to a POE camp up there. Some of the instructors really pushed you over the hill. We lined up before they took us out. One of the lieutenants was talking real serious about

John Dumnich: Somewhere in Italy.

what he thought would help us. One smartie Irishman from our group said "Blow it out of your ass!"

The lieutenant heard him and gave the guy two weeks punishment. The sergeant really pushed him around. Everyday he would march him for a couple hours. We figured the guy would drop from all that walking all day long, carrying a full pack and gun, but this young Irishman just stayed right with him. After the sergeant quit, the Irishman said, "Got anybody else to holler at me? Send him out here and see if he can jog!"

After training we headed for Newport News and shipped out from there, on a Liberty ship filled with high-octane gas and ammunition! We were on that boat for a month. In the Straits of Gibraltar on the Mediterranean Sea a munitions ship about 200 or 300 yards away from us got hit by a torpedo. It blew up and disappeared. The impact of the wave caused our boat to go under water like a submarine. A flaming generator from the ship that was hit crashed down onto our ship. A lot of other debris started to fall. I got nicked on the nose from pieces coming down. We were down in the ship with all that gasoline and everybody went up to the ladder to get out of there. A few guys shooting craps on top deck got hit pretty bad. We had to dock in North Africa to get the wounded off.

We trained on the M10s[175] in North Africa. At night they'd have us place guard duty on the vehicles. We worried about the Arabs stealing things. One guy booby trapped his barracks bag. An Arab took it and was running when it exploded, killing him. Mostly, the Arabs were after white mattress covers, which they would use for gowns.

There were a few guys around who had seen combat in North Africa, but they didn't do much talking about it. Our camp major was at Kasserine Pass. He was a bugger, too. He would take nothing from nobody. I think all the officers under him were just as strict. We hung around there for awhile, then went to Sicily to mop things up. Then we went to Salerno, and that's when the action started for us. The Germans and the Italians were thick as thieves at the time. As the war went on, the Italians drifted away from the Germans. Here and there, Italian people would provide you with a place to sleep. The Army would give us passes to town. I went to Naples with a couple buddies. We were standing around and the kids came up to us. We would give them candy, cookies, or fudge. One of their fathers came and invited us to supper. We tried to pay him for the meal, but he didn't want it. It was like an insult, me paying him. I had the feeling that we should offer it to him because he may need it. He finally took it. After that it was "Goodbye, Jack!" "Goodbye, Jack" meant that we were moving out. It could also mean you were moving out, period, to the Great Beyond. They gave us a little two-day break. Then, we took off again.

---

[175]Replaced by the M18 "Hellcat."

At Cassino, the Germans nailed our tank. We got out in time. The Army gave us another one. On the Rapido River, we were sitting in the tank, when an officer came back asking for two volunteers to go on outpost. I said, "I'll go."

The guys looked at me like they were thinking, "You must be nuts, volunteering to go up front!"

I was getting bored sitting back there. We were serving as the replacements at the time. I didn't even know what I was getting into. A guy told me, "You should never volunteer for anything in the Army, buddy. Let them pick *you*!

We went up front. Nothing happened. We just sat in the tank. We were lucky. Once German observers spotted you it was "Goodbye, Jack!"

Before the war ended for me, I had to abandon five tanks. We also flamed some German tanks. Once we turned the corner of a street and saw this Mark IV was no more than about fifty-yards away. The German was surprised, too. He was speeding along, and then just stopped dead. We let him have it. It was a little tank, but they all looked big when they were coming at you.

The only tank we were really worried about was the Tiger. We had one of our gunners bounce fifteen rounds off the front end of one. The rounds bounced off that tank like gumballs. We just ran away, that's all! Thank God, the Tiger was slow maneuvering. Our turrets rotated. If we moved behind them or to the side, the Tigers couldn't move fast enough to get us. We could still fire at them while we were moving because our turret went clean around. We'd fire while we were running away!

After Cassino they decided to take our outfit, the tank crews, and make a six-by-six truck battalion out of them. At Anzio, I was driving the food and ammunition to the Rangers who had made the beachhead. We were always under shellfire and air attack. A couple dozen of us got stranded up there for about thirty days. We were supposed to unload and go back to Naples. That was rougher than being in that tank.

I got caught in the open with a load. We parked in a trench dug out by a bulldozer. Bed-Check Charlie came over. I got underneath the truck. He dropped some bombs. I was so scared I started chewing on the axle. Anti-personnel bombs were falling all around us! A British anti-aircraft outfit up on a hill got the Hell knocked out of them. When I came back to Naples, I was steaming mad.

When they asked, "Where have you been?"

I said, "Where the Hell do you think I've been?"

When our Army started for Rome, they took our outfit out and sent us to France. In one attack around Lyons, we moved, fired, and moved again. German shellfire soon cratered the area we moved from. Four of us were going down a road doing this hit-and-run thing. We'd beat the Germans to the punch, then take off again. My driver, asked me, "Which way should I go?"

I told him, "Keep going right! Every time you see a crossroads, turn right so we can get away from this!"

I didn't get away. I got captured. A couple hundred of us got caught as we moved up in our tanks to free a bunch of infantry trapped in a schoolhouse. We fought our way to get to them, but we couldn't fight our way back out. The Germans had come around and had us all balled up. We did some fighting!

I got shot. Our tank got hit by a Panzerfaust, near the gunner's sight. I happened to be down on the floor picking up a shell for the gunner, when it hit. The lieutenant had his head out of the turret, and was decapitated. Then I tried to get another guy out of a hatch. I had a Thompson. As I was pushing the lid up with it a ricochet hit me in the right hand. After that, we exited from the bottom hatch. The gunner immediately got killed by a sniper. We ran into this building and out the back end. I and four others went over an eight-foot wall that had barbed wire on top of it. I don't know how the Hell I got over that wall. On the other side was a bunch of wounded guys. We landed on top of them. Some of them tried to get away. A couple of them started running between two buildings. We saw one throw his hands up. I think he took a bayonet.

So we said, "We're not running. We'll stay here and take what's coming."

We were totally blocked. One of our tanks in front of us got knocked out trying to get through another escape route. You could see German infantry coming up the street. They were dressed in GI clothes! Finally, we couldn't take any more and gave up. They marched us from there, across the Seine River. We kept walking and walking. Then they lined us up against the wall and a couple of German soldiers walked up to us with their burp guns. This guy from Buffalo grabbed me and said, "Hey, John, looks like we're going to get it!" and he started to cry.

I said, "What are we going to do?"

Just then a German officer came around and hollered at this guy. He pointed his burp gun at us, but then fired it toward a church steeple. Then they marched us off. They took us into a building where we were interviewed by German colonels who wanted information about different things. Then they called my name up to go in there with them.

The German said, "What are you fighting over here for? Your family comes from the Ukrainian country?"

I said, "You're fighting. They tell me to go to war, and I go to war. You go to war, too."

Then I said, "When are you going to give me a cigarette?"

He gave me one. We talked for a while. He wanted to know where we got our gasoline. I told him, "I don't know. I think we have a pipe line coming up the coast. I don't care." At that time I really didn't know, to tell you the truth.

We stayed there for a while. Then, sometime later, they marched us to Germany. Big snowfall. We walked right in line through the mountains, the guards in line with us. The old-timer guards thought, "You want to go run? Go! Where are you going to go with these big mountains all over the place?"

We kept walking all day long. One evening, they put us in an ice factory. We covered ourselves up with these wood shavings and sawdust to keep warm. We had ten guys sitting in a row trying to keep warm. Every so often we'd rotate; guys in back would come up front. During the day we'd march through these German towns and get stoned and snowballed by little kids.

One of the guys hollered at a kid, "Wait, we'll get you! My little brother's going to get you."

We laughed, and kept going. I was lucky. My group had a guy who talked perfect German. We marched to this camp in Moosburg. It was January 13. They threw us in there like cattle. We met some German guards who talked good English. One was a car dealer in Cleveland. Another one was from Cincinnati. He was also a car dealer.[176]

He said, "Well, I can't go back to America to sell cars."

We said, "We don't know if they're going to let you in or not."

We kidded like that with the guards, but they wouldn't give you anything to eat. We had strictly soup made out of meat, leaves or anything you could think of. Every so often we'd have Red Cross packages. We had one or two British guys who were "barrack leaders." They would be the first to open the Red Cross parcels, but a lot of those boxes would come to us already opened. We didn't know what was originally in them. We took what they gave us. We'd give each guy so much coffee and so forth. Six or seven guys would split a loaf of German bread. It was supposed to be rye but it was mixed with sawdust.

Every other day, they'd take a gang of us to the town to fix the railroads. When we weren't working, the bombers would come and destroy everything. The next day we go back and rebuild. It gave us something to do, plus we could do some black-market deals. We traded soap with German girls for bread. We were allowed to bring firewood back for our stoves. We made a big pole with a nail stuck in it. We'd stick the bread on the nail. We carried the wood in such a way that the guards couldn't see that we were carrying anything but a piece of wood. We tried every way to get stuff back into camp. Living conditions were terrible. Some of the barracks had double bunks, but in one barracks I slept on the floor. They gave us straw mattresses, and that was it. One day I saw a guy with "Greensburg, Pennsylvania" painted on his jacket. He was probably from the 110th Infantry, but we never got together.

My family got a letter saying I was missing in action. We had a chance to write V-Mail letters. I wrote quite a few of them, but I wasn't sure they got through or not. The Germans told us that they were going to send them to the Red Cross.

---

[176]German immigrants to the United States, visiting family in Germany before the war, were often conscripted into the German army.

One day, Patton's boys came.[177] Guys were picking up pistols and swords. After we were liberated the guards offered us some of their weapons. What the heck was I going to do with that now? If I had got any souvenirs I would have had to hide them and try to get them back to the States. I told them, "I don't want it. Just leave it here."

I weighed 160 pounds when I got to Moosburg. When I left, I weighed 130. The Army set up a big kitchen, and you ate all that you wanted of what they had. I was in line when they ran out of food. They did have some bread left, though. My buddy and I both grabbed some and went down the road eating bread. When we got out of there, they shoved us in a big POE camp in France. That's when they started delousing us. There we took all our old clothes off, and went through the showers. The doctors examined us closely.

When I got home they gave me a sixty-day leave. I took a taxi home. The driver asked, "You got any guns?"

"No, I don't, and I don't want any. I left all that stuff back there. I saw e-nough of it."

When I got there everyone in the house came running out. I was glad to be home, but I knew I would have to get accustomed to civilian life again. Go here, go there, go look for a job. I stayed at home for the sixty days, then departed for Fort Dix. I wasn't doing anything down there, except driving a reconnaissance car. I had to take care of it and clean it up. Every morning I'd run to some section where officers were training. I'd get out and say, "Here you are."

Then I'd get under a tree and sleep while they trained. I'd come back to camp, hose down the vehicle, gas it up, and park it. After that, I had the rest of the night free. We'd finagle our way into the officers' club to get better food.

I got out on 12 October 1945. I told this friend of mine, "Let's go down to General Motors in Pittsburgh and put an application in."

We did, and about a week later both of us got a call asking when we could start. I said, "I could start right now if you want me to."

The man said, "We better wait till tomorrow. We have certain time reports to fill out."

I was glad to get in. I worked until I had a bypass operation in 1987. I took a year off to recuperate. I went back down and talked to this girl from the plant who told me that I should retire altogether. I said, "Okay."

I was going to retire in two years anyway. While I was at GM there was this guy working there who was about seventy-one years old. He said, "I got nothing to do. I might as well work"

So I said, "No. I'm not going to do that."

---

[177]Robert Alexander Nelson, a Fifteenth Air Force lieutenant also at Moosburg, describes the liberation at Moosburg in his oral history *The Flag is Passing By*, conducted by the Center in 1996 and available from the Saint Vincent College Library.

For a long while after I came home, I would hit the dirt and crawl under something if I heard a loud noise. After a while, I would just turn around a little startled instead of jumping.

After fifty years, I'd say the worst thing I remember is being knocked out of those tanks. I tell those stories to my little seven-year-old grandson. He loves it. He wrote a big letter and read it in school. The subject was kids looking for heroes. He came right out and told them that his hero was his Pap-Pap.

1. John DiBattista takes a moment to pose during a lull in his sector at the Battle of Arracourt, September 1944. German 88s were still active in the area. "Don't be deceived by the smile," DiBattista said, "I was nineteen years old and scared shitless!"

2. (Left to right): Kellum, Dickson and DiBattista pose in front of an M8 armored personnel carrier.

3. Hohenburg, Germany. B Troop is the law in this remote Bavarian village. (Left to right): Boroski, Marek, Bates, Adamcyk, Stolfi, Roe and Cohen pose with German children outside the village school where they were billeted.
(Photo courtesy of John DiBattista).

1. Spring, 1945. German civilians, under orders from advancing American troops, collect bodies from a shallow grave for proper burial. The dead were executed by retreating Nazi SS troops. Here, they lift the partially decomposed body of a child into a coffin.

2. Stacked bodies of dead inmates at Ohrdruf Concentration Camp, April 1945. The camp was liberated by the 4th Armored Division.
(Photos courtesy of John DiBattista).

1. Harvey Farthing (left) and John Dudek near Stallbridge, England. Farthing was severely wounded during the Battle of the Bulge.

2. The main gate at Buchenwald.
(Photo courtesy of John Dudek).

3. Evidence of Nazi horror. The dead of the Nordhausen concentration camp.
(Photo courtesy of John Dudek).

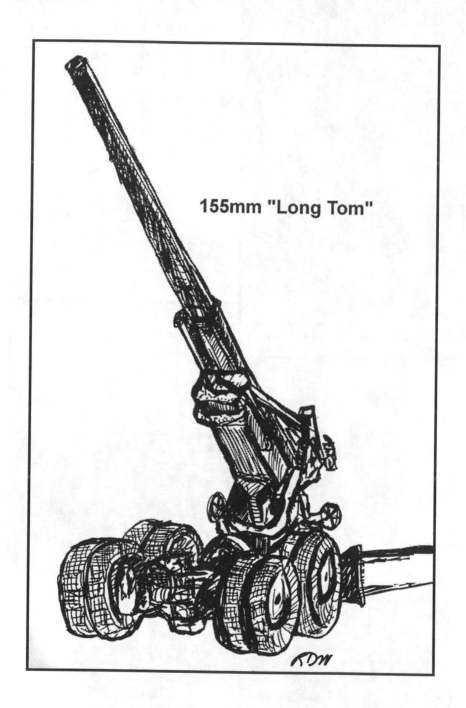

155mm "Long Tom"

"One Day Was Enough!"

Samuel A. Folby

United States Fifth Army
1st Infantry Division ("The Big Red One")
18th Infantry Regiment
1st Battalion, Company B

Latrobe, Pennsylvania, 4 July 1919

"You're walking for miles and miles, and your feet get wet, everything gets wet. If you don't have the temperament, then something is going to snap. The same thing in combat. I was in combat for one day. Then I got wounded. One day was enough!"

I was born down in Dorothy Coal Patch, by the railroad tracks in Latrobe. My father was John Di Fulvio. He was born in 1889 in Italy in a little town known as Fieroum Petri in the province of Abruzzi. He was a coal miner. I don't think he had any education at all. He came over here when he was fourteen with only a couple grades education. My mother was Mary Horwat. She was born in Austria-Hungary. She came here around 1910 or 1911. She was hospitalized when I was small, so I lived with my uncles and aunts on her side. There were eight brothers and sisters in that family. I was treated like a baby brother.

In my first job, I was a grease monkey on a coal tipple. Then I graduated to coupler. I did that from 1938 to 1941, for four dollars and sixty cents a day. While I was in school, I worked on a farm in the summer for one dollar a day plus meals. I pitched hay, loading it onto the wagons and getting it into the barn, but that was five in the morning to six or seven at night.

When the war came, I tried to get into the Air Corps, but I couldn't because of color blindness. I got drafted and passed the physical in December 1942. I was called about a month later, 30 January 1942. I left from New Cumberland for Camp Wheeler, Georgia, where I had basic training.

For the most part the town was rather shocked when the war came. Many of us volunteered, and a lot of others tried to get in, but because of their marital status they wouldn't take many of them. But I think the whole town was kind of mad that this was happening to us.

I got into Army Communications. My basic training consisted of laying lines, installing switchboards, field operations. I even operated a switchboard in basic

Sam Folby: Basic Training, 1942

training. We had to go to target practice regularly. If you hit the targets you were shooting at you got a badge saying you were a rifleman. There were different degrees of excellence. I don't think anyone ever failed. Even if they didn't hit the target at all they still got a badge of some sort!

My training was similar to a telephone lineman, climbing poles or digging trenches to get the wires hidden. We learned to conceal wires as much as possible so the enemy couldn't follow them. Once I got into a regular outfit, they made me a rifleman.

My dad was hurt in a mine accident while I was in basic training. A roof caved in on him and he was in critical condition for two or three weeks. I got leave to see him, and I missed almost two weeks of basic training. They gave me a three-day leave, and when I got home the Red Cross got in touch with the base commander in Camp Wheeler and they extended it to ten days. When my father recovered, I just picked up basic training where I left off.

At Camp Blanding, Florida, we joined up with the 1st Infantry Division, The Big Red One. I eventually became a platoon runner. It was my responsibility to keep our company informed as to where our platoon was and what we were doing, and sometimes I would have to go from company to battalion. Shortly after we joined the division we went to Fort Benning, Georgia for mostly night maneuvers. We did not sleep in the barracks. We had our own pup tents. Things were pretty tough. In fact, for a couple of days, the tents were blowing over. Even the mess tent was getting blown over. You just kept setting them up again.

The whole division went over on the *Queen Mary*. When we got to Liverpool, there were hardly any people around. We then went to Tidworth, the "West Point" of England. Then we went on to Pollock Estates near Glasgow, Scotland. That's where we started our training for the invasion of North Africa. Training in Scotland was tough. That was a lot of night stuff on the moors. That part of the country was very wet, and ninety-percent of the training took place at night. You know you get all this rain and stuff, and you're walking for miles and miles and miles, and your feet get wet, everything gets wet. If you don't have the temperament then something is going to snap. I think that's what happened to one fellow who went crazy. The same thing in combat. I was in combat for one day. Then I got wounded. One day was enough!

We had a guy in our platoon who was a native of Russia and he had this little instrument that looked like a potato with holes in it.[178] He would play this thing, and that kept me in good spirits. He was always close by me in the march.

We went to a naval base for more training. We jumped from the top deck of a ship into an icy North Sea. I never swam a stroke in my life so you can imagine how I felt. That experience was more frightening to me than the actual invasion. The ship was at least thirty-feet high, and you climbed up a rope ladder! We did

---

[178]These instruments were called "sweet potatoes."

this training in case we ever would get torpedoed. Whenever I made the climb up it was like, "Oh, God! I made it!"

We also practiced hitting the beach from landing craft. There was no simulation of enemy activity, because they didn't expect any resistance from the Vichy French[179] in North Africa. It was mostly preparing us to get out of the boats and onto the beaches, because sometimes the craft itself would be about thirty or forty yards from the beach and you had to get the Hell out of there and onto the beach as fast as you could.

When we boarded ship for the invasion we were in a convoy with another forty or fifty ships, including warships. We left from Scotland, and at one point we were within five hundred miles of Boston. This was merely a decoy tactic. Then we headed for North Africa. Our point was called Z Beach Green, which was actually in Arzue, but our main objective was the city of Oran in Algeria. We landed at Arzue in a very heavy surf.

Our personnel carrier was quite a distance from the shore, and quite a few of us got knocked on our faces. The surf hit us from the back. There was no resistance at all on the beach, thank God! A lot of us lost our rifles on the way in. Many other rifles were wet and filled with sand. The first thing that we did was tear the rifles apart and got them ready for service.[180]

When we got into the town of Arzue, there was a lot of sniper fire. We got into Arzue and lost a few people, killed and wounded. That night we headed for Oran, and as we headed toward this mountain we got an awful lot of fire, machine-gun, artillery, everything. As I reached back to get my shovel to dig a foxhole, I got hit in the top of my helmet. I was so angry that the helmet got penetrated I took the damn thing off and threw it away. I should have kept it, but I was just that mad. The bullet grazed my cheek. It missed my collar bone and went into my chest.

I started to pray that I wouldn't make noise and give our position away. Then I must have passed out. The next thing I knew I was in an evacuation truck. Damn if the thing didn't get hit with artillery! There were ten guys on the truck. Three of us survived. I was near the end gate, and I was blown clear into a field. A piece of shrapnel comes along and knocks my finger off! Somebody came along and got me to a hospital. I lost an awful lot of blood. In the hospital I received a couple of transfusions. These were person to person, not plasma. I got one transfusion from a black person, I don't know a name or anything, but I'm attributing my life to this guy. This all happened on 9 November. On Christmas Day I was still in the hospital. By Christmas Eve I could get up, and I was able to serve Midnight Mass.

---

[179]Vichy France was the unoccupied but pro-Nazi portion of France set up after the French surrender in 1940.

[180]During the rest of the war, American troops involved in amphibious attacks would cover the muzzles of their rifles with GI condoms.

I had a lung puncture, and they were draining stuff through my back. That damn suction needle had to be about six-inches long. That was kind of painful. Then it must have been some time in January when I was discharged from the hospital and sent to a staging area. They decided that I was not fit for combat any more. I had an awful lot of chest pain and shortness of breath. The fact that my finger was blown off was rather minor compared to my chest wound. I was sent into a limited service program, and assigned to the Central Postal Directory Service for the whole European theater. We had the names and supposedly the affiliation of all the troops that were in the area.

After a while it was my job to separate inquiries from people who were trying to find out where so-and-so was. I was a PFC, but I had master sergeants and staff sergeants under me. In Algiers, I got an inquiry from the general that said "John Smith." No serial number, no nothing. We looked through, and there were 211 John Smiths. So I just put down *beaucoup*, a whole lot of John Smiths! The general said, "I want this stuff, so find it out."

We got a location of where each John Smith was from, the state that he came from. From there we started checking serial numbers, and from there we narrowed it down to twenty-four. We sent the general twenty-four names and said, "Pick your own!"

We organized a softball team. In one game, I really hit one. I was rounding third base when I collapsed. They took me to the hospital. I went through five different hospitals before I got back to the States. They put me through all kinds of tests. I was probably still operating on one lung. The X-ray doctors kept saying, "What's all that stuff he's got in his chest?" None of them thought about removing the fragments surgically. They didn't feel it would do any good because more probing might have caused more damage.

When I got back to the States I was put in Ashford General Hospital in West Virginia. Today, it's White Sulfur Springs, a five-star resort. They had two golf courses. I lived like a king. They kept the chefs and the waiters busy. Mother and Dad came to see me in the hospital. They were in tears. When I got my Purple Heart, I cried, too. I was there maybe a month or two when they sent me out on limited service. I was in staging area making dogtags for the guys who were getting ready to go overseas. The dogtags were made with metal on a typewriter machine that embossed the metal plate. They checked me over periodically. Finally, they gave me the Certificate of Disability Discharge. They felt that the military would be better off without me. I got discharged on 20 June 1944.

I decided that I wasn't going to do a whole lot of anything for a while, but I did go to the Veterans Administration to make out the proper applications for any entitlements. At that time a person with a Certificate of Disability would be processed as eligible for some kind of compensation. We talked about school, and we talked about job opportunities that were available, and the gentleman that interviewed me said that I would be better off accepting one of these job opportunities instead of going to college. He thought I would make more money in a job.

I took his word for it, unfortunately. He sent me to the Addressograph-Multigraph Corporation. They wanted me to start the next day. This was like 10-12 July. It was after my birthday, at any rate, and I said, "Oh, Hell no, I can't do that!"

Two friends of mine were going fishing up in Canada, and they said, "You're going fishing with us. It's not going to cost you anything. We're going to supply you with everything!"

It sounded like a nice vacation. It was a ten-day-type thing, and this was going to happen sometime in September. So, I told the guy, "I can't start. I'm going to take this trip."

They said I could work until then, and I said, "You've got to be out of your tree. If you want my services I'll be available sometime after the end of September."

I did go to Canada. It was the first time I ever fished. I had a heck of a lot of fun. We had a guide who took us to a different lake almost every day. I caught some fish, and at lunchtime we would go ashore and the guide would fillet the fish. I got back from Canada around 20 September, and I got in touch with the people at Addressograph. I started with them on 25 September 1944, and I spent thirty-plus years with them. I took an early retirement.

When D-Day came in 1944, I was just saying prayers. I heard about it as it was happening. The media was that quick. My division was involved in the invasion and I prayed they didn't lose too many men.

I was in Pittsburgh when the war ended. I was still drinking. I had my last drink on St. Patrick's Day 1946. I belonged to the Moose and I was kind of a hero-type kid. Everytime I went to the Moose I couldn't buy my own drink. If I took a drink from one guy and not the other guy I was a shit heel. I was knocking off almost a fifth every evening. On St. Patrick's Day I walked in and said, "Leonard, this is it! Doctor's orders. No more drinks."

"Whoever Shot First Was the Lucky Guy!"

Michael J. Gatto

29th Infantry Division
116th Infantry Regiment
3rd Battalion Company M

Carlton, Pennsylvania, 24 November 1916

> "Many Germans tried to surrender to us that first day. They claimed that they were Poles who were forced to fight, but we couldn't trust anybody, so we shot them all. After all, they were wearing German uniforms. Whether they took prisoners behind us or not, I don't know, but our orders were to keep moving. If I couldn't stop and take care of a buddy who got wounded, then I sure wasn't going to stop and take prisoners."

We grew up with nothing. My dad, Charles, an immigrant from Italy, worked in coal mines until he finally got a job in Donora, Pennsylvania. My mother's name was Louise. I had five brothers and one sister. My brothers and I shared one bed. We used to pick up junk and sell it to the salvage man. I sold newspapers for a few cents. Anything to raise small change. My dad didn't work for three years during the Depression. He went on relief for fifteen dollars a week.

I was at a neighbor's house when I heard about Pearl Harbor. A bunch of us was playing Nickel Rum when the message came over the kitchen radio. Everybody screamed, and we all ran home. My mother was crying, along with everybody else. I was going with my wife at the time and we were going to be engaged on Christmas Day. When Pearl Harbor happened, we decided to get engaged, anyway. I had a high number in the draft. They used to sing, "I'll Be Back in a Year, Dear," because we all thought we were only going to serve for one year. I figured that I would never get picked, anyway. On 26 December 1941, I got my first draft notice. On 23 January 1942, I went into Pittsburgh for my final exam and sometime in February, I was in the service. That one year stretched into four.

When the war came lots of guys thought they were going to be left behind. They volunteered. When all the boys left, my younger brother said, "I'm not staying here. I'm going to sign up."

Michael Gatto: Bettendorf, Germany, December 1944

Very few people backed off from going into the service. When we got overseas, we found out about this kid in my outfit who was only seventeen years old when he joined. I used to joke with him about it saying, "I don't know how on earth your mother ever let you go to the service."

"Don't say anything to anybody," he said.

They would have kicked him out, especially because we were a combat outfit. He stayed with us. He got killed on 17 June 1944, eleven days after D-Day.

On my third day in the Army I went to Fort Meade. The sergeants who trained us were original 29th Division sergeants. They were all Southerners and were nice guys. We'd go out and have drills, and afterwards we'd go out and get drunk with them. When basic was over, we all hiked over to A.P. Hill Military Reservation in Virginia in five days.[181] It was a long way out there. When we got to A.P. Hill, we marched in formation, so that we could show off to the veterans who had served for years. We went from the nice homes that we had in Fort Meade to squad tents. We lived in them for about four weeks. We were getting ready for maneuvers in North Carolina.[182]

In North Carolina, we trained under combat conditions. One time we had a combat team showing us how to attack a pillbox. They had machine-gunners behind the guys attacking the pillbox. The machine-gun was positioned in such a way so that it would fire over the heads of the men attacking the pillbox. I don't know how it happened, but these boys were attacking the pillbox and the machine-gun fired into a group of men, killing three and wounding many others. Even when we saw these guys killed, we didn't get a real sense of combat. Nobody was shooting back at us.

We left New York on the *Queen Mary*.[183] The ship contained roughly 15,000 troops. There were bunks everywhere, but I was fortunate enough to be in a little cabin with six bunks. The day before we got to Scotland five Canadian anti-aircraft boats came out to protect the *Queen Mary* as she came into port. Apparently, one of the boats got too close and she ran it over. All these whistles started blowing, the doors were shut, and we started to get up and run. We were shooting craps downstairs and couldn't get out because the doors were closing. On the front of the boat were all our B bags and we were in the lower decks. We lost all the bags and our machine guns but not our rifles. Every one of those Canadians drowned.

When we got to shore, we were greeted by many Scottish people with coffee and donuts. From there we got on a train and went to Tidworth[184] to replace the 1st Division. We knew we were getting ready for D-Day. We practiced amphibious landings. We'd draw a line on the ground and put thirty men in that line and

---

[181]Around 22 April 1942.
[182]9 July 1942.
[183]5 October 1942, arriving England 11 October.
[184]18 October 1942.

practice running off of a pretend Higgins boat, because we didn't have any real boats at that time. We went to the Salisbury Plains. One night during maneuvers the paratroopers made a landing near Stonehenge. We were supposed to capture them. After we rounded them up, we took them all to a bar and got drunk.

We practiced for the invasion using English barges. Some of us were supposed to be American soldiers and others were Germans. We used live ammunition. We had airplanes come in strafing. While we were doing this, the real Germans came in with some torpedo boats and sunk one of our ships, and the English ships guarding our landing craft ran away. We lost seven hundred of our boys.[185]

On another exercise we attacked Dartmouth prison. It took a whole week. The ground was like muck. The men were all attached to each other by ropes in two-man teams. You couldn't go to the latrine unless two of you went; that way, if you fell in a hole, then your comrade could pull you out. We finally captured the prison, which had a reputation for having no escapees. Then we hiked forty miles all the way back to camp. The band played and the colonel stood right there as we hiked. By the time we got back, everyone was dragging his feet. When we went in there they told us, "Chow will be ready in a half hour!" When they blew the whistle for chow, everybody was sound asleep.

We got to know the English people pretty well. We drank their warm beer with them all the time. Did they love cigarettes! We had the cigarettes and they had a whiskey ration. We didn't have any PXs or commissaries. Most of that stuff fell off the ship on the way over. Each company had one person to take care of rationing. I ended up getting picked for my company. I went to get cigarettes, soap, chocolate bars, cookies, and shaving cream for 200 men. So when I came back the following month, I got about three or four cases of Twenty Grand, Chelseas, and Chesterfields cigarettes. I happened to see this Englishman, a cook in the officers' mess. I offered him a cigarette.

"Sell me some of those," he asked.

"No, I can't do that," I replied.

"I'll make a deal with you," he said "I'll give you a fifth of Scotch if you give me a carton of cigarettes."

"Yeah," I said, "When can we do it?"

"Any time you want."

"Here's what I'll do," I said. "I'll be gone in the morning. I'm in the second barracks. On my bunk you'll find a carton of cigarettes and you put that fifth of Scotch in my bag."

Over there we filled straw in a canvas bag to serve as a mattress against the hard wooden bunk. Every time I put a carton of cigarettes there, it would be gone, and there would be a bottle of Scotch. When trading time came, we knew

---

[185]Off Devon, 27 April 1944. This incident became known as the "Slapton Sands Coverup." Nine German E-Boats participated in the attack. News of the incident was suppressed by Allied Command for fear that German intelligence would deduce the scope of the impending invasion of the Continent.

that no one would be drinking water that night. Heck, for my buddies in the second platoon, I could get anything they wanted.

On the night of 4 June 1944, we went out in the English Channel, headed for Normandy. The water was so rough we had to turn back. We did the same on 5 June. We got on the upper deck of the *USS Charles Carroll* watching the departure and maneuvers. We could see flashes of exploding shells on the French coast. They told us to go back down and get some rest because we were going to be leaving pretty soon. So we went back down and I wrote a letter to my wife.

At 4:00 a.m. on 6 June we set out again. I hoped the Man Upstairs would be with me because my platoon was in the front row of assault craft. We walked to the boat and went into the water. The other boys who were down farther had to walk down the rope ladder, which required careful maneuvering. You had to wait until the boat was coming up to get into it, because if you got on it while the boat was low, it would come back up, hitting you and breaking your legs. We circled around until daybreak and then went into the beach. The boat bobbed in the waves.

I stood up in the boat, while most of the others were sitting down with their "puke bags." We were loaded down with equipment, including these vests on top of our jackets which contained equipment in its pockets. We had C-rations, K-rations, and chocolate bars, which we could nibble on if we ran out of food. I was ready to dump everything. I even had a 300 radio which I really wanted to throw into the ocean.

When we got in there, the shelling was so heavy the water splashed all over the place.[186] The 1st Battalion had already gone in and the 2nd Battalion was heading in according to plan. The former didn't arrive very smoothly, but the latter did. We wound up arriving right behind the 2nd Battalion. We stopped in two feet of water, just short of running aground. We didn't really know what to do, except to keep moving and to go up against the tide. One of our boys got a direct hit with a shell. A couple of others were killed as we were coming out of the boat. I never looked back. Boys screamed for their mothers, but all that I could think of was getting the heck off of that beach. They kept telling us, "Get off the beach!"

When we got over top of the beach, I saw a German soldier and dropped down. I guess he dropped down, also. It was all blurry that day. Everybody was scared as rabbits, shooting at anything that moved. I think that the artillery troops only got one gun in. We were all mixed up and it was hard keeping track of the - company and division. Everyone had a duty no matter who he was. We were no longer a heavy-weapons company. We were riflemen until we got settled.

---

[186]Omaha Beach. Pointe de la Percée to St. Honorine had been allocated to Major General Leonard T. Gerow's US V Corps. By nightfall, nearly 35,000 Americans were ashore, none as far as one mile off the beach. More than 1,000 were killed or wounded.

When guys got hurt, someone would take care of them. Each platoon had a medic. Our original plan was to go inland and then regroup before going toward the paratroopers who were dropped the night before.[187] Instead we got pinned on the beach. We traveled roughly half a mile, but we were supposed to go three miles before regrouping to meet with the paratroopers. My unit relieved some Rangers a day or so after the landing.[188] We didn't get to the paratroopers until two weeks later. Their wounded had gangrene from their wounds, because they couldn't get out to bandage them. There were still paratroopers hanging in the trees, and they had to be cut down. They laid out these elaborate plans, but nothing went the way it was supposed to.

Our battleships blasted away at those pillboxes, but they were so thick and heavy that we couldn't knock them out. We used satchel charges on them. On some of them we would put the charge on a pole and on others we would throw it. We didn't blow the pillboxes up, but we killed everybody who was in them. The riflemen threw the satchel charges because as heavy-weapons people, we were more familiar around bazookas, machine-guns, and mortars. I was doing a lot of firing. After the war, I thought about the Germans I shot. They had mothers and fathers like we did. I realized that we were killing people that had nothing to do with starting the war.

They gave us strict orders not to take prisoners. We didn't have time to take care of them. Whoever shot first was the lucky guy. German snipers sniped at our troops all morning. We brought up half-tracks mounted with four .50 caliber machine-guns and cut those trees in half to get them out of there. When that didn't work, we blew them up. These snipers were holding up the whole company.

On the first day, we trapped a German in a barn. Sergeant Jenner told us, "Keep me covered."

The German kept firing. Jenner ran across into the barn. The German ran to the back. As Jenner chased him, we looked up at the house we were hiding behind and noticed somebody poke his head out, preparing to shoot. We threw a couple hand grenades up to the window and it turned out to be a young woman. She had a gun and everything. She even had a wedding ring on. It seemed like she and this German lived on this farm for several years, so they could have been husband and wife. We killed them both.

Many Germans tried to surrender to us that first day. A bunch claimed that they were Poles who were forced to fight.[189] We couldn't trust anybody. We shot them down, anyway. After all, they were wearing German uniforms. Whether they took prisoners behind us or not, I don't know, but our orders were to keep moving. If I couldn't stop and take care of a buddy who got wounded, then I sure

[187]The 82nd and 101st Airborne.
[188]2nd Ranger Battalion at Pointe du Hoc.
[189]The Germans frequently pressed those they conquered into service.

wasn't going to stop and take prisoners. The worst part of the invasion was moving forward into the attack. We got hit with small arms fire and a lot of artillery. They even had rockets to fire at us. When artillery is firing at you, you don't run back, you run forward. If you turn back, you're more likely to get hit.

We were trained for the invasion, but not for the hedgerows. All the gates in the hedgerows were zeroed in by the Germans. Sometimes we could hear them talking at night. On top of the gates were many bushes, some of which were hard to get over. Somebody got the smart idea to insert a row of metal teeth on the front end of our tanks to smash the gates. This plan helped greatly because we couldn't go through the gates without the tanks, and if we tried to climb over it then the Germans would pick us off. So the tanks would run over the gates and we would follow them from hedgerow to hedgerow. There never seemed to be a front line. It was just one hedgerow after another.

A buddy of mine was killed in the hedgerows. It happened about the third day of fighting. I don't understand what made him do what he did because mostly everybody was telling us to stick to the edge of the hedgerows. He should have come into the gate, stayed low, and turned in the right direction. Instead he tried to cut across a sloping field toward another hedgerow. We knew a sniper was there. He had been there for a couple of days. He shot my buddy through the head.

The hedgerow fighting was a real test for some of our men in M Company. They were a great bunch of guys. There was only one incident that I remember that left a bad impression on me. During the hedgerow fighting we were ordered to send a patrol out because the rifle squads were short on men. Normally, the rifle squads would send a patrol out instead of M Company because that wasn't our job, but since we still had fifty percent of our men left, we got the job. I was one of them. What made this even worse was we had a new lieutenant leading the squad. When we got over about one or two hedges the lieutenant said, "Now, you boys crawl up and see where the Germans have positioned their guns. I'll stay here and wait for you. All you need are a couple of soldiers."

I said, "No, no, no, lieutenant. I'm staying back here. Your job is to lead the patrols!" We sat on our asses all night without anybody moving. It was really the riflemen's job anyway.

Even the enlisted man knew what an officer's job was, and could take over if necessary. Another thing that was good about our organization was each man in our five-man, machine-gun squad knew how to do each other's jobs. The men in a machine-gun squad included a PFC, who worked the gun, another soldier helped him, and another three carried ammunition and water. If the guy working the gun got knocked out everybody else knew how to take over.

I was wounded in the hedgerows. It was before the breakout at St. Lô.[190] Our 2nd Battalion was surrounded on top of a hill by Germans about a mile from St. Lô.[191] 3rd Battalion was ordered into the attack at 2:00 a.m. We followed the riflemen using nothing but bayonets and hand grenades. The Germans must have known we were coming because they were prepared and ended up trapping both us and the riflemen for thirty-six hours. We didn't know we were surrounded till later on. We thought we were winning!

After we got surrounded, a group of us, maybe squad-strength, ran down a depression in a field and gathered behind a mound of dirt. We could hear the Germans in the hedgerows in front of us. We joined up with some more of our men and were ordered to attack some Germans who were in a barn. We still did-n't know we were surrounded. During this assault, as I was running along this ditch toward the barn, I saw my chaplain laying dead over top of another dead soldier. My lieutenant was running in front of me and I tried to stick close to him because I was carrying that big 300 radio. If he needed to talk to someone then I had to be there. After all that running around I didn't want to carry that damn radio anymore. Besides I was the oldest man there! When this young boy came up, I said, "Here, take this radio." He was killed later that night in another assault going up a hill. Eventually, we had to use that radio, but we lost track of that kid. The lieutenant said to me, "Mike, go find that kid and bring the radio back."

I said, "How do I know where the radio's at? If the boy hasn't returned, he was probably killed back there."

He said, "Take a couple men with you and find that radio."

I said, "Heck, I don't need anybody to go with me for the radio."

I went back and struggled over a hedgerow. I found the radio along with the young man whom I gave it to. He was laying on top of it. I rolled him over, took the radio from his side and stood up. Something like a hot poker went through my thigh. I went down on one knee, but I could still move my legs. I grabbed his rifle, stuck it in the ground, but I didn't wait around long enough to put a helmet on it. Immediately, I grabbed that radio and took off in the direction I had come from. When I got back, I told the captain, "Jesus Christ, our men were shooting at me! I got hit!"

"Those are Germans back there," he said.

"Now you tell me! If you had told me they were in there, I could have avoid-ed getting shot!"

A buddy put his field dressing on me and said that I only had a hole on one side of my leg. He patched me up on that side, but the bullet had really gone clean through. The night wore on. My captain was sitting not far from me in a foxhole with two soldiers, one named Anderson and the other named Sheldon, when

---

[190]The 116th pushed on Martinville Ridge (16 June). The division took St. Lô on 18 July. Parts of the 116th were isolated on the Bayeux Road from 15 to 17 July.
[191]At Martinville Ridge, 12 July 1944.

suddenly three mortar rounds came in. My captain got hit in the hip, and Sheldon got all of the muscles torn out of his thigh and was killed by the concussion. That night I would say that we lost a few hundred men from our battalion, including Major Howie.

I was hit on July 17 and left combat July 18 to go to England. On July 19 I was in the hospital. I didn't realize that the bullet had gone clean through my leg until I was on an airplane for England. Suddenly I noticed that I was still bleeding. They asked me, "What's the matter?"

I said, "I feel more blood coming out."

So the nurse cut my pants open and there was blood. Luckily the bullet never hit the bone. I'll tell you, there were German snipers all around me that night and I didn't even know it, but I survived. Don't ask me how. I stayed in England about a month and a half. Then I returned to France. My sergeant was training some of the new recruits. He wanted me to stay, but I said, "No, I'm going back tomorrow. I want to be with my own outfit. I don't want to be with strangers. I don't want to teach these guys, anyhow."[192]

I got what I wanted. When I got back we moved out for Brest.[193] We were supposed to eliminate 75,000 or 80,000 Germans in about a week, but it took us almost a month. The Germans had pillboxes we couldn't overcome. It was mostly patrol fighting, because we had them trapped. There were three different divisions involved in this. The 5th Armored chased them into that pocket. The 2nd Division and the 29th assaulted the German positions. Finally they came out by the thousands, officers and all. We were loading the officers onto a truck when I saw one of the batmen[194] preparing to board with them. I asked him, "Where are you going? You're not getting on this truck. It's for officers."

They told me that this was a batman, and I responded, "You tell your officer that if he can't carry his own bags then the Hell with him. Those bags are staying where they are!" So he left and we finished packing the officers in. As we were going through town their civilians threw stones at them.

On the other side of Aachen, we arrived along the banks of the Roer River.[195] Our engineers set up pontoon bridges across the river. Meanwhile, we were digging in along the west bank of the river. We spent about two or three weeks preparing positions all along Holland and France before any movement toward Ger-

---

[192]One of the less enlightened practices of the American army was to send recovered wounded back to the front into units where they were needed, rather than to the units with which they trained. This practice did not help morale.
[193]The 29th began the attack on Brest 25 August 1944. The 116th assaulted Le Conquet Peninsula and the Battery Graf Spee. German resistance collapsed 18 September 1944.
[194]An orderly.
[195]October/November/December 1944. The 116th participated in the Uebach Bridgehead Battle on 5 October 1944, and the Aachen Gap fighting on 13 October, and frontally assaulted Wuerselen. The division began the Roer offensive 16 November. Setterich was taken by the 116th 19 November. On 1 December the 116th began the battle for two strongpoints west of the Roer opposite Jülich, the Hsenfeld Gut building-maze and the Jülich Sportplatz.

many could be made. While we were there, we got along with the people of Holland. I spent Thanksgiving with one of the families. There were three little girls, to whom I gave some GI soap so they could wash their clothes. Just before Christmas we attacked the Germans. They knocked our pontoon bridges out on three earlier occasions, but this time we finally got across. From then on the war wound down.

We weren't involved in the Battle of the Bulge. We were north of that. The 2nd Division, the 4th Division, the 29th Division and several armored divisions were preparing for our own attack up there before the Bulge broke out. We were all set to take off into Germany when the Germans attacked the Seventh Army. The next day there was nobody up there except for our division. The other outfits were sent south into battle. We were then attached to the British Eighth Army. We just stayed put in our holes. We had barbed wire strung out in front of us with tin cans, bottles, and anything we could imagine that would make noise so we could hear anyone trying to sneak up. We also dug our tanks in so that only the turrets were above the ground. We laid land mines all over, too. We were spread so thin they brought up cooks and clerks to help defend the line. Our job was to hold at all costs. We didn't know if we were going to get hit, but we sent a patrol out every hour on the hour. We never saw a thing. The Germans threw everything that they had into that Bulge. We stayed there until February.[196]

Our outfits would leapfrog each other and kept a steady stream of pressure on the Germans. Two battalions would attack and another would be in reserve to replace one of the battalions once they stopped to rest. In this manner we kept the Germans on the move. When that Bulge was broke the war was almost over. We went up to the Elbe River with very few casualties and continued to move day and night.[197]

In France and in Belgium the Germans really gave us a battle, but once we got into Germany we were fighting only fragments of their army. There would be a few people firing machine-guns. Once you'd throw a few shells at them you'd see that white flag coming out followed by groups of young kids and old men. The only problem that we had was with these Russians and Poles who we liberated from this camp. These people had been enslaved by the Germans and forced to work in coal mines in the area. They were given only bread and water. When we entered their camp there was no one around. We heard all this jibber-jabber coming from the barracks. We kicked the door open and all these people came running out. Their skin was all yellow from jaundice. Babies, old men and women. We rounded them up and deloused the older people. The babies they put in some ambulances to take to a hospital. About three or four days after we set these people free, we had to round them up and put them into the camp again because they

---

[196]The 116th and 175th combined to seize Munchen-Gladbach on 1 March 1945. The 29th then consolidated and went into reserve 3 March 1945.
[197]The division reached the Elbe on 24 April 1945, and relieved the 5th Armored Division.

were killing all the German people in the town, including the Burgermeister. These people weren't Jews. Another regiment in our division, the 115th, hit the Jewish Camp. Soon after this, the war ended.

Some of the Russian troops came over on our pontoon bridge to trade with us. We all drank their vodka, which they traded us for rifles. I don't know why they liked our rifles, but they did. On the second day they were not allowed on our pontoon bridge because they were getting drunk and shooting the German civilians. We didn't take anything from the Germans, either, and if they got smart with us they got shot. We shot a bunch of SS. When we *did* capture SS, they were placed in special POW camps because of their jobs at the death camps.

Most of the Germans wanted to avoid the Russians. We put up more pontoon bridges because Germans were coming across the river by the thousands and we didn't want them to drown. Before that, they would try to come across in boats or any way possible. At one place I counted 103 prisoners at the edge of the woods, all young and old people.

One of the soldiers asked, "What do you want me to do with them?"

"I don't care what you do with them," I said.

I asked them in German if anybody had any rifles. No one raised their hand so we decided to let them walk back toward the American lines by themselves. We didn't have anyplace to go so we just sat there and waited. We were in German homes. We chased all the residents into the church or town hall. We ate their eggs, killed their chickens and cows. Good steaks!

I came home at Camp Patrick Henry Virginia. I spent about a week there to have my teeth fixed and to sign up for pension. I asked the sergeant, "How long am I going to stay?"

He said, "About one more week."

I said, "Never mind, Sergeant, I'm going home."

In the war, you never saw a bunch of people work as closely together as we did. I can't say that today. It seemed like everybody wanted to go. When we joined our outfit, many already there were Southern and it was we Northerners who were joining. Pee-Wee Norton, a good friend of mind told me, "Mike, I never fell asleep until you fell asleep. I always thought you were part of the Mafia."

I lost a lot of good friends, and for what? Is it a better country? I don't think so. The government tells us anything and charges us for everything!

Safe conduct pass for surrendering German troops.

*Photos: Courtesy of
Richard R. Buchanan*

"I Thought It Would Be Good For Me."

Norman Haglund[198]

102nd Cavalry Group Mechanized
102nd Cavalry Reconnaissance Squadron Mechanized
Troop C

"I was carried to a plane, put in on a rack with other wounded, and given a shot. When I awoke, I was in an operating room in England. Someone was picking small pieces of shrapnel out of my chest. They said it looked like someone threw ashes at me. They also said they were going to put a cast on my right leg and put new bandages on my other leg, my face and chest. First thing I knew, I awoke in a bed, screaming. I was on fire! I thought my leg was rotting, because I picked up maggots coming out of the top of my cast! The doctors explained that the maggots were put in to eat the dead flesh *only*."

I was drafted into the United States Army on October 14, 1941 when I was twenty-one years old. I was only supposed to serve one year before being discharged. Little did I know we would be at war in two months! At the time I thought it was going to be a big adventure, yet there were some mixed feelings when I left my family. I was sad, but it was the first time I was leaving home and I thought that it would be good for me.

I was on guard duty at Fort Riley, Kansas when I heard that Pearl Harbor had been attacked. I was horrified the moment I knew I would be in the service for the duration of the war and not just one year. Still, I felt a great sense of pride in the fact that I would be taking a part in protecting my country. After Fort Riley, I took more training at Fort Jackson, North Carolina. I ended as a radio operator in an armored car. When we learned that we were heading overseas, we had no idea. I though to myself, "This is it. It's really going to happen." I think a lot of us were under the impression we would never get shipped overseas.

---

[198]Mr. Haglund passed away before his interview could be taken. His history has been constructed from a detailed questionnaire he prepared for the Center, and from some written notes he prepared during the pre-interview process. In a note to the Center, 17 November 1998, Mrs. Haglund wrote: "Thank you very much for including my husband's story in your book. I'm grateful that his sacrifice for this country will be remembered. I've always wondered about the [German] men who were killing the Americans, yet who saved my husband [when he was wounded.]"

Norman Haglund

We assembled at Fort Dix and boarded the East-Indies ship, *Dempo*, a small ship. I called our quarters, "The Hole." We had a large room with picnic tables anchored to the floor. There were hammocks for sleeping (I was too long for the hammocks so I found a mattress and slept under the picnic table.) The food was terrible. The bread wasn't baked all the way through. The crust could be eaten, but the inside dough was mushy. We rolled the dough into balls and tossed them around at each other like it was a battle! Unfortunately, real combat wasn't as much fun. After a few days down in "The Hole" our quarters started to stink. We had to carry the cleanup water through the corridors in a large tub, and inevitably we would spill most of it before we got to our quarters. So, we spent most of our time on deck. We exercised a great deal despite the size of the ship. We boxed and there was a lot of roughhousing. There was always a card game or a dice game somewhere on the ship. A good many were seasick, and stayed on deck day and night.

We arrived in England and stayed there for two years! In all that time we never knew where we were going or what we were doing there. It wasn't much different from the States. The civilians were always good, and they always made you feel welcome. The GIs fraternized with the local women.

During those two years in England there was a feeling among lots of the guys that we weren't doing anything important, because in all these other places, North Africa, Sicily, Italy and in the Pacific, there was fighting. I won't say I was eager to get into combat, or any of us for that matter! We were frightened more than anything else. There was a great deal of homesickness too. But morale was generally good, and our unit had an excellent camaraderie and discipline, even in combat.

Finally our time came. We were slated for the invasion of France. It was early June and we boarded our transport. It was an LST. Our armored cars and jeeps were put on board with us, and I found myself more frightened than I had ever been, because this time we knew for sure we were going into combat. This was the real thing!

We went across the Channel. The seas were rough. We approached the beach, Omaha Beach, and our LST came under heavy fire. This was our baptism of fire! I found myself praying like mad, "Just get me out of this alive!"

Then I had this horrible image of our ship getting hit and me being trapped inside my armored car as we sank to the bottom of the Channel. The fire began to intensify and it looked like my nightmare might come about, but luckily we were able to move out away from Omaha. The fire was so heavy we couldn't get in until the second day. At night some German planes came over, trying to attack the convoy. I thought they were all trying to get my ship. We shot them all down. The next day, 7 June, we went back into Omaha Beach. This time we got in. When we got on the beach, we saw how rough it had been for those guys going ashore in the first wave. There were bodies all over the beach and in the water.

Once we got established, our reconnaissance squadron's job was to seek out the enemy, report their position if possible, and to determine how many men they had and what kinds of firepower were in their possession. Then we were to race back to HQ. The trick was to not let the Germans see us. When we were going through the hedgerows though, you never knew where anyone was!

In August 1944, we were approaching Paris. The main army stopped because we were told that the Free French under General DeGaulle wanted to take over Paris. We were on the other side of the Seine River. Finally our troop was called upon to use reconnaissance. Usually we investigated every building as we moved forward. But this time we passed up everything because the French told us it was clear to a certain point. Our troop had three armored cars and six jeeps. The order in which the vehicles were on a patrol was: one jeep then an armored car and then two jeeps and then another armored car and two jeeps and then the last armored car and a jeep. We usually took turns being point. I was fortunate to be in the last car.

After traveling several miles, we came to a bend in the road. There was a high wall obstructing the view of the front cars as they went around the bend. As the second armored car turned firing broke out. We saw a ball of dark smoke in the sky, then more firing and another ball of smoke. When we reached the bend, the car commander told the driver to get behind the wall. The wall was too high to get our guns over. Even standing on top of the armored car, we couldn't see over the wall. Everything was happening so fast. Some of the men from the front cars came running around the wall. At the time I didn't know how many got around and how many were killed. I couldn't contact anyone on the radio. The car commander told everyone to get on top of the armored car and in the remaining jeep. We tried to get back under cover of the wall. We traveled through the field, but couldn't pick up any speed because the armored car was laboring under the extra weight.

The commander said, "We have to get back on the road."

We did and were doing all right until we came upon the farm houses we had first passed. Fire came from both sides of the road. The men on top of the car were screaming and hollering that they were hit. Then all of a sudden the armored car was hit. I thought my stomach blew out, and I gasped. The car went off the road and into a ditch. The driver and I opened our flaps and slid out of the car onto our faces. I couldn't believe I was conscious, but I couldn't move. I was sure I was going to die. I thought of what they would say at home. Then someone turned me over and I looked up and saw two Germans with guns. I closed my eyes and was sure they were going to kill me. Instead they took me under my arms and dragged me into a nearby barn.

I saw my leg bouncing awkwardly beneath me as they carried me. My clothes were smoldering. They laid me in the barn and left. I don't know how much time went by because I must have passed out. I woke up and a German was cutting off my clothes with a knife. He put bandages on my right leg. When he finished, he threw my clothes on top of me and left. Again, I must have passed out. I was awakened again to find two Germans putting me on an old door. They carried me out of the barn and laid me along the side of the road. How long I lay there I didn't know because again I was out of it. I found out later they had put a note on me saying, "Please help this wounded American soldier."

Someone said, "Are you ready to go back?"

I looked up and this time it was American soldiers! I passed out again. When I awoke I was in a first aid station being given blood. I was bandaged head to foot. I remember asking for water because I was burning up. I went to an evacuation hospital. It was a large tent. There was moaning and screaming all around me. The shock was gone, and I was in pain. Someone came by and I asked for something for the pain. They said they would get something.

I was carried to a plane, put in on a rack with other wounded, and given a shot. When I awoke, I was in an operating room in England. Someone was picking small pieces of shrapnel out of my chest. They said it looked like someone threw ashes at me. They also said they were going to put a cast on my right leg and put new bandages on my other leg, my face and chest. First thing I knew, I awoke in a bed, screaming. I was on fire! I thought my leg was rotting, because I picked up maggots coming out of the top of my cast! The doctors explained that the maggots were put in to eat the dead flesh *only*. They took my cast off and put my leg in traction. I had a compound fracture and the lower part of my right leg was burnt. Both legs had a lot of shrapnel (some is still in my legs and chest today!)

I had skin grafts on my right leg, but the graft didn't take around the compound fracture. The bone developed Osteomyelitis. In December I was sent to the States for further treatment. I had the Million-Dollar Wound! They put a cast on my leg and carried me onto the *Queen Mary* and put me in a room with a few other men. I had to stay in bed. I couldn't see out.

I was taken to Halloran Hospital. We were treated like heroes. They said we were not going to stay long but would be sent to another hospital. I called home. It was wonderful to hear the voices of my parents and sisters!

The doctors said I'd have to start walking, and when they saw I could get along with crutches they were going to send me home in a few weeks. For the next forty years they tried to treat this hole in my leg, but to no avail.

I went home by train. What a great feeling to be home! But after one week I got an infection in my leg and ended up in Indiantown Gap for six weeks. I asked to be sent to a closer hospital, but they said I had to go to Rome, Georgia. I stayed there for a few months and then was sent to Valley Forge Hospital, a plastic-surgery center. They couldn't close the opening in my leg. Finally, they said they would discharge me and I could go to a Veterans' Hospital in Pittsburgh whenever I needed treatment. I was discharged in February 1947.

I went to vocational school to learn drafting. I attended the Connelley Trade School in Pittsburgh. I used the GI Bill in order to do this. I owe a lot to the GI

Bill. It gave me the education that was necessary so that I could get married, support a family, buy a home and get on with my life. I thought at one time, because of my disability, I wouldn't be able to do all this. But all of my expectations have been realized, and they were great expectations!

I got a job in 1948 at Allis-Chalmers in Pittsburgh, the Electrical Division (Transformer) in drafting. At times I would go to the hospital to have the bone scraped. On another occasion I had a large piece of shrapnel removed from my groin. I lived this way until 1984 when there was a procedure they wanted to try if I was willing. They wanted to take a muscle and artery from my left side and transplant it onto my right leg, and then they would put skin grafts on. There was a fifty-fifty chance of it taking. I agreed and spent six weeks in the hospital. The procedure worked and today I have very few problems, compared to previous years.[199]

---

[199] The interviewer was told by a close friend of the Haglund family that even just before Mr. Haglund passed away he could not go out in the sun for long periods because his skin was extremely sensitive due to the burns he received when he was wounded. Consequently, if he did have to remain outside for an extended time he needed to carry an umbrella with him to shield the sun light.

Wings Like Eagles

James Walter Herrington

101st Airborne Division
327th Regiment
1st Battalion

Scottdale, Pennsylvania, 18 November 1920

"Yes, I shot a German. I shot some German people, yes. I think God has forgiven me for killing people. But it was a matter of either you or him. I think I was in a different world when I was doing this. I was interviewed by psychiatrists at Indiantown Gap when this all was over and we were being mustered out there. He really made me cry, that sonofabitch. That psychiatrist really brought it home to me. And I think the way he handled me when he talked to me made me think whether what I did was right or wrong, but it *had* to be right. This was just something that *had* to be done. But he was not a combat person. I don't think he understood what Hell the guys went through on the front lines. That psychiatrist bothered the Hell out of me for a while."

I grew up in Scottdale, Pennsylvania. Everytime the rent came due, we moved. This was the Depression! Finally we moved to Browntown, to the farm where my grandfather and grandmother lived and where my mother spent her youth. I attended high school in Weirton, West Virginia, and graduated in 1939.

The attack on Pearl Harbor is what made me go into the service. We had a lot of the guys who signed up then, because of all the stuff that was being said over the air, like, "What are we going to do about these Japs?" I think everybody kind of had the same sort of idea. "Hey! We got to go to war, and we got to get this thing over with and get back to our lives!"

My first outfit was the 403rd Anti-Aircraft Battalion. At Camp Wallace I trained on the 90mm anti-aircraft gun. They had what they called a 268, a radar as wide as a room and half as tall. The projectile was dependent on the radar focusing on a target. Then it would "tell" you when to fire. I and my crew set up a 90mm after it was unhooked from a big truck called a "prime mover." I was proud that we could get our gun ready to fire in six minutes. We practiced shooting at a target being pulled by an airplane. We were concerned about making a mistake and shooting the tow-plane down!

James Walter Herrington

We were on maneuvers in Palacios, Texas when a hurricane hit. We were told to get out of there, back to a town about thirty miles inland. Guns, the whole bit! I remember walking to a truck to get out of there, leaning forward at a forty-five-degree angle because of the wind, and the hurricane hadn't even hit us yet.

I had one two-week furlough from Camp Wallace, just before we left to go to Camp Hewlin just outside of Hattiesburg, Mississippi. When we got to Camp Hewlin, we were outfitted for combat, loaded onto a troopship and went to Camp Myles Standish, just outside of Boston, and from there we boarded the *USS America*, an old troop ship. I'll tell you those ships were the dirtiest things. The guys didn't get lice; they got the crabs. They had to shave every hair off their bodies! When the hair began to grow back they were scratching like crazy!

We were more than fourteen days on the ocean. Halfway out, about the eighth day, the German subs were looking for troopships. We had many troop-ships in this convoy, and I guess when we heard the depth charges, we knew there was something going on. And then the engine broke down. We were sitting dead in the water bobbing up and down! The depth charges appeared to be coming closer and closer. One guy was scared as heck! He said, "Man, I'm really scared! I'm afraid we're going to sink, I'm afraid I'm going to drown!'

The other guy said, "Don't worry you're only two miles from land."

"What do you mean?"

"Right straight down!"

I went through the campaign in North Africa, and was in on the invasion of Sicily and Italy. In Sicily, one of our guys tried to shoot me. There wasn't much resistance by then and we had a chance to let the guys go out on a pass into Paler-mo. They got their fill of booze and wine and whatever. This guy got himself a Beretta pistol from somebody and he came into the tent where I was making out the morning report. The light reflected off the pistol and got my attention. I turn-ed around and he had it aimed at me! I went underneath the back of that small wall tent. If I wouldn't have been knocked down by an olive tree just behind the tent, he wouldn't have gotten hold of me. He was a big guy, but fortunately he was too drunk to put up much of a fight. I managed to wrestle him to the ground. The captain came running down to see what was going on. They called the MPs, who came and got him and took him out. I didn't press any charges on him. I was lucky I was still alive and all. He was out of the outfit the next day.

Whenever the troops were not involved in combat there were crazy things happening. I had to sit on a court-martial case once where this guy from Alabama had taken advantage of an Italian girl. The Italian male relatives of that girl beat the living daylights out of him. I had to go visit him in the Army hospital. His face was almost blue from where he had gotten beat by these guys. I don't know whatever happened to him after that, because we had moved out, and he never came along with us.

After Italy surrendered,[200] we had a little Italian soldier who offered to do our cooking and KP. He said, "If you let me travel with you, I will leave you when you get to Rome, because I live in a little town called Terrormini Emerse, and then I'll be home." We gave him the job. Just like he said he would, he left us just before we got into Rome.

It was in Rome where I got my airborne training. I wanted to get into it because they were getting one hundred dollars for jump pay! Airborne training was rigorous. We'd run twenty-five miles every Monday, Wednesday, and Friday from our bivouac area outside of Rome. We got to be stronger than bulls! We could run our asses off! We'd run twelve-and-a-half miles into Rome, rest for a half hour, and then the same distance back. We did hand-to-hand combat. You got the shit beat out of you and then you'd give it back to somebody else! We had what was called boxing day and athletic day. We had baseball and football teams. As first sergeant, I did little of that. I had to plan for all those things.

We had to have cropped hair and no mustaches. The drill instructor was the one guy who had a mustache. It was beeswaxed and stuck up about an inch off his lips. He was mean. Once you started your sit-ups, he'd say "Okay! Sit up! One, two, three! On your left-side! On your right-side! On your back! On your belly!" I don't know how some of us ever stood it! We became the epitome of military prowess. A few good men, that's what we were, a few good men!

On my first jump, I almost pooped in my pants! As first sergeant, I had to be the jump master of the plane. I had to display some guts! I'd stand at the door and yell, "Follow me!" and jump out. And they would all follow me. The guy who was the Air Force person had to pull back the fifteen-foot static line attached to the plinny. Whenever everybody was out, he had to pull those back in and close the door.

After airborne training, we traveled north on the Appian Way from Rome to Florence. In Florence there was very little resistance. After a wait, we boarded a ship and went from there to Marseilles. There was an airdrop planned in southern France which didn't materialize. So we went in by land. We went north from Marseilles. In Arlon, we got into trucks, ready to go to Bastogne.

We were dug in at Arlon when the 705th Combat Command tank battalion came in to help us. We went with the tanks as infantry, searching for where the Germans were. I remember this little farm, called Kessler's, just next to the Arlon Road. Suddenly, I'm facing this German! I'm looking at him and he's looking at me. I aimed my piece at him and he aimed his piece at me, and before I could get a shot off somebody behind me shot him and he fell straight forward in the snow. I never found out who my savior was.

We were in a little area that was kind of a pine farm out of town about maybe two kilometers, no more. We were there digging in like crazy in that frosty

---

[200] August 1943. The Germans continued the war on the Italian peninsula.

ground. They brought in the mess kits, and the guys that fixed the food. The weather had cleared a little bit. There were German reconnaissance airplanes flying over at about 300 or 400 feet altitude. Then they radioed back to their artillery and then a barrage would come in. Then we heard the drone of Tiger tanks. I was scared by the RAT-TAT-TAT of the burp guns and the awful sound of the Screaming Meemies.

I was in a ditch when a Tiger tank went by. It could have run over me! The rumble was frightening! The Tiger was a big tank and heavily armored, but there was a spot about six or eight inches from the top of the cowling to the top of the tracks. And if you got your antitank gun into that area, it would break through the steel of that side. But on the front was an eight-inch piece of armor that hung down over that tank. Our bazookas could not pierce the fronts or backs of those tanks. An infantryman jumped up on the tank, pulled the turret hatch open, and threw a hand grenade right inside! That took guts to do that! I saw him come back off the tank. I don't know where he went from there. It was difficult to follow each of the guys who were doing their thing because we were all doing *our* own thing. We ran and when we heard burp guns and we hit the ground. Whenever it would stop, we got up, and away we'd go again. It was survival of the fittest. You would protect another guy if he were in trouble, but you had yourself to take care of first.

I threw a lot of hand grenades. I had them hanging on my ammunition belt. I could throw them thirty-five, forty yards.[201] I used them mostly against German foxholes. I killed some Germans that way. Well, I didn't kill them, the hand grenades did.

We respected our German counterparts. They were well trained. They had their cause, and they meant it. Once we got to the point that they felt or knew we had them beat, they altered their opinion about the American soldier. They became more submissive. They made really good prisoners.

After the Malmédy massacre, there were some paratroopers who were pretty damn mad about things and had no way of controlling themselves emotionally. The gun was their answer to it. I'll never forget seeing a paratrooper rifle-butt a German soldier who was laying wounded on the ground. What he did had to be accepted as usual behavior. I think the German was almost dead, anyway. There was a lot of that going on!

It was overcast in the Bastogne area a good part of the time until Christmas week when it cleared. Then our planes got out. One of them dropped a bomb that busted my right ear drum. It was a P-47. Some of our troops were killed by our own artillery. The lines were so ill-defined the gunners didn't know where we were as opposed to the German troops.

---

[201]Mr. Herrington was a professional baseball player, a star catcher for the University of West Virginia. He would ultimately receive a contract with the Pittsburgh Pirates. An injury to his thumb would end his baseball career.

The Army had to keep Bastogne supplied. In the underground command post in Bastogne itself, Colonel Crolls was to be notified if the aircraft had gotten out to help us from the air. One of the non-coms ran into the command post and said, "I hear the drone of airplanes!"

They didn't know if they were German airplanes or ours. They turned out to be our supply C-47s. Many were shot down. In fact I remember seeing a C-47 motor laying in the field where it was shot right off the plane. Sometimes the stuff that was dropped was not dropped exactly where we wanted it to be dropped. The Germans retrieved it. Just about everything you can imagine got dropped. It was ammunition we really needed. We were down to 200 rounds per man. I tried to fire only when I had a target. The artillery had some problems because the larger artillery shells were more difficult to transport by truck. Even though they were transporting some of the things like ammunition in the half tracks and two-and-a-half tonners, these were being shelled, and some of them were blown up. When an ammunition truck blows up, it blows up!

We used houses as battalion aid stations. Replacements cried. They held on to the veterans like sons to fathers. God, they were scared! So were we! But we had seen things before. Somehow we were able to say to ourselves, "OK, this is the way it is, man, now get with it!"

A Jewish boy was very concerned about what would happen to him if he was captured, so he threw his dog-tags away. At that time I couldn't understand it, but after I thought about it a while I realized what this kid was doing was trying to save his life! Guys got combat fatigue. Very non-committal. Non-conversive. Gazing off into the distance. Walking in a daze. Kind of a faraway look, and really having a Hell of a time with their heads.[202]

After Bastogne got liberated, we went into the Colmar Pocket. There was very little resistance there because the German army wasn't what it used to be. The soldiers we saw after we left the Colmar Pocket were mostly old men and young boys. We were right down on the Moder River. The Moder wasn't all that wide and we could hear the Germans talking on the other side. They did throw some real heavy artillery shells into our area, but we were close to the edge of the river and they were going over our heads. It reminded us of ashcans flying through the air.

I got frozen feet in the Colmar Pocket. I appreciated it when the doctor told me my feet were bad and that I had had enough. I was emotionally upset about things, too. I don't remember crying, but I did tell him that it had been damn difficult and that I needed a little rest. He said, "Don't worry, you're going back to England to get those frozen feet taken care of."

---

[202]Even troops not suffering combat fatigue were characterized as having the "thousand-yard stare" as described by Mr. Herrington.

We loaded up in an ambulance from a field hospital and went to Nancy, France. From there I went to Cherbourg. From Cherbourg we took a medical ship to Southampton. From there to Ellesmere, on the southern border of Scotland, a real nice community with a nice big lake and a walkway around it. We went to dances there. The English girls were very pleasant. We used to have hamburgers, and accused the people who were making the hamburgers of putting sawdust in them. A nurse kissed me. In the hospital the guys used to lay head to foot, head to foot. She came in one morning, bent down and kissed me. I hadn't had a kiss from a girl in a long time. I really felt good about that!

I was there for about two and a half months while my feet reestablished their circulation. One evening we were playing cards and I had my legs all bent up on this cot. All of a sudden I felt a very warm feeling in my right foot and in my left foot. Circulation was back! After I got better, I went back and ended the war in Berchtesgarten. Things were wound down by then. We were really on a high. I was pleased to not have to look anybody in the eye and have to shoot them, or they you.

There was one encounter we had with an SS trooper who was in the cellar of this home in the mountainside in Berchtesgarten. The family that lived there thought for sure there was going to be a killing. They got out of the way. We took care of him, then we marched some guys who were with him down over the hill, back to the brig. We had no difficulty with them. It was a pretty impersonal thing. Here they are, put them in the brig, goodbye! That was all there was to that!

While we were in the area, we did a demonstration jump for Churchill. The Army kept us pretty busy. We weren't worried about that anymore! We played poker, we chased girls. There was a resort there, and the ladies used to walk by in their bikinis, pat themselves on the behind and say, "Verboten, Yankee!"

Coming home, we boarded the transport *USS Mariposa*, at Marseilles. We landed in Boston Harbor. They fired water cannons from fireboats. Thousands of people were on the docks. On our dock they were selling ice-cream cones. We got onto buses that took us out to Camp Myles Standish. We weren't there more than a few days, then we loaded on a troop train, and came back to Indiantown Gap where we were interviewed. We had medical exams and psychiatric. I was given bus fare from Indiantown Gap to Weirton, West Virginia. That's where my mother and father met me.

I remember being very happy to be home, but I had an upset stomach for about two weeks. I was concerned and so were my parents. I was screwed up in the head a little bit. Kind of separation anxiety. My feet were still not completely recovered. I had a car, and I went to King's Creek in Weirton Heights to wash it. I drove it right out into the creek, used a bucket, threw the water up and washed it off. I was in my barefeet and they began to hurt, especially the parts that got frozen.

I would stay up with my family and talk through the night. My mom hugged me constantly and cried. We had a lot of conversations about my experiences, especially during the first night home. They did not completely understand. I had to hesitate many times, because I broke down, and so did they. My dad was a tough egg. I don't remember him crying any, but he was upset about it. "Boy," he said, "you must have had a rough time."

Things haunt me. Thunderstorms sound like shellfire to me. I used to say, "Okay, so it happened, so what." But not anymore. Any time something happens that is confrontational or threatening, I have a panic response. There are flashbacks. I was riding an elevator once. It had a glass front and I could see the landscape. I panicked. Maybe that came from looking out the door of an airplane and jumping. I don't know.

When I came back, I immediately signed up to go to school at West Virginia University. There were a lot of veterans there, so there was some comradeship in the dormitories. We got seventy-five bucks a month, all tuition was paid for, books were paid for. I think I adapted as well as most guys. I enjoyed going to school.

These days I join veterans of the Battle of the Bulge and the 101st Airborne Division. I speak to various groups using slides I took on a trip back to Bastogne. It's not something that I derive a great deal of egotistical benefit from, because I know what's going to happen when I show them these things. They say, "Geez! You did all this?" I don't do it to glorify war, but because it is necessary for people to understand what happened back then.

I once went to hospitals in Indiana and Illinois when I was training to be a physical therapist. We were concerned with the emotional effect blindness had on soldiers. We trained them to walk with canes. They didn't have many seeing-eye dogs in those days. My feeling toward them was that it would have been best if they had been killed in the war. That was the wrong way to look at it. Eventually, I came to realize that there is a lot of potential in people who are disabled. I learned that when I became a physical therapist. Maybe way down deep someplace they said, "Boy, I wish I would have died. Don't let God hear me say that!" That kind of thing. I'll never forget one guy who had both legs and one arm taken off. His nurse married him!

After having been in many campaigns, coming home with six Bronze Stars, a piece of shrapnel in my hip, a busted right eardrum and bad feet, and a Hell of a lot of time in a foxhole, I have no concern what the future holds for me. I'm just like a cat. I really had nine lives! I was lucky. Over there, you really didn't want to be a killer yourself, but it was kill or be killed! I remember shooting point blank at German soldiers. Yes, I shot a German. I shot some German people, yes. I think God has forgiven me for killing people. But it was a matter of either you or him. I think I was in a different world when I was doing this.

I was interviewed by psychiatrists at Indiantown Gap when this all was over and we were being mustered out there. He really made me cry, that sonofabitch.

That psychiatrist really brought it home to me. And I think the way he handled me when he talked to me made me think whether what I did was right or wrong, but it *had* to be right. This was just something that *had* to be done. But he was not a combat person. I don't think he understood what Hell the guys went through on the front lines. That psychiatrist bothered the Hell out of me for a while.

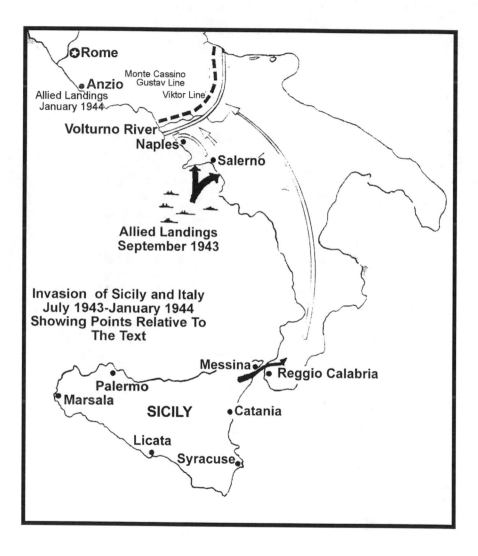

Rome

Anzio
Allied Landings
January 1944

Monte Cassino
Gustav Line

Viktor Line

Volturno River
Naples

Salerno

Allied Landings
September 1943

Invasion of Sicily and Italy
July 1943-January 1944
Showing Points Relative To
The Text

Messina

Reggio Calabria

Palermo
Marsala

SICILY

Catania

Licata

Syracuse

The Kid From Brooklyn

Joseph Kay

United States Seventh Army
63rd Infantry Division ("Blood and Fire")
254th Infantry Regiment
Company G

Brooklyn, New York, 15 August 1926

"We were behind a hill unloading our gear when the sergeant came around and told us to move it out. Some voice piped up, 'Is it all right to load our weapons now, Sergeant?' Then he laughed. That was the moment of truth because we were now at a place where no one would give us a hard time for having a bullet in our rifle with which we could kill someone. All the old rules had gone."

I was eighteen on 15 August 1944. From then until 15 August 1945, I fought as a combat infantryman, earned two battle stars, the Combat Infantry Badge, and returned to the United States in my nineteenth year!

My father was native-born. He died when I was sixteen. My mother was Winifred Brown. She died when I was six-months-old. I don't know much about her other than she was convent-raised. My full name is Joseph Vincent DiPaul John Kay. You can see that I came from a good Irish-Catholic family! My father's name was James Joseph Kay. His father was called "Big Jim" Kay. When my father came along he was known as Joe because he couldn't be Jim: his father had already taken that name. When I came along I was Joseph Vincent so I couldn't be Joe! That's how I came to be "Vinny!"

I dropped out of high school in 1942 and went to work at defense plants. I took whatever jobs were available at other places. There were a lot of pressures that pushed me toward quitting school. I lost my dad, and economically our family needed whatever we could get. But, in a way, the economics of it was more of an excuse than a reason. The family certainly needed my wages, and they certainly got them, but, really, I was disenchanted with school. I had gone the whole route with the Irish-Catholic deal. I went to Catholic schools. I was an altar boy. I was rebellious and unhappy at home because my stepmother and I never had a good relationship. That was probably as much my fault as anyone else's.

I worked in a factory that made wooden ammunition containers. They were intended for use onboard ship, because wood is a non-sparking surface. I worked at that and that was the closest I came to something that was definitely for the war

Joseph Kay (left) with "Bud" Greene (KIA).

effort. I ran through a whole series of jobs. If I was late or overslept or didn't go to work, I'd quit and just get another job.

By 1944 there weren't too many young fellas around but there were lots of girls. As a result I found myself the target of a lot of teasing on the part of many of the young women because there wasn't anybody else. Most of the guys were in the service, so the competition was very slim. Even so, I was not by no means very good at the social game. Even though the girls were willing, I was not much of a Lothario.

The boys my age were outraged over Pearl Harbor. We were convinced that the Axis was dreadful, which in fact they were, and we were going to be sure we won this one. When I heard about Pearl Harbor, I was sitting on the front stoop, playing cards with a bunch of kids. We heard somebody inside say, "Hey, listen! Listen!" We heard the news broadcast about the terrible event taking place. From there on out we were caught up in it like everybody else.

This was Brooklyn, and you know every outfit in the service had a kid from Brooklyn in it. Since Brooklyn had the Brooklyn Navy Yard there was a semi-tradition that young men from Brooklyn would join the Navy. Back then, with permission, you could enlist early, at seventeen. There were a number of boys who took advantage of this. Over the next several years I saw many of my compatriots gradually begin to vanish. By 1944, when I went in the service, there had been a hefty cut in the number of young people still in the area.

For two years we who were left followed the course of the war. We heard about Doolittle's Raid from the *USS Hornet* on Japan,[203] and various other things. We read the stories in the papers and saw the newsreels. We were good targets for propaganda. It was okay to call the enemy "Nips," "Japs," "Slant Eyes," "Huns." Hitler was "Schickelgruber." The real enemy seemed to be the Japanese. "Get them Japs!" That was really the thought at that time. We saw images that came out of China after the Japanese invasion. There was one particular *Life* photo of the little child crying on the railroad station in Nanking that had been bombed.

My stepmother was not anxious that I go into the service. She had a much better appreciation of it than I did, but the young guys didn't take much advice, especially since our whole society had a "Go get 'em" attitude. By the time I came to my eighteenth birthday I signed up and asked for immediate induction. I went in in September. I found a home in the Army and stayed for twenty-six years. The Army took me in hand, it disciplined me, it encouraged me, it educated me. I finally retired as a colonel.

I went to Grand Central Palace in Manhattan for induction. It was a cavernous hall and the line wandered hither and thither and everybody was kind of nervous and naked or down to their shorts. Back in those days we were a little more modest. There was a certain amount of embarrassment and "comparison"

---

[203] 18 April 1942.

and so forth. You couldn't process all the images that were being thrown your way, but I kept them as living memories.

Once in the service I went to Fort McClellan, Alabama, an IRTC (Infantry Replacement Center). Because I was a high school dropout without a specialty, I automatically fell into the most needed category, an infantry rifleman. I was left-handed, and they had to teach me to shoot right-handed. I became an Expert Marksman. Because of casualties and the need for replacements, they curtailed our training from sixteen weeks to eleven or twelve weeks. They gave us a five-day Christmas vacation then sent us to the port of embarkation. We were to replace casualties from the Battle of the Bulge.

Bayonet training appealed to youthful violence. There's nothing like sticking six inches to a foot of steel out in somebody's face and then somebody saying, "Yeah, go ahead! Try it!" We learned some rudimentary Judo for defense and also a way to disable and kill an enemy as quickly as possible. We were taught to kill. That's what it came down to. I thought it was great! A soldier wasn't trained to participate on a debating team. I never felt, "Pity the poor Germans. I can't shoot that guy."

I went over on the *Queen Elizabeth*. As we marched down the dock to go aboard, there were all these wooden rifle cases. They gave each of us a brand-new rifle packaged in cosmoline and wrapped in this green waterproof casing. Before we packed the rifles, we loaded our duffel bags and noticed an additional two sets of woolen underwear. When we got off the ship, they had packing cases at the dock where they took the rifles back. The Army managed to get 5,000 rifles across the ocean without paying transportation charges. They did the same thing when we got to the repo depo. Once we starting sorting out our clothing they took back the two sets of underwear. That was 10,000 sets of underwear without charge! I thought that this was marvelous! Everything that I possessed was either on my back, in my pack, or in a leather camera case that I had picked up along the way. By the time we assaulted the Siegfried Line, I was wearing a set of ODs, my combat boots, my field jacket, my GI sweater, a knit cap, my steel helmet, and a pair of gloves with inserts. There weren't any fatigues or cams then.

We landed in Scotland, and eventually entered France through Le Havre. I really didn't know where I was going until I got to the division replacement center. Then they assigned us to a company and a regiment.

I was scared. But I was scared from the first day of basic training, when my life became a mixture of fear, anxiety, and patriotism. I wanted to be a good soldier, but I was also beginning to learn about and see all these dreadful things. Some of the people who taught us were wounded vets. They told us about the realities of war. They made us more aware of how fragile our lives were.

I didn't arrive in the 63rd until the second or third week in January. I was assigned to a half-empty regiment. The regiment assigned me to a company. I became a scout for my squad. On the line near Sarreguemines on the Alsace border, Squad Leader Clark said, "Show the kid where to go."

From that point on, I buddied up with the people in the squad. We were behind a hill unloading our gear when the sergeant came around and told us to move it out. Some voice piped up, "Is it all right to load our weapons now, Sergeant?" Then he laughed. That was the moment of truth because we were now at a place where no one would give us a hard time for having a bullet in our rifle with which we could kill someone. All the old rules had gone.

By the time we first kicked off for the Siegfried Line, I had been on a few daylight patrols without any action. I had also been subjected to artillery fire of varying intensity. I experienced some sniper and machine-gun fire, but no determined action. We moved down through the dragon's teeth of the Siegfried Line and assaulted the bunkers. We came under small-arms fire from entrenched German infantry units. That experience made a real believer out of me. When we kicked off, we had thirteen men in the squad. By the time we had passed through the Siegfried Line we were down to seven. Two of the six we lost I knew for certain were dead. One died immediately and the other died on his way to being evacuated. The other four were evacuated with shrapnel wounds. One of the guys who died was a big BAR man. I was with him at the moment of death. We were coming up a draw leading up to the emplacement of a fortification. At that point we were subjected to everything that they could throw. The BAR man got hit in a couple different places and I'm not quite sure what killed him. I just remember cradling his head and watching him die.

I don't remember thinking of revenge. I wasn't so gung-ho that I wanted to go forward at all costs in the pursuit of vengeance. I wanted to get the job done and reduce the enemy's emplacements. I wanted to kill the enemy, but I didn't have any mind set of "kill the sons of guns." I was grimly determined to accomplish the task.

We moved out and I left the dead BAR man where he was. We pushed forward and made it through the dragon's teeth. Then we burst through the final fortification. The enemy was withdrawing in good order, fighting a delaying action. We were pursuing them all the while. Sometimes people don't realize that wars stop because everybody is tired. Troops that have made an assault or have been closely engaged, eventually stop or regroup to catch their breath. When we stopped, we went into a defensive mode, dug in and spent the night. Then when we got up in the morning, we abandoned our hole and continued to move on.

Very often they would leapfrog the reserve units through the forward units so that everyday the retreating, tired Germans were faced with fresh troops. We would motor people up in convoys. They would do this for a couple days until encountering the next strong point of the Germans. Then we would engage to reduce those strong points. Afterwards we would continue the pursuit. This is what went on from there on out. Instead of having pitched battles there was a series of skirmishes. That's what we encountered after going through the Siegfried Line around 17 March 1945.

We continued leap-frogging all the way from the Siegfried Line down to the Rhine River, which we crossed in the vicinity of Heidelberg-Mannheim.[204] Mannheim was an industrial town. Mannheim was totally destroyed. It was a contrast to Heidelberg which was hardly touched. It was declared an open city. Heidelberg was a university town of great historical importance.

We went swinging more or less to the southeast until we touched the Danube around Ulm and New Ulm.[205] We barely crossed the Danube before the war ended. We regrouped and moved back into the heartland of Germany.

That was our route. A lot happened along the way. As a grunt your outlook is, "Hey, don't do anything that's gonna get you killed! Don't do anything stupid!" But at the same time, you follow orders and protect your buddies. But it is the NCO and the officers who are going to give the orders and they have to be aware of their men. You don't want to waste your people on something stupid. It was the sergeants who won the war.

Our platoon officer was a godlike figure that I rarely, if ever, had anything to do with. The only time I saw him was when he'd come up to me and say, "Hey, Kay, what's going on?" and so forth. That's it! I had much more direct contact with my platoon sergeant, Tech-Sergeant Murphy, and with my squad leader, Dillon Clark. Clark was very important to me and we became very good combat buddies. As time went on I began to feel a great deal of confidence in his ability to keep my ass in one piece.

Once we were coming up through an orchard somewhere, and I got some fire from this village on the other side of the orchard. I hit the deck behind a tree and managed to smash a little finger between a tree root and my rifle. I just looked at it and muttered a little bit. It hurt, but I didn't realize that I had broken the bone and it grew back crooked. You didn't realize the seriousness of such things at the moment. People who got wounded very often did not understand the severity of their wounds until after the adrenaline shock had worn off. They would often keep firing and fighting unless it was really something massive that put them down and out.

The Germans had Schu mines and they littered the ditches with these things. If you were coming up the road and they hit you with shell fire and you hit the ditch, BANG! We looked for them. Booby trapping in villages was extensive. Most of them were not trip-wire types but dead-pull types. You open a door, BANG!

Most of the German army toward the end was made up of wounded, savvy, old soldiers who were smart enough not to get themselves killed, but shrewd enough to really give you trouble. Then there were old men in reserve units. Then finally there were the Hitler Youth, the young men. They wanted these kids

---

[204]28–30 March, advancing behind the 10th Armored Division.
[205]The 254th crossed the Danube on a damaged bridge in Riedheim 25 April. It repulsed a German counterattack.

to resist to the death. You had to be careful if you came across them because they were fanatical and very often would do stupid things which the veterans would not do. The vets were defending their country but they weren't about to throw their lives away, where the kids very often would.

I remember one time we chased this sixteen-year-old kid into a house. He was really intent on killing me. He really, truly, hated us and that kind of guy you couldn't have running around loose. I hit him pretty hard with my rifle and then someone else came in and picked him up. We didn't stand around and debate, "What are we going to do with this young man?" You take him out of a threatening mode and then move on.

Much of my combat experience was in close in built-up areas. We'd come up on a town and they would fight us from the outskirts. Then we would try to outflank them. We always had casualties, but we didn't have major losses. When you fight in a built-up area the best thing to do is make a high-point-entry and descend. What you don't want is to make a low-point-entry and ascend, because you hate like Hell to go up a flight of stairs and have someone throwing things down at you. If you could, where there were connected houses, you could go along the roof-line, or sometimes you'd blast a hole through the wall so you didn't have to go out into the street. Usually you took two or three guys into a house with you. One would be up, one would be down, and one would stay in place to protect your butt. If you went up the stairs to check things out you'd yell, "Secure!" Another guy might move up there and you'd check out the next floor. Another guy would find the entrance to the cellar and clear it out. It depended on the size of the house. If you're talking about a standard house then a three-man-team was adequate.

If you ran into a tank in a town you'd try to get on a roof with a bazooka, or you called up for antitank support. For a long time our antitank defenses were not adequate because the Germans had the best tanks in the world. In many cases if the Germans committed their armor they ran out of fuel and then it became an armored pillbox and you had to knock it out. If you blew up a track you could keep them in place. First you "fix 'em then fight 'em then you kill 'em!" That was the logic. After stopping them we aimed for the junction of the turret and the hull to immobilize the turret. Then the gunner could only shoot in the direction the gun was pointed when it became immobilized. The nicest solution we had were thermite and phosphorous grenades. It was not a happy end for the tank crew, but the tank would no longer be a problem. The fumes and flame would get inside a buttoned-up tank through the ventilation system and disable a crew. If you could get above a tank, one thing the crew couldn't do was open the hatches and take a look at you, especially when you're shooting at them. Usually we had someone pinning them down in the turret. If you had artillery support and vectored it in you could blow a building down on a tank and bury the whole thing.

The Germans had an excellent antitank weapon called the *Panzerfaust*. We used to call them "horse-cocks" because that's what they looked like, a big penis. They had that hollow charge which would direct all the force through one point.

It was hard to pin down the number of times you aimed at an individual. Generally speaking, you returned fire into an area from which you were receiving fire. Sometimes you were firing at trees, and sometimes you were firing at likely places and sometimes you were actually firing at individuals. I fired at individuals, many times. On none of these occasions did I act like a sniper, where you take your time, coolly checking the wind. I fired from the hip or fired from the shoulder. You might see an individual go down, but you seldom went to check. Sometimes you would advance through the exact place where he fell, and then get to see if he was dead or wounded. I was never sure, anyway, because I was just one of many firing into the same area.

There are two things that every soldier learns. One, it is not his job to tend to the wounded, and two, it is not his job to regret the death of the enemy. It is his job to accomplish his mission. I became hardened to the sight of the dead, especially the enemy. A dead German was just one less German who was likely to kill me. I didn't individualize somebody torn apart, bloody, and covered in mud. With American dead I felt an overwhelming sense of sorrow that I had lost a comrade. If I actually knew the guy, it was much more of an impact. Most of us would rather have been killed than become a burden on someone.

I went through a slave-labor camp, filled with mostly Eastern Europeans. We met these girls at this camp, and like young soldiers everywhere it was time to party, time to dance. The weather, as usual, was not cooperative. We were walking down this road and it was muddy and we came to a puddle, and I scooped up this little girl and carried her across the puddle and we all laughed. We came to another puddle and she picked me up!

I was delighted when the war ended but I knew that I was bound to go to the Pacific. I was an ideal candidate for redeployment. The point system was in effect and you got so many points for your service, you got so many points for combat, you got so many points for decorations, and you got so many points for families. I think the magic number was sixty-five. I had something like twenty-seven. I had my deployment orders for the 2nd Infantry Division and I was going to join them in Fort Lewis, Washington for shipment overseas for Operation CORONET, the invasion of Japan. I knew where I was going and what I was going to do. I had grown pretty cocky and felt seasoned, but it was going to be a new world out there in the Pacific. I wasn't quite sure I liked the idea of making a D-Day invasion because I had heard about the Normandy D-Day from people who had participated in it. Any landing in Japan was bound to be horrific!

We were reassigned around Mannheim, Germany. They divided people into two groups. The senior vets who had sufficient points to be eligible for demobilization, and the junior vets, like myself, who were not essential in some way. I was a rifleman and like most riflemen I was shipped back through the replacement chain with the object of going back to the States, getting a leave, reporting to the West Coast and going overseas again. When I was on the ship coming back to the States the Russians entered the war against Japan, then the Atomic Bomb was dropped. I was euphoric! The war was over! "God, I'm out of it!" I wasn't gonna have to think about making an assault on Japan.

I wasn't in any great hurry to get out of the Army, because now I could enjoy being an adult and away from home without being in fear of my life. I came home on leave and I reported to Camp Swift, Texas, then went to the West Coast in early 1946 to participate in the Army Day Parade. After that I went to Fort Lewis in Washington state, and was discharged there in June of 1946.

If you didn't reenlist within ninety days, you lost your rank. I was a T-5, so after being home for eighty-seven days I reenlisted. I found the civilian world not as keen as I thought it would be. In the Army I had found a place for myself. In the Army I had a job, some skills and a certain amount of respect and responsibility. The best I could do at home was get a job through my brother-in-law in a machine shop. It wasn't the future I wanted.

In September 1946, after reenlistment, I went to Japan, where I stayed for three years as an occupation soldier. I was promoted to technical sergeant. I came back to the States and was assigned to an armored division. When the Korean War broke out, I volunteered and went over with a tank battalion. I was in Korea from August 1950 to November 1951. I came back, was promoted to master sergeant, then assigned to the Pentagon. Then I went to OCS school at Fort Benning. I did another tour in Europe and two tours in Vietnam.

When I came home from Vietnam the second time, I got assigned to the ROTC at the Philadelphia campus of Penn State. My family was living here in the Indiana, Pennsylvania area and the commuting home on weekends was horrendous. I knew that I was actively under consideration for promotion in the next four or five years. I wasn't happy and I couldn't work a transfer so I decided to retire as a lieutenant colonel. I came back to Indiana and picked up my masters in history. My original idea was to get a job as an instructor at a community college, but there weren't too many of those jobs loose. I took the necessary courses to be certified as a high school teacher and at the end of a two-year period I started looking for a high-school job. I became a high school history teacher. I did that for fifteen years and I retired at age sixty-two. I taught in the Armstrong School District.

When I came home from World War II, I was a hero. Almost every vet I knew was a hero, simply because they did what they did. We didn't go around sticking out our chests. We got on with our lives. We all knew that we had done a great and wonderful thing. After I came home from Japan I turned right around and went overseas again.

The way people felt about Korea was that it was a job that we should have gotten done earlier. "Now we have to clean up the dirty mess," they thought. People were generally supportive, but the Korean vets' experiences were not nearly as "good" as what World War II vets experienced. When we "won" in Korea we did not have a feeling of winning anything essential. In Korea you fought over the same damn landscape time after time until it was just a muddy mess! There was a lot of heart lost there.

In the 1960s the military was no longer looked upon with respect. By the time Vietnam came and went people had taken on the attitude, "It isn't brave and patriotic to fight for your country and if you can get out of it, do it. If you can't get out of it flee to Canada." The boys who went to Vietnam were called "Baby Killers" by some of the American population. In World War II the Germans were depicted as the voracious "Hun" and the "Japs" as the "Wily Orientals." We would direct that same kind of propaganda toward the common soldier of our country. When they came back they were treated not with respect but with loathing. Professional soldiers were considered to be nothing but hired killers.

We Wuz No Heroes

William David King

United States First Army
99th Division
393rd Infantry Regiment
3rd Battalion
Company L

Derry, Pennsylvania, 3 March 1920

"The books that have been written, all the books that I've read concerning the Bulge and Remagen Bridgehead, Central Europe, these books, they're all heroes. I didn't see any heroes in the war. The guy that's carrying the rifle on the front lines, for him there's no glamor, and the food is terrible. The living conditions are horrible. You're just like a groundhog and treated like dirt under their feet. And you're expendable. They would much rather lose a man than lose a tank or a jeep."

A guy named Pat Johnson used to tell us stories about World War I. Me and my friends would go out and dig trenches in the backyard. Dad would come home from work and chew me out. The whole back yard was fortified! During the Battle of the Bulge, when we didn't have time to dig very good holes or the ground was frozen, I told a buddy of mine, "Hey, when I was a kid we had better fortifications in my backyard than we do here!" We could have done a better job with them Germans if we had been in my backyard!

It was 1:30 in the afternoon, 7 December 1941, and the family was sitting in the living room. My sister, who was visiting a friend down the street, came in and said, "Switch on the radio!" That's when we heard about Pearl Harbor. At first I thought like a lot of other people, "They asked for it now they're gonna get it." That's what they led us to believe, you know. The fleet is sailing out to meet them. They're really gonna give it to them now. Little did we know, but the fleet was half sunk at Pearl Harbor! I knew we were really going to get into the war, and I was sorry. Because I had signed up for the draft in 1940, I knew very well that I'd have to go and I didn't want to. My number was eventually called up. I was exempt the first time around because I had bad teeth.

It was very sad when I left home, but we celebrated a little and that took some of the sadness off the whole thing! When I told the interviewing sergeant at New Cumberland that I wanted to be in a fighting unit, he looked right at me like

William King and German Civilian

there was something wrong with me. He was probably right. That was the first mistake I made in the service.

They loaded us on another train at New Cumberland. Nobody knew where he was going. The Army *never* told you where you were going. It was December. We got to Effingham, Illinois on the Pennsylvania Railroad. Then they put us on the Illinois Central Railroad heading south. The ICR ran us as a freight train. From Effingham down we had no heat, and it was cold, and the toilets froze up, and the water froze up. They gave us Army rations to eat. When we got into the south, the toilets all started thawing out. The stink! We ended up in Camp Van Dorn, in the lower part of Mississippi, right outside of Centerville about five miles from the Mississippi River.

In camp there were a couple of guys wetting their beds. They put a big tent for them at the end of a big field between barracks where we drilled. We were all laughing at them. One night after we had been in basic training a month, this bed wetter came in in his Class A uniform. I said, "Boy! You're all dressed up! Where are you going?"

"Hey, I'm going home. I'm getting discharged."

It made me wish that I, too, had wet the bed. He was getting out! I discovered the Army didn't want you if you were a little goofy.

It would get cold in Mississippi at night. Camp Van Dorn had been a Civilian Conservation Corps camp. It had tarpaper barracks with no indoor latrines. The latrine for the company was outside, across a little boardwalk. We had two pot-belly stoves for heat, one at each end of the barracks, in which we burned coal. We had big, empty peach cans and used them for butt-cans. Everybody smoked cigarettes. We had water in the bottom of these cans, and a lot of times you'd get up in the morning and the water would be frozen There were no sidewalks, so we built wooden sidewalks to get around in the mud. There was no PX. Camp Van Dorn was pretty close to being the asshole of the world! As new recruits we thought that all Army camps were that way. Later on, we found some camps were pretty nice.

We were down at Van Dorn for six to eight months. After that we went on maneuvers in the Mississippi woods and swamps. We kept company with the snakes and the chiggers. Then they moved us to Louisiana,[206] just outside of Alexandria. We were there for about a month in the woods, playing war.

From Louisiana we went to Camp Maxey,[207] outside of Paris, Texas. Maxey was a well-established camp. They had double-decker barracks, and a latrine right inside. They had PXs and movies there. You could get a pass into Paris, a pretty good sized town, to go to a restaurant. Or you could go to New Orleans or Baton Rouge, if you got a weekend pass. I went to both.

---

[206]16 September 1943.
[207]The 99th "closed in" at Camp Maxey on 19 November 1943, a little more than one year after its activation.

Training was rough on me. I would do ten-mile hikes with a pack almost as heavy as I was. I had the stupid idea that I could do just as well as the other fella. They weren't gonna show me up! That's the way the Army did the whole thing! They brainwashed you into believing that you could do just as well as the big fella.

I hated bayonet training. They made you think you were some sort of an animal. They set up dummies stuffed with straw or hay. They insisted that you growl like a dog. GRRRR! GRRRR! GRRRR! Then you did the thrust. I told a couple of sergeants that I'm not a sonofabitch of an animal! There's a funny thing about a bayonet. It's not very nice to talk about, but when you stick a guy with a bayonet one of the hardest things is getting the bayonet out, because apparently when it goes inside it sort of forms a suction. They taught you when you stuck it in to bang the end of it, then pull it out. That was supposed to release the suction. I always said, "Hey, I'm not sticking nobody. I'll always have a bullet to hit 'em with!"

When I was at Camp Maxey, me and Sergeant Ronnie Johnston[208] got into communications. Basically, it was studying the Morse Code. You didn't pull any kind of KP or any extra duty. All you had to do was be at that school at eight o'clock in the morning and then you were dismissed at four in the afternoon. Good deal! You had these ear phones on and you heard that "ditty-dum-dum-ditty" all the time! It was a six-week course. When it came time to graduate, I said to Johnston, "I'm not graduating! This is the best deal I ever had!" So we failed! We never did graduate from that school! We had our pencils and a little notebook and we'd cross the firebreak into the school. One day we were crossing after lunch and saw Colonel Mackelroy, our L Company commander, who had a job at battalion headquarters. Everybody else was out in the field playing war, digging holes and running around. Johnston and I give him a big salute, and he says, "How come you fellows aren't out in the field with the rest of the battalion?"

"Oh, Sir. We're going to communications school."

"You fellows still going to communications school!? You ought to be teaching it!"

Johnston said, "Its coming! Its coming!"

You talk about goldbricks; we were two of the biggest!

There was always a poker game going on somewhere. I never gambled, or played cards or shot craps. One fella came in, and he had a whole bundle of money. He threw it out on the bed. He must have had four or five thousand dollars that he won. The next night he came in and borrowed twenty bucks from me. He lost that whole bundle in another game.

I said, "Where's that big handful of money you had last night?"

"Ahhh, that's all gone."

---

[208]Johnston would be evacuated with trenchfoot during the Battle of the Bulge.

That's the way it was. One night you'd be rich, the next night you'd be broke. What difference did it make whether you won or lost? There was a war on. What good was money if you were probably going to get killed?

We were at Camp Maxey close to six or eight months. We were notified a week or so in advance to prepare for shipping out, the whole 99th Division. The 36th Texas Division shipped out about six weeks before. They needed some replacements in the Texas Division, so they were going to take some men out of the 99th to fill up the 36th. We were all sweating it out because the 36th was going to go overseas in a week. There were no Gung-Hos. As long as you could stay away from that shooting, the better off you were. A friend of mine from Derry, Paul Fritz, was in I Company; I was in L Company. He came over to me and said he got orders to go with the Texas Division. It wasn't a very nice thing to say, but I told him I was glad he was going and not me. The Texas Division landed at Anzio. Paul was killed on the second day. I was the last person to talk to him. The poor bugger. He didn't last long.

When we got ready to ship out, they put us on alert. We were packed up and ready to go, but we couldn't leave the company area. I said to my friend Johnston, whose wife was staying up at Hugo, Oklahoma, a town about ten-miles North of Camp Maxey, "I don't think we're going to ship out tonight, why don't we sneak off for Hugo?" We did.

We sat in her apartment, drinking a little beer and talking when someone knocked on the door. It was our first sergeant, Selders.

"What the Hell are you doing here?" he asked. "We're on alert!"

"What the Hell are you doing here?" I said.

Selders told us his wife also had an apartment in Hugo. He went to see her. She wasn't there, so he went to Johnston's wife's apartment thinking Selders' wife may have been there, since they were friends. He never reported us, because we would have reported him!

The whole division shipped out by rail.[209] Of course we didn't know what direction we were going, whether to the west and the Pacific Theater or to the east coast. Everything was a secret. We had to keep the blinds pulled down so no one could see that it was a troop train. It was stupid. The Army did so many stupid things. I think the civilians knew where we were going before we did.

When we got into Chicago, I knew we were going east. We went up into Canada, then into Buffalo, New York. We ended up at Taunton, Massachusetts, at Camp Myles Standish. We stayed there ten days. Everything was still a big secret. They told us that all the telephones were monitored. Even in town we had to wear field jackets so that nobody in these towns—Boston, Taunton,

---

[209]At 0130 on 10 September 1944. Eight trains were employed. Mr. King accurately remembers the route.

Pautukett—would talk to you or ask you any questions. You were a marked person. You were getting ready to leave.

I was a runner and radio operator in company headquarters. The company clerk, a fellow named Brewer, had these passes. Half the company would get a twenty-four-hour pass and then the next night the other half would get one. I told Johnston, "I see a whole book of passes. There's no reason why I can't put that book in my pocket and write out our own passes."

So we went every night, Johnston and I. All we had to do is make sure we were back in the morning for reveille. Nobody could understand how Sergeant Johnston and I were going to Boston every night. We'd get the train back out of Boston at about five or six o'clock in the morning and make it back for seven o'clock reveille. They'd all be lined up and we'd be staggering up over the firebreak! When they called our name, we'd yell, "Yo!"

We got some more shots at Camp Myles Standish, and packed all of our equipment. We put our guns in cosmoline so that they wouldn't get rusty from the salt water. They built this two-storey replica of a ship on a lake they had there. They took us all up on the top of this thing, gave us a life preserver, and told us we were all going to have to jump off into the water in preparation of "abandon ship." I told Johnston I wasn't going to jump off. We finagled our way out of that!

One afternoon, they loaded us on a train, took us up to Boston Harbor and loaded us on this converted cruise ship, the *SS Argentina*. We got stuck in the hold. The bunks were about six high[210] A lot of guys got seasick. It never bothered me any. There were hundreds of ships in our convoy. We had air support over the convoy as long as we were along the coast, watching out for submarines. Then after we left the coast, we didn't have any air support, but we did have destroyer escorts. German submarine Wolfpacks were all over the place, trying to sink those convoys. Every day on the ship we'd have "abandon ship" drill. There weren't any lifeboats. I said to Johnston, "What's the use of coming up here?!"

On ship they'd give a potato boiled with the skins on and nothing else. Terrible food! We were up on deck one night and saw these cooks dumping leftover naval-personnel food off the end of the ship. This guy had this big huge tray of Jello and asked if we were hungry. We said, "Yeah, don't throw that Jello over. We'll eat it."

He said to come back every night and anything the Navy wouldn't eat, he would have for us. So Johnston and I and a couple of other guys ate Navy food going over, and the other guys just ate boiled potatoes.

The first ship ahead of us was a destroyer. We followed that destroyer, never varied a couple of yards, just kept the same distance. One morning we saw what looked like geysers up in front, and I told Johnston there must be a whale up

---

[210] The 99th Infantry Division departed Boston on September 29—30, 1944.

there. It was really a destroyer stalking a submarine and dropping "ash cans," what we called depth charges.[211] The convoy didn't stop, but the destroyer did, still dropping ash cans. A day or so later here comes the destroyer steaming past us to take his place in the convoy. Talk had it that there was a submarine and they got it.

We arrived in Southhampton, England.[212] They loaded us on a train and took us to Dorchester, south of Southhampton. Then they put us in trucks, along with all of our equipment. We had two duffle bags, full field-pack, gun, and close to 100 pounds of equipment on our backs. On these Army trucks they had staves across the top where they stretched canvas covers. The canvas was pulled back so they could stuff more guys in the trucks, and the staves were exposed. Ed Matheson had his pack caught under one of these staves, and he couldn't straighten up. He didn't know it. He just thought the pack was that heavy! He was in this cramped position for about five miles.

They hauled us to a camp in Puddletown.[213] Not much of a camp. Originally it was a dairy farm. As was usual in England, it was half rain, half snow. They gave us all a mattress cover, and told us to fill it with old, wet straw. After that we got our weapons ready for action. We could get passes to London but Johnston and me were scared of the buzz-bombs. Instead, we went overnight to a little town in the south of England and saw some of the countryside.

Eventually, they took us back down to Southhampton on a train,[214] where they put the whole regiment on an LST. The boat was crowded, so Johnston and I and some others decided we would sleep up on deck. It started to rain. We were in the middle of the English channel. It's night. We went back down to join the other guys. The bunks were stacked about seven or eight high, and were like hammocks on chains. *Everybody* climbed in, guns, bags, and everything else. The weight was too much. The whole hammock-rack collapsed. Johnston and I ended up on the bottom of the guys and their equipment. We thought we were torpedoed!

Rumors were that we were going up to Norway to make a landing. Instead, we went into Le Havre, France.[215] The port was all blown up, and ships were sunk all over the place. We zigzagged around them. They ran our ship up close to the beach and dropped the front end down. We were supposed to step off the boat and walk up on the beach. We stepped off and—PLOP!—down in the cold water with all of our equipment and weight. There were a few goofball German snipers still shooting, but it didn't come to anything.

---

[211]Few aboard the convoy knew about this incident, which occurred on October 6 (Lauer, 105).
[212]On or around 10 October.
[213]Other units were deployed at the nearby towns of Piddlehinton and Downhouse.
[214]2 November.
[215]Between 3 and 7 November.

We moved out on trucks. The next day we got up into Aubel, Belgium, about twenty miles from the front.[216] They put us in a barn. We could hear the guns going off and see flashes of explosions. They'd keep the cows outside at night but would bring them in the barn to milk them. One morning a young farmer girl was milking this cow and she gave me a squirt of this milk right in the face to wake me up. We both laughed!

After a few days, we left for the front line, to a little town called Krinkelt, Belgium, on the Belgium/German border.[217] We unloaded and marched to relieve this other outfit. We were all clean-shaven, but the withdrawing troops were all filthy-dirty with beards. They had been living in holes. They gave us advice. "Now this hill up here is Rath Hill (we called it Rat Hill). This is a quiet section. The Germans don't bother you as long as you don't bother them. German patrols will come through looking for prisoners. Every night they'll send a shell or two over. We took the hill once, but the Germans chased us off. We said 'the Hell with it!' The Germans didn't want us up there, and they don't want to stay up there either, so stay off of Rat Hill!"

That would have been good advice to follow, but we didn't have any say so about it. That was up to the higher-ups. Company L set up headquarters in a little hunter's cabin. The officers stayed in the downstairs, where they had a potbellied stove. It was pretty nice, in out of the weather. Enlisted personnel drove nails in the side of the cabin so they could climb up in the eaves and sleep. It was warm and dry, but Johnston wouldn't stay in the eaves. He dug himself a hole outside. He was afraid the Germans would shell the building, but the place was down in a valley between hills and I figured there was no way the Germans could drop a shell in and hit the cabin. I said, "C'mon Ronnie. This cabin has been here for weeks and weeks and the Germans haven't blown the thing up."

It was cold and snowing. Johnston was outside in his hole. It was a holiday and I had some cookies from home. We had little individual heating elements for heating cocoa or coffee. I asked Johnston to come up for some Thanksgiving dinner. We're up there having a big time eating cookies and all at once here comes a shell. KA-BOOM! It hit away from the cabin. Then here comes another KA-BOOM! It hit on the other side. They were zeroing in. The next one would hit the cabin for sure! Johnston, when that second shell hit, knocked the stove over, spilled everything, and hustled to his little hole in the ground. I was close behind him. That was the end of Thanksgiving dinner!

I had wired phones to each platoon, back to the Command Post in the little cabin. Shells were always breaking the wires, so it was my job to find out where the breaks were. Sometimes German patrols would come in and cut the wires. Then they'd wait for somebody to come to fix them then grab you.

---

[216]The route was through Normandy to Amiens, through Picardy, Flanders, Bapaume, Cambrai, Valencienes to Belgium, then through Mons, Charleroi, Namur, Liege, to Aubel, some 285 miles.
[217]This is in December 1944, in the area of the twin-villages, Krinkelt-Rocherath.

I said to Johnston, who was still in his little hole, "The wires are out at the 1st Platoon, I'll go splice it together."

He said, "You better take somebody with you."

I said, "There's no Germans around these woods."

I wasn't brave or anything, because I didn't think there *were* any Germans around. I got about 100 yards up and I ran into a patrol of Germans! They didn't see me. I beat it back to the CP and told the company commander there was a patrol of Germans up in the woods. He right away got a hold of a platoon to get some other guys. By the time they got up there the Germans were gone.

There were only three divisions, the 99th, the 28th, and 106th, holding the whole Western Front opposite the Siegfried Line. The First Army had driven up that far, then got low on gas. We were pulling guys off the line and giving them a little rest. They were supposed to attack up around Aachen and bypass the Siegfried line. The higher officials, all the way to Eisenhower, and even Division Commander Walter Lauer, figured that the Germans weren't going to attack.[218] We had them on the run, and we thought the place was thinly occupied. Our division was to protect the southern flank of the attack at Aachen. There were two dams north of our section. The 395th regiment, was to go up and protect these dams so that the Germans wouldn't blow them up. If they'd blow these dams up it would flood this whole area.

They told our company to take Rat Hill. The night before the morning we were going to make the attack the commander said that somebody was going to have to stay in the cabin with the telephones. "Then after we secure Rat Hill," he said, "you can bring the wire and the telephone up to where we are." He made me and Matheson stay with the phone. I was very glad to do it!

They took Rat Hill without too much problem. We decided to go up and see what was going on. We left the cabin and took the wires and telephone. It was night. When we got there the company was digging in. There was a little alcove dug out on the side of a hill. It wasn't even underground. So we waited there. The rest of the company was spread along the top of Rat Hill.

The next morning, December 16th, at 5:30, the shells started falling.[219] Holy Criminy! I told Johnston that it was probably our artillery that was falling short because they don't know we're up here. We didn't think the Germans had all that much. For a good twenty to thirty minutes, they just pounded Rat Hill. I said, "We made them mad all right!"[220]

---

[218]The official story has been that Allied Intelligence had no inkling of the impending attack because no German messages had been sent through code, but rather over land lines. This is challenged and reassessed by Whiting in *The Last Assault*.

[219]The preparatory bombardment lasted until 7:00.

[220]When German shells started to fall, the Americans sensed that they represented more than just the expected harassing fire. The story goes that when an officer phoned his battalion commander and informed him that he thought major German forces were approaching, he was interrupted in midsentence by someone speaking in a German accent—"We are here," the voice said.

We were pretty secure on the side of the hill. There were some fragments, but that's about it. They just peppered the whole thing.[221] None in our immediate outfit got killed. All the time we thought it was our own shells. Word came back that there was German movement. Johnston took me down along this road and stationed me in an old German fox hole. I told him, "If you guys pull out be sure to let me know. Don't let me stay down here."[222]

Finally we got orders to pull down off Rat Hill, where we had good firepower. In the meantime, our company commander, Paul Fogleman, had gone back to regiment for R&R thinking that nothing exciting would be going on. The second in command was a fellow by the name of Lieutenant Neudecker, Acting Company Commander.[223] I was with the Assistant Company Commander, Lieutenant Barr, as his radio man and runner. We got to a certain place and the company took back up into the woods. I stayed there with Barr to make sure that there were no stragglers. There was me, Barr, another lieutenant, and another runner by the name of "Popeye." I never knew what his real name was.

After everyone got in, we looked down, and here comes the whole German army![224] One lieutenant told us to jump into these holes until they went by. But those Germans were no dummies. They got there and followed our footprints in the snow. Every hole they came to they'd stick a burp-gun in and BLLLUUURP, BLLLUUURP, just to make sure there was nobody hiding in the hole. They got Barr. He was all bloody. Then they fired in this next foxhole and got the other lieutenant and "Popeye." Then the Germans came to my hole and I just jumped out. They took my helmet off, then smashed my rifle against a tree. They looked at division patches. One guy said, "Ninety-nine?"

I said, "We are a secret outfit."

Nobody knew about us in the States. We were supposed to be a secret movement, but the Germans knew we were there! The Germans continued the attack. They told me to follow. They left a guy guarding me with a machine-gun. I kept telling them to evacuate me and get me out of there. But they didn't have time. I was laying face-down in the snow. Our forces started to push the Germans back.

I thought to myself, "You know what they do. They don't leave prisoners. I'm going to get it right in the back."

---

[221]An American sentry on the Ardennes front phoned his command headquarters with the report of many "pinpoints of light" appearing in the area of the German lines. These were the flashes of German guns, which consisted of traditional artillery plus rockets and projectiles from railway guns.

[222]In the first German rush, *all* of 393rd Company K, except for one platoon, were killed. By 9:30, the Germans reached the battalion command post. Colonel Jack G. Allen ordered Companies I and L to assemble. At that moment, American 81mm mortar crews delivered a devastating 1200 round barrage forcing the Germans to swerve to the west.

[223]Rolland L. Neudecker.

[224]What Mr. King was seeing was the approach of the 989th, 990th, 991st Regiments of the 277th *Volks Grenadier* Division, moving against the right flank of the 393rd, after 7:00 AM.

The German guard spoke a little English and said, "What are you doing over here? This is my country. Why don't you go home?"

I said, "Hey, I can't go home. I go to run and the MPs would grab me. I can't run. How about you?"

He said, "I was drafted into the German army. I can't run. I run and the SS gets me."

I said, "What's the difference between you and me?"

He said, "Right now I got you captured."

Then the Germans just pulled back and left us! It was our company that came through. I asked our guys what happened to the German who was guarding me.

They said, "There he is."

He had a bullet hole in his head.

They said, "We knew you were captive down there, and we were all shooting at that one guy!"

After things quieted down a little bit, the Germans started peppering us with mortar shells. I jumped in a hole, and who is there? Ed Matheson! I jumped in on top of him, and the closer those mortar shells would get, the closer I'm trying to squeeze down on top of him. Matheson says, "I think I'm shot in the leg."

I told him I'd look at it. He had a flesh wound in the back meaty part of his leg. I told him his whole leg was shot off! He said his wife wouldn't like him with only one leg. Then I told him it wasn't bad. I sprinkled sulfa powder on it and bandaged it up. We had little packages of tablets, about ten tablets, and if you were wounded you were supposed to take one of these sulfa pills, chew it up good, and drink a canteen of water. The purpose was to prevent internal infection. You didn't do that, though, if you had a stomach wound. They didn't have penicillin there; everything was sulfa. He took all them pills and got really sick. We didn't have any water. After I got him fixed up, I looked around and there was nobody. Where's the German army!? Where's the American army!? Everybody had pulled out.

There we were in the middle of the woods, and the first thing we heard were some German tanks![225] We hid. We were behind the German lines for a good eight to ten hours hiding, trying to work our way back to our own forces. We didn't have any guns. Matheson was crippled up. I had no helmet. He had a makeshift cane and was trying to hobble along. We didn't walk on the road, because every once in a while there would be a whole convoy of Germans. I never saw so many Germans in my life. There was incoming artillery, but it was ours. We followed the sound. We got up to this big open field, and saw troops dug in. I said, "They must be our troops. We are going to walk right across this field standing straight up. Don't try to run a little bit then hide, otherwise they might think we're Germans."

---

[225]See Cole, *The Ardennes*, 98.

We just paraded right through the field. They had all these guns aimed right at us. When we got up there, the first thing they did was arrest us. They thought we were German soldiers in American uniforms because there were a lot of Germans in American uniforms sneaking into the lines. They even had American dogtags. I told them "Company L," but the company commander said they heard all that before. I think it was the Intelligence and Reconnaissance platoon, maybe the 394th Infantry. They shipped us back to the headquarters. They gave us a hard time. They were talking about shooting us as infiltrators. Finally, we convinced them we weren't Germans.

The first familiar face I saw in this town was the battalion chaplain, Truesdale. I asked him where Company L was. He said Company L had all been captured or killed. We asked what we should do. He said, "Save yourself, save yourself."[226]

All stragglers, sixty of us, went over to a big building and spent the night. We got a gun and a helmet. This was about the second day of the "Bulge." A friend of mine from Company L, Dinsmore, was there. He said the 393rd was packing up its gear, burning papers, and preparing to evacuate the town. There was a tank battle going on about two miles out. Command figured the Germans were going to be in the town in the next few hours. They were going to leave the stragglers in the building. Dinsmore said we better get out. The rear-echelon troops headed away from the front. We went with them.

It was pitch dark. A shell exploded close to our truck and knocked it off the road. We got onto another, smaller truck. They stopped in the middle of the night and made everyone go into a big building. You couldn't even see the hand in front of your face. The only time you could see is when shells were going off. Everyone was whispering. I told Dinsmore I thought I heard Germans talking on the other side of the building. I still think I was right. Dinsmore and I got out of there before first light. We made it to the town of Elsenborn, a few miles to the rear. Dinsmore said that we should get connected with the kitchen, because if the Germans were coming, Americans would evacuate the kitchen right away. Later on in the day, the division headquarters started packing up. They were going to pull back. The Germans had come that much closer.

There was a warehouse full of Army rations. They were going to pull back and leave those Army rations! Everything was frantic! I told Dinsmore I was going up there and bust open the rations and take the goodies out, all the cigarettes and candy. Dinsmore said he was going someplace else. In about a half-hour, he rode up in a jeep he "borrowed" from the 2nd Division, which was preparing to go to the front. He said he didn't want to wait on the trucks. They didn't move

---

[226]Truesdale, from Pottersville, New York, was truly a remarkable man. During the combat he went from foxhole to foxhole holding services until he was ordered to desist. One evening, he mixed up a batch of pancake batter for the men in an old bathtub. He organized hospital convoys, festooning the vehicles with Red Cross flags. None of these were fired upon by the Germans.

fast enough to get out of here. Meanwhile, it got dark again. We loaded these rations on the jeep and took off. We got into a convoy. We didn't know if we were going up to the front or the rear. The roads are going in all different directions.

After awhile I got a strange feeling. The little lights on the back of the truck in front of us looked different somehow. I said, "Dinsmore! Look at the back lights on that truck. I think we're in the middle of a German convoy!"

We knew that there could be German sentries checking out their vehicles. We wrapped our coat collars as high as we could around our necks. I told Dinsmore to turn off at the next crossroad. He did, and gunned the jeep. Damn if the rest of the convoy didn't follow us! We finally lost them.

I said, "Let's go to Upen." The town was twenty miles from the front line as we knew it originally. When we got there one of our MPs yelled, "Get that goddamned jeep out of here in a hurry! We're under air attack."

We drove toward what we thought was out of town. German airplanes were flying over dropping flares, and lighting up the whole sky. We both jumped out of the jeep and hit the ground. Someone said in English, "Don't move." Everything was confused. I figured it might be one of those English-speaking Germans. I told Dinsmore that as soon as the flares went out "I'd hit him high and you hit him low." He turned out to be one of our MPs. This poor guy never knew what hit him. Thankfully, we didn't kill him.

We spent the night there. The next morning we went into town and had a good breakfast and talked the whole thing over. We were beginning to feel a little guilty that we were running. We decided to go back to see if we could find out anything about our outfit. We didn't really know the expanse of the Battle of the Bulge. We thought it was just a small battle going on in our section. If we would have known the expanse of it, we probably would have gone to Paris, because we both were "missing in action," anyway. I was reported to the first sergeant as "killed in action." We didn't realize that the whole western front had cracked and the Germans were trying to go to Antwerp, Belgium. We went over this big bridge over a dam and asked these guys if they knew where the 393rd Regiment was. They said they didn't know, but for us to get back over the bridge because they had it all wired with dynamite and were going to blow it up in about ten minutes. We found out that the 393rd was going to assemble at Elsenborn Ridge. We found what was left of Company L— 75 guys out of 150. A lot of the guys were lost as stragglers like us, or had been captured. We went up to Elsenborn along with these other companies, and set up a defensive line.[227]

There was a Jewish guy in Company L. He was a fighter. He *wanted* to kill Germans. He carried a Browning Automatic Rifle. I saw him chase a German tank

---

[227]The 2nd and 99th Infantry Divisions at Elsenborn and the 4th Infantry Division and elements of the 10th Armored Division near Echternach would anchor the ends of the American front in the north and south.

"Camerino was a heavyset fellow and he
kept squirming trying to get deeper."

one time with that gun. He was down low and so close to the tank that they couldn't shoot him. For some reason, the tank withdrew! When we were up in Elsenborn ridge living in a hole for a month, nothing to wash with, pretty filthy, Lieutenant Neudecker went back to the rear to a house to wash and shave.

He came back and said, "You feel so good after you wash and shave. I'm giving the order everybody in the company has to wash and shave!"

We didn't have any water, only snow. Maybe there was one razor for twenty to thirty guys! This Jewish fellow said, "I'm not going to shave."

The rest of us washed and cut ourselves shaving with that old, dull razor. Neudecker went around and checked everybody to see that they were all cleaned up. He came to this Jewish fellow and gave him a direct order to get cleaned up before he came around again. So this fellow said to me, "I wanted to fight, I wanted to kill Germans, but if this is the way the American army is going to be, if that's how chickenshit they are, that's the end of it for me."

He took his glasses off and just smashed the devil out of them and went back on sick call. He couldn't see a thing. That's the last we ever saw of him.

It was difficult to dig foxholes. We had these small shovels. When the Germans broke through, we took cooks, or clerks, or anybody we could get to fill in the front lines. One of them, a mess sergeant named Camerino, came up and said, "I'll help you dig, King."

He was as lazy as me. Mess sergeants never did any work, anyway. So we started to dig this foxhole under this pine tree. We'd stop to smoke a cigarette, talk a little, dig a little. We finally got a hole in that frozen ground that wasn't more than six-inches deep. In the meantime, a German tank that sneaked up in the draw down below started with his cannon. We dived for the hole. I got in first. Camerino dived in on top of me. He was a heavyset fellow and he kept squirming trying to get down deeper. The tank gunner kept aiming for the tops of the trees because he knew treebursts were worse than the round itself. Branches and fragments were coming down all over the place. I wasn't too concerned because I knew that all that stuff would have to get through Camerino first. The tankers kept it up for about five minutes, then pulled back.

Camerino said, "That's it, King! That's enough of this shit!" He went back to the Company Commander and said he wanted to go back to the rear to see if he could find some kitchen equipment and set up a kitchen because the guys needed hot meals and coffee. Camerino took off, leaving me by myself. I left, also. I wasn't going to monkey around with that hole any further.

I found another hole. It was full of debris. I cleaned it out and stayed in it for the rest of the Battle of the Bulge. We never moved from that defensive position until we went into the attack and drove the Germans back. We were in defense to hold the north shoulder, protecting a direct route to Liege.[228] Then, Hitler's army ran out of gas!

By 1 January it was over. The Germans started pulling back, and we started moving up. Patton's outfit came up from the south and closed the hole in the Bulge. We fought our way down to meet with Patton's outfit. We went back to Krinkelt and Rocherath. We started to collect our dead. When they died it had been cold. Now the holes would be full of water. The bodies didn't smell, but most of the skin was all shriveled up. We pulled them out and put them on a stretcher, took them and dumped them on the side of the road. Burial details later came up in trucks and hauled them back. One fellow was stiff as a board with rigor mortis. One arm stuck out over the stretcher, and every once in a while it would catch in a bush and flip him off. Some guy said, "I'll fix it," and he just grabbed that arm and snapped it.

"That was an awful thing to do," I said.

"Don't worry about it," he said, "he never felt a thing."

After awhile, they took us back to Aubel, Belgium for a rest. We had been in constant contact with the enemy for close to 2-1/2 months.[229] During the winter fighting we had long underwear. We had combat boots that were like high-top shoes. The uniforms were warm. They were as good as clothes could be when your're living out in a hole in the ground. But nothing could really keep you warm. Occasionally they would bring clean underwear up. Nobody took the old stuff off. They just put the clean on top! We must have stunk like Hell! Everybody had diarrhea. The Army rations kept us opened up. If we were out taking a crap, pulling our pants down in a snow storm, we're not gonna mess around and wipe too well. But, everybody smelled the same! We went for weeks and weeks without washing! When they put us in warm buildings and let us clean up, and when they gave us good meals, we knew they were fattening us up for the next battle.

Food was the main source of our will to fight. Most of the time, we couldn't blame the Army because we were moving too fast for the kitchen to catch up. What they would do while you're moving and you're chasing the enemy and you're walking over the hills and so on, cleaning out towns, they'd say, "Well, the chow's on the way." Before the chow'd get there they'd say, "All right we're moving out! We're gonna chase them up through the fields, the hills and dales and take another town!"

---

[228]The Germans were interested in the small crossroads at Baraque di Fraiture, where they mounted a threat at the same time a tank battle was developing at the Bulge's tip. From this crossroads, the road north was a perfect tank road. Taking the road would allow the Germans two advantages: they could continue to Manhay and Werbomont and onto Liege, or they could wheel west to support the breakthrough of General Manteuffel.

[229]The 99th had by now earned the nickname of "Battle Babies." Lauer writes (160): "Life was good at Aubel, life was great, life was something to enjoy; and enjoy it they did."

By the time the chow would catch up it would be cold. Half of it would be spilled in the jeep which brought the food up in big containers. On one occasion they brought up bacon and hot cakes. They cooked this stuff at three or four o'clock in the morning. Here it is three or four o'clock in the afternoon, and they finally catch up with us! We got our mess kits and they threw in one old shriveled-up piece of bacon, a measly hot cake and hardly a teaspoon of syrup. The rest was on the road or all over the floor of the jeep. It really broke our hearts because we were looking for bacon and hot cakes. Holy Criminy! Troops stationed behind the lines had better food. The officers back there ate like kings. If the food didn't get spilled on the way to the line, it got stolen. Everybody from the landing wharf inland got a piece of the pie, until there was little left for the boys on the line. I suppose they had to keep accounts, but anything could get put down as lost or spoiled.

Sometimes the leadership was as touch-and-go as the food. Captain Paul V. Fogleman, the first of our company commanders, was good. He got it during the Bulge. His second-in-command took it over. That was Neudecker. I don't think Neudecker should have even been in the infantry. His platoon leaders were good, and that's what made him look good. I was with him most of the time because I was acting communications officer. He was no John Wayne!

One time we were in a defensive position during the Bulge. Neudecker and I were in a command post with the phones that were connected to the different platoons. Guys were all hollering over the phones that they wanted support, that they wanted this and that. They figured that the front lines were breaking, and that they couldn't hold.

I'm a PFC, and Neudecker says to me, "I'm going back to battalion headquarters (which was about half a mile if it was that) to get tank support. We need tank support up here!" So he took off.

Here in the heat of the battle, all these officers asking me what I'm gonna do! I'm covering up for Neudecker. I didn't tell them that he took off. I learned later that when he got back to the battalion CP the battalion commander, a fellow by the name of Studebaker, told him if he didn't get back up there with his men he's gonna send him to the stockade. I also learned through a friend at battalion that Neudecker really got straightened out. Neudecker could have called battalion on the phone. He went through the biggest part of the war over there and didn't get a scratch on him, and I didn't know any company commander who went that far. They didn't last too long! After Neudecker, we got a fella by the name of Jones.[230] Nobody ever knew what happened to Neudecker. Somebody said he cracked up. Rumors you know! One of the rumors was they made him the jeep driver for the chaplain! That sounded a little far-fetched to me.

---

[230]Captain Floyd O. Jones.

Jones was gung-ho. He wanted to fight and kill Germans. They said he was a West Pointer. Whether he was or not I didn't really know. Anyhow, he was a fighting fool. I couldn't keep up with that guy. When on the approach march, you have two scouts out ahead of the company. Jones would be out ahead of the scouts running over the hills saying, "I'll find them sonofabitch Germans! I'll find 'em someplace! We'll get 'em, won't we King?!"

I'd say, "Yeah, go ahead! Get 'em!"

Jones was outstanding. He wouldn't ask anybody to do anything he wouldn't do himself. The fact is he would have *rather* have done it himself. I don't know whatever happened to him, except he came through the war OK. After the war was over, we were on guard duty. They were breaking up the whole division and sending them away. I said, "I don't want to leave this outfit. I've been with these guys ever since the beginning."

Jones said, "We're all getting out of it. But I'm gonna take care of you."

After the Bulge they took us up to the Erft Canal,[231] on the Cologne Plain.[232] The Cologne Plain is a flat area of ground that extends across to the Rhine River to where Cologne is, near Düsseldorf.[233] We moved up there at night and were waiting to jump off for a morning attack, so I thought that with all this flat ground, as soon as it gets daylight these Germans are going to see us over here and start bombing us. So I started digging a hole. Someone yelled at me that someone along the road was looking for me. So I went over and here was a friend of mine from Derry, Bricky Toner, from the 370th Field Artillery. He had a panel truck with a radio in it, and his job was to radio back to the guns. He asked me if I was scared. He said, "You're in the attack now, you have to dig those Germans out of the holes."

He said he had a quart of dry gin. He asked me if I wanted a drink and I said, "Yeah."

So we started to drink this dry gin straight. After we got about half of it done, he manipulated his radio and got the Armed Forces Network from England and they were playing Glenn Miller and everything else! We were sitting there drinking up a storm. After awhile I said, "I better see what my outfit is doing." I went out and the whole outfit had moved out across the Erft Canal into the attack.[234] We went to find out where they went, as far as he could go with the truck. I got

---

[231] At Cologne, as part of Operation LUMBERJACK, attacks between Koblenz and Cologne north of the Moselle which began 23 February -1 March 1945, by the First and Third Armies.

[232] At Elsdorf.

[233] A city in the Ruhr, Düsseldorf was a developed industrial complex in which an attacking army could get bogged down. There was a great potential for deadly street fighting as the enemy could protect every inch of every factory and railyard.

[234] 2 March. The 393rd Infantry led, with the 4th Cavalry Group, now attached to the 99th. The units crossed near Glesch, and drove northeast, along the Erft Canal. They secured Neurath, Winkelheim and Buchholz. By 3 – 4 March, units had captured: Allrath, Heyderhof, Barrenstein, Erftwerke factory area, Munchausen, Faurmeiler, Rath, Vanikum Rommerskirchen Huchelhoven, Gill, Sinsteden. Many German prisoners were taken.

out and they were in a small fire fight. I was feeling no pain. I was wandering around yelling, "Where is L Company!" I guess it's true, that God watches over drunks. If I had been sober, I probably would have been shot.

We started across the Cologne Plain and the Germans were running.[235] We stopped at a crossroads, and they started shelling us with 88s. Everybody hit the dirt. I was standing beside three guys, and they all got it, but I didn't.[236] I don't know if they died or not. I wasn't sticking around to find out. The company got scattered with all this shelling. Some of us moved on down the road. We went down along side a railroad track, and there was a passenger train sitting there. It was an industrial town that had a big factory, a big steel mill. There were these broken up cranes laying all over the place. It was a horrible mess. We went by the office of the steel mill, and I could hear Germans talking in there. I thought, "Boy, when it gets daylight, there is going to be quite a good fight."

The company commander said that half of Company L got scattered and wanted me to go back. I wanted to get out of there before it got daylight. When I went by that train again, and got a notion to go in. But then I thought there were Germans in that train. I don't know. I was always hearing Germans talking.

I got back to the crossroads and found a barn and one of our lieutenants. He had rounded up the stragglers from L Company. I told him we were in the town up-a-ways. So we spent the night in the barn. The next morning we did have a little bit of a firefight in this steel mill.

The rest of the trip across the Cologne Plain was not very exciting. We had tanks; we were on cement roads, flat roads; we were out of the forest. The towns were four or five miles apart. You'd take one town and then you'd get orders to move up to the next. The tanks led the way. The company commander asked me if I wanted to ride on the side of a tank. I got on. We rode up close to this next town. The tanks all started to button down, and then they started shooting. Crimeny! Those muzzle blasts were something! We jumped off the tank. The next time they asked us if we wanted to ride on the tank I said, "I'll walk. I'm in no hurry."

---

[235] By 5 March, General Hodges' troops were upon the city of Cologne. Cologne's airfield was defended by sixteen 88mm guns. The guns were depressed to be used as ground weapons instead of anti-aircraft weapons. The fire was not as devastating as it could have been if regular infantry artillerymen had been using them, instead of Luftwaffe anti-aircraft crews.

[236] At Rommerskirchen, when German resistance stiffened. American units were facing the 9th Panzer, the 363rd *Volksgrenadier*, the 361st *Volksgrenadier*, the 59th Infantry, the 11th Panzer, and the 340th and 476th Infantry Divisions. The enemy's lack of success indicated that they were confused and disorganized (Lauer, 172).

Our company was the first company of the 99th Division to hit the Rhine River.[237] The Division Commander said for us to ship a couple bottles of Rhine water back, and he'd ship us a couple bottles of champagne back, which he did.[238]

There was a railroad yard all blown out and there was a couple of steam-engines up there. I said to this one fellow that I bet I could get those steam engines going. We got some steam in this one old German locomotive and got her going and then jumped off. It wrecked. Everyone wondered how those steam engines got going, but we never told.

The Germans were pulling back across the Rhine River opposite Düsseldorf. We were up there from five to ten days. It was like a rest camp. We got kitchen equipment, trucks, and so on. We got orders to move to Remagen[239] across the Rhine River. We crossed the bridge.

In the meantime, Ed Matheson had come back. On the other side of the Rhine River we turned south and went into Linz.[240] There was a big champagne factory there. We were in Linz for an hour or so and they told us we were taking off to chase the Germans out of the woods. We took off, and Matheson disappeared. Someone said he probably got killed because there was a lot of shelling and bombing going on. A week later, while we were driving up through a woods, Matheson came back. The Company Commander asked Matheson where he had been. He said he had gotten lost. Matheson told me he broke into a champagne factory, got drunk and just stayed there!

Neudecker told him to consider himself a deserter under arrest. Matheson was worried. I told him they always shot deserters at sunrise. He got awake in the morning and he had yellow jaundice. I'd never seen anyone so yellow. They evacuated him and that was the last I saw Matheson. From there we drove the Germans back and fought for two weeks in the Ruhr Pocket,[241] a section of Germany where they have all their industry.

We had these stupid gas-masks. They were bulky and awkward and a pain in the neck. After a while everybody started stuffing whatever they could into the gas-mask pouches—apples, cigarettes, different fruits, anything. Some guys even

---

[237]The legendary Rhine River was the last major obstacle facing the Allies in their northwest advance into Germany.

[238]This honor went to Captain Felix Salammagi's (Brooklyn, New York) company. The senior aide, Captain Frank X. Gallagher (Wilmington, Delaware) delivered the bottle of Rhine water, and Salamaggi received six bottles of Scotch in return.

[239]The most famous Rhine bridge of World War II was located at Remagen and misnomered the Remagen Bridge. Its real name was the Ludendorff Bridge.

[240]Around 16 March. Linz, Germany, not Linz, Austria.

[241]The 99th was assembled at the town of Germunden, preparing to deliver a final blow to German forces in the Ruhr who had become encircled by VII Corps and V Corps. The drive commenced on 5 April, and was finished by 16 April. The 99th called it the "Battle of Flak Hills." The area was full of hills, on many of which were German emplacements of 88mm flak guns, now turned toward ground defense.

threw the gas masks away to make more room in the pouches. We were moving through a field when we started to take some mortar fire.

I was laying beside my buddy and I said, smelling the air, "I smell garlic. I smell garlic."

He said, "Yeah, them sonofabitches are gassing us!"

They always told us if you smelled garlic that was mustard gas.

So I hollered, "GAS!"

Everybody around me hollered, "GAS!"

Everybody goes for the gas masks. Out comes apples, oranges, candy, bananas, cigarettes!

This officer comes up and says, "What the Hell is going on!"

I said, "Its gas! GAS!"

He said, "That's not gas, that's garlic. This field is full of garlic!"

These shells were stirring it up. Talk about a dumb Army!

We got into a town where there was a sniper. The other Germans had moved out, but this goof was up in the second story just picking guys off. The company commander said, "Hey, so on and so forth, go up and get that guy!"

So we went up a street, and the sniper shot one guy in the squad. The rest of them fired, and pretty soon the Kraut comes walking out with his hands up. Here's our dead guy laying there, and the German just more or less kicked him. That was the wrong thing for him to do! The squad opened up on that poor guy. Everybody took a whack at him. That was *his* problem! He shouldn't have been up there shooting at us in the first place. I don't know if he was SS or what. You couldn't really tell after what the squad did to him!

The last town we were in was Altena.[242] Our company, back up to 100 guys, captured a whole German division, about 10,000 men with their guns and tanks.[243] The Germans sent someone in and said that they wanted to surrender. We paraded them into town. We stationed our fellows about one every block. The German civilians were crying, and running out and kissing these German soldiers![244]

They shipped us down to the Third Army and General Patton. Talk had it that Hitler was going to go down to his Alpine retreat and make a last stand. We reached Landshut. The war was about over.[245] We could tell because there was nobody left to fight.

---

[242]In the valley of the Lenne River in the Sauerland. Around 15 April the 393rd overran Utterlingsen, Dahle, Vettenscheid, Evingsen, Nette, and Altena.

[243]The surrender was made to the 3rd Battalion of the 393rd Infantry. They captured the 13th Panzer Lehr Division under Colonel von Hauser. This occurred at 1900 on 15 April.

[244]See Lauer, 263 – 264.

[245]On 30 April, 1st and 3rd Battalions pulled up to the banks of the Isar River and 3rd Battalion (I and L Companies) infiltrated troops onto an island in the vicinity of Landshut. German defenses were stubborn. The town of Landshut was captured on 1 May. In Landshut on 8 May, the official announcement of VE day was made.

We billeted in an apartment building right in the heart of town. The residents had moved all their belongings into the basement. Through the course of checking out what was in the cellar worth stealing, I came across this big crock. It was full of eggs with some slimy stuff on top. So I covered them back up. I went up and told Orville Hastler. Orville had been the manager of an A&P before going into the service.

He said, "Is that crock full of eggs?"

I said, "Yeah. It has some kind of slimy stuff on top."

He said, "That's waterglass on top of it. That's the old fashioned way of preserving eggs."

I said, "You mean those eggs aren't rotten!"

He said, "Yeah. They'd be good!"

So I went down there and got a couple dozen, came up and we started frying eggs. Nobody could understand it! Here we are in the heart of a town that had no chickens. Where were we getting eggs? Finally, Captain Jones came into this room and he said, "I know the American army can do almost anything, and the American soldier can do almost anything, but where in the Hell can he find eggs in a city with no chickens?"

I said to him, "Do you want some eggs? I'll get you a dozen."

Every morning I'd get Jones a dozen eggs. I never told him or anyone else where I was getting those eggs! In the Army, you kept your mouth shut. Orville Hastler and I were the only ones who knew where those eggs were.

When we took a town, the first thing we did was get all the civilians and put them in these buildings, made sure there are no soldiers dressed in civilian clothes, process the civilians, then turned them loose. We also looked for people you thought might be sympathetic to the Nazi cause. Most of the Nazi civilians weren't Nazis when the Americans came in. As soon as we left, they'd be Nazis again!

A lot of those Germans, especially the officers, could speak fairly good English. In Bavaria we captured a high-ranking German general. He wanted to surrender to an officer. We had him in this house, and I went to Captain Jones, who was a fighting guy, and I said, "We've got a German officer over there. He's captured but he won't surrender. He wants to give his gun and all that, but he wants to make a formal surrender to a high-ranking officer."

Jones said, "I'll go over and get his gun. If he doesn't give it to me, I'll shoot the sonofabitch!"

While we were talking to him, the general was more or less bragging about how great the German army was. One of us said, "If the German army is so great, how come you're getting licked? We're licking you. We're beating the Hell out of you!"

He said, "The American army is so f----- up it has the German army f----- up! You set up a defensive position and the American army gets lost and comes in behind you! How are you going to fight a war that way!?"

And he really meant it! And I believe he was right!

Twelve and fourteen-year-old kids were mixed in with the older German soldiers. They had grown up being brainwashed by Hitler. We didn't care how old they were. We treated them same as everybody else. If you knew how to pull a trigger you could kill just as good as an adult.

After you checked the Germans out we'd say, "Hey, you can go back to your homes."

By the time they got back, their houses would be looted. I once got a pair of binoculars. On the outskirts of town was a mansion. The German who lived there was one of the high Nazis in control of slave labor for the whole district. I figured that if this fella had binoculars they'd be the best. I took them and brought them back to the States with me. Then, someone stole them off of me!

Of course, the Germans didn't like looting and they caused a little trouble. When you first went in they were scared to death of you because the German propaganda told them that the Americans would kill all the civilians. That was the last thing on our minds! As soon as they found that out they got pretty independent. They wouldn't listen to you. We finally put in martial law.

We were in this house and this poor old German comes back to the house and he didn't want us in there and he was raising cane.

Jones was in there saying, "What's that sonofabitch yelling about!"

We said, "He doesn't like us in here."

And Jones said, "Go out and shoot the sonofabitch! That'll teach him!"

I said, "You're not gonna shoot a poor old guy like that?"

He said, "That'll shut him up! Somebody go out and shoot that old sonofabitch!"

Somebody went out with a gun and when the German saw it, he took off! But Jones was that way. He had no love for the Germans.

About one o'clock in the afternoon we were told to get all the civilians off the street again. We were mad about that. We had already taken the town in the morning. They told us to get them off the street because Patton was going to come and personally take the town. Soon, a truckload of movie-camera guys rolls in. About a half-hour later here comes General Patton riding on his tank, leading the troops. Patton took Landshut with a strictly Hollywood setup. It's a wonder somebody didn't take a shot at him! I didn't even bother to go and look! I was kind of disgusted.

We ran into some Polish people. They were slave labor. The Germans had them in a stockade like a prison camp. When we turned them loose they really went wild, looting and raising Hell with the civilians. We had to go round them all up and put them back in the stockade!

After Landshut, we went down toward the Alps, just riding around looking for Germans. We went into a couple of old castles. When I first saw the Alps I thought they were clouds, and the closer we got, here it was the snow-capped Alps.

We pulled back to Landshut.[246] Then they told us the war was over. The first thing we thought about was getting home. I got to go to Paris five days after the end of the war. I was always interested in history and things, but I didn't see a doggone thing in that town except beer joints and a couple of shows. Finally, I thought I better see something, and I took a paid tour. They took me to Napoleon's tomb, to Notre Dame Cathedral, the Eiffel Tower and Arch de Triomphe. In about three hours I saw more of Paris than I had in the whole doggone five days. At Napoleon's tomb this guide said, "The reason we have these wooden walkways over top of the marble is because the German soldiers had hobnailed shoes and they would scratch up the marble."

Then he said, "The German soldiers were very good tippers."

I thought to myself, "You sonofabitch, you don't care what army's in here. You're showing them around. Today it's the Americans. Last year it was the Germans."

They broke up the 99th Division. They sent guys to all different divisions. By then, I didn't want to leave the 99th. I'd been with those guys for so long! True to his word, Captain Jones took care of me. He got me into the 90th Chemical Mortar Battalion. I went down to this rallying point in Nuremburg (Nürnberg). The 90th was a far cry from the infantry. Those guys threw away enough food to feed a whole company. The first morning I went in to breakfast and saw gigantic skillets filled with frying eggs.

The fella says, "How many do you want?"

I said, "What do you mean?"

He said, "I mean how many do you want! Quit your bullshit!"

I said, "Well, give me three." I went a little bit farther and the fella who was cooking pancakes said, "How many of these do you want?"

I said, "Give me a half a dozen."

"All right, come on!"

I loafed around there, and after four or five days I wondered what I was supposed to be doing in this outfit. So I went up to the colonel and asked him what I was supposed to be doing. He said, "You came out of the infantry, didn't you. You came across Europe with the 99th Division? You did enough!"

I never did a stick of work from that day until I got out of the Army. L Company originally had 150 men. When the war was over there were only seven of us left from those who went into Le Havre, France. They shipped us to the North Sea coast, to Camp Lucky Strike. We waited for a couple of weeks until our ship came in. I came home one the *SS Manhattan*, to Boston. A boat that came out to meet us. It had a band on it. Flags were flying all over it. They loaded us on a train there and took us back down to Camp Myles Standish. As soon as we got

---

[246]Near Moosburg, site of a prisoner of war camp. Landshut and Moosburg were opposite flanks of the 99th's zone of advance along the Isar River. The area was heavily defended.

there, we went into this mess hall and they told us we could have anything we wanted. I got a chocolate milk shake. Most other guys ordered steaks.

They gave us a forty-five-day furlough to go home. The war was still going on in Japan. We were told to report to Columbia, South Carolina, Fort Jackson. We went down there for a day or so, then I went back home on a furlough.

After the furlough, I went back down, loafed around, and came back home. August came around and the Japs surrendered. There was nothing to do at that camp. I was coming back and forth between home and camp, but I was running out of money. They shipped some of us to Indiantown Gap in December 1945. Then I got discharged and came home around Christmas, on a train.

In Greensburg I got a local train. My father was the conductor. He broke up when he saw me. We got off the train in Derry and walked up the street together. My wife was my girl friend then and she lived in Latrobe. I went down to her place in Latrobe and she was decorating the Christmas tree.

I walked in and I said, "I'm a civilian! I'm through with that military stuff!"

I jumped right back into civilian life. No problem at all. I had bought an automobile in 1941, and my sister drove it while I was in the service. So, I had a good car and a couple bucks from the 52/20 Club in my pocket and I enjoyed myself.

Eventually, I got a temporary job as a mail carrier on an RD route. Then I got a job on the Pennsylvania Railroad as a locomotive fireman. I worked that job until 1949, then I transferred over to a Block Operator. I worked on the railroad until I retired in the 1980s.

You know it was fifty-years ago, and there's a lot of things I'd like to remember, but I can't. The 99th Division has a reunion every year, and I've been to quite a few of them. I never see anybody who was in L Company. When the war ended I thought, "Well, I made it through this sonofagun and didn't get shot!" I lost a lot of buddies, but I made it!"

I really didn't have any ideals about the war. It was mostly a matter of survival. You got as much on your side as you could, including religion. I went to services. I don't know if I got anything out of them, but anything I could get a hold of as far as the luck went I tried! We had a guy who was always reading the Bible. He never cussed like the rest of us. After the first or second shot that was fired up in the Bulge, he was killed deader than a door nail. I thought that there was a fella who was a real nice, good, honest and religious fella, and he gets shot. I thought if there was anyone who would get through that war it would have been this fella.

It was more like making your own luck. You know, every battle you would go in there would be so many casualties. You'd come through that without a scratch and think, "Well, probably the next one I'll get it." You go through another one and you come through that, and there's so many casualties there. You figure, "I must be pretty lucky. My luck's gonna run out sometime."

After each fight your chances got worse. I was advised before the Battle of the Bulge by a fella who said, "The only advice I can give you is when you're going along the road, when you're in the approach march, just keep your eyes peeled along the side of the road for a little ditch, just something. Always be watching for something like that. Then when you hear them shells coming, you don't need to look around for where you're gonna hide. You just dive for that."

I hear about guys having nightmares about the war when they got home. Some still do. I sometimes dream not so much of the battle, but of them trying to draft me into the Army again! I try to explain to them in my dream, "I'm too old!"

They say, "We're going to take you right into the Army again!"

I didn't like the military. I never liked people telling me what to do, when to go to the bathroom, when to brush my teeth. It's rotten! I don't think much of war. I guess you realized that! I guess people in the rear echelon who weren't under fire probably had a different idea altogether. The books that have been written, all the books that I've read concerning the Bulge and Remagen Bridgehead, Central Europe, I don't think any of them portrayed really what war was like. These books, they're all heroes. I didn't see any heroes in the war. The guy that's carrying the rifle on the front lines, for him there's no glamour, and the food is terrible. The living conditions are horrible. You're just like a groundhog and treated like dirt under their feet. And you're expendable. They would much rather lose a man than lose a tank or a jeep. The hardship and the worry about being an infantryman at the front!

It's not really nice to say, but you more or less were glad it was them and not you. You hated to see someone get killed. You never got used to death, but it was far worse to see some poor bugger laying with his stomach blown open or half an arm blown off, crying in pain. We all wanted the magic bullet between the eyes rather than have that happen.

"I Guess We're Soldiers, Now?"

Alex ("Howitzer Al") Kormas[247]

United States First Army
69th Infantry Division
879th Field Artillery Battalion
Headquarters Battery

Cleveland, Ohio, 19 May 1921

"The dead must have been some part of a unit caught in the Bulge. We looked pretty dirty and crummy, but compared to these guys we dressed well. There was this one guy sharpening his knife on a whetstone. I'll never forget that sonofabitch. He said, 'Half of you guys are going to be dead.' When we got back, we rested for the remainder of the day and began combat after that. We learned that no matter how much training we had combat was different. I saw many frozen, dead Germans. That was the first big scare that I got. Another one was when I once went into the basement of a house. There were three young Germans laying under a couple of blankets. Their guns were upstairs. I noticed that their faces had a very pale, olive color, indicating that they had froze to death. I got out of there. Really, I was down there looking for some wine, because every German house had great German wine."

They called my father Nick the Greek. He owned a couple of restaurants. He passed away just before the Depression. Who knows, we might have become famous restauranteurs. My people came from North Macedonia. There's Bulgarian Macedonia, Greek Macedonia, and Albanian Macedonia. They all hated each other! My mother was Stella Chase. It really couldn't have been that last name, but the immigration man just wrote down what he thought it sounded like.

I was just an ordinary kid. I thought that everyone was poor. When my dad passed away, we lost the business and had to move to a poor section. After that we'd move every couple months because we didn't have rent money. There was my mother and five kids dragging the furniture around.

School was a struggle. At the beginning of the year we got a new pair of pants, a couple pairs of shorts, and a sweater that would last until summer. In the

---

[247]Mr. Kormas' oral history is supplemented with material he wrote for his division bulletin.

"Howitzer" Al Kormas: Camp Shelby, Mississippi, 1943

summer, we would go to the barbershop and get "baldies," because the haircut would last longer. We got two pairs of tennis shoes, a cheap pair for week-time use and a pair of Keds for Sundays. The cheap shoes cost forty-nine cents; the Keds cost eighty-nine cents.

The Shopping News came out two or three times a week advertising items from department stores. I got the route. One Christmas day, a woman on the route gave me two homemade donuts. I took them home and they became part of our Christmas dinner! One Thanksgiving Day we had potatoes, onions, tomatoes and maybe a pound of hamburger. I don't know how many times we asked, "Aren't you eating, Mom?"

"No," she replied, "I ate mine already."

It took me a long time to realize what was going on. That was the reality in those days. We made it by hook or crook. I think it made us better people for it. We realized the value of the things of life.

When I was eighteen, I lived near a hospital and dated some of the nurses from the nursing school. There was a confectionary across the street. Drinks were a nickel. I took dates there, got one drink with two straws, and we would share the drink. I was in a booth with one of the nurses when news of Pearl Harbor came over the radio. There was dead silence. I looked at the girl and she looked at me. We realized that our lives were going to change forever. I will never forget that moment. I felt fear.

Before the war started for us, things were going pretty good. We all got jobs making supplies for Britain. I was feeling pretty good until I got my draft notice. I got a cheap, mimeographed paper saying that I had been "selected by your friends and neighbors." I had to report on a certain day. I started to cry because my brother had already gone in. I had a month to prepare.

I reported to an auditorium in Cleveland where they were examining 400 guys a day. They spent all morning examining you. Then they took you out for a lousy meal. On the way back to the auditorium, all the office girls were standing around. "Don't worry. Be quiet. We'll get you processed," they would say.

They called three or four guys out who looked like football players. They got rejected! The hours dragged. At about 5:00 p.m., the sergeant asked us to be quiet. After he swore us in, his attitude changed. He really spieled out a lot of cussing. We were in! They gave me a week to prepare. Whether or not you were ready by then, they shipped you out.

My mom said, "Tell them that next week is your birthday, and you can't leave on that day."

I wasn't very bright. I told my sergeant about my birthday and he said, "Yeah! I'll speak to the major about it."

My mother asked, "Did you get the date moved back?"

"No, Ma. If I don't go on time, they are going to lose the war."

"Well, I'll call them!"

"Ma, please don't call them! I'm in enough trouble."

It was horrible when I left. My sisters had said goodbye early and headed off to school. My stepfather said good-bye and left for work. My mother and I just sat there at the table until it was time to go. I had my little brown bag and about three dollars in my pocket. They told us to take as little luggage as possible. I was trying to say goodbye and she was hanging onto me. She went down when my little brother left, but she realized that it was better to say goodbye at home. She wished me Happy Birthday. I got to the corner, turned around and saw her on the porch. I waved goodbye.

I was scheduled to leave Cleveland Union Terminal downtown at 12:30 p.m., but we left about 3:00 p.m. Some of these mothers were there for nearly three hours. The FBI was there to make sure nobody went AWOL. We finally got on the train. At the first stop a bunch of guys from Elyria, Ohio were waiting outside a saloon that was next to the station. It was a hot, muggy day, and they had been left unsupervised. They got on the train totally drunk. We got down to Columbus. We thought we were going to board some busses, but instead they walked us over to Fort Hayes, an old Civil War barracks.

We were still in civilian clothes. When we walked into the fort, we saw guys who had been there a couple of days. They assigned us to these big barracks. We had a couple tests and later some shots. Word got around, "Wait until they get you with that square needle."

They lined hundreds of guys up across the gym. They used the same syringe, but changed the needles. They said, "Keep your hands on your hips and just keep walking. If a guy falls down then just step over him." A few guys fell.

On the second day they gave us uniforms. By this time they had us singled out near this long table with rags and clothing on it. They gave us two empty barracks bags, one marked A and the other B, where we put all of our stuff. They told us, "Stand back and don't dare touch that counter."

We moved along with our bags. If a guy told you to put it in your bag then that's what you did. Whatever you picked that's the size shirt you got, and so forth. Most of the time the size was pretty close to your own. At the end of the line, they gave us ankle-high Army shoes. They were big and heavy. The test was to pick up one foot this way and pick up the other that way and those were your shoes. We got two pairs. I went back to where I started and tried to sort some of this stuff out. I tried the clothes on for the first time. The uniform didn't fit. There were tags all over the stuff.

Then we went on to tests and interviews. A score of about 117 would qualify you for officer's school. I think that I hit a score of 127. It didn't mean anything because they had all the officers they needed. After a day they started calling guys out for KP. They had these tremendous mess halls which served a few thousand guys. Some guys were working and others were standing around with shotguns. The workers, we found out, were guys being punished for going AWOL or whatever. If you were there Friday noon and you were not called out for KP, then you could get a pass to go home for the weekend. On Friday morning we were sweating it out. Noon came around and I called my mother and told her, "I'm coming home for the weekend, Ma."

Half an hour later we got notices saying, "This whole area is locked off. You're shipping out. Listen for your name." The phones were shut down, too. There were hundreds of names there, including mine. Everything was a big military secret, so I couldn't call my mother back. I explained the situation to the sergeant and asked him if he would mind calling my mother. He said he would. So I wrote the number down and gave it to him, but he never called. I can imagine how she felt.

The train arrived Saturday, about 4:00 a.m. We sat on our A&B bags. At 8:00 a.m. we were still there. Finally we got on the train. All the shades were drawn. They told us, "Don't you dare pick up those shades."

We went south, south, south. We were all apprehensive, suspicious. The sergeant in charge of the train walked back and forth. They had a clever way of feeding us. The mess car was right in the middle. They would take the guys from one end and walk them all the way back to the other end and let them get their food on a paper plate as they were walking through.

We speculated that we were going to Keesler Air Field in Biloxi, Mississippi which was the basic school for the Air Force. I thought, "Well, okay, I'll be a live coward."

Carefully, we backed into the swamps. Then the sergeant came down and said, "All you guys thought that you were going into the Air Corps, but you're really going to the infantry in Camp Shelby, Mississippi."[248]

We called it "giving us the shaft." It was crude humor. You could hear a pin drop on the train. They put us on trucks and took us to Shelby. The barracks were crude huts that held twelve guys. The sergeant in my barracks had just come back from the South Pacific and he was a little whacked. He told us, "In six months half of you guys are going to be dead. Then six months after that the other half of you guys will be dead. I'm lucky that I came back!"

Shelby was known as the "Asshole of the Camps." We didn't know until later that it was the biggest Army camp in the country. It held about 70,000 guys. Hattiesburg was about twelve miles away. We weren't very welcome and the way some of our guys behaved I could see why. It was a miserable area. A day or two later we started training. We didn't know how to put our leggings on or how to put our packs together. We wore our leggings over our boots. I don't know why the Army had them in the first place. Tents were this way and that way, falling down. It was like a Laurel and Hardy[249] movie, but we soon learned. Eventually we got to the point that we could do things in the dark.

---

[248] The 69th was activated at Camp Shelby 15 May 1943.
[249] Stan Laurel and Oliver Hardy, famous comedians, popularly known as "Fatty and Skinny."

There was some crazy stuff going on at Shelby. "Streaky" Wilcox got the latrine detail. After cleaning the latrine, he assembled twine and nails and went to work rigging up all the toilet seats so he could yank these strings and all the seats would come to attention. At inspection he said, "Latrine ready for inspection, Sir!"

All the seats snapped to attention. The officer said not a word nor did he change his expression. He and Sergeant Ed Stark quickly left. Nevertheless, Streaky was shipped out on the first opportunity!

Eventually, I was put into K Company of the 271st Infantry. The first night I heard some guys crying in their sleep. The first couple of days we didn't talk to each other. We were all wondering what we were doing there. About the third morning the first sergeant called me out after breakfast and told me to come to his office. I was scared to go in since I thought that this meeting entailed some kind of punishment. He told me, "Look, you don't belong here. You belong in the artillery. It was a mistake. Here are your papers. Be up on the corner about 11:00 with your A&B bags and they'll pick you up." I went to the artillery detachment that was at Camp Shelby. The guys in the barracks wouldn't talk to me and I don't blame them. The truck was about a mile away and I sat up there in the corner sweating bricks. Later I was glad, because Company K got slaughtered in Europe! We backed them up with artillery.

I wanted to go home to mother, but we knew we were going to be on our way. Everything was hush-hush when we left Camp Shelby. The whole town knew where we were going! The county had to make links for railroads, railroad cars, and trains. Word got around. The Army gave us a Thanksgiving dinner before we left. Since we were training for the Pacific, we figured that we were going to the jungles. Then we started going northeast. We thought that we'd probably go to New York then go around South America to the Pacific. We stopped in this small town to let a priority train go through. My buddies and I saw a liquor sign. Juggy Powers asked these sixteen-year-old colored kids, "Could you kids get us some liquor?"

"Yeah. We always get liquor for the troops. Just give us the money."

So we gave them about thirty bucks.

"We'll be right back."

The kids started running and kept right on going. They took off with all the money!

On Thanksgiving morning we pulled into Chester, Pennsylvania. It was a cold day and we were all homesick. There were all these homes along the tracks. Fathers were out there with bottles and mothers showed you big turkeys. We pulled into Camp Kilmer that Thanksgiving Day.[250] They gave us twenty-four hours off in New York. One of my close buddies had a girlfriend who worked for

---

[250]23 November 1944.

"In the morning, none of us ate the scrambled eggs."

the Manhattan Project.[251] Nobody knew what it was, not even the workers. This girl had three friends, so my buddy arranged a gathering for all of us. We pooled our money, but one guy, who was at least slightly drunk, handled it. We got into a Packard and headed for New York City. Before we left they took all insignia away. It didn't matter. The civilians knew, anyway. The cabbie, a real New Yorker said, "Yeah, you guys from 69th are from Shelby. Don't talk, that's okay."

My buddy told us to call him about 3:30. We'd meet the girls and go out for the evening. We didn't get a room. Instead, we got smashed! We were still smashed when we met the girls. He kept bawling us out. Then, once he started drinking, we went to Club 21 and enjoyed the rest of the night. People kept buying us drinks. My buddy proposed to his girl. She accepted. They never got married, but that was some night. He got a Dear John letter. He couldn't stand up. She said to me, "Honey, will you please take Dave to the men's room?"

We slept on the floors of this apartment. At 6:30 a.m. we were down at Penn Station where we said goodbye. It was emotional.

Our last night in Kilmer we were restricted to an area, but I, "Bigfoot" Parker, "Filthy" Gray, "Juggie" Powers and "Shorty" Hartman got caught drinking beer in an off-limits PX. We were marched under escort over to a large mess hall and put to work. Every time the mess sergeant separated us, we would be together in five minutes retrieving pitchers of beer we had stashed in different places. Finally, in desperation, the sergeant told us, "I know you are shipping out tomorrow morning. I will give you an easy job. Just do that, and I will not bother you again."

To this we all agreed. We were in a room and we were to crack eggs into large GI cans for breakfast. This was for a few thousand men. Somebody yelled, "Fire mission!"

We all proceeded to send a few eggs crashing into a wall. In the morning, none of us ate the scrambled eggs, since many went into the GI cans, shells and all. The men seemed to enjoy them!

When we left Kilmer, a train took us to the Staten Island Ferry out of Bayonne. We were so jammed together that if our noses itched we couldn't scratch. The officers were upstairs in RHIP (Rank Has Its Privileges). When we arrived at the dock there was a big ship called the *SS Lejeune*, a navy boat named after Camp Lejeune. It was a captured German liner from South America. When I looked at that thing I was shocked. The gangplank had a steep angle to it. Sergeant Stark blew his whistle and we formed ranks. "Mail Call" Hoch, the battery clerk, carried all of our 201 files in a box. He started to falter. I carried it the rest of the way. He never said, "Thanks, Buddy!"

---

[251]Code name for the American development of the atomic bomb. The name was taken from the first office in New York City that formed part of the Manhattan Engineer District.

They got us in! When we got underway, everyone ran out to see the Statue of Liberty because we were afraid we would never see Her again.

To speed things they had these sailors who would grab you and throw you in a bunk. The bunks were a little bit more than six-feet long, a couple-feet wide and maybe about fourteen-inches in between. We had to fit everything in there. They kept loading men for about three days and nights. We ate twice a day. It was a Navy ship, so we thought the food would be good. There were a couple-thousand sailors onboard. These guys sat on benches where they got eggs, nice biscuits, and sausage. When they got to us, they gave us wieners and beans. By the time we got to England, the wieners were green and the beans were awful. The coffee was horrible. It was tough going through that darn Navy mess hall watching the sailors eat like that. We starved on that ship and when we'd look on the deck above we'd smell food. Parker was an ox! He was about six-six and wore size seventeen-and-a-half shoes. He said, "Let's go get something to eat. Forget them!"

Five of us went up there. There was a sign that read, "Chief Petty Officer's Mess." When we opened the door there was a passageway with paintings and lights all over. We went through some swinging doors. Four chief petty officers sat at each table. Filipino stewards were fixing their breakfasts. They looked at us, but we just picked up some food and left. We had toast, meat, and eggs. The next day they had a Marine guard on the door!

We were allowed to buy a box of Ritz crackers or Hershey bars to keep from starving. We had about 9,000 troops on board and facilities were very limited. If you wanted to go to the bathroom, you sat on something like the gutter on the roof. There was a long trough which moved right along with the ship. If you weren't careful then you would get a wet keister. Some guys sat and "things" dropped down on other guys, who would holler and cuss. The water was so hard you couldn't shower. We all smelled, anyway. The guys did things with grace and humor.

I got called to KP one day. They took two artillery battalions to do all the heavy work. So there were about three of us put down in a room with four-wheeled skids full of six-pound cans of Spam. We used meat cleavers to open the cans. It got to the point that we couldn't hold the cleavers because of the grease. I never ate SPAM again!

We got into Southampton late in the afternoon.[252] A bunch of English stevedores were working the docks. It finally sunk in that we weren't going to the Pacific. They blew a whistle and all of a sudden the dockworkers disappeared. It was tea time! They came back half an hour later. We stayed aboard that night. Some of the guys blew up their life preservers for pillows. Most of them leaked!

We finally debarked and got on a blacked-out train. We weren't supposed to touch the shades, but we peeked anyway. At the stops girls were laughing and

---

[252] 12 December 1944.

giggling. We unloaded at night in the middle of nowhere, and around 2 a.m. we got to this old, castle-type place.[253] It had no conveniences. The question was where were we going to sleep? The beds were made of two-by-fours, steel strapping tape, and old mattress covers full of moldy straw. That was it. There were no officers, so about 6:00 a.m. guys started to get up. My buddy, who had been in England before, said, "Let's go. Everyone else is going to town."

At 9:00 a.m. we went to a Barclay Bank and converted some money. At 10:00 a.m. he said, "Come on, Al, let's hit the pubs."

When we walked into this pub, there was this old British lady playing the piano. As soon as they saw us the old people said, "There's a couple Yanks." The lady played *Roll Me Over in the Clover*. I got embarrassed and laughed. We were gone all day and returned just in time for supper. The two guys that came in after us really got in trouble. That was our initiation in England.

Our enlisted men made more money than a British second lieutenant. Naturally, the girls hung around the Yanks because we had money, but also because we were very aggressive compared to the English guys. The English girls said that the Englishmen took them on six dates before they'd ask for a goodnight kiss. Americans would take six minutes. The pubs were fantastic, especially the dart games. Englishmen carried their own darts. The Yankees would go up there and beat them at their own game. Oh, they'd get mad! On top of that, our dates were British girls![254] The average British citizens, at any rate, were nice to us. Of course, they would tell us, "You Yanks! We've been carrying the ball for so long."

Our favorite pub was the "Jolly Bird." One night I was escorting an ATS[255] girl back to her barracks. My buddies were following, catcalling. I yelled for them to wait while I walked the girl to her door, but they got lost in the fog. I couldn't catch up, and got lost myself. It was like a Sherlock Holmes movie. Finally, I heard footsteps. It was a policeman, a "Bobby." He took me back. I gave him some cigarettes for himself and some candy for his kids. I yelled at my buddies for leaving me. They only laughed.

We would go over to Newberry C-47 base. We got some old cargo chutes there that had two-inch felt bottoms. We converted these into our fartsacks. Stark came around and said, "I don't know where you guys got these, but I want one!"

And he did!

I'd go to Newberry quite often because I drove our pilots there. I'd bring along some of the guys and park in front of a large mess hall where there were big signs saying "No Parking." There would be a hundred guys in line, but we'd just saunter in. The people in line just moved aside and avoided eye contact. I think they thought we were some sort of frontline killer troops. At our own mess hall

---

[253]Brock Barracks, Reading, the home of the Royal Berkshire Regiment.
[254]To many of the British males, American military personnel were "Bloody Yanks," who were "Oversexed, overpaid, and over here."
[255]Auxiliary Territorial Service.

it usually was a spoonful of this and a spoonful of that. But at Newberry we really ate. There was ice cream, bread, jam, anything you could think of, and as much as you wanted. When we left, we would fill our pockets and helmets.

On our last "raid" on Newberry, we put on quite a show. We mounted my .50, radio, gas cans, put shiny, new bullets in the gun. We also mounted a carbine rack and wirecutter. Those Air Corps men just wondered at us. We gave them no conversation at all!

Most of the time the English didn't have much food. I'll never forget Patricia Hutchinson, my girlfriend. Her mother worked in a cookie factory, and Patricia worked in a bullet factory until 9:00 p.m. I would pick her up at work and buy her a single drink before the pub closed. Then we would go and buy some fish and chips, which her mother served up with some tea. They had a little fireplace and maybe two or three pieces of coal. They didn't have stockings and their legs were always blue. Her mother could really slice thin bread. I gave them some immense, orange, nylon, cargo chutes from the Newberry base. Pat's mother made underclothes from them.

On Christmas Day, Filthy and I had KP. We served mess for two battalions, about 1,000 guys. We had all the turkey we wanted. My buddy Gray got us some beer. We were doing pretty well, but what a filthy, depressing kitchen it was. Sergeant Payne, the mess sergeant, was exasperated with us. I still think Fowler the Cook deliberately burnt the chocolate pudding in a large stone pot and made me clean it up. We had a lively discussion about it! That night I was going over to Patricia's house. I picked up a twenty-five pound turkey and threw it out in the snow in the back. I also threw out fruit and packages of tea. When I went to the girl's house, the mother asked, "Do you mind if I invite the neighbors?"

I said, "Bring in the neighbors."

The house was full of kids and people. One of the kids about five-years old picked up a piece of fruit and asked, "Mother, what is this?"

They didn't have fruit! They used the whole turkey and drank all the tea. Of course, we had a surplus of all that stuff. I don't know how those people did it. They took it for years. I don't think that the people in the States could have withstood it as much as they did.

We went to the Salisbury Plain[256] on maneuvers. The moors on the Plain were home to the legendary Hound of the Baskervilles from the Sherlock Holmes movie. It was pitch dark, eerie and foggy. Some clown there used to howl like a mad dog. It gave us goose bumps.

It didn't take us long to find out that the Army would starve troops as they got closer to combat. It was supposed to make them "lean and mean." Parker and I got KP. We did our work and then disappeared. Payne would find us in the latrine, the barracks, wherever, and finally in empty huts back of the camp. He

---

[256]The Salisbury Plain was and remains an important area for armor training.

was so upset he couldn't talk. He just dribbled and walked out. This did not please our first sergeant. It was entered in the duty roster that Big Foot and I could no longer serve KP together!

Two of my friends from the Merchant Marine visited me at Salisbury. They spent a couple of days with me. When they left they said that they would rather take their chances on the high sea than put up with our chow and living conditions.

I got a three-day pass and went to London with my buddy from the Air Corps. We had a wild time, sightseeing and carousing. We went to Piccadilly Circus, which was filled with "questionable ladies of the evening."

One midnight they called us out and said, "Load up your vehicles, we're leaving."

The next morning the camp was empty. You didn't get a chance to say good-bye or anything. That was the Army. My jeep had a flat. The outfit left without me. My riders and I fixed the tire and caught up with the rest miles down the road, just before being met with our secret destination orders for Weymouth, a staging area. Terrible accommodations there. Torn tents and just C-Rations. We had some kind of farcical physical exam, after which we boarded LSTs for France.

It was supposed to be a twenty-hour trip, but it took almost three days. A big storm delayed us. We crossed the Channel and landed in Le Havre, France.[257] That's where we started seeing a lot of destruction. It didn't take guys long to learn what was going on. The French minegate openers had gone for the day. We were sitting ducks! We sailed on to Rouen. A couple of sailors wanted to go with us. Stark grabbed his old clipboard and started to write them up. They disappeared, never to be seen again. As we came ashore, we were greeted by a raggedy-assed kid who said, "Hey, Joe, cigarettes for papa? Candy for me?"

When we got to the old World War I battlefields, we quartered in a small chateau. It was cold, there was no firewood, and we were told that no one leaves except for special duty. Along comes a young kid and Big Foot. Filthy and I sampled this hard cider they were carrying, and made plans to visit the kid's folks' farm to make a trade. We had to jump over a high, spiked fence, make our deal, and get back. We each shoved three bottles through the fence, and started to cross it. Who should appear but Stark and Captain Thomas. We got reamed out and our cider was confiscated. The next morning at chow, Stark told us to keep a low profile, because the officers found out that the bottles contained only sweet cider![258]

We set up in a tent city, and it was cold. Some wise guy in Washington thought the war was going to be over by Christmas, so we didn't have the best winter clothing. When they realized it wasn't they sent a lot more stuff but it

---

[257] 24 January 1945.

[258] Hard liquor rations were reserved for officers. What the officers might have expected the bottles to contain was what the French called "Calvados," a potent liquor made from cider.

didn't materialize yet. All the guys carried a carbine and seventy-five rounds. The guys said, "We can carry more!"

One miserable, sleety night I was driving a jeep. Two buddies had blankets over their heads and weren't concerned with what was going on. I saw the light of the artillery against the sky. The clouds were low and I could really see a flash, then all of a sudden I heard the guns. We finally realized that this wasn't Camp Shelby and the artillery range. We stopped at a schoolhouse for a break. When the guys went in there they saw a room full of GI bodies ready for burial. It scared the living Hell out of us. This was going to be no baloney!

The dead must have been some part of a unit caught in the Bulge.[259] We looked pretty dirty and crummy, but compared to these guys we dressed well. There was this one guy sharpening his knife on a whetstone. I'll never forget that sonofabitch. He said, "Half of you guys are going to be dead." When we got back, we rested for the remainder of the day and began combat after that. We learned that no matter how much training we had combat was different. I saw many frozen, dead Germans. In a basement I saw three young Germans under a couple of blankets. Their guns were upstairs. I noticed that their faces had a very pale, olive color, indicating that they had frozen to death. I got out of there. Really, I was down there looking for some wine, because every German house had great German wine.

We were passing what we called "Purple Heart Corners."[260] There was all this mud and crap. Jeeps had a hard time getting through because trucks had made big ruts. While I was driving the Germans let go with some Screaming Meemies. When I looked over, the officer was running. I thought the heck with it, and ran the other way. As I ran I lost my helmet. Later, I realized I had wet knees. I had peed my pants. After awhile, at a first aid station, I asked this medic if I could have a helmet that was laying around. He said, "Take it."

When we got to the Siegfried Line, the guys stayed in the pillboxes.[261] The Germans were methodical. Every morning at 7:00 a.m. they would shell the area completely, then they would shell at noon and later at 5:00 p.m. So we had chow at 10:00 a.m. and maybe at 8:00 p.m. Our command post was in a large pillbox. The Germans had an outside privy, and it was overflowing with frozen contents. Sergeant Stark got Bob "Mail Call" Hoch to help him clear it out. They took a putty explosive, lit the fuse and took cover behind a boulder. It blew, scattering hard contents all over. A frozen turd hit Hoch on the back of the neck, forming a large bruise. Hoch went over to the medic, T/3 Glenn Ellefson, who said that although he was sorry, there was no broken flesh, therefore no Purple Heart. Ellefson suggested a special award called the Brown Heart!

---

[259] This was at the forward observation post of the 99th Infantry Division, known as "Checkerboard."
[260] Around Carentan, northern France. See the Louis Simpson poem "Carentan O Carentan."
[261] 11 February 1945

We were seventeen days on the Line and then we broke through with a lot of artillery. Then we rested a couple days at a town called Schmidtheim.[262] When we got to Schmidtheim, it was dark. The sergeant said, "You guys go and sleep in the church. Keep your own guard."

It was ice cold in the church, and dark. We laid down about five hours. I was facing my buddies. "Should we keep guard?" someone asked.

"The heck with it," we responded.

I woke up toward dawn. I looked around and saw five German bodies waiting for burial. One of them was an officer. Their burial detail had wooden crosses waiting for them, but we got there too quick. The officer had a blanket, but the other four had no blankets because they were enlisted men. Well, RHIP!

Sergeant Stark told me to take the jeep and trailer full of empty water cans back to the water point and hurry back with water for noon chow. My mistake was taking my good buddy "Bigfoot" Parker along. It was a few miles back over lousy roads. We came upon a large winery with all kinds of GI vehicles all hauling out wine. We got back hours later and all the water cans were full of wine. Some had not been properly closed and wine was all over the trailer. Of course, we opened one in the jeep and Bigfoot was just about passed out. This did not sit too well with the brass. Sergeant Stark and Captain Thomas issued an order for the men to bring their canteen cups. Parker and I got the usual reaming out and extra duty.

We used Piper Cubs for artillery observation. The pilot was usually a first lieutenant. There were two planes per battalion.

One morning, after we got to the Rhine,[263] the captain came by and said, "You're going to ride with me."

"Like Hell I am!" I said. His pilot was sick with pneumonia.

"You're going to ride with me in the observation plane."

"I'm only a PFC right now."

"You're riding!"

I went up in the observation plane. Nothing much happened. It was quiet going over the Rhine. We went up to Remagen to defend the bridge from German attacks.[264] At night the skies were red with tracer rounds being fired at German jets.[265] The Germans also tried underwater men, but were unsuccessful. We then crossed the treadway bridge. This had a sign on it signifying that it was the longest in the world. Vehicles were supposed to cross it thirty-five yards apart, but it was bumper to bumper. The thing really sagged! When we got to the east bank, we found a couple of our engineers shooting craps!

---

[262]6 March
[263]The division arrived on the Rhine 21 March.
[264]The Ludendorff Bridge.
[265]The Germans used Arado Ar234 "Blitz" B2 twin-engined bombers of III Kampfgeschwader 76 against the bridge.

We were usually two or three miles behind the front line. We never did get too much sleep, but we were young, strong, and healthy. Sleep was never a big factor. You could sleep anywhere, even standing up. We drank all the time, though. Man, did we drink! We never got a good buzz on until late at night, though. We got cognac. What we would do is get cans of grapefruit juice and mix it with the liquor. A canteen cup would hold eighteen fluid ounces. We would drink right in front of the officers. Look, you might be dead the next day!

One day, coming back from recon with a pilot of one of our Maytag washing-machine airplanes (Piper Cub), we passed our survey crew setting up the 105mms in an apple orchard. We blew the horn and they followed. They started to take artillery fire and piled out of the three-quarter tonner into a deep ditch. A few minutes later, Juggy runs across the road with a few bottles in his hands and jumps into the ditch. He told his buddies that if he was going to die, it wouldn't be while he was sober!

There was always food around. We would find potatoes or eggs in straw hidden in attics. We found broomsticks with all types of sausages hanging on them. We also had our regular rations. Whenever possible the Army would give us a hot meal. The GI was great for foraging. They called it, "boodle hunting." One time we got into a German officers' ration dump. There were boxes of Danish cheese, little, stubby cigars, cigarettes, and skinless, boneless sardines. We took all that we could carry. One time we killed some chickens. We plucked the feathers off and cooked them. We were sitting around talking, waiting for the chickens to get done, when this great stink rose. We plucked the chickens, but forgot to clean out the innards.

One night, we were assigned to a house. We sat around a table with our feet propped on top of it. The Frau of the house came in and with a clear voice said in English, "Will you soldiers please keep your muddy boots off my table!"

We were surprised, and pulled our feet off, all except for "Big Foot" Parker. He started to question her. She told him her husband came over from the States in 1939 as a paid engineer. They were forced to stay in Germany. We figured this was a lie. Parker told her to leave on the double. She got the message. We left the next morning. Some of the guys thought we should demolish the house, but we didn't. We had to leave in a hurry.

On the road one day, we came around a bend and there was a dead German lying on his stomach. His whole keester was blown away so perfectly that we could have fit a football into it. Amazing! Back home we viewed whole dead bodies, not as we saw them in combat. A couple of times I ran my jeep over enemy dead that were in the mud. There would be so many vehicles doing this that the corpses resembled filthy, muddy, flattened rag dolls.

Anyone could trace the path of the US Army. We would leave a trail of ration cans, boxes, cigarette butts, candy wrappers and empty bottles. If you saw a clear road ahead of you, you knew you were the first GIs in the area. That was a little scary.

We would not bathe for months. Nobody noticed. We all had the same stink. Once we got to a portable bath facility. We had three minutes to wash, two to rinse, and five to get out. There was a pile of clean, used clothing in the corner and we were allowed to help ourselves. I used up all of my soap. God! It was heaven! I washed off pounds of dirt, until I saw pink skin! None of us took any of the used clothing. Our great Army wouldn't even provide us with new stuff. We yelled our old battle cry, "Forty-eight, forty-nine, fifty, same old shit!"

In our last big battle at Eilenburg[266] we were having some trouble with the SS. Word came down to pull the men out and then blow the town to Hell with artillery. We fired day and night for about two or three days. The gun tubes were hot! We blew that town apart. Then we went in. We got to a German farm hall, which can be very big, especially the kitchens. A bunch of us were down in the basement. Also with us was the fire-command post. We were in our "cups" and my buddy, Juggy, and the rest of us were hungry. We found a ham and five potatoes, and a great pot of stew. Some guys found some onions and tomatoes, which we added to the stew. We ate it at about 3:00 in the morning. Some officers said, "That smells good! Do you have any for us?"

We did.

Another time on the Rhine, on a hillside near Remagen, a guy named Oberst got into a basement and found a bottle of cherries, flour and lard. On the second floor there was a big kitchen. He told us, "I'm going to make a cherry pie."

He found some crude sugar and cooked with the lard. He always said that his favorite desert was cherry pie. So we were downstairs drinking a little bit, while he was cooking. All of a sudden shells started coming over, but they landed in the river. One came over short and went through the roof and bounced off to the river. It was an armor piercing shell. If it had been a regular shell it would have exploded on the roof. We ran down to the basement. Someone called out, "Hey, Dave, get down here!"

"I'm watching my pie," he responded.

To this day, when I see cherry pie I can't help but think of Dave. We ate the whole thing and it was good. It reminded me of cobbler.

Despite the ugliness going on around you, you relaxed when you could. One time we encountered a beautiful little castle. We decided to stay in it for the night. The place had winding staircases and knights in armor. The guys would run through the place like crazy to see what they could find. My buddies and I went through the basement windows. My goodness, the bottles! The first thing we did was to get some boards and nail the cellar door. That night we filled the survey truck and a couple of jeeps full of bottles. The first sergeant told my gang, "You

---

[266] 21-23 April.

guys go upstairs. There's a little apartment way over in the corner. You stay there tonight."

We went up there and it looked like a place for romantic meetings. It had a nice little living room and a nice kitchen as well. It also had the biggest bed that I ever saw in my life. It looked like it was the size of the room! I think that there were about six of us. We drank a bit, then argued about who was going to get the bed. Somebody figured out that only two guys should get the bed out of six. Parker and I got the bed. We pushed everyone else off telling them, "Get off of our bed."

The next morning when we woke up, we were all on the floor! We went behind the castle and saw two small lakes that belonged to some Nazi bigwig. We figured there might be some fish there. Juggy had some lines and hooks with him. He said to me, "Come on, you and I will go fishing."

So we cut saplings and went to this stable where we found manure worms. I caught five fish. Juggy didn't catch any. The next thing I know, I'm in the water half way up to my face. Juggy's beating on me beating me. He's yelling, "You son of a gun, I carried these hooks and lines 3,000 miles, and you catch all the fish with them!" It was just one of those things. Juggy was some guy. He came into the Army at thirty-eight and made every hike. When Juggy was born, they broke the mold. I still write to his widow. They had a military wedding back in Shelby.

Our patrols met the Russians.[267] I was a little apprehensive. The Russians were filthy. They weren't very disciplined. I was on a jeep patrol with Juggy and someone else and as we passed this bridge we ran into a couple of Russian soldiers. The Russian officers drank vodka. I drank some first and, whew! Then I passed it to Juggy, who would drink anything. He refused it. We offered them a bottle of our cognac. They drank some, then laughed and said it was like water! Once we found out that it was Russian territory we got out of there as fast as possible. The German people were hollering and screaming, "Don't leave us!"[268]

The Russians were our allies, but we didn't trust them.

After VE Day in May, Major "Squirrley" Johnson, who came with us just before we went overseas, had an accident. Johnson was likeable and easy-going and a little flaky. Most of his time was spent taking pictures of many aspects of the war and riding horses. He liberated many saddles in the three-quarter tonner, plus large quantities of wine and cognac. Private Oberst worked with Squirrley and could be counted on to help find the beverages. One humid day, some GI poured gasoline into our two-holer latrine because he didn't appreciate the odor. Johnson came along, sat down and produced a smoke. He lit it, threw the match into the other hole. POOF! Johnson received no serious injuries, but he did go to the hospital. He never returned to the outfit.

---

[267] 23 April.
[268] The Germans knew they could expect harsh treatment at the hand of Russian troops.

We got into Berlin on Thanksgiving Day about 3:00 p.m. We found out we were going to go to the 78th Infantry Division. The officer grabbed us and told us, "Leave your bags right here. You're all on guard."

We told him, "We just got here. We're cold, hungry, and miserable."

"You guys are on guard so our guys can have the day off."

We guarded coal piles, and didn't get fed until the next day. That was our Thanksgiving! That was the Army! Nearly all of Berlin was destroyed. Down in the black market area, in the Tiergarten or near the Brandenburg Gate, I'd see old, fragile couples trying to sell stuff. Russian soldiers would carry their machine-guns off duty. We carried some type of a side arm. Now the Russians, who hadn't been paid in three or four years, were now getting paid in the same money we had, but they couldn't take it home. They bought suitcases and would buy any-thing—spoons, knives, old clothes. They'd fill those suitcases up. They really liked to buy GI watches, because they could get three horses for one watch back home. When we captured some Germans they told us, "You're fighting the wrong peo-ple. You should be helping us fight the Russians."

"What are these guys talking about?" we thought.

Later on, their comments seemed to have a little merit. When the Russian army got toward Berlin, Zhukov was their commander, and he kept some disci-pline. Then they pulled out their troops and put in a whole bunch of Mongolians. They were bad people. No one got away. They raped German women right in front of their families. These Mongolians had never seen a house of more than one or two storeys. They were filthy. They had diseases. There were a lot of Russian women troops. We called them oxen!

Christmas Eve, 1945, we spent at the Titania Palast, a big theater. We were waiting for enough points to take us home. The Titania had bars and restaurants which served only coffee and donuts. It was for occupying forces only. We were served by Red Cross gals. We also saw the latest movies from home. I went there with Gunner Sparacine, Ed Freel, and Roger Merling. The place was filled with GIs, WACs, Nurses. Not an empty seat! A German orchestra played holiday and classical music. There wasn't any heat. We were bundled up and wore mittens or gloves. There was a double-feature. Bing Crosby was in both. Just before mid-night, when Bing was singing "White Christmas," they passed out small candles and started singing with Bing. Out came the OD hankies. We were deep in thought. Then a boys' choir sang. We encored them until they became hoarse. The orchestra members all got a good meal. The German performers went home with many goodies. We all left about two or three in the morning.

We left Berlin with the 78th Division. They brought in some rookie replace-ments so we could go home. They lined them up in front of us. We looked at each other and thought, "I guess we're real soldiers!" They looked so scared and imma-ture. I guess that's the way we looked when we started. Some of us told them horrible stories that made them afraid to go out at night.

We knew it was over, but it was still kind of a shock. You'd see really close buddies hugging each other and crying. A lot of these guys had German girl friends. Those poor girls would be crying their eyes out. "Oh Johnny, my Johnny's going home!"

Then when I would see those same ladies with someone else, I would ask, "Hey, what happened to Johnny?"

"Shut up!" They'd say.

There weren't hardly any German males around after the war, and after a while females want a man. They were available, and we spread around a little Democracy!

On the way home I stayed at a German naval barracks in Bremen for awhile. They had a big mess hall and you could eat from about 6:00 a.m. to midnight. Most of us were so thin that you could see our ribs. We'd be there about seven and have a big breakfast prepared by the German cooks. We'd eat, go outside in the nice warm weather, lay on the grass for a few hours, and then go in and eat again. We ate about five meals a day. That helped us to put on a lot of weight because people back home were concerned about how skinny the guys were.

On April 1, 1946, I left Germany on a boat. I had $200.00, but I lost it in a crap game. When I got to New York, I called my mother. She cried. I told her, "Mom, I'm in New York. I should be home in about two weeks."

We spent about five days at Camp Kilmer. Then went to Camp Atterbury, Indiana where we were processed. They had us go in groups of fifty to get new uniforms. Then they gave us a final blood test. There was quite a hubbub in the papers about guys coming home diseased, so the Army was keeping them to get treated. This farm boy got called out and when he came back he was as green as a goat. We asked him, "What happened?"

"I got syphilis!"

This brand-new second lieutenant tried to convince us to join the Reserves. He told us, "If you guys sign then you can drink all the beer you want for free."

I thought, "The heck with that."

Finally they gave up and we got our discharges. Some of the guys grabbed their bags and went to the bus station. I said, "Heck, I'm going to wait until morning."

When I went into my barracks there were only two of us left. In the morning I got up, had breakfast, and walked outside to see a huge line. I figured that I stood in lines for three years so I'm not standing in any more lines. So I went back and had lunch and returned only to find the same line. After supper I went back and saw the same line. The next morning I got in line. Then finally I came home on a train.

The guys were drinking and passed me the bottle, but I didn't want any. I just wanted to get home. I got home on a Saturday. My mother was crying and hugging me. Sunday morning my mother had my uncle, aunt, and a bunch of relatives over. My mother had a bottle. She poured everyone a drink, but when she came to me she said, "No."

My uncle Jim said, "Give him a drink."

"I spent three years in the Army. Why don't you give me half a shot."

I didn't realize that after three years overseas I learned to cuss. My mother prepared a lamb and turkey for about twenty of us. I said, "Pass the f--ing tomatoes." It got really still. I said it again, only louder. My brother passed me the tomatoes. My mother went out of the room and my brother kicked me. Later, he took me out on the back porch and asked, "Do you know what you said?"

I said, "Yeah."

My mother was crying in the kitchen. I didn't know what to do. So for a couple weeks at home my family was afraid to talk to me, and if they did I would wait a while before I gave an answer. To your mother you always are innocent. I could never bring myself to apologize, because I just didn't know how to. She thought that I was going to Hell. That was my homecoming.

On Sunday we headed to the Greek Orthodox Church. Prior to the war, they used regular chairs. The women sat in one section and the men in another. So I got my old, gray, herringbone sport coat, my slacks, and my penny loafers. My mother asked, "Where are you going?"

I said, "If you want to go to church, then we'll go to church."

She said, "No, you're putting your uniform on."

"No, no," I said.

I ended up putting my uniform on. They had pews! I couldn't believe it! It happened during the war. Also, the women could mix, although my mother still sat in the women's section. The priest gave the sermon welcoming the guys home. Then my mother mentioned that I should go to confession. Now in the Catholic religion, which I am in now, Confession is important. For the Greek Orthodox, it was once a year and really isn't a big deal. Also, you stand by the side at the altar for confession instead of going in a little chamber. My mother said, "You go up there."

"No, Ma," I said.

I got in line with six other guys. What on earth am I going to say? When my turn came, the priest put his hand to my head and said, "How long were you in the Army?"

"Three years."

"Were you overseas?"

"Yes."

"Now you're home. Behave!"

My mother stood there, smiling.

I went to school for about a year and a half. Then, like an idiot, I went out and went to work. That was the biggest mistake of my life. I was taking a business administration course. I took a quiz to see what my aptitude was. They told me that I should either go into selling or writing. I should have gone into writing. I went to work selling X-ray and physical-therapy equipment. I got married when I was thirty-two years old. My first wife passed in 1971. She said, "Al, the only reason that you married me was because there were no other girls on the corner."

About six years ago we were at Cape Cod for a reunion. I was talking to our captain. We had our 69th cap on. Two girls came up. One, a graduate student in psychology, said, "Can I ask you two a question?"

The captain said, "Yeah."

"Are you guys part of a labor union on holiday?"

Did he get mad! He asked her, "What do you know about World War II?"

"Not very much. I never really went into anything about World War II."

She had no idea! A lot of other young people didn't want to hear and didn't care. We were old fogies!

That war was the greatest three years of our lives! If only once more we could hear Stark whistle us to formation. Nobody was closer to you than your buddies. Fifty years later, many are gone, many are ill. Thinking back now, we never knew when the war would end. It seemed like forever. But we all said the same prayer, "Please, God, no more!"

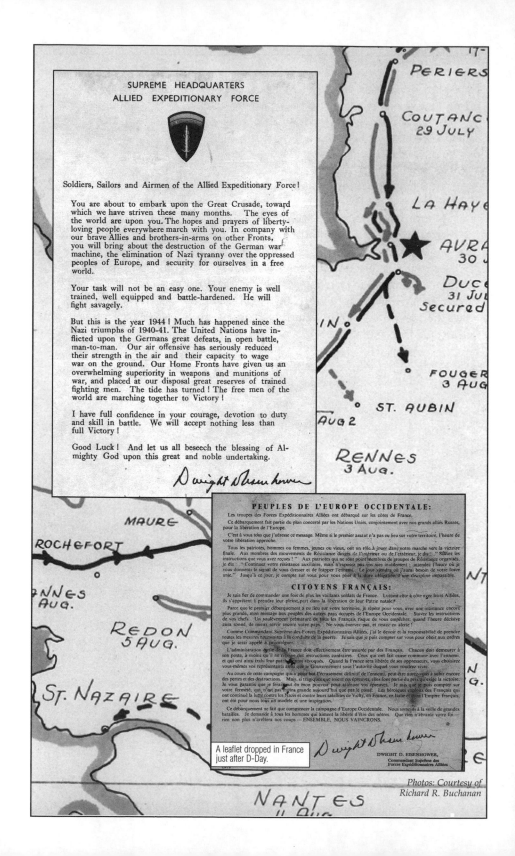

SUPREME HEADQUARTERS
ALLIED EXPEDITIONARY FORCE

Soldiers, Sailors and Airmen of the Allied Expeditionary Force!

You are about to embark upon the Great Crusade, toward which we have striven these many months. The eyes of the world are upon you. The hopes and prayers of liberty-loving people everywhere march with you. In company with our brave Allies and brothers-in-arms on other Fronts, you will bring about the destruction of the German war machine, the elimination of Nazi tyranny over the oppressed peoples of Europe, and security for ourselves in a free world.

Your task will not be an easy one. Your enemy is well trained, well equipped and battle-hardened. He will fight savagely.

But this is the year 1944! Much has happened since the Nazi triumphs of 1940-41. The United Nations have inflicted upon the Germans great defeats, in open battle, man-to-man. Our air offensive has seriously reduced their strength in the air and their capacity to wage war on the ground. Our Home Fronts have given us an overwhelming superiority in weapons and munitions of war, and placed at our disposal great reserves of trained fighting men. The tide has turned! The free men of the world are marching together to Victory!

I have full confidence in your courage, devotion to duty and skill in battle. We will accept nothing less than full Victory!

Good Luck! And let us all beseech the blessing of Almighty God upon this great and noble undertaking.

Dwight D. Eisenhower

PERIERS

COUTANC
29 JULY

LA HAYE

AVRA
30

DUCE
31 JU
secured

FOUGER
3 AUG

ST. AUBIN
AUG 2

RENNES
3 AUG.

MAURE

ROCHEFORT

NNES
AUG.

REDON
5 AUG.

ST. NAZAIRE

NANTES

PEUPLES DE L'EUROPE OCCIDENTALE:

Les troupes des Forces Expéditionnaires Alliées ont débarqué sur les côtes de France.

Ce débarquement fait partie du plan concerté par les Nations Unies, conjointement avec nos grands alliés Russes, pour la libération de l'Europe.

C'est à vous tous que j'adresse ce message. Même si le premier assaut n'a pas eu lieu sur votre territoire, l'heure de votre libération approche.

Tous les patriotes, hommes ou femmes, jeunes ou vieux, ont un rôle à jouer dans notre marche vers la victoire finale. Aux membres des mouvements de Résistance dirigés de l'intérieur ou de l'extérieur, je dis : " Suivez les instructions que vous avez reçues ! " Aux patriotes qui ne sont point membres de groupes de Résistance organisés, je dis : "Continuez votre résistance auxiliaire, mais n'exposez pas vos vies inutilement ; attendez l'heure où je vous donnerai le signal de vous dresser et de frapper l'ennemi. Le jour viendra où j'aurai besoin de votre force unie." Jusqu'à ce jour, je compte sur vous pour vous plier à la dure obligation d'une discipline impassible.

CITOYENS FRANÇAIS:

Je suis fier de commander une fois de plus les vaillants soldats de France. Luttant côte à côte avec leurs Alliées, ils s'apprêtent à prendre leur pleine part dans la libération de leur Patrie natale.

Parce que le premier débarquement a eu lieu sur votre territoire, je répète pour vous, avec une insistance encore plus grande, mon message aux peuples des autres pays occupés de l'Europe Occidentale. Suivez les instructions de vos chefs. Un soulèvement prématuré de tous les Français risque de vous empêcher, quand l'heure décisive aura sonné, de mieux servir encore votre pays. Ne vous énervez pas, et restez en alerte !

Comme Commandant Suprême des Forces Expéditionnaires Alliées, j'ai le devoir et la responsabilité de prendre toutes les mesures nécessaires à la conduite de la guerre. Je sais que je puis compter sur vous pour obéir aux ordres que je serai appelé à promulguer.

L'administration civile de la France doit effectivement être assurée par des Français. Chacun doit demeurer à son poste, à moins qu'il ne reçoive des instructions contraires. Ceux qui ont fait cause commune avec l'ennemi, et qui ont ainsi trahi leur patrie seront révoqués. Quand la France sera libérée de ses oppresseurs, vous choisirez vous-mêmes vos représentants ainsi que le Gouvernement sous l'autorité duquel vous voudrez vivre.

Au cours de cette campagne qui a pour but l'écrasement définitif de l'ennemi, peut-être aurez-vous à subir encore des pertes et des destructions. Mais, si tragiques que soient ces épreuves, elles font partie du prix qu'exige la victoire. Je vous garantis que je ferai tout en mon pouvoir pour atténuer vos épreuves. Je sais que je puis compter sur votre fermeté, qui n'est pas moins grande aujourd'hui que par le passé. Les héroïques exploits des Français qui ont continué la lutte contre les Nazis et contre leurs satellites de Vichy, en France, en Italie et dans l'Empire français, ont été pour nous tous un modèle et une inspiration.

Ce débarquement ne fait que commencer la campagne d'Europe Occidentale. Nous sommes à la veille de grandes batailles. Je demande à tous les hommes qui aiment la liberté d'être des nôtres. Que rien n'ébranle votre foi; rien non plus n'arrêtera nos coups — ENSEMBLE, NOUS VAINCRONS.

Dwight D. Eisenhower

DWIGHT D. EISENHOWER,
Commandant Suprême des
Forces Expéditionnaires Alliées

A leaflet dropped in France just after D-Day.

Photos: Courtesy of Richard R. Buchanan

"I Was Young, And This Was The Big War."

John "Jack" McDaniel

United States First Army
86th Infantry Division ("Black Hawks")
341st Infantry Regiment
2nd Battalion
Company C

Uniontown, Pennsylvania, 12 September 1925

"I always thought it would be so much better if we knew where we were going. As I look back on it now it really didn't make that much of a difference if we learned the big picture. Keep the rifleman ignorant and gung-ho. Young, dumb, virile kids make the best soldiers. They're too dumb to know they can get killed."

Combat soldiers were a close bunch, whether they wanted to be or not. You saw buddies get killed, but that didn't stop you from having buddies. What would draw me close to a guy? Maybe he liked the same kind of music. I used to steer clear of guys who liked country western; it drove me crazy! I always liked the big bands and jazz. If I found another like that, that was a guy I could knit with. Or if I found a guy that liked to shoot pool, I loved that. You couldn't help but get a little closer to some guys moreso than others. The thing that kept you from not getting so close is that everything happened so fast. There were times when guys were taken out and moved for whatever reason and then some other guys would come in. Sickness, ill health, wounds or death, and they'd be gone.

I remember many of the guys to this day, like Jouriles, who called me recently. There was a guy by the name of Ted Boik, a good buddy, from Detroit. He was an original hippie back then. I remember my assistant BAR man. He was six-four, and compared to him I was small. Here I was carrying that heavy gun and he was carrying my ammunition! He and I spent many a night in a foxhole together. He was the orneriest, rottenest guy, morally, I ever met in my life. Good grief! He was bad. But he would have taken a bullet for me!

I'll never forget Don DePhillips, our platoon sergeant, and Captain Hensley. I remember Captain Hensley because he was a brave, sonofabrick of a guy! There was one German that we brought back to Captain Hensley. Hensley called a corporal over who spoke German. The corporal interrogated the prisoner. The

Jack McDaniel: In trainig with BAR

German just kept repeating his name, rank and serial number, which, under the Geneva Convention, was all he was required to say. Captain Hensley, a southerner, said, "Hain't he gonna answer no moah?"

The corporal said, "I don't know. I'll ask him again."

Hensley pulled out his combat knife, handed it to the corporal, and said, "Stick him!"

I almost fell on the spot! It didn't happen, but good Lord I thought Hensley meant it! That German quaked and he talked a little bit. I remember Hensley on twenty-five mile forced marches. He'd run backwards for a half a mile alongside of us. He was a physically hard man, God bless me! He scared the death out of me!

I'm known as Jack. I got that name while I was a kid. There's a lot of Jacks in the family. My father's name was Emmet J. McDaniel. He was born in Columbus, Ohio in 1894. He was a lawyer and a judge. My mother's maiden name was Beatrice Daley. She was born in 1896 in Dunbar, Pennsylvania, which is not far from Uniontown. My mother was a legal secretary.

I had a very happy childhood in Uniontown. We weren't affected by the Depression, because my dad was a lawyer. I spent a lot of time at the country club, swimming and playing golf. That used to bother me a little, because the majority of my friends came from working-class families. The first job I ever had was as a soda-jerk. My dad didn't believe I should be taking jobs from other people, so he didn't encourage me to work.

I heard about Pearl Harbor during breakfast after Sunday-morning Mass. We were in our second-floor sun parlor. My dad, a World War I veteran, had a big map on the wall and had pins stuck in it showing where the Allies and Germans were. Pop turned the big radio on. The broadcast was interrupted by the announcement of the Japanese attack. Hawaii didn't mean much to me other than we "owned it." My dad, a big, gung-ho, patriot-type, became enraged. I picked up what I heard from him and felt the same. I was only seventeen. I said to him, "Pop, I want to go into the Army!"

He said, "You let me see what your marks are at the end of this year, and then maybe I'll sign for you."

Our country immediately engaged in propaganda to drum up patriotic feeling. The Germans and Japanese were the "Huns" and the "Japs," not politically correct terms today. It got to all of us, adults, kids, and all of my friends couldn't wait to get into the Army. Let's get in and get over there and get 'em and fight, fight, fight! The so-called "draft-dodger" was a rare-bird and was universally disliked. My dad was on the draft board. He would bring home stories about so and so. He'd say, "There's nothing wrong with him, damn it, but we had to give him a deferment."

A guy by the name of Martin Skelly, who was a year behind me in school, was only sixteen. He was not a good student, but he looked older. He lied about his age and his parents signed for him. Martin was killed about a year later. I guess they weren't real precise about checking birthdays. The Army was interested in live bodies, warm bodies.

When it came time for me to go in May 1943, I passed the Army Specialized Training Program. I was still in school. I graduated in June, and in late July I was sent to Indiantown Gap, sworn in, and sent right down to VMI in Lexington, Virginia. Even though I was gung-ho to get in, it didn't take long before homesickness set in. At VMI I'd leave my room at night and go down to the "sinks," the big toilet area. I'd sit on the can and cry like a baby! I thought I was a grown man, but I really wasn't.

I took engineering and military courses. We learned how to drill. I learned the so-called Rat System. A "Rat" was an incoming freshman. I learned to dislike it. The rats had to eat a square meal, turn square corners when they walked. There was "lights out." We used to put blankets up over our windows to cut out the light because we had to study. If we got caught we would do punishment walks. All of this was to instill discipline. I never resented it.

Slovenliness was a breach of discipline. Some guys wouldn't wash. They started to stink. One guy from the south wouldn't do anything. He wouldn't wash, he wouldn't train, he wouldn't do this, he wouldn't do that. So a bunch of us, pretty much at Sergeant Scruggs' recommendation, took him bodily and scrubbed him down with a brush. He didn't fight back. If he had struggled, I don't know what we would have done.

There were guys that just had two left feet and couldn't drill, couldn't do this, couldn't do that. That was usually left to the sergeants. They gave them extra training and tried to whip them into shape. Some of them just never became good soldiers. Some guys hated the Army and then were recalcitrant all the time they were in the service. Some couldn't run an obstacle course, some were physically unfit, uncoordinated guys. The ones that were just hardheaded, they got a hard time, not just from the non-coms, but from us, too, because we suffered along with them. We all took pride in looking good. It was a different mind set then. We were young and this was the big war and we all wanted to do well. I thought I would be at VMI for four years, but it was just one semester. They closed the program. They needed the troops. Casualties overseas were mounting. They shipped us out to Fort Benning, Georgia, for three months of infantry training.

We got a lot of bayonet training at Benning. Thank God I never had to use one! When we got overseas, we used our bayonets mostly for opening cans and cooking! We got hand-to-hand combat training, as well. I worked hard on that, and got to be pretty good at it. First, you went through it slowly. I learned how to make a hip turn. I learned how to break a person's neck. I wasn't big, like my brothers. I remember my dad telling me before I went overseas, "You learn and get in as good as shape as you can, because your life might depend on it."

Sergeant DePhillips, my first sergeant, was with me all through the war. He was the toughest and the best. He was an influence also, for good! He'd cuss like a trooper, but he was a good man. If he thought you were screwing around in town, drinking too much, he'd sit on you. He was like a father. He was only about four years older than me, but I thought he was a lot older. You know when you're eighteen and a guy is twenty-two, that's older!

After Benning, we went to Camp Livingston, Louisiana. We were there about three or four months for more training. That's when we really started to get together as a unit. When we were at Camp Livingston we became part of the 86th Division, where I stayed for the rest of the war.

After Livingstone, we went to Camp San Luis Obispo, California,[269] for Pacific training. We trained for island hopping at San Clemente. Training was dangerous. A lot of guys gave themselves self-inflicted wounds on the firing ranges. Other guys got careless. One guy panicked and guy dropped a grenade. DePhillips grabbed that thing. I think the grenade had a six or eight-second fuse on it, and there were only two seconds left. DePhillips flung it as far as he could. When it exploded a couple of guys got some fragments in their legs.

I got hit in the head with shrapnel from an artillery shell. Four or five guys and me ran up the side of a hill. We had live ammunition. We were popping away at rabbits and things like that. I turned on my side, and my buddy next to me was smoking a cigarette. I looked and saw a 105mm howitzer about 100-yards behind us. The muzzle of the gun raised and then dropped. I heard THU-THUNK! The shell hit the hillside. Fragments blew the thumb off the guy who was smoking, put another guy's eye out. Something hit me in the head. I jumped up with my helmet in my hands. I held it in front of my face, and saw daylight where the shrapnel went through. Then blood got into my eyes, and I thought I was blind. I yelled, "Oh, my God! Get me the chaplain!"

I didn't remember anything else. They got me in an ambulance and put me in a hospital, where I stayed for two weeks. My mom and dad came to visit me. I bled like a stuck pig, I was told. I had a concussion. The other two guys who were wounded with me were discharged from the service because of their injuries.

We expected to go to the Pacific, but at the last minute we were sent to Europe. There was a lot of secrecy about the move. I recall we had to remove our Black Hawk division patches. We were told that we shouldn't discuss at any time what outfit we were with, or where we were going. As a matter of fact, we weren't absolutely sure we were going to Europe, but traveling across the country like that we all presumed that we were. Most of us did talk. I told my parents. I was filled with an anxiety when we got to our POE. We knew that this was it! I felt exhilarated, but I was also afraid. We just wanted to get over there and get those Germans!

We went over on a Liberty Ship.[270] Guys were laying sick on the deck, their vomit rolling back in their faces. We had no fresh water for showering. We had to

---

[269]1 October 1944.
[270]From Boston, 19 February 1945.

shower in salt water, and the soap just wouldn't come off. Just before we debarked, they gave us thirty seconds of fresh water to rinse with.

We finally got to Le Havre, France, after the Battle of the Bulge.[271] My brother, Larry, an officer, was in charge of a pre-invasion raid. He was in charge of a black company. His DUKW[272] had been blown out of the Channel. The family was told he was KIA. Medics put him in the bottom of an LST with a dead-tag. Somebody saw him moving, and they got him out of there. When I first got to Le Havre, I was supposed to have a day before we got in our trucks to head out. A jeep came up with an aide of his to pick me up to see him. But we never got to see each other. Immediately, we were put on trucks and driven to the town of Aachen.[273]

I couldn't believe it. Aachen looked like a huge giant with a scythe just went whoosh and chopped off the tops of everything. It was a badly destroyed town. We got off the trucks and began our march. We marched and marched and marched. We knew we were in the infantry! We got Benzedrine to stay awake. I was so dog-tired once! We were marching and I walked into a six-foot hole! I was dead asleep on my feet! I damn near broke my leg! We got to the Bastogne area just after our troops there were relieved. It was pretty much cleaned up, so we went on to Cologne. We dug in on the banks of the Rhine.[274] We could see the Germans across the river. We'd pop away at each other. I don't know if anyone ever got hit. They'd throw 88s over at us. Usually in fours. You'd hear them go THUNK! THUNK! The shell that came closest to me was a dud! Thank God! It was only twenty feet away.

We knew we were going to get into combat right after Aachen. That's where I saw my first dead American soldier. His rifle and bayonet were stuck in the ground, his helmet on top of it. I knew then, my God, this wasn't cops and robbers! We weren't playing cowboys and Indians! The Germans really meant to kill you! It was then that I almost had an involuntary bowel movement. I saw my first dead German there, too. I shouldn't have. The cleanup crews should have removed those bodies. The dead had grotesque expressions. Blood was everywhere. We were behind the lines, but we could still hear the artillery five miles in front of us.

The soldier, the actual dog face, a guy like me, didn't get the "big picture" as much as DePhillips did. The company commander got even more information. From battalion on up, they got the really big picture. We never knew exactly where we were headed. We just followed the guy in front of us. We all had been

---

[271] The 86th landed in France 1 March 1945.

[272] A "duck." A six-wheel-drive, two-and-a-half-ton amphibious truck. The name is from the model number of the manufacturer, General Motors. D = year of origin (1942); U = utility; K = all-wheel drive; W = six-wheeled. First used in the landings at Sicily, the DUKW carried twenty-five men on land and fifty at sea.

[273] Entered Germany 27 March 1945.

[274] The 341st was detached on 5-9 April to reinforce the 97th Infantry Division in the Sieg River assault.

given map reading in basic training, but none of us ever really had a map. DePhillips did, your platoon sergeant and company commanders had maps. Just before an engagement, if we knew the enemy was in that town, we got information on what they had in there, how many troops, artillery, maybe tanks. I always thought it would have been so much better if we knew where we were going. As I look back on it now, it really didn't make that much of a difference if we learned the big picture. Keep the rifleman ignorant and gung-ho. Young, dumb, virile kids make the best soldiers. They're too dumb to know they can get killed.

My first experience in combat was near Cologne. We moved from Cologne and crossed the Rhine on a pontoon bridge.[275] For the most part it was their artillery and our artillery, but there was also small arms fire. You didn't see a guy, but you shot in the direction of the sound. There was a truck load of Germans stopped about 100 yards away. They dropped the rear gate of the truck and they started coming out. I let all twenty rounds of my BAR go and I know I got a lot of them. Geez, I didn't like knowing that I killed someone. I didn't care how much I thought I hated them. That was my personal first.

We went up into the Ruhr Pocket. It was a big industrial area. We hit a lot of towns up there. There was hard building-to-building fighting in Essen. Some of the resistance in street fighting was pretty stiff. A good buddy of mine was killed in a house. He was in one room and I was in another. I heard him firing away. I just fired into the dark. I think that he got the person that got him.

In house-to-house fighting you spread out and the sergeant directs you. "Get over to that area! Over to that area!"

Then when you hear the Pop! Pop! Pop! You know they're shooting. You hit the dirt. You crawl. You go for cover. You zigzag. Even in the daytime you could see the muzzle flash of a weapon being fired at you. That was one of the reasons why it was bad to carry a BAR. It drew fire, because of its muzzle flash, and because it was fast shooting. Usually I headed for a doorway and made sure that house was secure and no one was in it. We'd go running in like you see cops do on TV shows. We'd go from room to room. I was fired at down a flight of steps. One of my buddies threw a hand grenade down the stairs. The grenade wounded some Germans, but just about ruptured my ear drums. The rest of the Germans immediately gave up. It was always a pain in the neck getting prisoners together, hoping someone would take them back somewhere.

We were always concerned about tanks coming around. They made a scary noise! We'd fire away at them though. Ping! Ping! Ping! Our bullets would bounce off their armor. Usually we'd wait for the bazookas, or our own self-propelled 105s. When the tanks got hit, they went up big!

It was in Essen that I helped to deliver a baby! We were going from basement to basement. There was a sloping cellar door, and I heard something. I pulled it

---

[275] 5 April 1945 at Eibelshausen.

open and threw in a grenade. After it exploded, I went in with some buddies and, my God, there was nothing in there but a couple of nuns and some pregnant women! None of them, thank God, were hit! They were huddled in the corner. I'm sure their ears were shattered. This one woman started screaming in pain because she was delivering. I helped hold her legs down while a nun reached in and pulled. The baby was fine. I spent about half an hour in that basement. Outside there was still all this shooting going on. The mother was scared to death. She never stopped screaming. The one nun could speak a little English. She would say, "Ach! Don't push! Don't push!" I told the nun I was a Catholic. That seemed to soothe her a little bit.

After the Ruhr, we were attached to Patton and we moved fast toward the mythical Nazi redoubt area in the Austrian Alps. That's when I absolutely thought in my mind that I was going to kill Sergeant DePhillips. We were on a hillside and there was a big open valley of about 200 yards and another hill on the other side, and there were Germans on that hill, firing at us. They had good small arms, Schmeissers and machine-guns, and they were just peppering us. DePhillips was sitting up there with our platoon and he says to a buddy of mine, "Jimmy, go!"

Jimmy goes running, and you could see the splatter of bullets all around him. Two guys got hit in the legs. You could see them fly into the air and then crawl like Hell to get behind something. Jerry Jouriles, a Greek kid, got hit and he really flew into the air. I thought he was dead. I thought, "DePhillips is crazy! They can't miss us!"

It came down that I was the last one to run across the field. I had been firing support with the BAR. I put a new magazine in. DePhillips said, "McDaniel!"

I was going to shoot him, I swear, because I thought he was crazy. But I ran so fast Jesse Owens couldn't have caught me. I was zigzagging and praying, "Please, God, hit me in the leg! Hit me in the leg! Hit me in the leg!"

We took the other hill, and took prisoners, but we lost a lot of men. I carried about eight magazines with me and I emptied them all. Hotaling, my assistant BAR man, kept shoving them to me. My BAR barrel was as hot as a firecracker! We ran into some mortars and behind them was one 88 emplacement, but our first bunch of guys disabled it. The whole incident took only thirty to forty-five minutes, but it seemed like two days. You don't think much about what's going on until after it happens. When you saw someone get hit, it filled you with such a hate for who did it you wanted to go savage and get 'em! You might not have even known the guy that got killed. I cried like a baby over some guys that got shot up. There were times I wept uncontrollably and wet myself. I remember I came close to shooting myself in my own foot! I had a service .45 and I aimed that thing at my foot. I didn't do it because I was afraid I'd blow my whole foot off!

Just over the brow of the hill was a little village which we liberated. It was the first time that we slept overnight in a village. DePhillips told us, "You two guys go into that house. You two guys in that house."

When we got a house to sleep in we displaced the owners and took over the beds. I got in this house where my friend and I were billeted for that night and, my God, the man and woman in there were cowering. They looked like my parents! "Hell's Fire! I can't put those people out of bed!" I said.

After DePhillips went down the street we went into their barn. It was hard because the people looked so much like us. They were Catholics and they had little shrines in their house. That got to me.

The next morning a little ray of sun woke me up. I had my combat boots on, but I had unlaced them to air my feet out a little bit. I felt something here in my pant leg. A mouse was running up my leg! God Almighty, it was worse than getting shot at! I squashed the mouse and it fell out.

There were four or five chickens around. The farmers needed them more than we did, but we were hungry. We had this southern guy with us and I saw him grab a chicken and wring its neck. We all plucked the feathers off that thing and stuck it in hot water. I think we forgot to clean it. It stunk bad! He was a good cook. We had chicken that day.

When we were brought back for a rest, that was the time to write letters home. You could only do that when you had half of a day or a day. The Army really tried hard to keep the mail up. That was a great thing when the mail clerk came around with his stack of mail. I got letters from my parents and sometimes girls that I knew. I always liked getting letters from girls. My parents were real good. They wrote me often. I seemed to get most of their letters. Some guys got ten letters at a time. Other guys would be sitting around with none.

After R&R, going back to the front was a real downer! The worst part of combat was the anticipation. Once you were actually in a fire fight you didn't have time to think about anything. The worry and the anticipation about what you were going to run into occurred while you were walking up to the front. You heard artillery and small-arms fire. That's when your stomach started to churn.

In combat you would see things you would rather forget. Once, near Ingolstadt, several guys captured twenty Germans. They weren't SS, they were regular army. We were in behind a hill so we were pretty safe from small-arms fire. Our blood was real high that day. Sergeant DePhillips told this guy, a southerner who was a little crazy, "Take these prisoners back."

We had set up a place where they were keeping Germans. He took them over the hillside. He had a BAR. I heard the BRAPP! BRAPP! BRAPP! I didn't see it happen. I saw him come back. I didn't ask him anything. He wasn't gone long enough to take them back. He just mowed them down. He was a little crazy and a dimwit, but he was shaking when they told him to take the prisoners back.

I saw a sergeant who, at the time, I thought was a damn coward. This happened in Cologne. My assistant and I had a foxhole just on the banks of the Rhine. I came back and I'm standing behind this building and 88 shells were coming in. The sergeant was standing alongside this building. Part of the corner of the building near the top came down from the shelling and he began to shake like a leaf and he ran. I thought, "My God!" Later on, he acquitted himself well, at that time I thought, "Boy, you yella sonofabrick!"

I saw one guy who couldn't walk. He was down on his hands and knees. No injuries at all, but he was catatonic. I was absolutely sympathetic. Guys were trying to get him up. They were going, "Come on! Come on!" But he just sat there and stared. We had to leave. The medics took care of him. I don't remember where that happened. One day just blended into another.

The fighting in Ingolstadt was very heavy. I had my shoes shot off from under me! I think I should have been in for a Purple Heart for that because it drew blood, but I didn't push it. I had screwy ideas about honor. If you didn't get hit bad enough, you didn't deserve the Purple Heart. I was running from one side of street to the other, and ricochets hitting my boots just pulled them off my feet. I ran in my bare feet until I could get into a building. Within twenty minutes our supply truck came down the street and I got a new pair of combat boots right there on the spot. I would have been dead in the water without any shoes because it was cold out.

Like Essen, Ingolstadt was house to house. Every house seemed to have a German in it. You'd see them in second floors. When we were fighting in that town, we thought we were surrounded. You should have seen us, me especially, getting rid of my Luger and German paraphernalia, which we would stuff in wherever we could! I was sure I was going to get captured and I didn't want to get captured with the German stuff on me. Later on I tried to retrieve it. I did find some of it.

That was a time when three tanks were coming down a very broad street. One in the front and two to the rear of it. They were wreaking havoc. Buildings were going up all around us from those tank cannon. They were leveling buildings wherever they saw small-arms fire. The rubble slowed them. There were some areas they couldn't get through. These were Tigers. Big tanks! Even a rifle grenade bounced off them. Bazookas finally got them. But they gave us trouble for well over an hour. I remember one bazooka guy went to the top of a building and was able to fire directly down at them. I saw the treads fly off this one tank and it kind of lurched it to the right and stopped the other tank behind it, making it a sitting duck. I can't remember what happened to the third one, but it took about an hour before we could get through. I was providing cover fire for the bazooka guys as best I could. It at least kept the tank commander's head inside the tank. They could only see through a slot in the turret and often they would raise the top turret and put their head out to find out where they were.

Once there was a young girl walking in an open field we were trying to cross. There was small-arms fire everywhere, and she would hit the dirt. "Don't fire," we yelled. She got up and artillery fire came in. One of our guys shot her. She was probably fifteen. We figured she was a spotter for the Germans. She absolutely was a spotter. We were sure.

I saw young kids in German uniforms. I saw old men, too old to be in the service. They couldn't do hard marching. Guys my age now! Close to seventy! They had guns, they had some kind of makeshift helmets. I saw guys with World War I helmets on, the ones with the spikes on top. They looked anachronistic! Most of them had no ammunition on them. If they had, I'm sure they would have used it.

It's hard to isolate certain instances in time. There were a lot of old civilians in Ingolstadt. That's one of the first places we heard them all say, "Kein Nazi, kein Nazi!" They were scared to death of us, but after they saw us they seemed to warm up immediately. They saw that we weren't quite the monsters that they expected.

Near the end we had an engagement on the Isar River, not far from Munich. We crossed in wooden boats, a hard crossing. It was just a little too deep and too wide to do it on foot. When we got to the other side we just spread and ran! Like with most river banks there's a broad, flat area, the kind of place you never wanted to get caught in. We were getting covering fire from our artillery and from .50 caliber and .30 caliber machine-guns. A bunch of us were told that there was a concentration camp nearby.[276] It had already been freed by other units, but we went there to relieve them. As we drew closer, I could smell burned flesh. Inside the camp there were living skeletons, people with legs no bigger than my fingers! Sunken eyes! But the smell was what got to me. I had never smelled anything like burning flesh. There were rows of huge incinerators. Most of the prisoners seemed to be Poles.

Toward the end, none of us wanted to get shot. We wondered, "Why aren't they quitting!?" When we finally heard that the war was over, we wondered if the Germans knew it was over. Two or three days after the war was declared over we relaxed. Whether we should have or not, I don't know. We all still carried ammunition in our weapons, but we got a little lax. We looted. We fraternized. It was forbidden, but we did it anyway! I met a girl that I thought I was in love with! Really, in just the one day that I met her. She was a nice girl. Her name was Erika. I don't remember what her last name was. I always tell my wife that story, and she hates it! I didn't do anything with Erika because I was a good, innocent boy!

We got into Austria, then back to Germany. We stayed only two weeks, and then went by truck to Heddesheim, then Mannheim. Mannheim was a big town. We stayed in that town for about a week, and in another week we were back to Le Havre and on our way out.

When we got back to the States we had a thirty-day furlough. That was a great time! They must have had ten big boats with their fire hoses shooting water into the air. I recall a USO boat with girls dancing on it. I got up real early because our ship stopped way out in the harbor so that it could come in during the

---

[276]Dachau

daytime. It was a big publicity thing. I remember that when the sky started to get bright I could see the Statue of Liberty! We came steaming in with the tug boats pushing us. When we landed, the Red Cross and USO were there passing out goodies to us and patting us on the back! We felt great!

I couldn't wait to get home. My dad welcomed me. He wasn't a real emotional type, but he gave me a big hug and that was great stuff! My brother Larry hadn't gotten home yet. My brother Bob had gotten a medical discharge. He was at home and in law school. Pop got out his maps and we went over the whole thing! I saw a lot of buddies, did a lot of dating, did a lot of boozing!

Then we got word to report to Camp Gruber, Oklahoma, for transfer to the Pacific. We were on the boat going over when the Bomb was dropped on Japan. We thought we were going to turn around and go home, but we went to the Philippines! We were there nine months! We landed at Leyte. I had my birthday in Manila. We had a little bit of fighting there, but mostly rounding up Japanese who wouldn't quit or didn't know the war was over. Our biggest job down there was keeping the Filipinos in my squad from killing the Japanese.

I was a sergeant and we would take forays into the hills to flush out Japanese. Generally the Filipinos knew where the Japanese were. The Japanese lived in squalor. In their own filth. Very little eating. They were emaciated and crazed. They had swords and rifles, but if they had two rounds apiece they were lucky! Once a Japanese group surrendered they became very complacent, very nice, they bowed and scraped, but the Filipinos would cut their throats. Absolutely! I had to tell them, "No! No!" That went on for about a month. After that my only job was to guard the AFWESPAC civilian banks.[277]

When I got home for good, I had no trouble adjusting to civilian life. Later, my sons said I had dreams because they heard me scream in the night. I embraced civilian life with open arms. Some other guys just couldn't handle not having the regimen and the assurance that they were going to be fed, clothed, get a check and be taken care of. For me, getting away from that was great.

I came back whole, but I would have rather been killed, I think, than crippled. I belonged to a singing group, the Pax Choral, and every Christmas we sang at hospitals and different places. One year we went to the veterans' hospital in East Liberty. A couple of the girls who sang with us would go to the patients and say, "Jack was in the service."

As soon as they heard this, these fellas would seek me out. Some of them had been in the hospital for thirty-five years! They'd talk to us as though they were talking about something that happened yesterday! They'd say, "Were you at such and such! Did you see this!"

I tried to go along with them. It was pathetic! They weren't there, mentally. I would not want to live that way! If I was sure that I'd have a nice little minor

---

[277] Armed Forces Western Pacific.

injury, maybe a limp I guess I could get along with that, but major problems where I'd have to be dependent on everybody? No, I wouldn't want to live that way! I think I would have rather taken a bullet. In combat, everyone prayed for the Million-Dollar Wound. "If I get hit, I hope it hits me in the fatty part of the thigh!" You were faced with the sights of guys dropping around you and you thought, "Maybe it will be me next!"

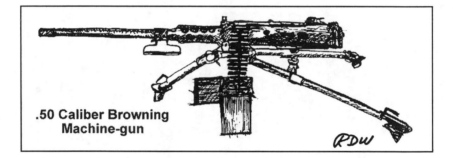

.50 Caliber Browning
Machine-gun

RDW

Who Knows the Dead?

Richard Radock[278]

United States Third Army
80th Infantry Division
319th Infantry Regiment
305th Medical Battalion
Company C

Fairhope, Pennsylvania, February 4, 1921
Belle Vernon, Pennsylvania

"I told a lot of people that the soldiers in our company were more than brothers to us because we knew more about them and they knew more about us than our own brothers did. It was like a family. If you live at home a long time, then you see your brother once at the dinner table. Then they go their way and you go your way. That's it! But your life depended on your buddies in the Army. The Army would emphasize this. They had to know what each other was thinking, especially if they were riflemen."

I was twenty when Pearl Harbor happened. I was fit to be tied because I wanted to enlist right away. My mother said, "Settle down. You'll get your chance." I was so mad at the Japs, I wanted to go over there and kill them right away. We lived in a different era when citizens were more patriotic. We had parades and used to walk two miles to the cemetery up the streetcar track in Belle Vernon to attend memorials for the dead World War I soldiers. We were flag-wavers.

My father was Nicholas Radakovich, a carpenter and blacksmith, but when he came to this country in 1914 from Dolgani, Yugoslavia, he had it changed to Radock. My mother's name was Radinovich, but they changed it to Radish when she came through Ellis Island 4 September, 1906. A lot of immigrants lost their identity because of that. My mother was born 11 July in Garsnica, Yugoslavia, about 200-miles north of my father's town. She grew up in the town of Cheria.

My dad worked all around Greensburg in coal-mining towns, then he moved to Fairhope where he got a job hammering coal, and that's where he met my mother. The mining towns were populated mainly by Yugoslav, Russian, or Polish people. Neighbors shared things out of the gardens as well as the bread

---

[278]Mr. Radock's history combines taped interviews with written materials submitted by Mr. Radock.

Richard Radock; Camp Forest, Tennessee, 1942

they all made. My grandfather had a couple barns where they kept some cows, chickens, geese, and rabbits.

My first job during the Depression was with the National Youth Association. I delivered papers for eight years, too. With the money I earned, I bought all my clothes for school, and my bicycle. After high school, I got a part-time job with American Window Glass Factory in Belle Vernon. In 1940 I got a job at Pittsburgh Steel as a laborer in the open-hearth furnace department.

I didn't want to wait for the draft, which would have meant being in the infantry, so I enlisted on 2 July 1942. The guys that I ran around with, about seven or eight of them, all enlisted in the Marines, Coast Guard, the Air Force. I joined as a diesel mechanic, because I took a correspondence course at home in engineering. I was going to use that for my lifelong vocation.

I was supposed to be shipped out of Pittsburgh to Camp Edwards, Massachusetts in the Amphibious Engineers, but they had a big push on for the European Theater. I was shipped down south to the 80th Division at Camp Forrest, Tennessee. I ended up in the infantry after all!

My mother was a little nervous about me going to war and never coming back. Dad thought that I should go. My brother, who was in the first draft, went to North Africa. They were supposed to serve for a year. As a matter of fact a lot of guys that he went to school with in the Army were sent home because their enlistment was up. When they found out that they were going to have the big push in Europe, they recalled all of them. So my brother never did get to come home during the war.

I didn't get a send-off because I went to Perryopolis, where our district draft board was. One man ran away from the bus when we made a stop. They put us up in the Fort Pitt Hotel. Our physicals were the next day. I never did get to come home on furlough. As soon as the physicals were over they swore us in. We left immediately for Camp Cumberland for clothes and shots, and then they shipped us down to Camp Forrest, Tennessee.[279] They put me in a combat medic battalion. I also had to go to school to learn first aid and other things necessary for a combat situation. They showed us pictures about venereal diseases and combat wounds. Then we practiced putting splints on each other. I didn't want any part of it. I wanted to get in the motor pool. I didn't know what was going to happen. I thought, "What am I in for?"

As combat medics we weren't part of the field hospital. Our purpose was to take immediate care of wounded infantry soldiers and evacuate them. They decided arbitrarily, for the most part, who would be part of the combat medical battalion, unless you were good friends with the sergeant.

---

[279]The 80th Division (Blue Ridge Division) was activated at Camp Forrest 15 July 1942 and redesignated the 80th Infantry Division 1 August 1942. The division arrived at Camp Phillips, Kansas 8 September 1943 and went to the Desert Training Center No. 4 California Maneuvers 9 December 1943.

During training, one of the infantrymen panicked while crawling under live machine-gun fire. He stood up and got cut in two. We had an ambulance there from my company to evacuate him and take him to the camp hospital, but it didn't matter. He was dead. There was another incident where they had dummy tanks made out of wood. They were setting charges to blow one up. One charge didn't go off. The guy that set the charge went back, and as soon as he approached the dummy tank, it blew up and killed him.

We were opposite the 30th Division, and were the first division that took Ranger training in Army maneuvers. The Army was going to use 82nd Airborne for the first time with infantry troops. So the 82nd Airborne was to be with my division for the first week, and then for the second week they would be with the 30th. During maneuvers, these guys were dropping down from 400-feet, breaking their legs and landing in trees and getting all battered up! They were so ferocious that they were hitting each other in the heads with their rifle butts. After a week of that they had to tone things down because of too many casualties. Guys down at Fort Bragg told us that 82nd soldiers would hide behind buildings at night and shoot live ammo. They were crazy!

The Army set goals for the 82nd, and the officers wanted the best men they could get. There was more rivalry when it came to company and platoon levels. It was easier to notice there than in an infantry division. They didn't like to see the medics though. They called us "pill roller" and "doc," but they changed their minds when we got overseas.

Camp was near a small town. I don't suppose it had more than 6,000 people before they broke camp. Then they built houses for the soldiers' families and so forth. If you calculate the division in there plus other troops stationed at the camps there would be about 30,000-40,000 people in that town. You couldn't get a drink at bars because people would be lined up six or seven deep!

Guys would go into town to raise Hell. Some of them got drunk, but we used to steer away from town once we became familiar with the area. Sometimes we'd go to Chattanooga or Nashville on the Chattanooga Choo-Choo.[280] One nice thing about the people was that they took the soldiers into their homes. They would also block off streets in their towns to have dances. Ten years after the war, the public changed their attitude toward soldiers and didn't want them around. This was especially true of the people who lived near camps.

The guys who were in the motor pool still had to keep going to classes. We used our new skills a lot of times also. For instance, we had to give shots of morphine, or prepare dressings. We had first-aid kits with us. We also had to do ambulance duty at the camp hospital for about two days. We'd sleep right in the hospital. If somebody had appendicitis we'd take them from the camp hospital to another hospital where they had nurses and doctors for surgery.

---

[280]Made famous in a popular song of the day.

From December to March 1944 we were in Camp Laguna in Yuma, Arizona for desert maneuvers. I was on a ten-day furlough and didn't get to Yuma until December 13. The country was nothing but wasteland. There was no one around for miles. There were a few head of scrawny cattle with hides scarred from cactus needles. They had burrs stuck to them. Yuma was populated mostly by Mexicans, Indians and cowboys, but not the Hollywood type. Most of the buildings were adobe, and there were not many of them. There were a few stores, saloons, gas stations and motels.

Camp Laguna was a temporary camp of pyramidal tents twenty-five miles east of town, close to the Mexican Border. It was dry and warm in the daytime and cold enough for blankets at night. We were four to a tent. We slept on cots with no sheets or mattresses. Each tent had a coal-burning stove. No wood was available. We tied our shoes to the tent poles to keep out the scorpions. Kangaroo rats stole anything shiny and buried the stuff in their holes. There were no refrigerators. We ate C Rations and dehydrated food. Our mess tables were four-feet high with legs stuck in the sand. There was no electricity, so we used candles. Generators provided power for the collecting station and motor pool. We bought all the beer we wanted in the PX, as well as toothpaste and soap. At night we would sit in the sand and watch movies on a screen. The power was supplied by one of the portable generators. We went to classes every day, did exercises, went on long marches through the desert, did close-order drill. The motor pool section learned to drive in the desert.

I became a full-fledged corporal, driving a three-quarter-ton weapons carrier which I used to haul supplies. We cleaned and serviced our vehicles. They were filthy because we inherited them from another division who used them in maneuvers. The sand took a toll on the engines and the paint was worn off by sand particles. We had no water to wash the vehicles. Instead we blew off the dust with an air compressor.

We would drive in a sixty-mile convoy across the desert in combat conditions—no lights, not even blackout lights. I was acting sergeant and I accompanied PFC Herbie Haupt as his assistant driver on a three-quarter tonner. We ended up in a bomb crater about eight-feet deep and thirty-feet wide. We were airborne for a few seconds! Our motor sergeant, Phillip Elko, who was bringing up the rear of the convoy, flagged a five-ton battalion wrecker which pulled us out. This was in the Yuma Proving Grounds for Artillery and Bomber Aircraft.

We had classes about both the Pacific Theater and the Japanese army. We began to train for the Pacific since the North African desert war was over.

On Christmas Day we had canned fruit, turkey, yams, peas, corn, stuffing and cranberry sauce. In the evening we went to a church service conducted by the chaplain of the 305th, Chaplain Ball.

On 28 December we went on a three-day field trip into the desert. We marched eighteen miles into the wilderness and set up tents and concealed them with brush. Motor-pool drivers were transported back to camp to pick up their vehicles. We drove all night during a blackout. We drove to Castle Dome, about forty miles from our bivouac. We ate cold C Rations and made a small fire for instant coffee. My buddy and I had six blankets and two comforters that we borrowed from the supply truck. We kept warm. The rest of the guys had only two GI blankets. Our mess truck finally arrived and we had a good, hot breakfast. We spent the day learning how to camouflage our vehicles and digging foxholes.

We had New Year's Day off, but were constantly busy cleaning vehicles. I was put in charge of a coal detail with three other GIs. We went to Yuma and shoveled coal from a gondola car into an Army dump truck, about eight tons of it.

I went to Mexicali, Mexico with three buddies. It was about thirty miles away. It was a filthy town with open sewers, lots of flies. The streets were mud. There were no screens on the doors and windows. We had to change dollars into pesos.

We were now maneuvering in the Southern California desert. We went in a night convoy over the mountains. It was hard to breathe in the desert. The high winds blew fine dust around. The only relief from the sand storms was to kneel down and place a blanket over our heads to keep the dust out of our eyes and nostrils.

I went to Hollywood with one of my squad. We had a three-day pass and hitchhiked up and rode back on the train. We stayed at the Hollywood Guild, a canteen that had beds for servicemen. The hostesses were young Hollywood starlets. We took a tour of Hollywood and Beverly Hills and saw all the stars' mansions.

We worked out a lot of combat problems in the desert. Our "enemy" was the 104th Infantry Division (Timberwolves). We had a mock war in the Palen Pass area of the Palen Mountains. We won decisively. The "battle" ranged near the Salton Sea, into the Chocolate Mountains, Blythe, the Palens, the Needles area, the Whipple Mountains near Parker Dam, the Turtle Mountains, the Chuca-wallas, the Eagles, the Palo Verdes, the Old Woman Mountains, to Indio, Palm Desert, Indian Wells, Borrego Springs.

When we got back to Laguna we had lots to do cleaning up. Then I was put on the advance unit to New Jersey to prepare Fort Dix for the division. When we got to Fort Dix[281], we knew that we were going to go to Europe. We got some training there, and then went to Camp Kilmer.[282] We were so tired of training, and we were anxious to get into combat.

We departed from New York on 1 July 1944 on the *Queen Mary*, from Pier 16. We were moved by train under heavy security from Camp Kilmer. We march-ed to get on the boat, where we stayed for one night below decks. Everything was

---

[281]20 March 1944
[282]23 June 1944

secured. We had to take off all our identification patches. I was in charge of eighteen people in a state room, where they had bunks four-tiers high. The portholes were all blacked out. I was up on deck and somebody opened the porthole in my stateroom. There must have been secret service men with binoculars looking off the Statue of Liberty, because they identified which porthole was opened. We had to go before the captain. I didn't know who did it, but one guy confessed. He had to mop the deck for the five days it took us to go over.

We had sent an advance party to get our camp ready at Knutsford, England South of Manchester, where General Patton had his headquarters. We had about 1,800 people from different companies. There were probably about 13,000 soldiers from our division plus 500 WACS and 500 nurses. The nurses were under tight security. They were put way down at the bottom of the ship near the boiler room. The MPs would bring them up at night for air. Everyone started flirting with the nurses or the WACS. There were also 800 British crewmen.

The *Queen Mary* and the *Queen Elizabeth* were priority targets for the German submarine wolf-packs. We left New York, and traveled along the coasts of Newfoundland and Nova Scotia. We had blimps, which were good at submarine detection because they could see the submerged submarine's shadow. When we got to Greenland, the American Air Force gave us protection with their bombers. After Iceland the RAF escorted us. We had a storm in the North Sea. Forty-five foot waves rocked our boat. Everyone was vomiting in their helmets. One British soldier told me, "Son, eat!"

We had to eat British food. Imagine kidney stew for breakfast! We also had horse meat which they called "bully beef." The mutton, which was imported from New Zealand, was tough and greasy. One day we'd sleep down in the state room and the next day we'd have to sleep in our sacks on one of the three covered decks. They decided to have ack-ack practice when we were trying to sleep. We thought, "Oh no, the Germans are after us!" We were right underneath the gun decks, and it was noisy!

We landed in Greenock in the Firth of Clyde, Scotland. Of course, the *Queen Mary's* home port was Southhampton, but they couldn't land there because that was too close to where the Germans were bombing. We went in on small ships because the harbor wasn't deep enough for the *Queen Mary*. When we got into the bay area we saw all these little aircraft carriers, along with cruisers and destroyers. There must have been a thousand ships up there, all on our side!

When we got into Glasgow, a Royal Highlander Kilt Band played for us. A general greeted us. We also had a big steak dinner at which they told us what we were going to do. Then we departed by train from Scotland for Manchester, England. On both sides of the tracks there were thousands and thousands of shells and bombs stored in what looked like open-ended huts. At that moment we knew we were in a war zone. When we got to Manchester, we were trucked to our camp, Knutsford. There were English Home Guards at the gate with bayonets. They were older fellows, maybe in their sixties. Then we knew for *sure* that we were in a war zone. We knew that this was it. It was total blackout. If we lit a cigarette or used a flashlight we'd get shot. They had orders to shoot anybody.

After we got settled, the officers told us that next door was Patton's residence. We'd be part of his Third Army. Before this, they had given him a fictitious army at Dover, because the Allies wanted to deceive German intelligence. Since Patton was the most prominent of American generals, they made it look like he would be invading the French coast at a different point from the actual invasion site.[283] He had Sherman tanks made out of balloons. The Germans would send reconnaissance planes over, and the British ack-ack would keep the German planes at about 25,000 feet up. When the Germans took aerial photos these balloons looked like real tanks. The Army used phonographs and amplifiers to imitate the sounds of moving tanks. They even used landing barges made out of rubber. We learned later that this deception made the Germans keep five armored divisions at Calais. Had Hitler released those armored divisions like Rommel wanted, then we might never have been successful at Normandy.

We stayed in camp for about a month, and did a lot of marching through towns. We went to classes taught by British and American men who had landed in Normandy. Some of them were recuperating from wounds. They told us many things about the German way of fighting.

We went by truck in units to Southampton. When we got to the middle of town, the air raid siren went off. We hit the deck right on the road where we were marching. Then we heard a great big bang about two blocks away. We could see the smoke and the flames. The whole block was obliterated. You didn't hear any whistle or anything. It was a V-2 rocket. They went high, then dropped. You couldn't hear them. Everybody was scared.

We loaded up and stayed in the port until evening. We left as a division on LSTs with all accessories—nearly 30,000 personnel, including officers, support troops, tank battalions, tank destroyers, and artillery, medical battalions, even field hospital people. We knew the Channel was rough because we heard stories about D-Day.

Some of us from the 319th landed at Utah Beach[284] with the French 2nd Armored Division. We fought with them halfway across France. The rest of the division landed on Omaha Beach. We had to split it up in order to prevent too many troops from being concentrated in one area.

When I left New York, I thought that I'd never come back home. That was in my mind the whole time. Then when I got into England that reinforced my doubts. Then when I got onto Utah Beach, I thought, "I'll never make it to shore!" Fortunately, the beach was secure. We didn't make camp the first night.

---

[283]This was part of Operation COCKADE.
[284]3 August 1944, assembling at St. Jores 7 August.

We just slept on the ground. German bombers came over to bomb the supplies on the beach. The concussions were so great we were lifted off the ground!

On the second day, we went through to St. Lô with the First Army. We were driving south. On the second night, the Germans counter-attacked with two Panzer divisions. Of course we heard the shooting all around us through the hedgerows. The Germans always attacked at night because they were scared of our air power.

That first night the guys in my platoon were in this hedgerow. We heard that the German counterattack was coming our way. What they were going to do was to cut across Avranches and trap some of the troops who were ahead or between the two sections of the Army. One of my guys lost his trench shovel, so I gave him mine, while I dug in with a knife. I was going like a beaver! We were really scared. Everybody was hollering, but we didn't want to make too much noise because the Germans might have been in the next hedgerow. Then a V-1 came over and totally changed our way of thinking. The first thing that came to our minds was either we kill them or they kill us. There was no other way around it, unless we were taking prisoners.[285] We dug in for a while and then got an all clear and moved out.

When we moved at night, we used blackout lights on the vehicles, except when the enemy was in the vicinity. We kept fifty-foot intervals when we were in total blackout. Sometimes the MPs, who ordinarily made us keep that distance, would get us to get as close as possible to avoid getting lost. It depended on how clear the night was.

In the little towns the Germans would put snipers in the steeples and belfries. Patton gave orders for the tanks to shell the steeples in case they housed snipers. We would throw hand grenades into other possible hiding places, like basements. Around the third night this kid got shot through the head. There was nothing we could do for him. I don't think he ever got a chance to fire his rifle. We felt very sad because we didn't know anything about him. Not having really known the dead is the worst part. You knew if they were in your outfit or that they were in the infantry, but you didn't know them on a personal basis.

Our doctors were good with the wounded. If it was a major wound, they knew that the patient would die, but they did everything in their power to make sure that they got the best treatment. In France, they brought in a young second lieutenant. He was unconscious. His skin was clammy. We couldn't find any wounds. The doctor, another technician and I started giving him resuscitation on the way to the field hospital. There they found a little red spot on his chest, close to his heart. It was made by a small piece of shrapnel that went through and hit his heart. He died.

---

[285] At this point Mr. Radock added the aside: "Even then, German prisoners were shot. Guys would take four or five prisoners, shoot them and then say, 'Well they tried to run away!'"

The Army had aid stations set up in tents or any kind of building. Reconnaissance would find the best spots. There were doctors, technicians and aid men, two aid men with stretchers per company. We also had litter bearers from my company who would work with them. These groups would go into three battalions and they would rotate every couple of days. They lived right with the infantry men in foxholes. The aid man would patch a man up as much as possible and maybe give him a shot of morphine for pain. They had big field dressings. Of course, stomach wounds were pretty tough to wrap. Then we'd try to get them back to the aid station where the doctor worked right away on stopping the flow of blood. That's the first thing they try to do because blood loss could lead to shock and death.

We had an ambulance with each battalion aid station. Along with the ambulance was a driver and an assistant. They would bring the wounded back to our collection station. There we'd redress the wounded and give them blood plasma. Then the four doctors in the collection station would reevaluate the wounds, and maybe give more plasma or new dressings. Then we shipped the wounded to the clearing station about five miles away, where there were more doctors and technicians, or to the field hospital about ten miles away, depending on the seriousness of their wounds.

We treated German wounded, as well. Some of the hard-core Nazis were tough. In the Army there were soldiers from twenty-six different Native American tribes. They would use them for night patrols, since the Indians liked that. They wore nothing that would make noise. They even wore socks over their boots. They would bring back prisoners. One day an Indian master sergeant brought this wounded SS officer in. He was a typical SS soldier with blonde hair and blue eyes. We doctored him, then called Intelligence. The German didn't want to talk. The major questioning him was Jewish. The Indian master sergeant shot his submachine-gun in front of the soldier's feet. When the rounds got close enough to the German's boots, he talked. He told us that he was a tank commander who was wounded two or three times. He got decorated for destroying a Russian tank with a hand grenade through the turret hatch. I think he was only about twenty-one years old. He was a tough nut to crack, but they cracked him.

We went across the Our/Sauer on a pontoon bridge.[286] There we set up a bigger collection station. We were faced with more trenchfoot and respiratory diseases than combat wounds. Many of the guys had to ford streams that were up to their waists, and they didn't have time to change their shoes and dry out. Patton established rules that required us to set up drying stoves wherever we could to dry our clothes out. This was standard procedure for the infantry because they didn't carry a change of clothes in their combat gear. A full fieldpack con-

---

[286]7 February 1945. The 319th at Wallendorf.

tained an extra set of clothes and shoes, and socks. You didn't carry a full field-pack unless you knew that you were going a greater distance, maybe thirty miles.

Our collecting station was maybe four or five miles behind frontlines, because we had to get as close as possible to cut down travel time. One time in a small village we were helping armor, a dangerous job because tanks drew heavy artillery fire. To make matters worse the Germans were only a few hundred yards away on a ridge, hammering away at us with big mortars. The Germans also knew the terrain and had maps we didn't have. They knew where we would be and where our defenses would be set up and other things.

I was in this room at a house where our billets were. Our collection station was a couple doors down. We had a German trailer with a generator plant, which we towed with the kitchen truck. We used it to set up electricity for our station and headquarters. In fact we provided electricity for some of the other units by this means. During battle a shell hit that trailer, but it was still functional. I was in the room nearby and the glass blew up all over me. Every time I left the building or headquarters, they would lob a couple shells. They knew when our chow time or mail call was and that's especially when they would shell us. The first sergeant and our commanding officer told me to stay inside the building. Those Germans had me buffaloed. I really got scared because I thought that the next one was going to be for me. Fortunately, that didn't happen.

Troops coming to the aid station would be tired, wet, and muddy. The relieved troops would go to the rear and get a shower in portable showers the Army provided when we were halfway through France. They would set up big tents with showerheads, near rivers. It wasn't like home, but it was some relief to bathe the entire body. Most of the time the guys washed using helmets as sinks. Clothes were a different story. Our only laundry services were provided by rivers.

We got a lot of wine and cognac which we carried in our supply trucks. We'd give each wounded soldier a drink, if they drank, to warm them up and keep their spirits up. If we had them, we would offer them cigarettes. What they really needed was hot food.

A lot of wounded guys though, wanted to get patched up and go back to the front. One of our guys got shot and lost his testicles. He said, "I got a young wife at home. What am I going to do?" Sometimes, if a soldier had his legs blown off, his buddies would tell someone to shoot him, especially if he lost his legs clean to the hips. You could see why they wanted it done. Maybe if some soldiers had small arms, they'd do it. Sometimes guys would shoot themselves just to get the "Million-Dollar Wound." One guy shot down at his ankle and blew his whole heel off. They had to amputate. Some of them shot their trigger fingers off.

Patton wanted explanations of suspicious wounds. Self-inflicted wounds meant court martial. In a way, I understood the actions of guys who shot themselves. They were consistently fighting day and night in horrible weather under constant bombardment from artillery and mortars. They saw a lot of buddies get killed. The combination of these factors eventually affected the soldier mentally.

When the weather was bad, even tanks got stuck. Sometimes they built roads out of trees and logs. We'd take the four-wheel drive jeeps as far as possible, and put the wounded litter soldiers on them. From there we'd evacuate the wounded to an ambulance or sometimes to the aid station. Winter took its toll. There were a lot of frozen feet. The doctors and nurses did the amputations back at the field hospital. The soldiers didn't suffer as much from amputations or wounds in the cold because they didn't bleed as much as they would have in warm weather. The temperature was usually below zero, so as soon as the blood was exposed to the atmosphere, it gelled. However, one went into shock right away, and a lot of soldiers died from shock. Many times, you just couldn't get to them. One time we got a call and I went with the ambulance driver to get a GI in the field. While he was laying there a sniper got him. He died in my arms from a gunshot wound to the head. There was nothing that we could do for him.[287]

Icy roads made evacuation difficult. On top of that, we didn't know where a lot of places were. What the Germans used to do was turn signs around. A lot of signs were down anyway from shelling. Some of the roads and villages had been shelled more than once, and when the Germans came back through[288] they shelled them again. Not much was left standing.

We were at St. Avold when Hitler launched his *Wacht am Rhein*, the attack through the Ardennes, the Battle of the Bulge. Patton decided to send the 4th Armored, the 80th and the 26th up to the Bastogne area where our 101st Airborne was trapped. We were getting ready to breach the Siegfried Line, but that was canceled. We were ordered to move north to Luxembourg with all speed and protect it from the enemy. We pulled out of the line, loaded our vehicles, gassed up, and pushed off. The roads were icy. We drove in a blizzard with headlights on! Our armor, the 702nd Tank Battalion was with us. The MPs kept the convoy closed tight. The engineers went first to check for mines and to check out the bridges. All tired vehicles had chains.

Thirty-six hours later we arrived in Luxembourg to relieve the 28th Infantry Division's rear echelon troops, mostly cooks, bakers, clerks and medics. They were glad to see us! On 22 December we attacked. We caught the German Wehrmacht's Seventh Army by surprise and slaughtered one of its divisions. The second day after Bastogne was liberated, the ambulances went in. They were waiting for the armored support and the troops to have cleared certain routes.

During the ridge fighting,[289] our infantry took this one town, but the Germans, who were across the ridge, were shelling us pretty hard. The billet that I had for my troops was a two-and-a-half-storey house with red tiles for a roof. One

---

[287]The 80th Division suffered 3,038 KIA, 12,284 WIA. 442 personnel later died of wounds.

[288]16 December 1944 during the Ardennes Offensive (Battle of the Bulge).

[289]This incident occurred around 23 December 1944 in Heiderscheid where Mr. Radock set up an ambulance shuttle post for the Company C Combat Team, servicing the 319th.

of our artillery observers said, "I want to go upstairs and poke a hole through the roof, set up my periscope, and call in for artillery fire."

I said, "Sure. Go ahead."

I was there with him while he was getting things set up. Across the ridge he noticed a Tiger tank set up in a three-storey hospital. There was a hole in the wall through which the tank would ease its gun, fire three shells, then withdraw. We'd hear the 88s go whistling over our heads. He told me to take a look and I saw the same thing happen. Our infantry was ahead and down in a ravine trying to out-flank the Germans. He called this artillery outfit, who called the 19th TAC. They sent four P-47s who came in and bombed that Tiger. Fortunately the hospital was empty. It was a civilian hospital for the townspeople, but the Germans probably used it as well. I still maintain that if they had the right to use that building for a hostile engagement then we had a right to bomb it!

Each division had both a tank battalion and an antitank battalion. They had a hard time going up into that town because it was windy and filled with icy narrow roads. A couple of them went over the embankment and guys got killed. I was running an ambulance post. They brought the ambulances from the aid stations to me and I would transfer the casualties to another ambulance. We evacu-ated everyone, but our troops came first, then the civilians, then the Germans, but they got the same treatment. Some of the guys got so mad waiting for German prisoners to be evacuated to POW camps that they wanted me to take them out and shoot them. One staff sergeant volunteered to take six to eight prisoners back to the POW camp in the rear. He took them over the ridge. We heard shots. He killed them all.

Some of the Germans were disgusted. A lot of them where either much older or younger than the normal age of recruitment. Some Hitler Youth, who volun-teered in the Battle of the Bulge, were only thirteen years old. When we came to bandage their wounds they were scared of us, because their propaganda said we didn't take prisoners. They got better medical treatment from us than we got from them. The German doctors did amputations and treated severe wounds with no painkillers. They also didn't have plasma.

Our litter bearers suffered because they were right up there with the infantry. In combat, our litter bearers were exposed to constant gunfire. Quite a few of them received Distinguished Service Crosses. One litter bearer was a Catholic chaplain. There was a white flag up for truce, but the Germans kept shooting. This Chaplain picked up a guy on his back and carried him out of the line of fire. Then he went back to get another one. He rescued four men. He received the DSC.[290]

---

[290] Awarded to any member of the United States Army, regardless of rank, who "shall have distinguished himself or herself by extraordinary heroism."

We lost a lot of men at the Siegfried Line and during and after the Rhine crossing.[291] One time we stopped at a barn. We had a tough time bringing casualties in. As the ambulance was backing up, I was guiding it to the door to unload casualties. The driver gunned his engine too much and pinned me against the side of the barn. I thought that I had broken legs, but I didn't. They carried me on a stretcher, which I stayed on for about a week. My knees were blown up like balloons.

Once we got across the Rhine, we hit the Autobahns. We headed for Kassel.[292] When we were about thirty miles south of Kassel, one of our lieutenants, who was in charge of the ambulance platoon told me, "Sergeant Radock, you go back with the maintenance truck, with the maintenance sergeant, and keep the convoy closed up there. I'll ride in the jeep in front."

He made a left turn and went across a stream and then made a right turn, which he shouldn't have done. We arrived at a battle between American and German tanks. The town was burning up. The German infantry was shooting burp guns. Germans were on our right flank in the woods shooting at us. We were on a little sunken road, and this gave us some protection. The tankers and the armored infantry were dug in on our left. One of our infantry soldiers said, "Where in the heck are you guys going? There's Germans all over the place."

Then the lieutenant said, "Sergeant, you'd better take the lead."

So we unhitched all the trailers and turned all those vehicles around. On that narrow road, everything was chaotic. Tanks were shelling each other and everybody was scared. We got half of that convoy turned around. We didn't have any casualties. I took charge of the convoy. Further on the road to Kassel, about 7:00 a.m., we saw vehicles, a six-by-six jeep and two armored cars, both ours. The Germans were breaking out of the Ruhr Pocket. I think they had about a half-million troops in there. They would leave the Pocket at night to mine the roads. These vehicles that we saw were blown up. A convoy, which I believe was the 86th Chemical Company, came up behind me. The colonel got out and asked, "What happened?"

I said, "The Germans mined the roads."

He asked me where I was going. I told him that we were heading for Kassel. He said, "That's where we're going too. You lead the way, but first let's get these vehicles out."

So with our six-by-six kitchen truck, we pushed the vehicles out of the way. As we were going, we were buzzed by four RAF Spitfires. We had panels on our vehicles, though. Then we saw a German patrol of eighteen men about a mile from the road. The truck driver said, "Let's shoot them."

---

[291]14 February–27 March 1945. The 319th crossed at Bischofsheim.
[292]2–4 April 1945. After the expansion of the Mainz bridgehead, the 80th followed the 6th Armored Division to Kassel, where there was fierce house-to-house fighting.

I said, "With what? We only have one M1. Don't worry, they'll run into our troops. We're not going to get into any engagements!"

We got to Kassel and there was some pretty tough street fighting. There was a German Tiger tank factory near there. Some of the civilians were taking those tanks out. The paint was still wet on them. Our troops killed about 400 German civilians, who were armed with shotguns and hunting rifles. They had orders to fight to the death.

One of our aid-station jeeps was transporting a badly wounded German officer. A German nurse was giving him aid right on the jeep while they were traveling. When they passed through town a young German soldier about fifteen years old shot a Panzerfaust from the basement killing everyone on that jeep. After that happened, the infantry threw hand grenades and killed the kid.

As we got further into Germany, Hitler ordered *all* the population to defend the country. We didn't have to kill as many civilians because our general had a plan where he'd call up the 19th Tactical Air Command. TAC would send about eight P-47s over to circle the town, dropping surrender leaflets. Then they'd send in a couple emissaries under guard to tell the burgermeisters to meet in the town, where they would give them ultimatums, "Now you go back and if there are any Germans in the town, tell them to leave. Our aircraft are going to bomb the town."

Meanwhile, the P-47s kept circling lower and lower. Artillery and tanks starting moving as well. It worked! Of course, the Germans were desperate at this point. It's a shame that they didn't give up sooner because they would have saved a lot of their own people, but Hitler and those SS troops were nuts!

It wasn't long before we started to come upon the death camps. We already knew about them from people who were captured and escaped. The word was out that we would see a lot of things in our life that we would never see again. Before we arrived, a lot of the SS guards took off. At Ohrdruf this one guy, who weighed about 230 pounds, was demonstrating how they killed some of the inmates if they disobeyed. They would have to bend over a table while the guards hit them all over their body with a club. Somebody said, "He can't be a prisoner. He's too heavy. He's eaten a lot."

He turned out to be one of the death camp guards. One of the inmates pointed him out to us. The MPs took him and locked him up.

At Buchenwald, I was standing close to one of our infantry colonels when an inmate took our colonel's trench knife and cut a German major across the throat. Then another inmate grabbed the carbine off a soldier and pumped a few bullets in his stomach. Me and the colonel were splashed with his blood. That's how close we were. We didn't stop them. They had the right to revenge.

Seeing the death camps changed the attitudes of our troops. After that they no longer took many prisoners. There were a lot of Germans who surrendered with their hands up, holding a white flag, but got shot anyway.

When the war ended, we thought for sure that we were going to the Pacific. We thought, "Well we didn't get killed here, so we're going to go to the islands and get killed by the Japs."

We were elected to stay for the occupation. That's when we were really happy! We went into Austria, to Lake Traunsee. We were in a boathouse on the lake. My platoon slept upstairs on the floor. There were a couple bunks, but it was pretty tough to house a whole platoon. Then we had twenty-six Arabian horses which we used for riding. From there we moved into Bavaria for occupation. Once again we had to clean up our rooms because we were in a hotel. We divided the rooms up. We had classes about the occupation, a review of first aid procedures, a critique of the whole war. We had close-order drill and did maintenance on our equipment.

I had seventy-two points, and I elected to go home, even though I had the opportunity for a promotion to staff sergeant. I had enough of the war. Me and this other guy joined the 242nd Field Artillery Battalion. They trucked us into France, to Camp Phillip Morris. I was one of the sergeants, so I had to get the guys up and do guard duty, and other things. At that time they had a ship strike on. So we got stuck there. We had six men in a tent, with a stove, but no fuel. We had already rationed it out. We could only get so much wood a day, but it wasn't enough. It was so cold we slept in overcoats.

We were there from September until the end of November. They had a flu epidemic and the hospitals were jammed full. I was sick for six weeks. They had technicians coming around to check on everyone. They gave us flu shots to combat the flu, but I got sick from that, too.

We finally got on a Victory Ship and bounced across the ocean through a storm. We got into New York, the ship was covered with ice. A lot of us were on deck to view the Statue of Liberty, and when we got closer to the pier, we heard an Army band playing military music. As soon as we got off, they took us into a huge hall. In Camp Shanks, New York, a general welcomed us back to the States. Then we had a big steak dinner. From there we got a series of shots. They checked on the troops then shipped them out to different Army camps in their own states. I went to Indiantown Gap, where we stayed for about a week or two. We had lots of entertainment, dancers, singers, guitar players.

When I got home, we all felt kind of numb. I didn't have too much to say other than greeting everyone. All the relatives came. My brother, Joe, had come home about four or five months earlier than me. We talked a little about the war. That was a big journey. I think that I traveled about forty-one of the States and seven countries. I never expected to travel overseas like that.

It was tough at first. I wasn't used to a soft bed. I had stomach problems for about two or three years. I couldn't hold a lot of food down. We got a 300-dollar bonus. Then we signed up for the 52/20 program. I went back to the mill about six weeks after I got home. After I got married, I decided to go to trade school in Pittsburgh to study diesels.

1. Bethendorf, Germany. Michael Gatto, John Hoffman, Virgil Grimshaw, J. Grumpler, Pop Newsome, mechanic, kneeling.

2. Michael Gatto and driver Pete Dolan, Bethendorf, Germany

3. Unknown location. German soldiers crowd around a downed British fighter plane. Michael Gatto "liberated" the photograph.

Example of World War II V-Mail from Michael Gatto to his family.

1. Corporal Andrews readies Sam Folby's detail for the return to camp after a long march during basic training. 1942.

2. Sam Folby's unit presents arms at retreat during basic training.

3. Sam Folby with a nurse Lt. Kurley at 7th Station Hospital, Oran, 1942.

1. Joseph Kay (front) with buddies from 1st Squad, 3rd Platoon, Company G, 254th Infantry.

2. Joseph Kay and buddies, just after war's end.

3. Joseph Kay and a buddy take a Lunch break in a town square in Germany. "Hey, Joe, you got chocolate?" the kids would say.

1. Ron Johnston of Indiana, PA (left) and William King, Camp van Dorn, Mississippi, 1943.

2. William King watches over Orville Hastler napping in a basket. Germany, 1945.

3. Orville Hastler of Richmond, Virginia at Vilsbiburg, Germany.

1. A discussion over what the map says. Southern Bavaria, 1945.

(Photo courtesy of William King)

2. Officers of the 99th Division check maps at Elsenborn Ridge during the Battle of the Bulge, 20 December 1944.

(Photo courtesy of William King)

3. William King in his foxhole, Elsenborn Ridge, 20 December 1944.

1. The Big Three! Al Kormas (right), Ed Freel and Harry Truman at the Brandenburg Gate, Berlin, 1945.

2. After three weeks in the swamp. Camp Shelby, Mississippi. Left to right: Unknown, "Big Foot" Parker, Al Kormas, Unknown, Sal DiMascio.

3. "Juggy" Powers, Al Kormas, Dale Kilzer on Saturday KP.

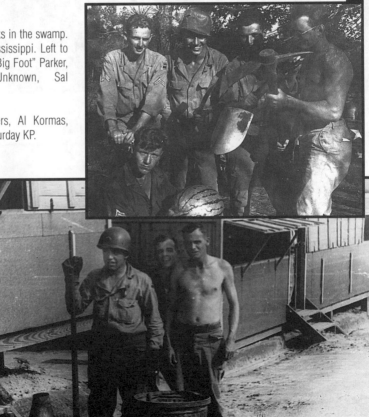

1. Jack McDaniel "surrenders" to two Frauleins in Heddesheim, Germany.

2. (Left to right); Sergeant West, Sergeant DePhillip and Jack McDaniel. Camp Livingstone, Louisiana.

3. McDaniel and buddy at a Lister Bag, Manila in the Phillipines.

4. Jerry Jouralis, "Snake" Carter, Jack McDaniel and Laverne Hotaling at San Luis Obispo, California. McDaniel is perched on Hotaling's right arm.

1. Richard Radock's Ambulance Platoon jeep. Driver Milton Dieter is inside with mascot "Cognac," Wimsbach, Austria, 1945.

2. Richard Radock's "That Old Gang of Mine." Company C, 305th Medical Battalion Motor Pool.

Photos: Courtesy of
Richard R. Buchanan

German troops firing the dreaded 88. "Doc" Buchanan made the print from film he found in a "liberated" German camera.

"I Was Just A Guy With A Uniform."

William Smolcic

United States Seventh Army
45th Infantry Division
179th Infantry Regiment
2nd Battalion
Company E

Yukon, Pennsylvania, 9 April 1925

"We had just piled it up when two 88 rounds came in. I knew they would hit very close. I dove through an open cellar window. I landed on something soft and immediately after I heard those shells go off in the courtyard, followed by screams. I dug myself out of what I was in, came out into the sunlight, and saw that I was covered from head to toe in red! I thought it was blood, but it turned out I had dove into a bin of over-ripe beets! I looked around the courtyard and two of us were the only ones left standing. I had a little nick on my knuckle, but that was it. Everybody was yelling, 'Medic! Medic!' The medic was holding his eye in his hand. He said, 'I can't help you this time, boys.' Me and the other guy set about patching up the wounded, using our medical kits and the medic's. My foxhole buddy, Jim Ritchie, was hit the worst with wounds in his head and all over his body. We patched him up first. I said to the kid I was with, 'You make these guys comfortable, and I'll go to the rear and see if I can find stretcher bearers to haul these guys out.'"

I started hunting when I was twelve. You could always tell it was the first day of hunting season. Every one had a hunting dog and as soon as guys came outside wearing their hunting clothes the dogs all over town would start barking. All those days spent in the woods helped me as an infantryman. I was in good physical shape, and I had no fear of firearms. Most of the city kids were petrified of them, and held their rifles like they were holding snakes.

My father, Joe, came from Czechoslovakia around 1909, from a peasant family. My mother and dad were from the same town, but met and married in the States. My dad spent most of his life working in coal mines. During World War II he went to work as a motor winder at Westinghouse. He was a go-getter.

William Smolcic: Off the line in France, 1944

When one mine shut down he would go to another mine that was still working and pester them until they hired him. We didn't live in any grand style, but we had food on the table.

Uncle Sam took me July 1943, after I graduated high school. I was eighteen. The minute I graduated from high school I started applying for jobs, but no one hired me because of my draft status. When I got my draft notice, I felt fear and apprehension, but also anticipation and excitement. I hadn't done anything or been anywhere. I had no idea of what fighting was all about. A month after I got my notice, I was in basic training.

I took a test, and was accepted to the ASTP (Army Specialized Training Program). After basic training, all the ASTP guys were grouped together for another test. I flunked it, along with another guy from home. We were the only ones who flunked. They threw a word at us called "calculus." It was Greek to both of us. The rest of the guys in the company came from Belle Vernon, Monessen and Charleroi where they had bigger schools and were more conversant in higher mathematics. All the ones who passed went to New York City College, my future brother-in-law among them. My buddy and I were ultimately sent to Florida to teach recruits basic training. In a way, flunking the test was a blessing. The ASTP folded because of high casualties overseas. My future brother-in-law and the rest got into combat much earlier than I did.[293]

I went to Fort McClellan, Alabama for basic training. We would do long marches in ninety-degree heat. We once did a thirty-two-mile hike with full field-pack and M1s and it took us twelve hours. We took a ten-minute break every hour. That was at night but it was even hot at night. Our feet bled from broken blisters. Afterwards, I marveled how fast the Coke machine emptied. If you weren't one of the first forty or fifty you got no Coke.

Our drill sergeants were "Panamanians," peacetime soldiers who had served in Panama. They were rougher than a cob and did their best to make life miserable for us, but it was for our own good. They taught us was how to use initiative in case our officers got killed. The worst punishment they handed out was to make guys clean out the grease trap in the kitchen. The stink was unimaginable. It took them four days to get back to normal after cleaning that thing. Fortu-

---

[293]Mr. Smolcic added as an aside: "My brother-in-law had been on the train with me from New Stanton to Fort Meade. He was a little guy, probably was five-foot-six at the most. At the time I had no idea he would end up being my brother-in-law but we became rather fast friends. On twelve-mile hikes at night he would start to poop out after about three miles. So I would carry his rifle and pack as well as my own. That may be one of the reasons he fixed me up with his sister! I remember one time I was by his bunk and he had arrayed six or seven pictures of girls, and they were all nice looking girls. One especially appealed to me and I said, 'I would really like to meet this girl!' He said, 'That shouldn't be any problem, that's my sister.' He wrote to her and said, 'There's a guy here who would like to write to you.' Her name was Louise Zema. We started corresponding and I went to see her when I came home for a five-day furlough just before I went overseas. Within a few months after I was out of the service I was married to her."

nately, I was able to avoid that punishment. KP was a regular duty for everybody. One of the benefits of KP was we could sneak all the food we wanted!

After basic I was sent to Camp Blanding, Florida to train recruits. I was tough but compassionate because I had already been through the grinder. I taught one recruit how to use the bayonet. At first he broke down and cried. I convinced him that either he killed or he would be killed. After a lot of cajoling, I finally got him to participate in the drill.

I went through one training cycle with the recruits, then in July or August of 1944, I got orders to go overseas. I got a leave, after which I shipped out from Newport News, Virginia, as a replacement. I had no idea where I was going to end up. I was just a guy with a uniform.

We went over on a rust-bucket Liberty Ship. It took seventeen days, and on most of them the sea was rough. We ate standing up at a steel table with no chairs. We had our food in front of us and every now and then the ship would hit a swell and everything on the table would fly to one side. If you happened to be the unfortunate guy on the end you got clobbered with all that greasy food! I was prone to seasickness, so I had a pretty miserable seventeen days. My head was hanging over the rail most of the time. As a child I got sick on the merry-go-round, so you can imagine how I felt on a ship! There was a joke going around at the time. This GI has his head over the rail and some salty sailor comes up and says, "What's the matter, buddy? Weak stomach?"

The GI responds, "Hell, no! I'm throwing it out there as far as the next guy!"

Our ship docked in Naples, Italy. I ended up in a repo depo in Casserta. We took over Mussolini's son-in-law's dairy farm estate as a replacement center. We'd lay around with very little to do. Every once in a while a guy you got to know would get called and he'd be shipped out to a unit. They wouldn't take large groups of men. It was piecemeal.

The food was nothing to write home about. It was stew every day, and very bland. Not like the food my mother made, seasoned with garlic and onions. I was at the depot three weeks and started to hope that I would spend the rest of the war there. Then I envisioned having to eat that awful stew every day. I wrote a letter to my dad saying, "This stew over here is horrible tasting. Could you possibly send me some onions?"

I got a letter back, "The onions are on the way."

The mail system was so slow I was long in combat before the onions arrived. My dad was very meticulous and wanted to make sure the onions were in good shape when they arrived. He got small onions of the same size. He made a carton out of quarter-inch plywood about the size of a cigar box. He drilled holes all through that so that the onions would get air. Three months later the onions caught up with me on the front line. I was in a hole on the side of a mountain. I heard the mailman yell my name. "Yo! I'm up here," I yelled back!

He was laughing like Hell. "I got a package for you," he said.

He showed me the box. Every one of those holes my dad drilled had a green onion sprout coming out. I had no stew this time. The onions ended up over the other side of the mountain!

One day it came my turn to leave the depot. I got on a ship at Naples for Marseilles, France. Again I was thrust among people I didn't know. I could never make any friends. This was my entire history in the army! Replacements would come in and would be dead before you even got to know their names. Anyway, you really didn't want to get too close to somebody because it would be too tough on you if they got killed.

In Marseilles we boarded forty-and-eight box cars.[294] We traveled through the night into the northern part of France. I was put in the 45th Division.[295] The only thing I heard about them was that they were comprised almost entirely of Indians. By the time I got to them, only one Indian was left. All the rest had been killed or wounded.

We came up at night in big, canvas-covered trucks with blacked-out lights. Those of us in the back of the trucks could see that we were traveling through woods and were going up into the mountains. The trucks pulled to the side of the road and the sergeant hollered, "Okay, hit the deck!"

I got into a ditch, right next to a dead German soldier. He was all bloated. It was frightening for a nineteen year old to see that, but within a couple of days that kind of thing became commonplace. Dead horses always got me gagging, though. When a horse got hit by a mortar shell there was an awful pile of blood and guts. The Germans used a lot of horses. We didn't. *We* were the horses!

The sergeant led us up into the side of a mountain. It was pitch black out. We had our first baptism of fire. Our artillery was firing behind us over our heads. Unbeknownst to us they were trying to soften up the area we were to take the next day. We were scared. The sergeant then told us to drop our packs and dig in. All this time the 105s and 155s were firing. After a couple of hours of sleep the sergeant rousted us up and said, " Okay, boys. Saddle up! Load your rifles! We're going to attack!"

We had no idea where we were. They pointed out, "This is the way you want to go." And that's the way we went. We were on the crest of a mountain. All of our attacks started at pre-dawn, but we could see a little town in the distance, across some fields. That was our objective. Always, when they sent replacements up, they dispersed them among the units. Two for this platoon, three for that platoon. They experimented with our group. They put us all in one platoon. They put two seasoned sergeants in charge. The sergeants made us rush down the hill toward this town, screaming like a bunch of banshees and firing our rifles as we went. They figured if we couldn't kill the Germans, we'd scare the Hell outta

---

[294]Forty men or eight horses.
[295]Oklahoma National Guard.

of them! The town turned out to be deserted. We spread out and checked each house. We kicked doors in and all the usual stuff! I'm not pretending that our screaming and shouting had anything to do with it. The Germans probably pulled out the night before! I had no targets so I started shooting doorknobs off of doors and little balls off steeple tops! It was something to do. We were making a lot of noise hoping if there was anyone left they'd get the Hell out! Where the Hell all the civilians went, I have no idea. We felt pretty good about ourselves after that. We took our first objective and never lost a drop of blood! It all went down hill after that! Of the thirty-two men I moved up into the line with that first night, by war's end I was the only one left alive.

My combat experience was almost a hundred percent in the Vosges Mountains in northern France. Most of the towns we went through were like that first town. They had 150 inhabitants at the most and sometimes only two-dozen houses. We fought from dark to dark. We got up, got a K-ration breakfast and as soon as it got light enough we'd move out. When it got dark we dug holes and teamed up with someone. One man had a pick and the other had a shovel. The digging was tough! If you could go down five or six inches without hitting a big rock, that was a big evening for you! Many times those holes weren't really holes at all but slit trenches. Often a guy couldn't get any further in that hole and he'd have his butt sticking up in the air when he'd lay in it.

We were constantly fatigued! At the most we got four hours of sleep a night! One man guarded while the other slept, two hours on, two off. Once in a great while we'd be in an area for two or three days, but mainly it was moving and digging a hole every day! On those days when we were stationary we'd make renovations to our holes. Once or twice we were on the outskirts of a village where they had barns. We'd sneak in and occasionally we'd find a big, cross-cut saw. We'd cut big timbers and put those on top of our holes and pile dirt around them. That made us feel secure from 88mm tree bursts.

Nighttime in a foxhole was a good time to write a letter home. Our K-ration boxes were covered in a wax-like substance. I would take my knife and scrape the wax off the box. After I accumulated enough of it I made a candle. I would then pull a thick blanket over the top of my hole so no light would shine out. Then I would write. After a while the blanket would start to drip with water and there'd be blotches on the paper. I never told my parents the truth about what was happening to me in my letters. My mother was a highly nervous person and I didn't want her more upset than she had to be. Whenever I wrote home I made up some cock-and-bull story.

Once we occupied a pillbox on the Maginot Line. It was luxurious. The Germans had it first, and then we took it. When we left, we made damn sure we didn't have to fight for it again. We put all our excess ammunition and TNT inside. We set a fuse and by the time we were on the next mountain we heard this big explosion and saw a fireball as the top of that thing blew off.

We were always cold and wet. Sometimes it was so cold the receivers on our rifles would freeze. We just peed on them to thaw them out. After that, they would fire all day. We were ordered not to take our boots off, because our feet would swell. My longest stint without taking a shower or a bath was twenty-eight days. During that time those boots never came off! Another thing that I dreaded was frozen blankets. You got a bed roll every night, but you never got your own back. I always tried to keep mine as dry and clean as possible, but some of the guys weren't that particular. Sometimes those bed rolls were as hard as rock and broke when you tried to unfold them! They were pretty rank, too! So were we. My God, the stink was enough to gag a maggot!

Our steel helmets were versatile things. We washed in them, cooked in them, even crapped in them, because you didn't want to crap in your foxhole. If you were under fire and had to go, you just crapped in your helmet and dumped it outside.

We did some crazy things. There were all these "dares" and "double dares." One time we ran across a dead German. He was pretty ripe and his stomach was all bloated up. One of the guys challenged me to sit on the dead guy's stomach while I ate my breakfast. I took the challenge. When I sat on him all that air in his stomach went, Whoosh! That was a horrible experience!

In Fall 1944, the combat got pretty rough. We had just taken this little village, after a lot of resistance. Most of our ammunition was gone. Usually I carried as much of it as possible. I likened myself to Pancho Villa. I carried bandoleers across my chest. I had an ammunition belt full of shells. I stuffed my pockets with bullets and hand grenades. I still had some ammo left. Some guys had none. The sergeant in charge gathered thirteen of us into this courtyard. There was a six-foot-stone wall around it. He said, "Okay, guys. Dump all your ammo in a pile and we'll redistribute it evenly."

We had just piled it up when two 88 rounds came in. I knew they would hit very close. I dove through an open cellar window. I landed on something soft and immediately after I heard those shells go off in the courtyard, followed by screams. I dug myself out of what I was in, came out into the sunlight, and saw that I was covered from head to toe in red! I thought it was blood, but it turned out I had dove into a bin of over-ripe beets! I looked around the courtyard and two of us were the only ones left standing. I had a little nick on my knuckle, but that was it. Everybody was yelling, "Medic! Medic!"

The medic was holding his eye in his hand.

He said, "I can't help you this time, boys."

Me and the other guy set about patching up the wounded, using our medical kits and the medic's. My foxhole buddy, Jim Ritchie, was hit the worst with wounds in his head and all over his body. We patched him up first. I said to the kid I was with, "You make these guys comfortable, and I'll go to the rear and see if I can find stretcher bearers to haul these guys out."

I got to an aid station. I went into a little tent that had a red cross on it. There was a lieutenant on duty, no one else. I told him, "We have eleven men wounded about a quarter of a mile away and we need stretcher bearers to carry them out."

He said, "I can't help you. All my guys are already out. I'm the only one left here. What I can do is give you a stretcher."

I high-tailed it back to the courtyard and we carried the guys one by one back to the aid station. We carried Jim Richie out first. It took us three hours. Throughout that time the Germans were still shelling the town. Several times we had to drop a guy in the middle of the street and duck into a doorway.

Once a guy left the front for the hospital you lost complete contact with him. You never knew if he died or lived or whether he was coming back.[296]

Being responsible for other men's lives was something I didn't want all the time. When they offered me a battlefield commission, I turned it down. I was all right taking orders and helping somebody but I didn't want to say to anyone, "Go do this," and then see them get killed.

I did lead some patrols. Whenever we were static we would send a patrol out to seek out the enemy. Really, we were sent out to draw fire! We were like sitting ducks. I never assigned anyone to point. I asked for volunteers, but they were scarce as hens! I was usually the first man in the patrol. We were fired on a couple of times. Once a guy got hit in the helmet and thought he was dead. He said, "I'm hit! I'm hit!"

He was off to my right side and a little ahead of me. I said, "Can you crawl back to me?"

He said, "I'll try." He crawled back and I pulled his helmet off and saw no blood.

I said, "Let me see that helmet."

The steel helmet had a helmet liner underneath it. The bullet hit the helmet at an angle, penetrated it, but didn't go through the liner. It went around that and came out the other side! He had one Hell of a headache for a few days!

One day, we were moving through a forest and there was a rutted road going through. We got some pretty heavy machine-gun fire and I ducked down in one of the ruts. Something struck me in the shoulder and I yelled to my buddy, "I'm hit!"

We were wearing these white parkas for winter warfare. I detested them because the soil was a reddish-orange color, and when you dug in and laid in the bottom of that hole your side or back was all red and stuck out like a sore thumb! Most of us discarded our parkas after a while. My buddy crawled over to me and got me away from the firing line. I took my parka off and opened up my jacket. He said, "Where are you hit?"

---

[296]Long after the war, in the 1990s, Mr. Smolcic discovered that Ritchie was living on Staten Island. At the hospital, a steel plate was inserted into his head. He suffered nine wounds altogether.

I said, "Can't you see anything?"

Whatever it was that hit me just left a big black and blue mark on my collar bone. I had a sore arm for two or three days.

I saw cases of what they called shell shock. One time we were sedentary while other outfits could straighten their lines up with ours. We were sitting in our holes. This guy took off his parka and laid it on the side of his hole. The Germans started to shell us with mortars and we got down in our holes as far as we could get. A shell exploded near that guy's parka, and it ended up in a tree about twenty feet above the hole. When he looked up at that parka, that was it for him. He started screaming and yelling and thrashing. He envisioned himself being in that parka, the way I figured it. That was the last we ever saw of him.

You cannot withstand hour after hour of shelling. You never got immune to it. Every day I thought, "What the Hell am I doing here!" I kept praying for the Million-Dollar Wound. I thought, "Why can't I get hit in the shoulder or the leg so I can get the Hell outta here and live?" I saw one guy who shot himself in the palm of his hand with a .45. It left nothing but the fingers hanging on like threads. He probably lost that whole hand. I guess everybody was tempted to do something like that. I didn't blame anyone who did.

We had some guys you might call heroes. One guy from Pennsylvania who was in an outfit next to mine on the line stood out from the rest. He was no more than five feet five, but he carried a big stick, a .45 Thompson submachine-gun. This was his weapon of choice. He never buddied up with anyone. He was a loner. Sometimes he would go out at night with his Thompson. Invariably he would come back with one or two six-foot Germans with their hands on their heads. If we had had more like him, the war would have ended sooner.

German soldiers were pretty tenacious. It seemed every one we faced had a burp gun. Like our Thompson, the burp gun was best for close fighting. We didn't experience a lot of close fighting where I was, but there did come a time when I knew for sure I had killed someone. My best high-school friend had been killed in combat in Italy. I got word of that by mail, and it really tore me up. The next day we went into an attack through this wooded area. I had blood in my eye, and wanted to kill somebody. There was a wounded German lying face down on the ground. In passing, I shot him in the back of the head and continued on. I justified what I did. If he wasn't mortally wounded he could have shot me in the back as I walked past him.

On another occasion I know for certain I shot two guys. Whether they died, or were wounded I don't know. I was in an outpost hole about seventy yards in front of everybody else. I would be the first to see a counterattack. If I did, I was to fire as much as possible to alert the guys to the rear. I was given charge of two greenhorn replacements. After several hours of digging, our butts still stuck up out of the hole. Shortly before dawn we saw movement ahead of us. There was an opening in the woods and Germans were running across it. I told the two guys, "Line up on that opening. Next time we see movement we'll fire."

Next time they came across we opened up and I'm sure I saw two figures fall from my fire. We kept this up for a couple of hours. The Germans were firing in our direction too, but all this while no one from our lines was coming up to help us. I had a radio with me and I called back to the CP, "We need tank support up here. There's a lot of enemy movement."

In the meantime we were running pretty low on ammunition. I told the two kids with me, "You hold tight. I'll try to bring some ammo up."

Finally, one of our tanks came up and fired off a few rounds. That dispersed the Germans in front of our position. I talked to the tank commander and showed him the area in the woods where we had directed our fire. I said to him, "If you would, go down and see what's in that open area."

He did and when he got back he said that there were five dead Germans laying there. We had no regrets.

Once the Germans were trying to get a tank up into our lines. They were throwing shell after shell at us. We were pinned down for several hours. Scuttlebutt said that there was more than one tank out there. I never actually saw the tank or tanks, but I wasn't about to stick my head up and take a look around! During all this our captain, who was from Montana (we referred to him as the "Sheepherder"), called up one of our Sherman tanks to see if it could deal with the German tank. Our tank came up, and the German turned his gun on him and fired in his direction. Our tank just stood fast and wouldn't move any closer. Our captain got up on the side of the tank and rapped the hull with the butt of his rifle. The hatch opened up and he started yelling at the lieutenant or captain inside, "What the Hell's the matter!? Get moving! Our boys our getting slaughtered!"

The tank commander said, "I'm not going any further than this!"

Our captain said, "All my men have is a steel pot on their heads and you're encased in it! You want our men to go forward!?"

It got to be a pretty serious confrontation and the tank commander just closed the hatch and started backing out. Our captain put his carbine up and sprayed the whole tank with rifle fire! That didn't do any good either! Eventually the Germans pulled back for the day. But we suffered quite a few casualties from that.

Only once did we get to sleep in a town we captured. They issued us sleeping bags, which was the only time I ever got one. We were billeted in a three-story brick school house. There were numerous rooms and they told us to take whatever room we wanted. Other troops were guarding the perimeter, so we didn't have to post guard. I chose a room on the second floor with three or four other guys, laid my bag out, and dumped all my gear. In came this young French girl about our age. She found one of the guys to her liking and wanted to climb into the sleeping bag with him. Whether it was his Christian upbringing or what, he kept pushing her away. All of the rest of the guys volunteered! She kept insisting she wanted to be in the bag with him, and it was getting rather raucous. I decided, "Hell, this is no place for me."

I gathered up my gear and went up another flight of steps to the third floor. I said, "Let them fight that out themselves. I want to get some sleep."

In the middle of the night a shell came in and completely demolished where I had been lying a couple of hours before. I don't know if the reluctant lover and his girlfriend were still in there or not. I guess it wasn't my time.

After a few days we were called up to replace another company on the line. We moved into their holes. Again, I was given the dubious distinction of manning the outpost hole. I guess I must have looked like the right kind of guy! Again, I was given two green guys. We were on the edge of a valley overlooking a ravine. The guys we relieved said, "Keep your eyes open because the Germans have been infiltrating through here the past couple of nights."

That left me and the other two a little on edge. A couple of hours before we moved up to this position we heard a terrific explosion some miles to our front. We thought it was an ammunition dump. It got dark. We looked out into the valley and made out a figure moving toward us. The two kids with me trained their rifles on the guy. They said, "We'll wait till he gets close enough and then we'll let him have it!"

I said, "Wait. Something just doesn't look right. He's just walking straight on up."

They said, "We can't let him get any closer! We're gonna let him have it!"

They kept insisting they were going to kill this guy, so I just shoved their rifles out of the way, grabbed my own and started down the hill towards this guy. I didn't know what the Hell was going on either. I started yelling at the guy,

I yelled "Halt" with the German pronunciation, and he replied in perfect English. I started saying all the usual things like, "Who plays for the Yankees?" "Who won the World Series?" and all that BS! After a few correct answers, I was half-convinced that he was an American.

I said, "Put your hands up and come forward." When he got close, I saw that we was wearing an American flyer's uniform.

"What the Hell are you doing out here? You know you just walked through the whole German army to get to us?"

"I wondered about that," he said. "I was going by these holes and there were these strange looking guys saluting me."

"Saluting you?"

"Yeah."

"Didn't the Air Corps ever give you any kind of training what a German infantryman looks like?"

"I had no idea," he said! And the Germans didn't seem to have had any idea what an American flyer looked like, either. They probably thought he was some big important officer coming by! The German helmet is very distinctive, but he didn't pick up on that, either. I took him back to my hole and I told the two kids, "Now you see who you wanted to shoot?"

The flyer was from Michigan. I told the two guys to sit tight while I took him back to the CP. The captain interviewed him, then got on the radio to all the outfits in our area to be on the lookout for the rest of the bomber crew. The following morning I got back to the CP and talked to the captain and he told me that all of them came through that night.

Our food at the line was miserable. Once, at Thanksgiving and again at Christmas, we got hot meals. The rest of the time we supplemented our rations with whatever we could find. At the first cackle of a chicken, everybody would go looking for eggs! I made rabbit stew once. I used my steel helmet as the cooking pot. I found the rabbit in the back of a barn, and killed him with the back of my hand, a "rabbit punch." As a hunter, I knew how to gut and clean it. I found a frozen carrot and cabbage head in the garden. I dumped it all into my helmet with some water and cooked it up. I could have used those onions for that!

I was a pretty big guy, but when I came off the front line, I weighed 137 pounds, fifty pounds less than my normal weight. When I came off the line, I came off for good. I had hepatitis. My urine looked like dark beer. It got to the point where I couldn't carry my pack, my rifle, or anything. We pulled back for a day or two to rest and get cleaned up. I was so weak I couldn't take a shower. I practically crawled over to the aid station and told the doctor I was sick. He took one look at my yellow skin and yellow eyeballs and said, "You bet you are!"

It was around February or March when I was evacuated to a field hospital. A few days later, I was sent to Marseilles. The wards were loaded with hepatitis cases. I was sent back to the United States, to the hospital at Staunton Military Academy in Virginia. I stayed there four months. The doctor came around every day and stuck his fingers up under my rib cage. If it was still tender you would yelp. Most guys cried out anyway, so they could stay in the hospital! But they could tell by your complexion and eyes clearing up that you were getting better. My blood became forever ruined. I'm not permitted to give blood.

I was given a ten-day furlough. My mother took care of things when I got home. Pigs-in-a-blanket, stew, good ol' Hunky cooking! I ate like the Pope! While I was home the Bomb was dropped. I was glad about that! I was what they considered, "cured," and had my ticket punched for the Pacific Theater! I was a veteran of combat and they were looking for guys like me. The way I figured it, I survived one, but I wouldn't survive another.

If it wasn't for wars, I often felt I would have made one Hell of a career soldier. For some strange reason I liked regimented life. They offered me an increase in rank if I stayed in, but I felt if another war broke out I'd be the first to go. I was finally discharged in 1946. Before that I sat down with an officer who went over my records. The army used numbers that designated what you were. Mine was 745, a rifleman. He looked at that and said, "You were a rifleman the whole time you were in the army? Al Capone's not doing any hiring. Your chances of finding a job with your MOS number are slim to none."

He was right. I constantly looked for a job, but no one was hiring people who didn't have jobs before the war. I lived off the 52/20 Club. I got married. I banged around from job to job. I worked the coal mines, rubber works in Jeannette and the steel mills. I took advantage of the GI Bill to study bricklaying. I went into the contracting business with my dad and brothers, but we were too particular, and you don't become successful by being particular. Finally I ended up selling insurance for twenty years. I could have gone to college under the GI Bill, but I couldn't picture myself being a twenty-one-year-old guy just coming back from killing people to sitting down with some snot-nosed kids in a class room! It just didn't ring true.

3-INCH GUN MOTOR CARRIAGE, M10

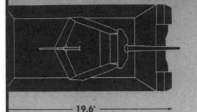

CHARACTERISTICS:

Turret: Undercut front and rear; narrow front mounting large gun mantlet; wide rear; front composed of V of two flat, inclined plates which joins in horizontal line; rear composed of two such V's set diagonally across rear corners of turret; sides are flat, inclined plates, pointed at both ends to fit into V's at front and rear; open top.

Hull: Long, flat top, from which flat plates slope down abruptly all around; inclined sides and rear join lower, undercutting faces.
Armament:
One 3-inch gun in turret.
One caliber .50 machine gun on rear of turret.
Traction: Full track; six equally spaced bogie wheels suspended in pairs; driving sprocket in front; three track support rollers.

INTEREST DATA: This vehicle mounts a 3-inch gun in a turret on a modified M3 medium tank chassis. It has been the standard tank destroyer weapon, but is being replaced by the T70. It performed well in North Africa, where it was of great assistance in stopping German tank attacks.

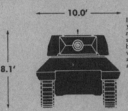

NOVEMBER 1943
FROM DATA CURRENTLY AVAILABLE
WAR DEPARTMENT FM 30-40

19.6'   10.0'   8.1'

Our M10 TD and later the T70 TD sure did look light in comparison, but of course we had "MOBILITY".

76-MM GUN MOTOR CARRIAGE, T70

The experimental T70 became the M18

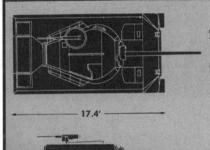

CHARACTERISTICS:

Turret: Low, conical, with large undercut projection in rear; set at center of hull; open top; has ring mount for AA machine gun at left rear.
Hull: Flat top, with slight upward bulge in rear of turret; extends beyond tracks in rear; sides flat, inclined in slightly at top; front flat, slopes down gently; front corners beveled.

Armament:
One 76-mm gun.
One caliber .50 AA machine gun on ring mount on turret.
76-mm gun extends well beyond front of carriage.
Traction: Full track, five equally spaced, medium-sized bogie wheels, independently sprung; four track support rollers; driving sprocket in front.

INTEREST DATA: This vehicle is the successor to the 3-inch gun motor carriage, M10 as the standard tank destroyer weapon. It is much faster than the M10, but is lightly armored. It has not yet made its appearance in quantity on the battlefield.

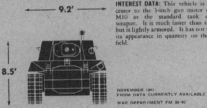

NOVEMBER 1943
FROM DATA CURRENTLY AVAILABLE
WAR DEPARTMENT FM 30-40

17.4'   9.2'   8.5'

GERMAN/AMERICAN ARMOR

These collages are taken from the scrapbooks of Doc Buchanan

The Foot Soldier

Anonymous[297]

United States First Army
112th Engineer Combat Battalion
Attached to the 29th Infantry Division
June 6, 1944

Greensburg, Pennsylvania, 16 March 1917

"I was there eight months. Eight months they kept saying they'd get me shoes. They made six pairs of shoes for me, and I was shipped over, but I didn't get the shoes until I got overseas. They sent me those six pair of shoes. They give me two pair and the supply sergeant got the other four. They said to me, "I don't know who's going to last the longest, you or the war."

They called me "Slim" because I was tall. My father was born in Greensburg on June 18, 1881. Mom was twelve years younger than him. Dad worked on the railroad in Youngwood, PA. He was a car inspector for thirty-four years. He used to work on a wreck train too. Dad didn't have very much education. I know my mother was a fifth grader, "fifth reader" they called it. Dad had about the same education, I suppose. My parents were married in 1911, when Dad was twenty-nine. They were married in New Cumberland, Maryland. Three other couples went down with them to get married. When I was a little kid, Mother sewed at a factory in South Greensburg. She also worked at the Penn Albert Hotel Annex as a cook and baker.

I worked on township roads when I was out of school to pay my dad's taxes. Then I got a job with the railroad in 1939, when I was 22. I worked with them until I was twenty-five, and then I went into the service. After the war I went back to the railroad. I started in Greensburg, but I worked in Jeannette and Pittsburgh. I traveled to Butler, Washington, all around. The whole time that I worked for the railroad I traveled 4,165,180 miles. I handled freight from different states. I always started at 4:30 in the morning. Then I got an over-road truck job as they

---

[297]This informant preferred to have his name withheld from publication.

called it. I traveled around 250 miles a day. Went home everyday, too. They didn't pay big money when I first started, only $137.84 a month. That's a start.

I was drafted 23 May 1942. I was told to report to the Greensburg Armory. When I left, the woman next door drove my mother to the train station in my 1940 Nash. My family took it pretty hard. My mother tried not to show it too much. I had a good mother. Good dad, too. They were both little people. When I went to New Cumberland, my mother came down to see me. She brought down a cake she baked. It didn't last long! I was a long time in the States while some of the guys were sent to Texas or were shipped out. There are several reasons why I was left behind in New Cumberland while all the other guys went to Texas. First of all, I have to go back a bit.

When I was a kid we had pick-up baseball games. I was swinging two bats on deck, and the guy in the box lined off a foul. The thing came right at me and hit me in the nose and broke it! The next day, I walked from there to Youngwood to see the doctor and he told me it was just badly bruised, but it was broken. Later, at the Armory in Greensburg, the doctor said to me, "I'm gonna stop you. I guess you know why."

"I figure it's my nose."

There was a possibility I would be 4F. I couldn't breathe through my nose. I'd breathe through my mouth, and it'd play me out. The doctor who delivered me said, "I'll tell you what I'm gonna do. I'll see if I get the Army to operate on your nose. If they don't operate, they'll send you back home."

They operated on me at Fort Belvoir. They told me the bones were crossed like an "X." They put my head in a headrest. Then they put a big sheet over top of me. The doctor put needles up my nose with anesthetic in them. The doctor, a captain, said, "Give me the chisel. Now, give me the hammer."

He used those to break my nose. He showed me the bones he took out. After that he shoved up something that looked like a lead pencil and stuffed packing in. I had that in for about three days. I went back to the hospital, where they pulled that packing back out. The doctor said, "This is gonna be the worst part of it."

"What's that?"

"I gotta pull that thing out of your nose. All that blood that has been clotting is going to come out."

He started pulling it out. Real slow! It hurt!

I said to him, "Hey, Doc! How about one quick hurt?"

"I think that's a good idea!"

He gave one quick jerk. I had to rest for five days. That was one reason I was left behind. The other had to do with clothes.

All the clothes they had for me in New Cumberland was too small. They give me a size-thirteen shoe, but I wore size fifteen. They said, "Try these on."

I said, "What! They'll fit you better than they fit me."

My pants where six inches too short. By this time the guys had shipped out. New guys came into camp. I didn't know any of them. I was there a long time, three months or more. Finally, I got a pair of sized-fifteen shoes, and they sent me to Fort Belvoir, to an engineering outfit.

I had only that one pair of shoes. I'd get out in the water, building Bailey Bridges.[298] I had those shoes on my feet all day. They would get soaking wet. I'd come back and stand formation in the same shoes. One day the captain came down the line with the sergeant. The captain said, "Soldier, your shoes aren't shined!"

The sergeant said, "Captain, this is the only pair of shoes he has. He can't shine those shoes. This guy was out in the water all day today and them's the same shoes he had on all day."

The captain didn't say a word; he just kept on going. I wore those shoes out. I was there eight months; eight months they kept saying they'd get me shoes. They made six pairs of shoes for me, but I didn't get any until I got overseas. They give me two pair and the supply sergeant got the other four. They said to me, "I don't know who's going to last the longest, you or the war."

Around camp, I wore my civilian shoes. In the barracks in the morning they'd come around and inspect. One day I'm laying in the bunk, and the captain came in and said to me "What are you doing in here?"

I just put my feet up.

"Well, that's all right, you're the guy who doesn't have any shoes."

The captain got to know me.

There was another reason I didn't get shipped out. One day I was leading the squad over an obstacle course. I fell off a barrier and broke my right wrist. The lieutenant came over to me and he said to me, "Slim, that didn't sound good. I heard that crack. I think you broke your wrist."

They took me to the hospital. When I come back the lieutenant said, "Just what I thought."

They had a cast on up to my elbow. The doctor said to me, "The cast will be on for six weeks. Then we'll take it off."

All the guys wrote their names all over the cast. I couldn't do anything, except go to the PX and the Service Club, or just hung around the barracks. I don't know how long it was till they said, "We're gonna check your wrist out."

They made the cast too tight, and it used to ache like a toothache. They had to take a pair of scissors and cut the cast. I wore that cast six weeks, and it turned out that they set it wrong. They had to reset it again. Six months I had a cast on my wrist. They said, "Well you might as well go home."

They'd give me weekend passes. I'd go home on Fridays and come back for Monday roll call. After they took off the cast, I went back into training. They

---

[298]An invention of Sir Donald Bailey, the Bailey Bridge was a light-weight bridge of interchangeable parts that could be easily transported, assembled and repaired. It was widely used by Allied engineers throughout the war in Europe.

"Soldier, your shoes aren't shined!"

couldn't ship me out, but they did take me out to the rifle range in my bare feet to qualify as a rifleman.

I also had pants six inches too short. I wore them the whole way through the war. I had to have a special overcoat made. I had to have special pants made. The first pair I had made were pretty nice. I didn't see anybody that had anything like them. When they got dirty the lieutenant told me to have them cleaned. I sent them to the cleaners.

The lieutenant said, "Your pants get back from the cleaners?"

"No. They didn't come in today."

We went down to check on them. "Oh, they'll be in next week," he said.

Next week came and he'd say, "Did they come in today?"

"No, I can't find them."

So he went down with me again. We searched the whole laundry. No pants. The lieutenant said, "You want me to tell you something? Somebody must need those pants worse than you do."

I wore those same six-inch-too-short pants overseas. Even my leggings wouldn't fit down in them, they were just too short. When I came back to the States with those same pants and I went to get discharged, I asked for a pair of pants to go home with.

The supply sergeant said, "What's the matter with the ones you got on?"

"You're kidding. Come here."

He looked and said, "Yeah, you do need a pair of pants."

I had a rough life in the service, I'm telling you! They didn't care about me. I had to have a special overcoat made, special pants made, special shoes made. They couldn't outfit me.

I wore those shoes from Normandy to Pilsen. I got trenchfoot because of that. They used to give me some kind of purple salve to rub on my feet. You couldn't take it off once you put it on. It had to wear off. I still get sore feet every summer. In the hot, humid weather, the blisters come back. I got discharged overseas and I asked them for the shoes the sergeant had kept back. Do you know they wouldn't give me those shoes?

On my way back home, I was wearing my special overcoat. There was a boat right across from me and I saw a soldier who looked about my size and I said to him, "Where's your overcoat? Where's your Army coat?"

He said, "They don't have one big enough for me."

I said, "They do now!" And I took my overcoat off and threw it over to him because I was going home. I don't know who I gave it to.

The guy next to me said, "Boy, you had a good coat! Why would you give that away?"

I said, "That guy needed one. I didn't. I'm going home."

Maybe the shoes and everything saved my life, I don't know. All the other guys who shipped out went to North Africa. Most of my guys I was supposed to go with got wiped out.

I went over on the *Queen Mary*. We left on November 3, 1943.[299] We landed in Glasgow, Scotland. We stayed there for maybe a day. Then we got on a train and we went to a place called Newkly, England. It must have been close to midnight when we got off the train. They sent us to a barracks they had up there. That's where we trained for the Normandy beach landing.

Nobody seemed to be excited. They just went along with their business. We would go out on Sunday night, but we always had to make sure that we got in before dark, because the Germans would bomb at night. We heard sirens all the time. When we were in the staging area for the invasion they had a loud speaker and they'd holler, "AIR RAID ALERT! AIR RAID ALERT!" When we were in Dorchester that's all we used to hear during the day, "AIR RAID ALERT! AIR RAID ALERT!" But that was just to keep us on our toes. We stayed there till we got all assembled to go over to Weymouth. We got on boats and laid over there I don't know how long.

I know we went on a dry run on the Channel once. We knew it wasn't the real invasion because there were no chaplains on the boat. Finally, one night they said to us, "We want everybody to get down into the hull of the boat!"

It was six o'clock and I saw that we're going to have pork chops. We never got pork chops before. I said to this guy from North Carolina, I said, "Hey, Cusper (Cuspersin), guess what? Pork-chops for dinner! What's that sound like to you? They're fatting us up for the kill."

Then we noticed that they had chaplains on the boats! This was it! They told us we were gonna hit the French beach at a certain time in the morning. We laid out there on the Channel in a storm. The boat was rocking all night. Each guy had a barf-bag, but I didn't use mine. One guy used his and mine.

Then we started off. As we got in closer the Germans shot big guns at our boats. We got on smaller boats, to bring us to the beach. A big shell hit near the side of our boat.

The lieutenant said, "Hit the water!"

We all got off. I never saw anything like it! It was like a hurricane. You were over here and a wave would hit you and you'd be over there. It didn't seem like we were making any ground. We were thrown around like matchsticks. It was awful that day. The Germans had these mines on poles. I was going to grab hold of one. This guy hollered at me, "Slim, don't grab a hold of that pole! It's got a mine on it!"

I heard a machine-gun the whole way coming in. But the way we were getting tossed around the Germans couldn't get a bead on us. It was a Godsend the surf was like it was. A lot of guys drowned because those inner tube things they gave us didn't work. How I finally found my outfit with all of those thousands and

---

[299]The rest of the unit left 19 August 1943.

thousands of soldiers over there I couldn't tell you! I must have just stumbled on them.

One guy lost his head. He was just so excited that he didn't know what he was doing. Every once and a while he'd grab hold of me and push me under.

I said to him, "Don't grab hold of me!"

He didn't even know he had hold of me. I was bigger than he was. He was about 175 pounds and I weighed about 235. I got him into the beach and told him what happened.

After I got on the beach, I saw guys from the 29th Division[300] bobbing in the water. I grabbed hold of two of them and pulled them up onto the beach. They were hit. This soldier said to me, "Slim," he said "I think it's too late. I think they're gone."

The soldier who said this had been a sergeant once, but one night in Dorchester he went over the hill and got busted. He come into the beach as a private. He started to give in. I grabbed him. "Come on," I said, "no Germans are gonna to stop me."

I brought him in.[301] I was calm on D-Day. I didn't think.

I said to one of the guys, "These Germans ain't going to keep me from going back home!" I got overhead bursts and everything else off the beach. I got a piece of shrapnel bounced off the beach and hit me in the leg, but just nicked me a little bit. They said we lost about 2,500 on that first day.

I had sixteen pounds of TNT on my back. We were supposed to blow some stuff up but we couldn't get to it because of the German resistance. We were walking bombs! I never thought about it. We were so mixed up on D-Day. We were pinned down for the biggest part of the day. We got moving off the beach the next day. We got a report that the German tanks were coming up a certain road off of the beach. Me and Cuspersin were supposed to guard this road. It ended up that the Air Force spotted them first. They took out the lead tank and then they came back and strafed a whole bunch. They had them all lined up whenever we got there. I didn't have to use my bazooka or nothing. I was glad I didn't! I don't know, at the time I don't think it would have penetrated one of those big tanks anyway.

So the first day was a bugger. Every vehicle we put on the beach got hit. There were Germans in a pillbox on the bluff. They had an 88 in there and every

[300]The 29th Division, under the command of Major General Charles H. Gerhardt, was a part of Force B, the follow-up for Omaha Beach. Force B was under Western Naval Task Force commanded by Rear Admiral Alan G. Kirk. On Omaha Beach (7 June) German resistance was so strong that the 29th could not expand its beachhead, still under fire by mortars and artillery. Moreover, there was so much wreckage scattered about that supplies could be unloaded in only a few places.

[301]In many instances, control of landing boats was lost before the men reached the beaches. Troops were forced to wade through the surf under withering fire. Casualties were greater among those who delayed progress to the beach. Wounded were drowned in the rising tide.

American vehicle that hit the beach got knocked out.[302] The Navy had big guns out on the water.[303] They blasted that pillbox. When we got up there, a German was thrown over the barrel. After that we could move.

When we were coming off the Normandy Beach this 29th Division guy had five German prisoners. They were all hollering, "Take me prisoner! Take me prisoner!" One of our guys said, "You're going as far as you're going to go!" He took them around a little hill and I heard five shots. I never saw those prisoners again.

On the first day, we were all mixed up. Nobody was with his own outfit. I was away from my outfit for a day and a half. I kept on moving. I know I was with the medics but I don't remember how I came to be with them. They put me on a water point on top of a hill after we got inland, and I was guarding it so the Germans couldn't mess up our drinking water. A German plane came over. Anti-aircraft guns hit him. The plane exploded right over me. I told the guys. One said, "I'm going to check it."

They went by this hedgerow where I said it was, but the only thing they could find was the pilot's skull. The plane was blown up.[304]

One day we were going to the line in a truck and got caught in a crossfire. Everybody had to bail out of that truck.[305] We asked some of the guys of the 29th Division around there where the front was? They said, "There isn't such a thing as a front. You're on your own. You just gotta keep your eyes open!"

We let that truck set there and we moved back. Three days later they said, "Who's gonna to volunteer to go up and get that truck."

I said, "I'm not bothering that truck. It could be booby trapped now. It's been sitting up there and they've got it covered."

Five guys said they'd go up. This kid, Shorty, a little guy from Johnstown, Pennsylvania, a transfer from artillery, was one of the volunteers. He carried his rifle slung over his shoulder with the barrel up in the air. I said to him, "Shorty, you're not in the artillery now. You're up here where it's rough. If you ever have to you use that rifle you ain't gonna be able to do it!"

He said, "You mind your own business!"

I said, "Okay."

---

[302]German coastal defenses, for the most part developed by Field Marshall Erwin Rommel, were of four kinds. *Two* types are explained here. The smallest and most unusual was the "resistance nest" *Widerstandsnest*, a single position manned by one or two squads armed with heavy or light weapons. When several of these were combined the defense was then called a "strong point" *Stuetzpunkt*. Omaha Beach was protected by at least six casemented 155mm guns.

[303]Could this be the instance described by Harrison, *Cross Channel Attack*, 325? "A pillbox west of the draw was reduced by skillfully directed destroyer fire at about 1130."

[304]Luftwaffe efforts on D Day and following were largely futile and directed mostly against shipping. The rest of their effort did not exceed 500 sorties (as opposed to 3000 sorties by the Allies), and were mostly fighter interventions inland.

[305]Note Harrison's account, *Cross-Channel Attack*, 328.

A little bit later some of the guys came back. I saw some sad faces. They said, "Did you hear the latest?"

"What?"

"Shorty got hit."

"I told him! And he told me to mind my own business."

"He never had a chance to defend himself. He went down flat on his face. He still had his rifle slung over his shoulder."

Shorty? He was careless. He was awful careless.

We were supposed to clear German mines. They would put them in the roads. We'd get them out and throw them alongside the road. The next day they were put back in again! What you did to disarm these mines was put a pin or a nail to interfere with the detonator. Those Germans got too smart, though. They put two triggers on. If you had it fixed for the first one, the second one would go off. We brought this tank up that had a series of chains attached to the front. It would throw these chains out against the ground and that would blow these mines up.[306]

We had a mine detector. We went around with it until it started buzzing. It would buzz louder and louder when we got close to a mine. That's when we knew to get out our bayonets and probe to find the mine.

When we got into hedgerow country we couldn't see much, but we could hear these "burp-guns." Some guys from the 29th had gotten hit. They were laying there when we went through. In fact we smelled them before we saw them.

At St. Lô we were supposed to dig foxholes. The guys were always teasing me. "Hey, Slim! What are you doing? Digging your grave?"

One guy from West Virginia said, "No Kraut is going to get me to dig a foxhole!"

Around dusk one day some German planes came over, dive bombing. Three or four guys behind me said, "Hey, Slim!"

"What?"

"We don't have no fox holes!"

"Well, jump in mine"

They said, "We won't tease you anymore about digging your grave. We'll help you dig!"

We got to know this German plane we called Bed-Check Charlie. One night Charlie came over, and I heard somebody digging and digging and digging. He said, "He's after me!"

That's the first time he dug a fox hole, that West Virginian! He was funny.

---

[306]One of the "funnies" developed by British Major-General Hobart to support the D-Day invasion. The interviewee is describing the "Crab," a mine-sweeping adaptation of a Sherman tank which could clear a lane ten-feet wide. A revolving drum fitted with chains and steel balls was fitted to the front of the tank.

One time we were going through an open spot and we had planes come overhead and they strafed us. They were our planes, our P-47s. A lieutenant said, "That's funny. They ought to know that these are American troops here!"

We had a guy in our outfit who had a .50 caliber machine-gun, and he wanted to shoot them down. The lieutenant said, "No, you don't want to shoot your own planes!"

Four planes came over every day and they strafed us. We couldn't figure out what the dickens was going on. Anyhow, some guy from another outfit, he didn't listen to anybody. He took a .50 caliber machine-gun and shot one of them down. We ran over to the wreck and found a German pilot! The Germans were flying captured American planes!

I also saw German planes in the woods. The wings were off of them. The Germans had them hidden and all they had to do was put the wings on them. They got so low in fuel, they couldn't use the planes. But we saw plane after plane after plane with the wings off them.[307]

Many times we went into German lines to put in trip flares and booby-traps. The trip flares had parachutes on them. If you tripped them they flew up into the air and came down lighting up everything. One night we were ready to pull out of a place, and a trip flare went off. We all got ready to take on whatever it was that tripped the flare. It was just a passing dog.

Some of the officers through all this were good. A lot of them were terrible. We'd be under fire, and the officers would be in the foxhole. When we were on Hill 192,[308] this nineteen-year-old 90-Day Wonder came up in the morning and said, "How's everything going fellas?" He wasn't there five minutes, and he took off.

The sergeants always stuck with us. No lieutenants did, except for Lieutenant Shepherd. Lieutenant Shepherd, he was the guy. He was one of the boys. Once, he and Jim Jordan, from near my hometown, heard this guy from the 29th Division hollering in a German mine field. Lieutenant Shepherd and Jim Jordan went out in that mine field out in the open, and brought that guy in! I never figured out why Jim and Lieutenant Shepherd didn't get medals for that!

Toward the end, Germans wandered all over the place. They *wanted* to be prisoners! A German I talked to was forty-two years old. He talked perfect English. He said, "I suppose you don't want to be any more in this service than I do."

"No. I had to go."

"So did I."

I caught him under a wood pile. I wondered what he was doing. I looked under and he was shaking. He thought I was going to shoot him. I asked him, "What are you doing under there?"

---

[307] Allied bombing was extremely successful in disrupting German resupply systems and the fuel production industries.
[308] July 1944, east of St. Lô.

"Potatoes, mister! Potatoes!"

"What?"

"Potatoes under there."

"Where?"

"Under there."

There were too. I don't know where they came from. I said, "Go ahead take them!"

"Can I have them?"

"Yeah, take 'em!"

Every time we took these German prisoners out for work, that one guy was always skipping into my bunch. He hung around with me. He said that if he had to go take a leak the other American guards would be kind of hard on him. Wouldn't let him go. I said, "If you've gotta go you gotta go! Go ahead!" I let prisoners go take a leak anytime they wanted. They always came back to the line. Some of the German soldiers were nice guys.

We once had 500 prisoners. We had to do something with them, like keep them exercised. We'd take them out on work details too. We'd take 500 out, and come back that night with 495. Next day we'd take out 495 and come back with 500. The others would be back! Maybe they had no place to go. We had them in our kitchens and everything, as cooks and helpers. They didn't want to leave us after the war was over. They had it made.

We also took some Hungarian prisoners who were in the German army.

They were scared to death. Sometimes it seemed like they were your buddies. Around where we had them there was a bakery. You could smell fresh-baked bread. Man, did that bread smell good! This one Hungarian guy says, *Brote, Brote!* I said to the sergeant, "They want bread."

He said, "Yeah, they can smell it. I don't know what I'm going to do."

I said, "Let's give them a slip to get bread."

One of the Hungarians spoke English.

So we told them that we'd give them a slip to get bread, but they had to come right back. We only let so many go. They came back with the bread and gave us back the slip.

In those German towns, everybody looted. Jim Jordan took a Luger off of a German captain. Of course, he had to shoot him to get it! I have some German coins in a bag. All kinds. But we couldn't get them exchanged.

When the war ended, they said we were going home. I came back into France and stayed at one of them Cigarette Camps. We stayed there, gosh, I don't know how long.[309] In fact I was in Paris first, for a week's vacation, I called it. Time off.

---

[309] A notation on the informant's Army Transportation Corps certificate states that he was at Camp Phillip Morris for seven days.

Then they called me up and said that I was going home. I went back to camp and stayed there for another month. I didn't go home right away.

In camp they had us in a big line waiting for the doctor, no clothes on, and women were walking around. We were standing there naked as the day we were born! The doctor checked us out to see if we had syphilis or any other "social" diseases. There was a bunch of colored guys who were going to be shipped home and they wanted to know if it was all right if they were shipped home with us. We didn't care. They fought the war same as us. We were all going home together. The colonel who was doing the checking examined this colored kid and said, "What do you have in there?"

This kid said, "Nothing."

He said, "Yes, you do!"

He had cotton stuffed inside of his penis because he had some kind of venereal disease. They held him out. Whatever happened to him I don't know.

I had a buddy who was running around with some German girls and everybody else. I said to him, "You better stay away from that one."

"Why."

"She's got all kinds chasing her."

"How'd you'd like to mind your own business."

"I just wanted to let you know what's going on."

It came time to ship out. He came to me and said, "I'm not going home."

"What's the matter?"

"I can't go for six months."

"She fixed you up with a dose didn't she?"

"Yeah."

"What'd I tell you?"

"I know!"

So I got home and got off the boat and this one woman, maybe his wife, came up to me and asked about him! She said, "Is he on this boat?"

I said, "No, something happened to his records. He'll probably be home later."

I couldn't tell her.

I saw some colored guys over there put a GI blanket down on the ground, loaded it with fruit and other food, and they were feeding the German girls. One guy from Tennessee said, "You know where I come from, if they do that down there, they're dead!"

He was mad. He was going to go out looking for them. I knew if he did *he* wasn't going to go home.

In camp there was a fifteen-year-old girl who came around for something to eat. A guy in the kitchen told her "If you give me some lovin' I'll get you some more food."

I thought he was dirty! I told the sergeant about it.

I came back to the United States on a ship called *St. Albans*. We ran into a storm coming back. I heard the Skipper talking, and he said, "We're gonna run into a storm. It's coming and we're gonna run right into it."

And so we did run right into it. The worst part about it was one of the rudders went bad. We rocked for a day and a half. You could look down the chow line, and there wasn't nobody there. Everybody was too sick to eat. It took us from 11 October to 20 October 1945 to cross.

My mother was glad to see me. She lost twenty pounds while I was away.

I couldn't tell you what I did when I got home. I know I didn't go to work. The boss found out I was home and he wanted to know when I was coming back!

I said, "I'm going to take off a week. To get situated."

It's a winter day today. When I got up this morning, I thought of how I once lived in a foxhole on days like this and survived. After fifty years I still look back and think, "I made it!"

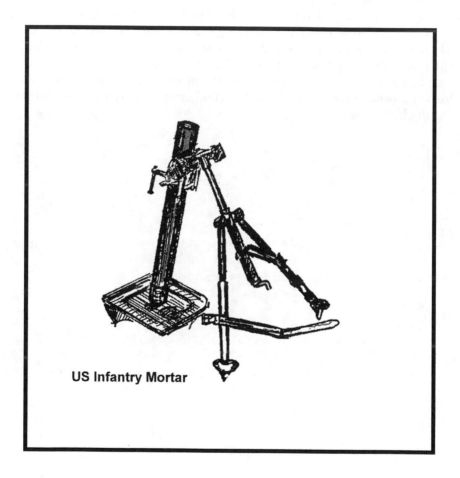

US Infantry Mortar

After a Visit to Buchenwald:
A Letter Home

Presly Richard " Bud" Dowler

Third Army
30th Special Service Company

April 20, 1945
East of the Rhine

My dearest Roberta,

I have more time to write and I'm not quite as tired from last night so I think that I'll write you that promised letter.

On Tuesday April 16, I was fortunate or perhaps unfortunate enough to visit one of the worst concentration camps that the Allies have yet come across. I assure you, Darling, that it was really horrible, and if I hadn't had the hardening that I received over the past eight months, then I'm sure that I would have left the place quite sick. As it was, I left quite mad at the Germans, and so very bewildered. Even today it doesn't seem possible that I witnessed such sights. It is far beyond anybody's normal conception. It all seems as though it was just a dream. However, it wasn't any dream, and I saw it almost as the Nazis left it.

You've probably seen articles on the camp in the paper, for there were plenty of correspondents and newsreel men around. The name of the place was Buchenwald, and it was near Weimar. Churchill says that he is going to come over and see the place for himself because it is so hard to believe. In fact, he has already appointed several members of the House to take the trip and see the camp of German atrocities. Man! And I do mean atrocities.

To get on with the story, we were very lucky to get a man [a prisoner at the camp] who had been there fourteen months. He was very well informed because he was a [dental surgeon] at the camp and also helped in any other surgery that might have been necessary at the time. First I'll tell you a little about him. He was from Antwerp, spoke excellent English, studied dentistry in Canada, and had a wife there to whom he was with only ten months before he returned to Belgium to fight in the Belgium [sic] army. He has been in prison camps for about five years and this was his last. He was much healthier than most of the people. He explained this with the fact that he had been acquainted with the damage and disease connected with the camp and that he knew how to combat them better than most men. He said that he used most of his allotted water to wash with while others used their ration to drink. The water was polluted so it just tore down the internees' health. He also was in the privileged class that was allowed to receive parcels from the Red Cross and home. This class [was] Dutch, French, English, and Belgium. Jews, Russians, and the rest were not allowed to receive [packages]. It was through these packages that he and some of his friends were able to keep alive.

They were permitted to take a shower about two minutes under the water once every three weeks. There were about 30,000 prisoners in what they called the upper camp that had one washroom, but no toilet facilities. In the lower camp, which contained about 20,000 prisoners, they had no washroom or toilet facilities. When we went inside, we saw boney men just squatting any place that they happened to be. They had very little food, as revealed by their daily ration of one loaf of bread to be shared by six men and a bowl of soup for each. Many of them were quite sick when we got there because the army increased their rations (still German food though) and they had overeaten.

I've gotten a little ahead of myself in this story, so I'd better stop here and explain that the camp had about 30,000 prisoners still in it when we arrived. The Germans had evacuated about 22,000 prisoners and had set April 13th to massacre the rest of the 25,000 in camp, but the American armor arrived on April 12th and the Germans had to clear out. The population of the camp was normally between forty and fifty thousand so you can just imagine the size of the place.

I'll tell you a little more about the things that they had to put up with, and then I'll give you a description of my trip through, with no feelings spared. They had no religious services...and no games other than chess and checkers. The types of prisoners in camp were Jews (who died quickly and received very harsh treatment), German criminals, German religious prisoners (priests, preachers, etc.,) German homosexuals, and the foreigners who opposed the Nazi party. The doctor said that the stealing was rampant and that life in general among the groups was terrible. We were told that, as a prisoner, you had to be on your guard every minute of your time there. When a man died, they often carried his body for four days, standing the body up in formations just so that they could receive the dead man's food ration. In doing this they also had to sleep with the body in their bunks. They would also use the dead man's clothes at night because they had no blankets or heat at night.

When as SS guard was killed the prisoners had to show up from their day's work with fifty bodies to pay for the death of the guard. Where they got them or how they were killed was not questioned, just so there were fifty dead men at the evening formation. Sometimes the guards would grab a hat off a man and throw it into a forbidden area and then order the man get it. When the prisoner stepped off of the grounds he was shot. Playful guys, these Germans.

Now I'll tell you step by step about my tour through the place.

First, we went into the lower camp where the hospitals were located. The first was the hospital for open wounds. The Germans had only paper bandages and these were changed once every three days, so most of the men usually died of infection. The doctors were not real doctors, but just SS soldiers who were too jealous of the real foreign doctors to let them do the work, so they just butchered the people at their delight. They had very little medicine and used less. A man had to have a temperature of 104 degrees before he was admitted. Anything less than that, and he was forced to work. Really, the hospitals were just a place to die.

Next we went into the whorehouse which was converted into a hospital ward (the girls in the house were German political prisoners only, and men had to have seven months of good conduct before they could have the girls). There were seventeen girls in all and nine were still there acting as nurses. They were Czechs, Poles, Russians, and Gypsies. In this ward, I saw about 400 living skeletons. Their limbs were so pitifully thin and their thighs were not as thick as my wrists. Several of the men here had bones sticking out because the skin had worn off and there just wasn't any flesh to cover up. They honestly looked like ghosts, the living dead.

From there we went into one of the barracks occupied by the Russians. Such a stinking sight, a space as wide as a double bed was the sleeping space for eight men. No mattresses were used, just plain boards. The beds were built in tiers and one barrack was about as long as the ceiling part of Graff's store. In that confined space they slept about 425 men. In fact, they often smothered each other because they had to sleep so close. Ordinarily, I wouldn't have believed that eight men could fit into the space, but on several of the tiers men were still sleeping. Moreover, when the doctor said that that was where they slept and I actually saw the men sleeping there, I had to believe him.

Next we entered the upper camp and the first place he showed us there was the human guinea pig laboratory. We didn't go in because there still may have been communicable diseases present. In this lab, a man never came out alive. The Germans tested new serums on the prisoners, and if they survived one, then another was tried, so eventually all of the prisoners died.

We went into a couple more barracks and then to the second worst sight of them all. It was in Block 61 where I nearly got sick. In this particular barrack they detained men who were too feeble to work so that they could die there. They didn't feed them or give them water. There were about 300 in the place at the time when we arrived (the American medics were treating them) and they looked so awful and the place smelled so bad that we could hardly tolerate it. In a shed along side of the barrack they stored the bodies until it was full and then they carted them to the crematorium. By the way, there were still two bodies in it [the shed] of men who had died the night before.

[The] last, but the most terrible sight was the crematory. Never again do I want to see that. Outside of it were forty to fifty-five bodies stacked as neatly as cordwood and in all the furnaces were the bodies of men already burned. In one furnace there was still one body only half-burned. There were six furnaces each burning three bodies at a time to ashes at a rate of about twelve times a day. Just figure out the death rate for yourself. One time last winter when the coal was short there were over 2,400 bodies in the storage yard outside of the crematory.

Underneath the furnaces was the torture chamber where they whipped and hung the men. They had hooks in the wall about eight feet off the floor. These hooks were used to hang a man. The procedure was that a man's hands were shackled behind him and they took a rope about three feet long and put it around the victim's neck. They then hung the other end of the rope over the hook and let the man strangle to death. No broken neck, just strangling. We could see the marks on the wall where men had strangled. They let the man hang there for fifteen minutes then if he wasn't dead then they break his brains out with a big club. The club was still there and we could see hair and blood on it.

That was my trip and this enclosed clipping may give you a little more of an idea how this place was. I saw German civilians saying that it couldn't be true, but nevertheless, it was true. I saw it with my own eyes and it made me so darn mad that if a German had said, "Boo!" I would have shot him on the spot.

Well, darling I'm all writ out so I think I shall say goodnight.

I love you darling and miss you so very much. I think of you constantly and just wish I could be out of this mess and with you again. Take care of yourself for me.

Lots of Love,
Bud

P.S. Read this letter to Mother and Dad for is too long to write over again

A Nurse's Story

Helen Talmachoff Metrisin

First Lieutenant
Army Nurse Corps
154th Headquarters Group
United Kingdom

Indiana County, Pennsylvania

I was born and raised in a small town in Indiana County I graduated from Homer City High School in 1938. In September 1940, I enrolled in Mercy Hospital School of Nursing, Pittsburgh, Pennsylvania, and graduated in September 1943. My decision to join the Army was a gradual one made over that time. My older brother joined the Air Force in 1943, and one of my younger brothers enlisted in the Navy. During my three years at nursing school many graduate nurses left for service in the Military, especially after Pearl Harbor. Then, there were only two classes of nurses in hospitals: graduate RN's and student nurses. We also had orderlies and nurses' aides who were assistants in transport and supply, but did not participate in direct patient care. Physicians were going into the service and they worked the remaining interns and residents to death. As a result, they required senior nursing students to take on more responsibility. They not only permitted but begged to learn intravenous fluid and drug administration. After graduation in September 1943, I remained as a staff nurse on a large postoperative unit at Mercy. On January 20, 1944, at age twenty-one, they inducted me and several of my classmates into the Army Nurse Corps in Pittsburgh. I left for Fort Meade, Maryland. My parents accepted my decision. Besides, my status as nurse would not put me in as much danger, compared with my older brother who was in training school as navigator on B-17's.

At Fort Meade, a large and busy post, I was picked up by jeep and driven to the station hospital, where I reported to the chief nurse. After welcoming me, the chief nurse asked me if I had a civilian nurse's uniform. Fortunately, I did. Within two hours of arriving at the hospital, I reported on duty to care for a female patient who was having seizures so severe she fractured several of her vertebrae. I worked with her for twenty-four hours until she was finally under control. So much for my induction into the Army Nurses Corps, and so much for orientation to military nursing! At this juncture, it seemed like a continuation of nursing in civilian hospitals, since there were no battle casualties yet. What stood out was the fact that we could use your own judgment on many items of care, and we did not need a written order. The ward physicians only expected you to keep them informed of major changes. Later, when I received my GI uniforms, I had no idea how to affix my second lieutenant's insignia. No one seemed to notice.

I cared for some nurses and other military personnel who were POWs of the Japanese in the Philippines. I can still see the one nurse, thin and malnourished, with fungal infections on her feet. She insisted that I be her maid of honor in her marriage to a young artillery officer who also had been a POW. There was no time for fuss-military uniforms. They were married and were both transferred closer to her new home. They were lucky to have survived the prison camp. It was so brave that they could put everything behind them. All of this took place in one day. I forget their names, but often over the years, I have wished them well.

A classmate from Fort Meade and I signed up for overseas duty. They accepted us in one unit almost immediately, but they dropped us from the roster when the T.O. changed from one-hundred to only seventy nurses for each general hospital unit. In April 1944, they assigned my classmate and me to another unit and sent us to Georgia to join a station hospital which became the 154th General Hospital Unit. Within two weeks, we were on our way to Fort Dix, New Jersey. From there we went to Europe.

In May 1944, we sailed from New York aboard the *Queen Elizabeth*. There were 15,000 troops on board, Air Force units and infantry, and two complete hospital units. We had a convoy escort for 500 miles because of enemy submarines. The ship's captain told us the ship altered course in a zigzag fashion every few minutes to avoid torpedoes. Five days later we reached Glasgow, Scotland, the only port other than Southampton that could accommodate this huge ship. They necessarily restricted us to certain areas. They served meals twice daily. Some of us volunteered for hospital duty. They much needed our services because respiratory diseases spread easily on such a crowded ship. The sick bay, where most of the troops were quartered, was located on a deck deep within the ship. It tended to be warm down there. Thankfully, the trip took only five days.

In Glasgow, our hospital unit disembarked early and boarded a British troop train. We headed south. At various brief stops, the British Red Cross served hot coffee which we drank along with our K-rations. Two days later, we arrived at , a railroad center midway between London and Bristol, and within the proximity of many airfields. The hospital was located about twenty-five miles from Swindon, near the little village of Wroughton. An RAF hospital was about a mile or so from the American site in Burderop Park (formerly a cow pasture). It was beautiful countryside. It was hard for us to believe that London, just 100 miles away, was being terrorized by V-2 rockets. In spite of their ordeal, all the British people, from the Red Cross workers, the military people, to the train personnel, greeted us cheerfully. When we arrived at 154th General Headquarters, there was an invitation on the latrine bulletin board inviting us to "Ann's Cottage" in Wroughton where they served us tea and biscuits. We did not learn until much later that the Brits had stringent rationing. That did not deter them from sharing their rations with us.

The first few nights we slept in tents on the hospital site, while the Nissen-hut wards were cleared and made ready. It rained steadily. Nevertheless, we made our cots and slept soundly, awakening in the morning to find our blankets covered with snails. What fun! When the enlisted men delivered our trunks, they showed us a trick to prevent this from happening again. We were good nurses, but lousy campers.

We moved into the hospital quickly. The arrangement was one medical officer and one nurse per ward. The concrete Nissen huts held forty-five cots, nursing stations, exam rooms, and a kitchen. Each hut had two others attached to it and fifteen cot tents for the walking wounded. Special wards were staffed accordingly: spinal cord injury ward, severe head injury ward, etc. D-Day had already occurred, and we got ready for casualties. Though we were a general hospital, we were initially to function much like an evacuation hospital. Of our surgeons, including two neurologists from the Midwest, some were experienced, while others were just out of residency. The ambulance convoys began arriving. All the doctors were in the triage area. Each nurse was in her ward ready to admit patients, assess them, start IV fluids, etc., I still see the gurneys rolling into the ward, one after the other. Six hours later we had admitted 1,000 patients. The hospital was full. Surgery went on around the clock. These men still had the dirt and sand from the beaches on them. They were evacuated to England on anything that could transport them. The most badly injured came by plane to the airfield. When the weather got bad, they came to us on ambulances. These soldiers were exhausted and dehydrated. Some of them had been lying on the hard gurneys so long that they had bed sores. Mess facilities got very busy because it was obvious that these men had not had any food for a long time, except K-rations.

We cleaned them up and dressed their wounds. The food carts arrived with hot wieners, beans, veggies, and apple cobbler. As I looked at the trays, my first thought was, "How can we serve these men wieners and beans? Is this the best that we can do?"

Their reaction was quite different. They ate ravenously with comments like, "Oh boy, hot food!" "You guys are great to go to all this trouble!"

We served them at 10 p.m. I will never forget them thanking us for those wieners and beans as long as I live. After eating, they fell asleep, exhausted. In the morning, the soldiers, most of which were from the Caen area, began to relive the battles. They spoke of the horror of hedgerows in Normandy that hid them from the enemy, but also hid the enemy from them. This group left us in a few days, some going to Bristol to hospital ships, and others going to rehabilitation hospitals, to recuperate. Eventually, some of them returned to duty.

Every week patients would undergo a process of being admitted into a full hospital, receiving surgery, having their wounds dressed and then moving on. Soon, wounded from the drive from Caen and Carentan to the assault on St. Lô started to come in. They talked about the battles, and about the German 88s. - They said, "You never knew when a shell was coming in until you heard the whistle followed by an explosion."

One young soldier became mute from battle stress. Instinctively, other patients seemed to know what to do. They gathered around his bed and talked of the battle, including details on the gunfire, artillery explosions, and men getting hit. They asked him yes or no questions about what happened to him. He responded by nodding his head. No one could have been more therapeutic than those soldiers. This caring for each other was evident in other ways. Sometimes we had a large number of patients with casts on their arms and legs, yet many would insist on getting up to help feed his "buddy" at chow time. They talked of their home state, or about family, and most had a picture of a wife or a girlfriend, or sometimes of their family. After a lot of sleep, they went to the Red Cross facility for games, materials to write letters home, and other recreational activities.

The soldiers were patient and good humored. A young man asked me if I would look at his eye because it was bothering him. I got set to flush out the eye with some sterile solution. He also said that he had a glassy stare. When I looked closely, he grinned at me and I could see that he had lost an eye. They had fitted him with a prosthesis at some prior hospital. They did the requisite flirting also. More than one would take the thermometer and hold it against a light bulb for a moment to be sure that he had a "fever" when I got back to him. Each thought he had invented the idea. One of the remarkable differences between service men overall and civilian patients was that service men were good-natured for the most part as they recovered, whereas civilian patients tended to complain more. When the sun shined we carried the non-ambulatory patients outside on the grass for a sun bath.

Once St. Lô was captured, the drive through France and the liberation of Paris became the topics of conservation. After awhile we heard that our casualties were getting lighter. Our hospitals started to receive German POWs. We also took in people from Nazi slave-labor units. All had to be handled as POWs at this point, since there was no time to sort them out. Our GIs told us that many German soldiers hid out so they could surrender either to British or American armies. They wanted to avoid the advancing Russians, at all costs. Many had wounds that had not been treated recently. Some had wounds that had never been treated. You could see a deterioration in their uniforms. Many had holes in their boots that they had filled in with cardboard. They had clothing that appeared to be made of some sort of paper. We did surgery and cleaned and dressed their wounds, just as we did for our own soldiers. Our supply of penicillin was pretty steady so we were able to use it to save limbs and treat deep abdomen wounds.

The POW's were very disciplined, quiet, and respectful. A couple of them had a limited knowledge of English. Our doctors and nurses had learned words and phrases from a couple of our enlisted men who spoke German. Like our men, these POWs helped their "buddies" during meal times. Without even being asked they would return trays to the kitchen and clean up afterwards.

Some Germans were in their fifties, and others were under the age of sixteen. One of the young people had been shot in the head and was paralyzed from the waist down. A corpsman and I were bathing him, and he insisted that Germany was winning the war. He said that German planes had bombed New York City about two or three months earlier. He did not believe us when we said that we had sailed from there in late May and saw nothing of the sort. This kid said that he was eighteen years old. It was so sad, because I knew that he was really fourteen or fifteen. Nazi propaganda had brainwashed him. He had grown up knowing nothing but Nazism. Occasionally, a young German officer, usually a lieutenant, would interfere with my work in an arrogant, sometimes flirting way. Nevertheless, for the most part, they seemed appreciative for the care that they received.

Then came the surprise of the Battle of the Bulge. We started to receive increasing casualties. Frozen feet were a major problem. Europe was having the coldest weather in many years. The Army told us that the enemy surrounded our boys at Bastogne, and the weather was so bad that Allied planes could not launch air strikes or drop supplies. The boys had no dry socks. Care was aimed at keeping their feet from cracking and getting infected. You knew that many of them would at least lose all or some of the toes on both feet.

We continued to receive battle casualties until VE day in May 1945. Hospital personnel were led to believe that they would send us to the Pacific war zone. In late July we went to Southampton and boarded the *Queen Mary,* bound for New York. They filled the welcome in New York Harbor with blowing whistles, flying flags, and cheering people. The Red Cross was waiting with coffee, donuts, and fresh milk. The ladies said that fresh milk was the most popular item, because all we had overseas was powdered milk. Moreover, the British had asked us to forego ordering milk in restaurants because they had barely enough for their babies and children.

Following our return to the States, they gave us two weeks of rest and relaxation. Then the war with Japan ended. There was jubilation. They sent me to Fitz Army hospital near Denver, Colorado. There they made me a charge nurse of the large post-op unit of 125 beds. We did reconstructive surgery, repair of bone/muscle injuries, etc. It was different because the men were a little closer to their homes. Some families were able to visit and the men could call home occasionally. There were some patients who had been prisoners of the Japanese. They told us that they had little or no medical care and very little food. They looked the part. They were emaciated and had many tropical infections. Many men talked about how awful it would have been if our armies would have had to invade the Japanese mainland.

I was proud to have cared for our soldiers during World War II. I did not join any of the reserve units or the veterans' associations. I was discharged at Fort Des Moines, Iowa in March 1946.

Last October, I attended the dedication of the Women's Memorial in Washington, D.C. Many World War II veterans were there. It was a great day, but no one else from the 154th was there.

Bibliography and Works Cited

37th Tank Battalion. "Battalion Diary." HQ 37th Tank Battalion, APO 254 US Army, July 15, 1944.

393rd Infantry Regiment Historical Association. *The 393rd Infantry Regiment in Review*. 1947.

4th Armored Division. *Combat History*. July 17, 1944–May, 1945. (Official US Army).

Allen, Robert S. *Lucky Forward: Patton's Third US Army*. New York: Manor Books, 1947.

Ambrose, Stephen. Citizen Soldiers. Simon and Schuster (Touchstone), 1997.

Ambrose, Stephen. Band of Brothers. Simon and Schuster (Touchstone), 1992.

Barnes, Richard H., Major, Field Artillery. "Arracourt—September 1944." Thesis, Fort Leavenworth, Kansas, 1982.

Berry, Craig. *The Legacy of the 4th Armored Division*. Paducah, KY: Turner, 1990.

Buchanan, Richard R. M.D., Richard David Wissolik, David Wilmes, Gary E.J. Smith. *Men of the 704: A Pictorial and Spoken History of the 704th Tank Destroyer Battalion in World War II*. Publications of the Saint Vincent College Center for Northern Appalachian Studies, 1998.

Clarke, Jeffrey J. and Robert Ross Smith. *Riviera to the Rhine*. Washington, DC, 1993.

Cole, Hugh M. *The Ardennes: Battle of the Bulge*. U.S. Army in World War II. Washington DC: US Government Printing Office, 1965.

Cooper, Matthew. *The German Army 1933–1945*. New York: Zebra Books, 1978.

Critchell, Laurence. *Four Stars of Hell*. Ballantine, 1947.

Eisenhower, Dwight David. *Crusade In Europe*. Garden City, NJ: Doubleday, 1948.

Ellis, John. *Brute Force: Allied Strategy and Tactics In The Second World War*. New York: Viking Press, 1990.

Evans, Thomas J. *Reluctant Valor*. Publications of the Saint Vincent College Center for Northern Appalachian Studies, 1995-1997. Contains the Mullen/Macomber Combat Diary.

Farago, Ladislas. *Patton: Ordeal and Triumph*. New York: Dell, 1963.

Fussell, Paul. *Wartime: Understanding and Behavior In The Second World War*. New York: Oxford University Press, 1989.

Mauldin, Bill. *Up Front*. New York: Award Books, 1968.

Patton, George S. *War As I Knew It*. Boston: Houghton Mifflin, 1947.

Ryan, Cornelius. *The Longest Day*. New York: Popular Library, 1959.

Stanton, Shelby L. *World War II Order Of Battle*. New York: Galahad Books, 1984.

Weigley, Russell F. *The American Way Of War*. Bloomington: Indiana University Press, 1973.

Whiting, Charles. *The Last Assault*. Sarpedon, 1994.

Index